U.S. Marine Corps

BIOGRAPHICAL DICTIONARY

U.S. Marine Corps

BIOGRAPHICAL

The Corps' Fighting Men · What They Did · Where They Served

FRANKLIN WATTS, INC.
575 Lexington Avenue, New York 22

DICTIONARY

by Karl Schuon

ACKNOWLEDGMENTS

WHEN PLACES and dates lie buried in dusty archives or hide illusively in myriad file cabinets at Headquarters Marine Corps, an author and his researchers would be helpless without those who guard such records of the past, ensuring that no Marine will be lost to the ages for lack of biographical material.

For their patient, cheerful, and untiring assistance in making this work possible, sincere gratitude and thanks are due to Miss Manell P. Brice, Division of Information, HQMC; Mr. Michael O'Quinlivan, Mrs. Clara Miller, and Mrs. Mickey McLain, Records and Research Section, HQMC; and to Mrs. Virginia P. White, Miss Ethyl F. Schurman, and Miss Wanda L. Graves, Decorations and Medals Branch, HQMC.

Finally, a vote of gratitude is due Gy.Sgt. Arthur J. McGowan whose research on this volume was invaluable.

PREFACE

COMPILING a biographical dictionary is a serious editorial responsibility, and those who undertake it must exercise the best possible objectivity. But unavoidably, the author of such a work — together with those he must necessarily work with — is faced with many differences of opinion concerning which names shall be included and which shall not — and for what reasons. In the present volume the task was far from easy, and certain criteria had to be determined in planning it.

First, it was decided to include the current Marine Corps generals who were on active duty when this work was assembled. These men are today's leaders of the Corps. Unquestionably, their individual careers are indicative of the priceless experience gained in command responsibilities. Every general's detailed biography is therefore included.

Second, there came the largest group of Marines by far — an extremely important group. These were the Marines who won the nation's highest award — the Medal of Honor. The list was long. The names spanned the many years of Marine Corps history. The battles in which these highest awards were won covered the globe. Each individual name was carefully researched and all the information that was available was duly included in the entry. In some cases only the name, rank, and a brief citation remained to remind historians that some gallant Marine crossed a river and demolished a fort, captured a flag, or — as so often in World War II — gave his life to save a comrade. But, famous or forgotten, the Medal of Honor winners are all in the pages of this book.

Third, no biographical dictionary of the U.S. Marine Corps would be complete without sketches of the lives of the Commandants. From Samuel Nicholas to David Shoup their biographies in themselves form a historic pattern of the development of America's élite force-in-readiness.

Then, having fully covered the generals, the Medal of Honor winners, and the Commandants, there remained the most difficult part of the job — choosing the well-known or colorful Marines who did not necessarily fall under the above categories. Again — a far from easy task.

This done, the resulting list was checked with every Marine qualified to help add to, or delete, from it. Of course, the list did not diminish; it grew daily, for the famous and the fabulous were legion.

Finally — and reluctantly — space limitations dictated a cutoff point. The Chesty Pullers, John Quicks, Lou Diamonds, Dan Dalys, John Glenns, and Herman Hannekens are here but, unavoidably, a gunny's top colonel and a colonel's top gunny may be missing from the roster. Only a library of many shelves could include them all. Anyway, future editions

v

and revisions of this dictionary will serve to correct whatever faults it may contain, update what needs updating, and add to the roster of those who make Corps history and tradition.

KARL A. SCHUON

WASHINGTON, D.C.
JUNE 1963

CONTENTS

KEY TO ABBREVIATIONS USED IN THIS WORK

AEF — American Expeditionary Force
Bn. — Battalion
CG — Commanding General
CMC — Commandant of the
  Marine Corps
CO — Commanding Officer
Co. — Company
Det. — Detachment
FMF (Atlantic or Pacific) — Fleet
  Marine Force
HQ — Headquarters
HQMC — Headquarters Marine Corps
KIA — Killed in Action
MAD — Marine Aviation Detachment
MAG — Marine Aircraft Group
Mar. Brig. — Marine Brigade
Mar. Div. — Marine Division
MAW — Marine Aircraft Wing
MB — Marine Barracks

MCAS — Marine Corps Air Station
MCB — Marine Corps Base
MCR — Marine Corps Reserve
MCRD — Marine Corps Recruit Depot
MCS — Marine Corps Schools (Quantico)
MIA — Missing in Action
MLR — Main Line of Resistance
NAS — Naval Air Station
Plat. — Platoon
POW — Prisoner of War
Prov. — Provisional
Recon. — Reconnaissance
Reinf. — Reinforced
ROTC — Reserve Officer's Training Corps
R&R — Rest & Rehabilitation
VMF — Marine Fighter Squadron
WWI — World War I
WWII — World War II

U. S. Marine Corps

BIOGRAPHICAL DICTIONARY

A

ABRELL, Charles Gene. Corporal. Medal of Honor: b. Terre Haute, Ind., Aug. 12, 1931; d. KIA, Hwachon, Korea, June 10, 1951. Charles Abrell, the 14th Marine to receive the Medal of Honor for Korean fighting, attended public schools in Las Vegas, Nev., before enlisting in the Marine Corps on Aug. 17, 1948 at the age of 17. Following recruit training at Parris Island, S.C., he was assigned to Camp Lejeune, N.C., and also served aboard the USS *Noble* before going to Korea with the 1st Mar. Div. He was in action at Inchon, Seoul, Wonsan, Chosin Reservoir, and Hanghum, before the assault on a hill near Hwachon in which he was killed. His citation reads, in part: "... Although previously wounded by enemy hand grenade fragments, he proceeded to carry out a bold, single-handed attack against the enemy bunker.... Sustaining two additional wounds as he stormed toward the emplacement, he resolutely pulled the pin from a grenade clutched in his hand and hurled himself bodily into the bunker with the live missile still in his grasp. Fatally wounded in the resulting explosion which killed the entire enemy gun crew within the stronghold, Cpl. Abrell, by his valiant spirit of self-sacrifice in the face of certain death, served to inspire all his comrades and contributed directly to the success of his platoon in attaining its objective...."

ADAMS, John Mapes. Sergeant. Medal of Honor: b. Haverhill, Mass., Oct. 11, 1871. Sgt. Adams' citation reads, in part: "... in the presence of the enemy during the battle near Tientsin, China, July 13, 1900, he distinguished himself by meritorious conduct...."

ADRIANCE, Harry Chapman. Corporal. Medal of Honor: b. Oswego, N.Y., Oct. 27, 1864. Cpl. Adriance's citation reads, in part: "... in the presence of the enemy during the battle near Tientsin, China, July 13, 1900, he distinguished himself by meritorious conduct...."

AGERHOLM, Harold Christ. Private First Class. Medal of Honor: b. Racine, Wis., Jan. 29, 1925; d. KIA, Saipan, Marianas Islands, July 7, 1944. After attending Racine public schools, Agerholm joined the Marine Corps Reserve on July 16, 1942, and received his recruit training at San Diego, Calif. On completion of his boot training, he was ordered to the 10th Marines, 2nd Mar. Div. The outfit embarked for New Zealand on Nov. 3, 1942, where it underwent training at Wellington for 11 months. In Nov. 1943, Agerholm participated in the bitter fighting at Betio Is., Tarawa Atoll, then went to Hawaii where he trained with his battalion for the forthcoming operation at Saipan. He landed on Saipan three days after D-Day. With the battle raging for three weeks, the enemy launched a frantic counterattack on July 7, 1944, and a neighboring battalion was overrun. For his conspicuous gallantry on that day, he was awarded the Medal of Honor. His citation reads, in part: "P.F.C. Agerholm volunteered to assist in the efforts to check the hostile attack and evacuate our wounded. Locating and appropriating an abandoned ambulance jeep, he repeatedly made perilous trips under heavy rifle and mortar fire, and singlehandedly loaded and evacuated approximately forty-five casualties, working tirelessly and with utter disregard for his own safety. Despite intense, persistent enemy fire, he ran out to aid two men whom he believed to be wounded Marines but was himself mortally wounded by a Japanese sniper while carrying out his hazardous mission." On June 20, 1946, at Boston, Mass. the USS *Agerholm*, a new destroyer, was commissioned — named for the young Marine hero.

ALLEN, Chester Robinson. Major General. Quartermaster General of the Marine Corps (1963): b. Somerville, Tenn., Feb. 6, 1905. Chester Allen attended school in Auburndale and Lakeland, Fla., prior to his graduation from the University of Florida in 1929. A member of the ROTC in college, he was appointed a Marine second lieutenant July 25, 1929, and was enrolled in the Basic School for Marine Corps officers at the Philadelphia Navy Yard. While attending the Basic School and serving there as a company officer, Lt. Allen was a tackle on the All-Marine Corps football team of 1930. He also played the same position on the Marine team at Parris Island, S.C., in 1931. From June 1932, to July 1934, he served with the Marine Detachment aboard the USS *Nevada*. During the next two years, he was stationed at the Marine Barracks, Bremerton, Wash. In March 1935, he was promoted to first lieutenant. He captained the Bremerton Marine Rifle and Pistol Team, which won the San Diego Trophy Match in March 1936. In Aug. 1936, Lt. Allen entered the Company Officers' Course at Quantico, Va. After completing the course, he was promoted to captain in Aug. 1937, and embarked with the 6th Marine Regiment for China. The following year he was detached to the 4th Marines, 2nd Marine Brigade, in Shanghai. Allen served there on special duty with the Marine Detachment at the American Embassy in Peiping in connection with Asiatic Division Rifle and Pistol

Competitions, and later as Officer in Charge, 4th Marines Rifle and Pistol Team. On his return from China in Aug. 1940, he was stationed at the Marine Barracks, San Diego, Calif., as Chief Range Officer. He joined the 2nd Barrage Balloon Squadron at Parris Island, S.C., in Nov. 1941, and in Jan. 1942, was promoted to major. He accompanied the squadron to Samoa in Apr. 1942, and was promoted to lieutenant colonel in Aug. 1942. He returned to the States the following month. In Feb. 1943, following temporary duty at HQMC, Washington, D.C., Lt. Col. Allen was assigned to the Marine Corps Depot of Supplies, San Francisco, Calif., as Chief of the Ordnance Division. He was promoted to colonel in Aug. 1945. The following year, he joined the 2nd Mar. Div. and served with that organization in the occupation of Japan. He moved to Pearl Harbor in July 1946, to begin a one-year tour of duty with HQ, Service Command, FMF, Pacific, as Assistant Chief of Staff, G-4. After his return from Pearl Harbor in Aug. 1947, he served for four years as Commanding Officer of the Barstow Annex, Marine Corps Depot of Supplies, Barstow, Calif. Ordered to Korea in June 1951, Allen earned the Legion of Merit with Combat "V" while serving as Supply Officer, 1st Mar. Div. He remained in Korea until May 1952, when he returned to the States to serve as Supply Officer, Marine Corps Base, Camp Pendleton, Calif. In July 1954, he was transferred to HQMC, Washington, D.C., where he headed the Operations Branch of the Supply Department. In Feb. 1955, he was promoted to brigadier general and assumed duties as Executive Officer of the Supply Department and Head of the Supply Branch. Gen. Allen served as Assistant Quartermaster General of the Marine Corps from Sept. 1957, until Mar.

1959, when he was named Director, Marksmanship Training Division. In Sept. 1959, he resumed his former post as Assistant Quartermaster General of the Marine Corps. He served in this capacity until Jan. 1, 1960, when he was named Quartermaster General of the Marine Corps and promoted to major general.

ANDERSON, Norman Jacob. Brigadier General. Combat aviator in both WWII and Korea. Deputy Chief of Staff (Air) HQMC (1963): b. Manitowoc, Wis., Feb. 7, 1913. After graduation from Glendale, Calif., High School, he attended the University of California at Los Angeles where he was a member of the ROTC unit, and graduated in 1934 with a Bachelor of Arts degree in history. In Jan. 1936, he was appointed an aviation cadet in the Marine Corps Reserve and the following month was assigned active duty as a student naval aviator at Pensacola, Fla. He was designated a naval aviator Feb. 26, 1937, and subsequently was assigned to aviation duty at Quantico, Va. and again at Pensacola. While at Quantico he was appointed a Marine Reserve second lieutenant. In Apr. 1940, when his active duty period expired, Lt. Anderson joined American Airlines as a pilot. A year before WWII broke out, he requested reassignment to active duty and returned to Pensacola as an instructor. He was integrated in the regular Marine Corps on Feb. 25, 1941, as a first lieutenant. When WWII began, he was serving as Aide to the CG of the 1st MAW. He was promoted to captain in Feb. 1942, and to major in Aug. 1942. Ordered overseas, he served as pilot and Assistant Group Operations Officer with MAWG 25 in the Solomons from Aug. 1942, to Sept. 1943. Later, Anderson flew more than 100 bombing missions as CO, Marine Bombing Squadron 423 in the Bismarck

Archipelago and Philippines campaigns from Feb. 1944, to Sept. 1945. For heroism and distinguished service during this period, he was awarded three Distinguished Flying Crosses and seven Air Medals. He was promoted to lieutenant colonel in March 1944. Following the war, Lt. Col. Anderson returned to the United States, and served until Feb. 1947 at the Marine Corps Air Station, El Toro, Calif., as Executive Officer, Air Base Group 2, and Commander, Aircraft Engineering Squadron 21, respectively. Assigned next to Marine Corps Schools, Quantico, he completed the Junior Course in Aug. 1947, then served for two years as Chief, Air Section, Junior School. In Sept. 1949, he returned to El Toro as Executive Officer of MAG-33, and the following Mar. became Deputy Group Commander. With the outbreak of hostilities in Korea, Lt. Col. Anderson embarked in Aug. 1950 with his group for the western Pacific. As Deputy Group Commander, MAG-33, and as a pilot in Marine Fighting Squadron 323, based aboard the USS *Badoeng Strait*, he earned the Silver Star Medal, his fourth Distinguished Flying Cross, and his eighth through tenth Air Medals. The citation for the Silver Star Medal awarded him for gallantry in action on Aug. 17, 1950, during the Pusan Perimeter fighting, states in part: "Organizing and leading a well-planned aerial attack against an enemy-held bridgehead across the Naktong River, south of Taegu, Korea, Lieutenant Colonel Anderson succeeded in clearing the area for later occupation by Marine ground forces. When advancing Marine troops became pinned down by intense gunfire from enemy positions along a ridge line, he daringly marked out enemy targets for his aerial attack group despite the defiladed and camouflaged nature of the hostile positions which necessitated the execution of extremely low passes directly over fire-spurting enemy guns. After the bombs and rockets of his aerial group were expended, he led his flight in bold strafing attacks against a cornered and desperately fighting enemy in support of advancing Marine troops." Lt. Col. Anderson was assigned to the Pacific Fleet Evaluation Group in Mar. 1951. While serving in this capacity, he was promoted to colonel in Dec. 1951, and the following June returned to the States. In Aug. 1952, Col. Anderson entered the National War College at Washington, D.C. Upon graduation in June 1953, he was ordered to head the Air Section, Tactics and Techniques Board, Marine Corps Schools, Quantico, Va. for three years. In June 1956, he was assigned to HQMC and served as Chief of the Policy Analysis Division until June 1959. In Sept., after six weeks of intensive flying with the Jet Transition Training Unit at Olathe, Kan., he reported to the 1st MAW in the Far East. In Dec. 1959, Col. Anderson assumed command of MAG 11, Atsugi, Japan which, during the succeeding 12 months, operated at various times from airfields and aircraft carriers throughout the western Pacific as part of the Marine Corps mobile ready forces. Reporting again to the National War College in Jan. 1961, for special staff work, Col. Anderson, in May, was assigned to a board convened to examine the organization of HQMC. In Aug. 1961, he became Deputy Assistant Chief of Staff (G-3), HQMC. He was promoted to his present rank of brigadier general on Nov. 1, 1961. In May 1962, upon the reorganization of the Office of the Deputy Chief of Staff (Plans), Gen. Anderson was designated as the Assistant to the Deputy Chief of Staff (Plans) for Joint Matters. He served in this capacity until July 1962, when he became Deputy Chief of Staff (Air), HQMC.

ANDERSON, Richard Beatty. Private First Class. Medal of Honor: b. Tacoma, Wash., June 26, 1921; d. KIA, Roi Island, Kwajalein Atoll, Marshall Islands, Feb. 1, 1944. Before enlisting in the Marine Corps on July 6, 1942, he graduated from Sequim High School and worked for 11 months in the Richmond shipyards in Richmond, Calif. Completing recruit training at San Diego, Anderson went to Camp Elliott, San Diego, for Infantry Training. Shortly thereafter he joined Co. E, 2nd Bn., 23rd Marines and, with this unit, he sailed for the Marshalls in Jan. 1944. On Roi Island, as a member of the invasion force, while on a sniper hunt, he chose a shell hole in the center of the Roi airfield as a vantage point from which to attack Japanese positions. In the shell crater, also occupied by three buddies, Anderson was preparing to throw a grenade at an enemy position when it slipped from his hand and rolled toward his comrades. Realizing that there would be insufficient time to retrieve the armed weapon and throw it, he hurled himself on the sputtering grenade and took the full impact of the explosion on his own body, thereby sacrificing himself for the lives of his friends. Seriously injured, the 22-year-old Marine — with "Death Before Dishonor" tattooed on his arm — was evacuated to a ship where he died of his wounds. He was buried at sea with full military honors. For his selfless act of heroism he was posthumously awarded the Medal of Honor.

APPLETON, Edwin Nelson. Corporal. Medal of Honor: b. Brooklyn, N.Y., Aug. 29, 1876. Cpl. Appleton's citation reads, in part: " . . . in action against the enemy at Tientsin, China, June 20, 1900, crossing the river in a small boat while under heavy enemy fire, he assisted in destroying buildings occupied by the enemy. . . ."

B

BAILEY, Kenneth Dillon. Major. Medal of Honor: b. Pawnee, Okla., Oct. 21, 1910; d. KIA, Guadalcanal, Sept. 13, 1942. Bailey received his second lieutenant's commission on July 1, 1935, and joined the 5th Marines at Quantico, Va. Maneuvers at San Diego and in the Caribbean preceded his assignment aboard the USS *Pennsylvania* as Detachment and Battery Officer. He became a first lieutenant on Jan. 19, 1939, while serving aboard the vessel. A short tour of duty as Range Officer at Quantico followed. Then he was off to the Recruit Depot at Parris Island where he served as Assistant Training Officer. The major was ordered to Guantanamo Bay, Cuba, in Dec. 1940, where he joined the 1st Mar. Brig. He was promoted to captain in Mar. 1941. At Quantico in June 1941, he joined the 5th Marines as a company commander. In Feb. 1942, his unit was redesignated the 1st Mar. Raider Bn. The unit was ordered to San Diego, Calif. in Apr. 1942, and, on the last day of that month, it reached Tutuila, Samoa. He was promoted to major on May 8, 1942, prior to the assault on Tulagi. Bailey made the bloody landing, then moved on with his unit to Guadalcanal, where he lost his life in the bitter fighting. His citation reads, in part, ". . . for extraordinary courage and heroic conduct as Commanding Officer of a Marine Raider company during the Japanese attack on Henderson Field, Guadalcanal, on September 12-13, 1942. With great resourcefulness, he stemmed a retreat against great odds, reorganized his troops, generally improved the position of our forces, and repeatedly led his troops in fierce hand-to-hand combat for a period of 10 hours despite a severe head wound. His

great personal valor, while exposed to constant and merciless enemy fire, and his indomitable fighting spirit inspired his troops to heights of heroic endeavor which enabled them to repulse the enemy and hold Henderson Field. He gallantly gave up his life in the service of his country."

BARBER, William Earl. Lieutenant Colonel. Medal of Honor: b. Dehart, Ky., Nov. 30, 1919. William Barber enlisted in the Marine Corps on Mar. 13, 1940. Completing boot camp at Parris Is., S.C. in May 1940, he remained there until Oct. 1941, when he entered parachute training at NAS, Lakehurst, N.J. He was a parachute instructor at Lakehurst, San Diego, Calif. and Camp Lejeune, N.C. from Mar. 1942 until June 1943, then entered the Officer Candidates' Class at Quantico. He was commissioned a second lieutenant on Aug. 11, 1943. After further instruction at Quantico until Oct. 1943, Lt. Barber was assigned for three months to parachute duty at San Diego. He joined the 26th Mar. Regt., 5th Mar. Div. at Camp Pendleton in Jan. 1944 as a platoon commander, and sailed with the regiment for Hawaii in Aug. 1944. In Jan. 1945, he sailed for Iwo Jima, where he fought with the regiment until Mar. 1945. The following month he was promoted to first lieutenant. Barber again served in Hawaii from Apr. to Sept. 1945, when he was ordered to occupation duty at Sasebo, Japan. Returning to San Diego in Jan. 1946, he served there briefly before he was assigned to recruiting duty at Milwaukee, Wis. That Nov. he was made a company commander at Camp Lejeune. In Sept. 1947, he was appointed Inspector-Instructor of the Marine Corps

Reserve's Co. D, 6th Infantry Bn. at Altoona, Pa. Following his promotion to captain in Aug. 1949, he was assigned to the MB at the Philadelphia Navy Yard the following month. In Oct. 1950, Capt. Barber was ordered to Korea where he took part in the Chosin Reservoir campaign during which he earned the Medal of Honor. His citation reads, in part: "...as CO of Co. F, 2nd Bn., 7th Marines, 1st Mar. Div. (Reinf.) in action against enemy aggressor forces in Korea from Nov. 28 to Dec. 2, 1950. Assigned to defend a three mile mountain pass along the division's main supply line and commanding the only route of approach in the march from Yudam-ni to Hagaruri, Capt. Barber took position with his battle-weary troops and, before nightfall, had dug in and set up a defense along the frozen, snow covered hillside. When a force of estimated regimental strength savagely attacked during the night, inflicting heavy casualties, and finally surrounding his position following a bitterly fought seven hour conflict, Capt. Barber, after repulsing the enemy, gave assurance that he could hold if supplied by air drops. He requested permission to stand fast when orders were received by radio to fight his way back to a relieving force after two reinforcing units had been driven back under fierce resistance in their attempts to reach the isolated troops. Aware that leaving the position would sever contact with the 8000 Marines trapped at Yudam-ni and jeopardize their chances of joining the 3000 more awaiting their arrival in Hagaru-ri for the continued drive to the sea, he chose to risk loss of his command rather than sacrifice more men if the enemy seized control and forced a renewed battle to regain the position, or abandon his many wounded who were unable to walk. Although severely wounded in the leg on

the early morning of the 29th, Capt. Barber continued to maintain personal control, often moving up and down the lines on a stretcher to direct the defense and consistently encouraging and inspiring his men to supreme efforts despite the staggering opposition. Waging desperate battle throughout five days and six nights of repeated onslaughts launched by the fanatical aggressors, he and his heroic command accounted for approximately 1000 enemy dead in this epic stand in bitter sub-zero weather, and when the company was relieved, only 82 of his original 220 men were able to walk away from the position so valiantly defended against insuperable odds..." Because of his wound, Barber was evacuated on Dec. 5 and hospitalized in Yokosuka, Japan, until his return to the States in Mar. 1951. That Apr. he was assigned as a company commander and, later, Executive Officer of the 1st Recruit Training Bn. at the Marine Corps Recruit Depot, San Diego. While stationed in San Diego, he was promoted to major in July 1952. In Aug. 1953, Maj. Barber entered the Infantry School, Fort Benning, Ga., and upon graduation in Mar. 1954, was assigned as S-3, 2nd Bn., 2nd Marines, Camp Lejeune. In May 1956, he embarked for Thailand where he served as Assistant Naval Attaché and Assistant Naval Attaché for Air at the American Embassy in Bangkok from June 1956 through Aug. 1958. He then returned to the States and served as an instructor and, later, Assistant Chief Instructor of the Junior School, MCS, Quantico. He was promoted to lieutenant colonel in Apr. 1960, and remained at Quantico until June 1962. Again ordered overseas, Lt. Col. Barber joined the 3rd Mar. Div. on Okinawa in July 1962 as CO of the Reconnaissance Battalion.

Barnett

BARNETT, George. Major General. 12th Commandant of the Marine Corps, and the first to serve under the policy of a four-year term. Appointed to his first term on Feb. 25, 1914, but retained because of the exigencies of WWI until June 30, 1920. As CMC of the Corps he guided it through its rapid expansion and demobilization after WWI: b. Lancaster, Wis., Dec. 9, 1859; d. Washington, D.C., Apr. 27, 1930. George Barnett graduated from the U.S. Naval Academy in 1881, and went to sea as a cadet-midshipman. He was commissioned a Marine second lieutenant July 1, 1883. After serving briefly at the Brooklyn, N.Y., and Mare Island, Calif., Navy Yards he was assigned in July 1884, to the USS *Pinta*. He was attached to that ship until Aug. 1887,

when he was ordered to the Navy Yard, Washington, D. C. In Apr. 1888, he entered the torpedo school at Newport, R.I., returning to Washington in Aug. of the same year. After brief tours of duty at the Washington Navy Yard and the Marine Barracks, Washington, he joined the Marine Detachment of the USS *Iroquois* in May 1889. Barnett returned to the Washington Navy Yard in May 1892. He was temporarily detached to the Marine Guard at the Columbian Exposition in Chicago from May to Dec. 1893, and completed his Washington tour in Mar. 1896, when he was ordered to the Marine Barracks, Portsmouth, N.H. In June 1896, he joined the Marine Detachment of the USS *Vermont*, and in Nov. 1897, was ordered to the USS *San Francisco*. In Apr. 1898, he was given command of the Marine Detachment of the USS *New Orleans*, serving aboard that ship throughout the Spanish-American War and participating in the shelling of Spanish forts at Santiago, Cuba. He was transferred to the USS *Chicago* in Nov. 1898. Barnett returned to Washington in Apr. 1901, served several months at HQMC, and in July of that year began a three-month tour of duty at Newport, R.I. In Oct. 1901, he was given command of the recruiting districts of western New Jersey, Delaware and Pennsylvania, with headquarters at Philadelphia. In Sept. 1902, he assumed command of a battalion of Marines sent to Panama to protect the railroad across the Isthmus. He returned to Washington with the battalion in Dec. 1902, and in Jan. 1903, accompanied it to Cavite, Philippine Islands, to join the 1st Mar. Brig. there. In July 1903, he was named Fleet Marine Officer of the Asiatic Fleet and commander of the Marine Detachment aboard the USS *Kentucky*. He took command of the 1st Mar. Brig. at Cavite in Dec. 1904, returned to Washington in May 1905, and two months later assumed command of the Marine Barracks, Navy Yard, Washington, D.C. From June to Sept. 1906, he was stationed at the Naval War College, Newport, R.I. Barnett was again given command of an expeditionary battalion in Sept. 1906, and accompanied the battalion to Havana, where it became part of the Cuban Army of Pacification. The expeditionary force was soon expanded to a regiment, which he also commanded. The regiment was sent to Cienfuegos, and occupied a large part of that island. When the U. S. Army relieved his unit in Nov. 1906, General Barnett returned to Washington, resuming his command of the Marine Barracks at the Washington Navy Yard. In Nov. 1907, he began a brief tour of duty at HQMC, and in Jan. 1908, was ordered to China to command the Marine Detachment at the U.S. Legation in Peking. Upon his return to the States in Oct. 1910; he was given command of the Marine Barracks, Philadelphia. His tour of duty at Philadelphia was interrupted three times by temporary expeditionary duty to settle domestic disturbances in Cuba. He commanded the 1st Mar. Regt. in Cuba from Mar. to June 1911, from May to Aug. 1912, and from Feb. to May 1913. In Dec. 1913, he was given the additional command of the 1st Advance Base Brig., with which he participated in the Atlantic Fleet maneuvers at Puerto Rico in Jan. and Feb. 1914. Upon his return from Puerto Rico, Gen. Barnett reported to HQMC in Washington and accepted his appointment as Commandant. Before the entry of the United States into WWI, he sent expeditionary forces to capture Vera Cruz, Mexico in 1914, and to settle domestic disturbances in Haiti in 1915 and the Dominican Republic in 1916. In Oct. 1920, Gen. Barnett became the first CG of the Department

of the Pacific, serving in that capacity until his retirement on Dec. 9, 1923, at the age limit of 64. He died Apr. 27, 1930.

Basilone

BASILONE, John. "Manila John." Gunnery Sergeant. Awarded the Medal of Honor for outstanding heroism at Guadalcanal: b. Buffalo, N.Y., Nov. 4, 1916; d. KIA, Iwo Jima, D-Day, Feb. 19, 1945. Attended parochial school at Raritan, N.J., then enlisted in the U.S. Army and was ordered to Manila which, later during WWII, gave him his famous nickname, "Manila John." In July, 1940, he enlisted in the Marine Corps. After duty at Guantanamo Bay, Cuba; Quantico, Va.; Parris Island, S.C.; and Camp Lejeune, N.C., he shipped out for the Solomons. At Guadalcanal, where he was serving with the 1st Bn., 7th Marines, 1st

Div., he used a machine gun and a pistol to pile up 38 Japanese bodies in front of his emplacement and win his nation's highest military decoration. The citation accompanying his Medal of Honor states: " ... while serving with the 1st Bn. 7th Marines, 1st Mar. Div., in the Lunga Area, Guadalcanal, Solomon Islands, on Oct. 24 and 25, 1942. While the enemy was hammering at the Marines' defensive positions, Sgt. Basilone, in charge of two sections of heavy machine guns, fought valiantly to check the savage and determined assault. In a fierce frontal attack with the Japanese blasting his guns with grenades and mortar fire, one of Sgt. Basilone's sections, with its gun crews, was put out of action, leaving only two men able to carry on. Moving an extra gun into position, he placed it in action, then, under continual fire, repaired another and personally manned it, gallantly holding his line until replacements arrived. A little later, with ammunition critically low and the supply lines cut off, Sgt. Basilone, at great risk of his life and in the face of continued enemy attack, battled his way through hostile lines with urgently needed shells for his gunners, thereby contributing in a large measure to the virtual annihilation of a Japanese regiment." At Iwo Jima, Sgt. Basilone again distinguished himself, singlehandedly destroying a Japanese blockhouse while braving smashing bombardment of enemy heavy caliber fire. For his exploit he was posthumously awarded the Navy Cross. While at Iwo Jima he was attached to the 1st Bn., 27th Marines, 5th Mar. Div. Following WWII Basilone's remains were reinterred in the Arlington National Cemetery. In July, 1949, the USS *Basilone*, a destroyer, was commissioned in his honor at the Boston Naval Shipyard.

BATTELL, William Putnam. Major General. Assistant Quartermaster General, HQMC, (1963): b. Mediapolis, Iowa, Dec. 26, 1906. Gen. Battell attended Iowa State College prior to enlisting in the Marine Corps in Apr. 1927. After completing radio school and serving as an instructor at the Naval Radio Materiel School, Anacostia, Md., he was selected for Officers' Candidate School in July, 1929. He was commissioned a second lieutenant on Jan. 31, 1930, at Quantico, Va. After brief duty at the Marine Barracks, Norfolk Navy Yard, Battell entered Basic School at Philadelphia, Pa., in Aug. 1930. On completing the course in June 1931, he was assigned to the Marine Barracks, Navy Yard, Washington, D.C., prior to sailing for China duty. In May 1932, he joined the Marine Detachment in Peiping, China, and on his return to the States in Nov. 1932, was stationed at Mare Island, Calif. In July, 1933, he began a year's duty aboard the USS *Saratoga*, and the following July was assigned communications duty at the MCB, San Diego, Calif. He was transferred to Quantico in Jan. 1935, and promoted to first lieutenant. In Sept. he entered the Army Signal School at Fort Monmouth, N.J. He completed the course in June 1936, then served a year as an instructor in the Basic School, Philadelphia. In July 1937, he returned to Quantico, and was promoted to captain. In May 1938, Capt. Battell began another tour of sea duty, serving as Detachment Commanding Officer aboard the USS *Arkansas* and USS *New York* successively. In July 1939, he reported to the Depot of Supplies at Philadelphia, as Signal Supply Officer, remaining there until Sept. 1941. That month he was assigned to the Radio Division, Bureau of Ships, Navy Department, Washington, D.C., to serve as Head of the Marine Corps Installation and Maintenance Group, until Feb. 1944. He was promoted to major in Jan. 1942, and to lieutenant colonel in Aug. 1942. Reporting to FMF, Pacific, in early 1944, Lt. Col. Battell saw duty in the Pacific area as Signal Supply Officer, Service Command. For service in this capacity, in support of the Marianas, Palau, and Iwo Jima operations, he received the Bronze Star Medal with Combat "V." In Oct. 1946, shortly after his return to the States, he was based at the San Francisco Depot of Supplies, where he served almost five years. He was promoted to colonel in Mar. 1948. Following his detachment from the Depot of Supplies in Aug. 1951, Col. Battell was enrolled at the Naval War College, Newport, R.I., and completed the course in June 1952. During the next two years, he served as Supply Officer at the Marine Corps Schools, Quantico, until Sept. 1954. That Oct. he moved to the MCB, Camp Pendleton, as Base Supply Officer. In Dec. 1955, he joined the 3rd Mar. Div. in Japan as CO of the 3rd Service Regt. He was assigned to HQMC in Dec. 1956. Upon his promotion to brigadier general in Jan. 1957, Gen. Battell assumed duty as Director, Materiel Division, Supply Department. Following this assignment, he served as CG of the Marine Corps Supply Center, Albany, Ga., from July 1958, through Sept. 1962. He was promoted to major general in Aug. 1962. He assumed his present assignment as Assistant Quartermaster General of the Marine Corps in Oct. 1962.

BAUER, Harold William. Lieutenant Colonel. Medal of Honor: b. Woodruff, Kans., Nov. 20, 1908; d. MIA, vicinity Russell Is., Nov. 14, 1942. Harold Bauer entered the Naval Academy from Nebraska in 1926; and after graduation in 1930, he was appointed a Marine second

lieutenant. Following his commissioning, Lt. Bauer attended the Officers' Basic School at Quantico, Va. He was then assigned as a company officer with the 1st Bn., 6th Marines at Quantico after completing the basic school there. He was later assigned to NAS at Pensacola, Fla., in Dec. 1934 where he won his wings as a Marine aviator in Feb. 1936. Bauer was transferred to NAS, San Diego, Calif. in June 1940 where he served as squadron officer of a fighter squadron. While stationed at San Diego, he participated in carrier group exercises on the USS *Lexington* and USS *Saratoga*. When the Japanese attacked Pearl Harbor, Col. Bauer was sent to Midway for duty as a squadron commander. He was transferred to Hawaii in Feb. 1942, and then was ordered to the south Pacific where he took command of Marine Fighter Squadron 212. On Sept. 28, 1942, Bauer's squadron was attacked by a superior force of Japanese planes and, undaunted by the odds, he engaged the enemy and shot down one of their bombers. Again attacking a superior force on Oct. 3, Bauer shot down four of the enemy and left a fifth badly damaged. While leading a reinforcement flight on Oct. 16 from Espirito Santo to Guadalcanal 600 miles away, the colonel was about to land at Henderson Field when he noticed a squadron of Japanese planes attacking the USS *McFarland* off shore. Although the long flight from Espirito Santo had almost exhausted his fuel and he knew no friendly planes were able to assist him, he immediately proceeded alone to attack the enemy and succeeded in destroying four of them before lack of gasoline forced him to return to Henderson Field. Col. Bauer was forced to ditch his plane over water on Nov. 14, after downing two of the enemy in an attack 100 miles off Guadalcanal. He was last seen in the water in his Mae West and did not appear to be seriously hurt. Days of intense searching by planes and Russell Is. natives failed to locate any further trace of him. The squadron under the colonel's command at Guadalcanal was officially credited with 92 Japanese planes and helping to sink two of their destroyers. Col. Bauer's citation reads, in part: "... as squadron commander of Marine Fighter Squadron 212 in the south Pacific during the period of May 10 to Nov. 14, 1942. ... His intrepid fighting spirit and distinctive ability as a leader and an airman exemplified in his splendid record of combat achievement, were vital factors in the successful operations in the south Pacific Area."

BAUGH, William Bernard. Private First Class. Medal of Honor: b. McKinney, Ky., July 7, 1930; d. KIA, en route from Koto-ri to Hagaru-ri, Korea, Nov. 29, 1950. P.F.C. Baugh's citation reads, in part: "... while serving as a member of an Anti-Tank Assault Squad attached to Co. G, 3rd Bn., 1st Marines, 1st Mar. Div. (Reinf.), during a night time enemy attack on a motorized column en route from Koto-ri to Hagaru-ri, Korea, on Nov. 29, 1950. Acting instantly when a hostile hand grenade landed in his truck as he and his squad prepared to alight and assist in the repulse of an enemy force delivering intense automatic weapons and grenade fire from deeply entrenched and well-concealed roadside positions, P.F.C. Baugh quickly shouted a warning to the other men in the vehicle and, unmindful of his own personal safety, hurled himself upon the deadly missile, thereby saving his comrades from serious injury or possible death. ..."

BAUSELL, Lewis Kenneth. Corporal. Medal of Honor: b. Pulaski, Va., Apr. 17, 1924; d. KIA, Peleliu, Sept. 18, 1944.

Bausell enlisted in the Marine Corps on Dec. 15, 1941, and was sent to Parris Island for recruit training. At Guadalcanal he went ashore with the initial landing and fought there for four months before sailing for Melbourne, Australia. In the spring of 1943, he embarked for New Guinea. Serving with the 5th Marines, 1st Mar. Div., he prepared for the next campaign and made the Cape Gloucester, New Britain, landing three days after the original invasion. With the conclusion of that campaign, the Division returned to Pavuvu Is. for rest and rehabilitation. The next chore for the 5th Marines was the Peleliu landing on Sept. 15, 1944. They were the left flank regiment on the division front. In the first hour of action, the assault waves fought their way 100 yards inland to the top of a small coral ridge, one of dozens on the island. Bausell was in a squad assigned to clean out one of the many Japanese infested caves which honeycombed the ridge. On one side of the cave, a Marine second lieutenant and several of his men were using a flame thrower to drive the enemy out through the other side where Bausell and several others waited with rifles ready. Two men stood at the entrance, firing into the cave. A Japanese charged out holding a grenade against his body and lunged toward the little band of Marines. The grenade exploded, injuring several Marines and killing the enemy soldier. Another Japanese came to the exit and was shot. Then a third appeared and hurled a grenade into the group. Bausell threw himself upon it, taking the full impact of its explosion. Evacuated to a hospital ship, 20-year-old Cpl. Bausell died of his wounds three days later on Sept. 18, 1944. On Nov. 19, 1945, at Bath, Maine, a new destroyer, the USS *Bausell*, was christened by the corporal's mother.

BEARSS, Hiram Iddings. Brigadier General (Retired). Medal of Honor: b. Peru, Ind., Apr. 13, 1875; d. Aug. 26, 1938. During his distinguished career, Hiram Bearss served in the Philippine Is. from Dec. 1899 to May 1902, and during this period he served with Maj. Waller's battalion in Samar from Oct. 1901 to Mar. 1902; in Panama from Dec. 1903 to Mar. 1904; in Cuba in Feb., Mar. and Apr., 1913; in Mexico from Apr. to Aug. 1914, during which period he participated in the occupation of the city of Vera Cruz and the engagement incident thereto; and in Santo Domingo from June 1916 to May 1917. He was awarded the Medal of Honor on Mar. 13, 1934, for "extraordinary heroism and eminent and conspicuous conduct in battle at the junction of the Cadacan and Sojoton Rivers, Samar, P.I., Nov. 17, 1901. Capt. Bearss, second in command of the columns upon their uniting ashore in the Sohoton region, made a surprise attack on the fortified cliffs and completely routed the enemy, killing 30 and capturing and destroying the powder magazine, 40 lantacas (guns), rice, food, and cuartels. Due to his courage, intelligence, discrimination and zeal, he successfully led his men up the cliffs by means of bamboo ladders to a height of 200 feet. The cliffs were of soft stone of volcanic origin, in the nature of pumice, and were honeycombed with caves. Tons of rocks were suspended in platforms held in position by vine cables in readiness to be precipitated upon people below. After driving the insurgents from their position which was almost impregnable, being covered with numerous trails lined with poisoned spears, pits, etc., he led his men across the river, scaled the cliffs on the opposite side, and destroyed the camps there. He and the men under his command overcame incredible difficulties and dangers in destroying positions which, according to reports from old prisoners, had taken three years to perfect, were held as a final rallying point, and were never before penetrated by white troops. Capt. Bearss also rendered distinguished public service in the presence of the enemy at Quinapundan River, Samar, P.I., on Jan. 19, 1902." During WWI, Bearss served with distinction in various capacities. He arrived in France Aug. 20, 1917, and was in command of the Marine Base Detachment, 5th Regt., until Sept. 7, 1917; then first commander of Base Section No. 2 (Headquarters at Bordeaux) serving in this capacity from Sept. 8 to Oct. 25, 1917. He was relieved from this assignment at his own request and was assigned command of the 5th Mar. Regt., serving from Oct. 30, 1917 to Dec. 31, 1917; then second in command of the 5th Regt. from Jan. 1, 1918 to Feb. 26, 1918, when he was temporarily assigned to command of a battalion of the 9th Infantry. He commanded the 3rd Bn., 9th Infantry in the Toulon-Troyon sector southeast of the city of Verdun, France. He was detailed to duty at 2nd Div. HQ on May 1, 1918. During his tour of duty at Div. HQ he was Assistant Provost Marshal and CO of HQ Troop and APO 710. He was relieved from this duty on June 13, 1918, and assigned to the 6th Regt., Marine Corps, as second in command. On Aug. 24, 1918, he was assigned to the 26th Div. for duty as a regimental commander. He commanded the 102nd Infantry Regiment from Aug. 26, 1918 to Oct. 14, 1918, Oct. 25, 1918 to Nov. 8, 1918, and Nov. 24, 1918 to Dec. 7, 1918. He commanded the 51st Infantry Brig., 26th Div. Oct. 15-24, 1918 and Nov. 9-23, 1918. His tour of service with the 26th Div. included the Rupt sector (Lorraine), the St.-Mihiel operation, the Troyon sector

(Lorraine) and the Meuse-Argonne operation. In the St.-Mihiel action, he commanded the leading elements of the 51st Brig. in a bold and successful march southeast from the Rupt sector, through Dommartin-la-Montagne, the Grande Tranchée de Calonne, Vigneulles-les-Hattonchatel and established contact with the 1st Div. which was advancing from the south, thus completing the reduction of the St.-Mihiel salient. He was placed on the retired list as a colonel, Nov. 22, 1919, having been found permanently incapacitated for active service by a Marine Retiring Board because of physical disability incident to his service, and was advanced to the rank of brigadier general on Jan. 16, 1936.

BERKELEY, James Phillips. Major General: b. Portsmouth, Va., July 1, 1907. James Berkeley attended school at Shepherdstown, W. Va., and Severn Preparatory School. He enlisted in the Marine Corps on Mar. 1, 1927, and served in Nicaragua from Jan. to Dec. 1928. After nearly three years as an enlisted man, he was commissioned a Marine second lieutenant on Jan. 31, 1930, at the Marine Barracks, Washington, D.C. He was then ordered to the Philadelphia Navy Yard, where he served as a company officer at the MB and completed Basic School in June 1931. Following graduation he served at the Norfolk Navy Yard, Va., before sailing for China in Apr. 1932, for duty with the Marine Detachment at the American Embassy, Peiping. He returned to the States in Dec. 1935, while serving as a battalion communications officer with the 6th Mar. Regt. at San Diego, Calif. In May 1935, Lt. Berkeley reported to Quantico, Va., where he headed the communications platoons of the Fleet Marine Force and the 1st Mar. Brig. Detached from Quantico in Aug.

1936, he entered the Army Signal School at Fort Monmouth, N.J. On completing the course in June 1937, he returned to the 1st Brig. and was promoted to captain. Berkeley headed the 1st Brigade's communications platoon until Apr. 1938, then served as Brigade Communications Officer until Mar. 1939, when he left Quantico to take command of the Marine Detachment aboard the USS *Wichita*. Returning from sea duty in June 1941, he was named Communications Officer of the MCB at Quantico. He was serving in this post when WWII broke out. In Jan. 1942, he was promoted to major. In Mar. 1942, Maj. Berkeley was ordered to HQMC, Washington, D.C., to serve as Assistant Officer in Charge of the Communications Section, Division of Plans and Policies. He was promoted to lieutenant colonel in Aug. 1942. While attached to that section, he accompanied the Commandant of the Marine Corps on an inspection tour of Guadalcanal and other South Pacific areas in Oct. and Nov. 1942. He also made an observation tour of the United Kingdom, Africa, and Italy from Aug. to Oct. 1943. He was an observer with the 46th British Inf. Div. at the Salerno landing, Sept. 9, 1943. In Nov. 1943, he reported to Camp Pendleton, Calif., where he commanded the Field Signal Battalion prior to becoming Signal Officer of the 5th Mar. Div. in Feb. 1944. Sailing again for the Pacific area that Aug., Lt. Col. Berkeley served as 5th Div. Signal Officer in Hawaii and at Iwo Jima. He also served as Executive Officer of the 27th Marines, 5th Mar. Div., at Iwo Jima in Mar. 1945, and in Hawaii during the following two months. In July 1945, he was named Signal Officer of the 5th Amphibious Corps, serving in that capacity in Hawaii and Japan. He was promoted to colonel the following month. He then served as officer in charge of the disposition of enemy material from Oct. to Dec. 1945, and then as commander of the 6th Marines, 2nd Mar. Div., from Jan. to Mar. 1946. Berkeley returned from Japan in Apr. 1946, and the following month was named Assistant to the Navy Secretary of the Joint Army-Navy Secretariat, Office of the Secretary of the Navy, Washington, D.C. He remained with that organization until Jan. 1947. In Feb. 1947, Col. Berkeley sailed for Buenos Aires to serve as Amphibious Warfare Advisor to the Argentine Naval War College and as an advisor to the Argentine Marine Corps. He returned to the States in May 1949, and, after brief service with the Troop Training Unit, Atlantic, at Little Creek, Va., entered the Armed Forces Staff College at Norfolk in Aug. 1949. Completing that course in Jan. 1950, he reported the following month to the Naval War College at Newport, R.I., where he served as a staff member, and later as Assistant Head and Head of the Department of Strategy and Tactics. He left Newport in May 1953, to serve in Washington for the next year as CO of the Marine Barracks and Director of the Marine Corps Institute. He embarked for Korea in June 1954, to become Chief of Staff of the 1st Mar. Div. and returned with the division to Camp Pendleton the following spring. In July 1955, he was promoted to brigadier general and began three years' duty as Assistant Chief of Staff, G-1 (Personnel), at HQMC. He was promoted to the rank of major general in July 1958, on assuming duties as CG, Department of the Pacific, in San Francisco, Calif. Following this assignment, Gen. Berkeley served as CG, 2nd Mar. Div., FMF, at Camp Lejeune, N.C., from Nov. 1959, until Oct. 1961. In Nov. 1961, he assumed the duties of CG, MCB, Camp Lejeune.

Berkeley

BERKELEY, Randolph Carter. Major General. Medal of Honor: b. Staunton, Va., Jan. 9, 1875; d. U. S. Naval Hospital, Beaufort, S.C., Jan. 31, 1960. In Staunton, Va., Randolph Berkeley attended grade and high school. He graduated from Potomac Academy at Alexandria, Va., in 1891, and was appointed a Marine second lieutenant on Aug. 8, 1898, for service during the Spanish-American War. He was stationed at the Navy Yard, Washington, D.C., until he was honorably discharged on Jan. 9, 1899. He returned to the Corps in Apr. 1899, and was appointed a first lieutenant. In addition to his service at posts in the United States, the general served on a variety of assignments at sea and abroad. He served aboard the USS *Oregon* from Oct. 1899, to Mar. 1901; in the Philippines from

Apr. to June 1901; aboard the USS *Helena* from July 1901, to Aug. 1902; on expeditionary duty in Cuba in Sept. and Oct. 1906; aboard the USS *Kentucky* as commander of its Marine Detachment from Dec. 1907, to Nov. 1908; and in the Philippines and China from Dec. 1908, to Oct. 1910. Berkeley then took command of the 1st Bn., 2nd Advanced Base Regiment, in Dec. 1913, at Pensacola, Fla., and sailed with it for Vera Cruz in Mar. 1914. Berkeley, then a major, was commanding the 1st Bn. of the 2nd Advanced Base Regiment when he took part in the action for which he earned the nation's highest decoration on Apr. 21-22, 1914. Relations between the United States and the Huerta government of Mexico had been strained for some time, and a landing force of Marines and sailors was ordered ashore at Vera Cruz after a Huerta officer had arrested several U.S. Naval personnel at Tampico. The 2nd Regt. was the first ashore, meeting resistance from Mexican troops about noon on Apr. 21. The citation for his Medal of Honor describes General Berkeley's part in the action as follows: "For distinguished conduct in battle, engagements of Vera Cruz, Apr. 21 and 22, 1914, was eminent and conspicuous in command of his battalion; was in the fighting of both days, and exhibited courage and skill in leading his men through action. His cool judgment and courage and his skill in handling his men in encountering and overcoming the machine-gun and rifle fire down Cinco de Mayo and parallel streets accounts for the small percentage of the losses of Marines under his command." He returned to the States in Dec. 1914, and was stationed at Philadelphia until June 1915, when he sailed for Guam to command the Marine Barracks. Returning from Guam in Nov. 1917, he served at the Marine Barracks, New York, N.Y., and

Charleston, S.C., during the next two years. Gen. Berkeley was again ordered to expeditionary duty in Oct. 1919, serving for two years with the 1st Provisional Brig. Marines in Haiti. After he returned from that country in Nov. 1921, he served at New York, N.Y., and Norfolk and Quantico, Va. He completed the Field Officers' Course at Quantico in Aug. 1925, and a year of study at the Army War College, Washington, D.C. in June 1926. Returning to Quantico, he served as a commander of the 1st Mar. Regt. He served in that capacity for the next two years, except for the period from May to Aug. 1927, when he was commanding the 11th Mar. Regt. in Nicaragua. The general was ordered to Nicaragua again in May 1928, serving there for a year as Chief of Staff of the 2nd Mar. Brig. After his return to the States in Apr. 1929, he commanded the Marine Barracks at the Norfolk Navy Yard, Portsmouth, Va. He served in that capacity until Aug. 1930, when he was ordered to Quantico, Va. There he commanded the Marine Corps Schools until Nov. 1931, when he was again ordered to Nicaragua — this time as commander of the 2nd Mar. Brig. He returned to the States in Jan. 1933, and from then until May 1936, commanded the MB at Parris Island, S.C. He was then ordered to HQMC, Washington, D.C., where he was President of the Marine Corps Examining and Retiring Boards until Dec. 1938. He reached the statutory retirement age in Jan. 1939, and was placed on the retired list the following month as a major general. Following his retirement, Gen. Berkeley lived in Beaufort and Port Royal, until his death at the U.S. Naval Hospital, Beaufort. He was buried in Arlington National Cemetery on Feb. 4, 1960.

BERRY, Charles Joseph. Corporal. Medal

of Honor: b. Lorain, Ohio, July 10, 1923; d. KIA, Iwo Jima, Mar. 3, 1945. Following graduation from Lorain High School, young Berry enlisted in the Marine Corps at Cleveland, Ohio, and was sent to Parris Is. for recruit training. From boot camp he was transferred to Quantico, Va., then to New River, N.C., for parachute instruction. On June 2, 1942, now a qualified parachutist, Berry was promoted to private first class. He sailed from San Diego in Mar. 1943, for New Caledonia where he served with the First Parachute Bn. In Sept. 1943, the outfit left New Caledonia for the Solomon Is. In Nov. 1943, he landed at Bougainville, and during that campaign took part in the raid at Koairi Beach and in the Empress Augusta Bay action. Prior to returning to the States in Feb. 1944, he spent a short time at Guadalcanal. Following his arrival at Camp Elliott, San Diego, he joined the newly organized 5th Mar. Div. in early 1944, and in July departed for the Hawaiian Islands with his unit. He was advanced to corporal on July 22, 1944. Berry landed on Iwo Jima on D-Day, Feb. 19, 1945, and was killed in action on Mar. 3, 1945. His citation reads, in part, "Stationed in the front lines, Cpl. Berry manned his weapon with alert readiness as he maintained a constant vigil with other members of his gun crew during the hazardous night hours. When infiltrating Japanese soldiers launched a surprise attack shortly after midnight in an attempt to overrun his position, he engaged in a pitched hand grenade duel, returning the dangerous weapons with prompt and deadly accuracy until an enemy grenade landed in the foxhole. Determined to save his comrades, he unhesitatingly chose to sacrifice himself and immediately dived on the deadly missile, absorbing the shattering violence of the exploding charge

in his own body and protecting the others from serious injury. Stouthearted and indomitable, Cpl. Berry fearlessly yielded his own life that his fellow Marines might carry on the relentless battle against a ruthless enemy. . . ."

Biddle

BIDDLE, Anthony J. Drexel. Colonel. Internationally known swordsman and distinguished master of jujitsu, bayonet, and knife fighting. Served with the Marine Corps in two world wars, training Marines in the art of hand-to-hand combat: b. Philadelphia, Pa., Oct. 1, 1874; d. Syosset, N.Y., May 27, 1948. Two of the oldest Philadelphia families were combined in the name Anthony J. Drexel Biddle. Young Tony began his education by attending first grade in Spain where he later developed an interest in knife fighting. He became amateur heavy-weight champion of Spain and, although of medium height and weighing less than 175 pounds, he held his own in sparring contests with many of the heavy-weight champions including John L. Sullivan. Prior to WWI he startled Philadelphia society by taking a job as a reporter in the waterfront district, and later by building a boxing ring in his back yard so he could box with champions "just for the fun of it." At the outbreak of WWI, he organized the Philadelphia Military Training Corps, a private corporation of 1600 subscribers which in 1917 had 12,000 men in training. Early in 1917, he quietly enlisted in the Marine Corps as a private and in Mar. of that same year was commissioned a captain in the Marine Corps Reserve. In June 1917, he went to Port Royal, S.C. for basic instruction. Following a tour of duty with the AEF in France he was ordered to the MB, Quantico, Va. Appointed a major in Dec. 1918, he was later transferred to the Philadelphia Navy Yard. He was relieved from active duty in July 1919. Col. Biddle traveled extensively during the years following the war, and boxed with Kid McCoy, and "Philadelphia Jack" O'Brien. He fought an exhibition match with Georges Carpentier, an event which required police to keep the throngs of spectators orderly. It was Tony Biddle who first taught Gene Tunney, later heavyweight champion of the world, how to box while he was a private at Quantico during WWI. In Dec. 1926, at his own request, Biddle was recalled to active duty with the Marine Corps. Ordered to report to the Philadelphia Navy Yard, he trained exhibition combat teams invited to appear at the Philadelphia Sesquicentennial. He not only taught these teams, but engaged in the hand-to-hand fighting per-sonally. In Sept. 1928, again at his own request, he was ordered to report to the Basic School, Philadelphia, where he taught newly commissioned officers hand-to-hand combat. Between trips abroad and on this continent, he interspersed his periods of active duty with various special assignments. He taught agents of the Federal Bureau of Investigation the art of jujitsu. Following the Philadelphia Sesquicentennial he also shared his knowledge of jujitsu with that city's police force. He was appointed lieutenant colonel in the Marine Corps Reserve in Oct. 1934, shortly after reporting for one of his active duty periods. In June 1937, he was assigned to duty with the 5th Marines, 1st Mar. Brig., FMF, at Quantico. Following the Japanese attack on Pearl Harbor, Col. Biddle requested active duty with his Corps — although he retired in 1938 and was now 67 years of age. He was ordered to Quantico and taught bayonet fighting primarily in training camps on both the east and west coasts. Col. Biddle died on May 27, 1948.

BIDDLE, William P. Major General. 11th Commandant of the Marine Corps: b. Philadelphia, Pa., Dec. 15, 1853; d. Nice, France, 1923. Biddle was commissioned a second lieutenant in the Corps in June 1875, and after short tours of duty in Washington, New York, and Philadelphia, he made the first of his many tours of sea duty. After three years aboard the USS *Hartford* and *Powhatan*, he again went ashore for duty at Philadelphia and New York. He returned to sea duty on the *Kearsarge* in Mar. 1882, and was promoted to first lieutenant two years later. With a break of fewer than three years at the same domestic stations as his previous shore duty, he again went to sea for three years on board the *Swatara*. He returned to Philadelphia for duty in Feb. 1891, where he was advanced to captain three years later. Biddle resumed sea duty aboard the *Baltimore* in June 1895 and was shortly afterward transferred to the *Olympia,* on which ship he served during the Spanish-American War. Biddle was with Admiral Dewey at the Battle of Manila Bay. Soon after the close of the war, he returned to Philadelphia for duty, but was soon called to join the 4th Bn. of Marines, organized for duty in the Far East. With that battalion he arrived in China to take part in the famous relief expedition to Peking in 1900, After the Boxer Rebellion, Biddle was transferred with his battalion to the 1st Brig. of Marines, Philippine Is. where he served for more than two years. He then returned to the States for duty at HQMC, Washington, D.C. He was advanced to lieutenant colonel on Mar. 23, 1903 and in Dec. of that year he was ordered to Panama in command of the battalion of Marines on the *Dixie,* which arrived in time to participate in affairs when the independence of that country was declared. He returned to the States soon afterward, however, and served for short tours of duty in Philadelphia and at HQMC. He was promoted to colonel in Feb. 1905 and during the following year returned to the Philippine Is. where he commanded the 1st Brig. of Marines for approximately two years. He reported for duty at HQMC in May 1908, and was soon assigned command of an expeditionary brigade, organized in Philadelphia, for service in-Panama to reinforce the troops protecting the construction of the Panama Canal, and for potential duty in Nicaragua. Biddle returned to HQ in Apr. 1910, where he continued to serve the remainder of his active duty. During the closing months of Gen. Elliott's term as Commandant, Gen. Biddle acted as

Commandant of the Marine Corps most of the time. He was chosen as Commandant of the Corps on Feb. 3, 1911. His tour of duty as the 11th Commandant was a comparatively short, quiet, and uneventful one. He concerned himself primarily with the routine affairs of the Marine Corps. Under his tenure, several minor expeditions took place, including the first intervention in Nicaragua. Following approximately three years in office, Gen. Biddle applied for retirement on the ground of having completed more than thirty years' service, and he was retired on Feb. 24, 1914. He was recalled to active duty during WWI and served primarily on court-martial duty in San Diego, Calif.

BINDER, Richard. Sergeant. Medal of Honor: b. in Germany, July 26, 1839. Sgt. Binder won the Medal of Honor while aboard the USS *Ticonderoga,* as captain of a gun during the assault on Fort Fisher. He was cited for performing his duties with skill and courage during the first two days of battle, and on Jan. 13, 1865, "he remained steadfast as the *Ticonderoga* maintained a well-placed fire upon the batteries on shore, and thereafter, as she materially lessened the power on the mound which had been turned upon our assaulting columns...."

BINNEY, Arthur Fremont. Major General: b. Big Rapids, Mich., Nov. 25, 1905. After completing high school, Arthur Binney entered the U.S. Naval Academy at Annapolis. On June 7, 1928, he graduated and was commissioned a Marine second lieutenant. He remained at the Academy until Aug. 1928, then completed Basic School at the Philadelphia Navy Yard in June 1929. After preliminary flight training at the Naval Air Station, Hampton Roads, Va., and at Quantico,

Va., he began his final training at Pensacola, Fla., in Nov. 1929. He was designated a Naval Aviator July 1, 1930, and the following month was assigned aviation duty at Quantico. In May 1931, Lt. Binney sailed for Nicaragua where he served as Communications Officer, Aircraft Squadrons, 2nd Mar. Brig. Subsequently, in Aug. 1932, he was awarded the Nicaraguan Cross of Valor for frequent flights over dangerous terrain to rescue a detachment of Marines lost in the jungle. Returning to the States in Jan. 1933, he was reassigned aviation duty at Quantico. In June 1933, he began a year's study in the communications section of the Postgraduate School at the Naval Academy. While there he was promoted to first lieutenant in Nov. 1934. In Aug. 1935, following temporary duty under instruction at the Submarine Base, New London, Conn., Lt. Binney was assigned another year of postgraduate communications training at Harvard. The following July, he was ordered to San Diego, Calif., where he served for three years in aircraft communications. He was promoted to captain in Oct. 1936. He returned to Quantico in Aug. 1939, and was stationed there when WWII broke out. During his three years there, he served as Radio Officer of the 1st MAG; Communications Officer of Base Air Detachment 1; and CO of the Base Air Detachment's Headquarters Squadron. He also completed the Senior Course while at Quantico, and was promoted to major in Jan. 1942, then to lieutenant colonel in Aug. 1942. He served briefly at Cherry Point, N.C., and San Diego, Calif., then departed in Mar. 1943, from Marine Fleet Air, West Coast, for the Pacific area. Overseas he served as Communications Officer of the 4th Marine Aircraft Base Defense Wing; Executive Officer of MAG 13, Ellice and Marshall Islands; and Commander, Force

Aircraft, Forward Area, Samoan Group. He was promoted to colonel in Dec. 1943, and remained overseas until July 1944. Assigned to HQMC, Washington, D.C., Col. Binney served as Head, Personnel Section, Division of Aviation, until Oct. 1945, when he was appointed Naval Attaché and Naval Attaché for Air for the U.S. Embassies in Guatemala, El Salvador, Honduras, Nicaragua, and Costa Rica. In June 1948, he returned to Washington and was assigned to the Bureau of Aeronautics, Navy Department, serving as Deputy Director of the Electronics Div. until Mar. 1949, and as Director until June 1950. He then completed the course at the Naval War College, Newport, R.I., in June 1951. The following month, Col. Binney departed for Korea where he served as Chief of Staff, 1st MAW until May 1952. Early in 1952, he was released from his Chief of Staff duties for three months to command MAG 33 in Korea. On his return to the States, he was assigned to Quantico and began a two-year assignment as CO of the Marine Corps Air Station there. In Sept. 1954, he was promoted to brigadier general and assumed duties as Assistant Commanding General of the 3rd MAW at Miami, Fla. In June 1955, Gen. Binney became Commander of Marine Air Reserve Training at the Naval Air Station, Glenview, Ill., serving there until Nov. 1956. Ordered to Japan, he assumed duties in Jan. 1957, as CG, 1st MAW, Aircraft, FMF, Pacific. While serving in this post, he was promoted to his present rank of major general in Apr. 1957. In Jan. 1958, he was named CG of the 2nd MAW at Cherry Point. He held this command until Dec. 1959, when he was assigned to HQMC as Director of Aviation. Following this assignment he assumed his current duties at Norfolk in Sept. 1961, as Deputy Commander, FMF, Atlantic.

BONNYMAN, Alexander, Jr. "Sandy." First Lieutenant. Medal of Honor: b. Atlanta, Ga., May 2, 1910; d. KIA, Betio Is., Tarawa Atoll, Gilbert Is., Nov. 22, 1943. After attending Princeton University, class of 1932, where he was a first stringer on the football team, "Sandy" Bonnyman left school to join the Army Air Corps where he became a Flying Cadet. He was honorably discharged on Sept. 19, 1932, and went to work with his father's huge coal mining company. In 1938, Bonnyman acquired his own copper mine in the mountains near Santa Fe, N. Mex. With the advent of WWII, he enlisted as a private in the Marine Corps at Phoenix, Ariz., and took his recruit training at San Diego. In Oct. 1942, he sailed for the South Pacific aboard the USS *Matsonia* with the 6th Marines, 2nd Mar. Div. Combat in the final stages of the Guadalcanal campaign followed and in Feb. 1943, Bonnyman, now a corporal, received a field promotion to the rank of second lieutenant. The next stop was Tarawa. Landing on D-Day, Nov. 20, 1st Lt. Bonnyman — having been promoted on Sept. 1, 1943 — was Executive Officer of the 2nd Bn., 8th Marines' Shore Party. When the assault troops were pinned down by heavy enemy artillery fire at the seaward end of the long Betio Pier, Lt. Bonnyman, on his own initiative, organized and led the men over the open pier to the beach. There he voluntarily obtained flame throwers and demolitions, organized his pioneer shore party into assault demolitionists, and directed the blowing up of several hostile installations before the close of D-Day. On the second day of the epic struggle for that strategically important piece of coral, Bonnyman, determined to effect an opening in the enemy's strongly defended defense line, led his demolition team in an assault on the entrance to a huge bombproof

shelter which contained approximately 150 Japanese soldiers. This strong point was inflicting heavy casualties upon the Marines and was holding up their advance. The enemy position was about 40 yards forward of the Marine lines. The lieutenant advanced his team to the mouth of the position, killing many of the defenders before they were forced to withdraw to replenish their supply of ammunition and grenades. On the third and final day, Bonnyman renewed his attack upon the enemy position, leading his men in the placing of flame throwers and demolitions in both mouths of the cave. He pressed his attack and gained the top of the structure flushing more than 100 of its occupants into the open where they were shot down. Assailed by additional Japanese, the lieutenant stood at the forward edge of the position and killed three of the attackers before he himself fell mortally wounded. His men beat off the counterattack and broke the back of the resistance. The island was declared secured on the day of Lt. Bonnyman's death.

BORDELON, William James. Staff Sergeant. Medal of Honor: b. San Antonio, Tex., Dec. 25, 1920; d. KIA, Tarawa Atoll, Gilbert Is., Nov. 20, 1943. After attending local schools in his hometown and graduating from Central Catholic High School, where he had become a cadet officer in the ROTC, Bordelon entered the Marine Corps on Dec. 10, 1941, and received his recruit training at San Diego, Calif. On graduation from boot camp, he was assigned to Company D, 2nd Engr. Bn., 2nd Mar. Div., where his promotions came rapidly. By July 10, 1942, he had reached the rank of sergeant and was transferred to Co. C, 18th Marines. On Oct. 20, 1942, his outfit embarked for Wellington, New Zealand, where they remained for six weeks before leaving for Guadalcanal aboard the USS *President Hayes*. Bordelon's organization remained on the Japanese-infested island from Jan. 4, 1943, until Feb. 19, 1943, and then returned to New Zealand, this time aboard the USS *President Adams*. The next few months were spent in preparation for the next campaign. Bordelon was promoted to staff sergeant on May 13, 1943, and transferred to Company A, 1st Bn., 18th Marines, on Oct. 10. One week later he boarded the USS *Zeilin*, but the vessel did not leave Wellington until Nov. 1. Making one stop at Efate, New Hebrides, on the 7th and sailing again on the 18th, the *Zeilin* arrived off grim, enemy-held Tarawa on D-Day, Nov. 20, 1943. During the subsequent landing, Sgt. Bordelon was one of four men from his tractor to reach the beach alive. The sergeant and a buddy, Sgt. Elden Beers, went over the tractor's side together and were immediately caught in the barbed wire entanglement. Extricating themselves under heavy fire, the two Marines and two others from their craft managed to hit the beach and secure a little protection behind a four-foot-high seawall. In their struggle to reach the beach, the Marines lost all their equipment except a few small arms and two packages of dynamite. Quickly forming the dynamite into demolition charges, Sgt. Bordelon personally put two pillboxes out of action. Assaulting a third enemy position, the sergeant was hit by enemy machine gun fire just as one of his charges left his hand. The backlash from the charge also wounded Bordelon and he had to be bandaged by two of his companions. The small band behind the seawall was still pinned to the sand by fire which was coming from a machine gun nest 200 yards up the beach. Gathering up the last two demolition charges,

Bordelon started to crawl toward the enemy gunpit. He succeeded in destroying the position but, in doing so, was again hit through the left arm. He returned and asked his men to apply a tourniquet. Taking a rifle, Sgt. Bordelon provided fire coverage for a group attempting to scale the wall. In the meantime, his companions had decided to try to rescue a group of wounded Marines who were floundering around in the water offshore. On their first move another enemy machine gun pinned them down. The sergeant, seeing his companion wounded, started off in search of a corpsman, but was unable to locate one. Instead he stumbled on a rifle grenade and immediately returned to take action against enemy machine gunners who were holding up the rescue of the wounded. As he started his next single-handed attack, his attention was caught by a badly wounded Marine whom the surf had thrown upon the beach. Immediately going to the aid of the Marine, he was caught in the shoulder by a burst of enemy fire. Although he was suffering from multiple wounds, he lunged toward the enemy gun and employing the rifle grenade, destroyed the nest before he fell dead from a final burst of enemy fire. This Marine hero was originally buried in Lone Palm Cemetery on Betio Is., Tarawa Atoll. He later was moved to the U.S. Army Mausoleum at Schofield Barracks, Hawaii. The Medal of Honor was posthumously awarded to him by President Franklin D. Roosevelt.

BOUKER, John Griswold. Brigadier General: b. Greenfield, Mass., July 27, 1914. John Bouker graduated from Greenfield High School in 1931 and Deerfield Academy in Deerfield, Mass., in 1932. He then entered Dartmouth College, Hanover, N.H. While still in college, he enlisted in the Marine Corps Reserve in June 1935, and completed Marine Platoon Leaders' Class at Quantico, Va. that August. Upon graduation from Dartmouth in 1936, he was awarded a Bachelor of Arts degree, and was commissioned a Marine Reserve second lieutenant on Aug. 6, 1936, to rank from July 1, 1936. During the next three years he was employed by the Liberty Mutual Insurance Company of Boston, Mass. In April 1937, he joined the 2nd Inf. Bn., Organized Marine Corps Reserve, in Boston. On Sept. 30, 1939, he was ordered to active duty as a first lieutenant, and completed the First Reserve Officers' Class at Marine Corps Schools, Quantico, that Nov. Assigned next to the Marine Barracks, Parris Is., S.C., Lt. Bouker served as a battery officer with the 4th Defense Bn., FMF, until Feb. 1941, when he embarked with his battery for Guantanamo Bay, Cuba. In Oct. 1941, he returned to the States, serving in the Artillery Section (later the Gunnery Section) of the Division of Plans and Policies at HQMC for 18 months. He was promoted to captain in Feb. 1942, and to major in Aug. 1942. In June 1943, after instruction in the Coast Artillery School, Fort Monroe, Va., Maj. Bouker embarked for the Pacific area. He took part in three WWII campaigns, including the occupation and defense of Cape Torokina during the Treasury-Bougainville operation, the consolidation of the northern Solomons, and the assault and occupation of Okinawa. He was promoted to lieutenant colonel in Apr. 1944, while serving with the 3rd Defense Bn. on Bougainville. In April 1945, Bouker arrived at Okinawa Shima, and participated in combat against the enemy as 3rd Amphibious Corps Artillery Target Information Center Officer. He returned to the States in Aug. 1945, and was integrated

into the regular Marine Corps while stationed at the Recruit Depot, Parris Is. In Oct. 1946, after completing the Advanced Naval Gunfire Course at Marine Corps Schools, Quantico, Va., he was assigned to Pearl Harbor as Naval Gunfire Officer, HQ, FMF, Pacific, until May 1948. For the next three years he was stationed at Marine Corps Schools, Quantico. During this time, he was 2nd Bn. Executive Officer of the PLC Training Regiment; an instructor in the Basic School; completed the Senior Course; and served as Director of the Officer Candidate Screening Course. In Aug. 1951, he was named CO of the 2nd Bn., 3rd Marines, 3rd Mar. Brig. (later 3rd Mar. Div.), FMF. Shortly after arriving at Camp Pendleton for this assignment, he was promoted to colonel, in Dec. 1951. Remaining with the 3rd Mar. Div., Col. Bouker served as Regimental Commander, 3rd Marines, and Assistant Division G-3 (Liaison), respectively, until June 1953. That same month he began a three-year tour of duty as Professor of Naval Science and CO of the NROTC unit at Cornell University, Ithaca, N.Y. In July 1956, he again embarked for the Far East where he joined the 3rd Mar. Div., and served as Regimental Commander of the 3rd Marines in Japan and on Okinawa. In Sept. 1957, Col. Bouker returned to the States and served a year as HQ Bn. Commander, MCB, Camp Lejeune, N.C., before entering the National War College, Washington, D.C., as a student. Upon graduation in June 1959, he was assigned to the Joint Staff, Office of the Joint Chiefs of Staff, serving there until Oct. 1961. Ordered to HQMC, Gen. Bouker was promoted to his present rank of brigadier general on Nov. 1, 1961, and that same month became Deputy Director of the Marine Corps Reserve. In Feb. 1962, he left HQMC to serve as CG, Landing Force

Training Unit, Pacific Fleet, Coronado, Calif.

BOWMAN, George Shepard. Brigadier General. CG, 1st MAW, Iwakuni, Japan (1963): b. Hammond, La., Dec. 24, 1911. George Bowman entered Louisiana State University, at Baton Rouge, and received a Bachelor of Science degree in Electrical Engineering upon graduation in 1936. Active in sports during his school years, he was a five-letter man at the university, participating in football and track. He was also a member of the ROTC unit at the university, and resigned his Army Reserve commission to accept appointment as a Marine second lieutenant, July 10, 1936. After completing Basic School at the Philadelphia Navy Yard, he was stationed at the Navy Yard, Pearl Harbor, Hawaii, from May 1937, to July 1938, then served with the 6th Marines in San Diego. In Feb. 1939, he was assigned as a student Naval aviator at the Naval Air Station, Pensacola, Fla. He was promoted to first lieutenant in July 1939. Lt. Bowman was designated a Naval Aviator in Dec. 1939. He reported to Quantico, Va., in Feb. 1940, and was later assigned to Marine Fighter Squadron 111, MAG 11. He was promoted to captain in Oct. 1941. When the United States entered WWII, Capt. Bowman was ordered with the squadron to San Diego. In Mar. 1942, he was named commander of Service Squadron 13, MAG 13, and embarked with the group for American Samoa. He was promoted to major in Aug. 1942. While stationed on Samoa, he served as Operations Officer of MAG 13 from Jan. 1943, to Sept. 1943, when he returned to the States. He was assigned to MCAS, Santa Barbara, Calif., in Nov. 1943, and was promoted to lieutenant colonel the following month. In Dec. 1943, he became Operations Officer, G-3,

MAG 42, Marine Fleet Air, West Coast, serving in this capacity until Sept. 1944, and as Group Executive Officer until Dec. In Jan. 1945, he arrived at Ewa, Oahu, Hawaii, as Assistant G-3, Aircraft, FMF, Pacific. That June he was assigned as Operations Officer on the Staff of Commander Naval Air Base, Okinawa, administering shore controlled air-sea rescue facilities. Following this assignment, he rejoined Aircraft, FMF, Pacific, in Nov. 1945, serving as a squadron commander with MAG 15 until Feb. 1946. In Mar. 1946, he reported to Marine Corps Schools, Quantico, where he completed the Command and Staff Course in Aug. 1946, then served as an instructor in the Aviation Section through May 1949. Upon leaving Quantico, he began a three-year tour of duty at HQMC in June 1949, serving as Assistant Head and, later, Head, Personnel Branch, Division of Aviation. While serving in the latter capacity, he was promoted to colonel in Feb. 1951. Col. Bowman was detached from HQMC in July 1952, and ordered to Korea. On his arrival in Korea he served briefly as CO of MAG 12, 1st MAW, prior to assuming his regular duties as Group Executive Officer. From Jan. to April 1953, he again served as the group's commander. For exceptionally meritorious conduct from Aug. 1952, to Apr. 1953, he was awarded the Legion of Merit with Combat "V." The Distinguished Flying Cross was awarded him for heroism while flying an attack bomber in a massed aerial assault on enemy supply installations in the vicinity of Chinnampo, Mar. 26, 1953. On his return to Washington, D.C., in May 1953, he was a member of a board studying the Marine Aviation-Ground Officer Program and, in Aug. 1953, entered the National War College as a student. He completed the course the following summer, and was transferred to Cherry Point, N.C., in July 1954. He served there as Chief of Staff, 2nd MAW, Aircraft, FMF, Atlantic, until Jan. 1956. Col. Bowman was assigned to Marine Corps Schools, Quantico, in Feb. 1956, and served as Director of the Junior School through June 1958. The following month he returned to HQMC where he served as Deputy Assistant Director of the Division of Aviation until Mar. 1960. In Apr. 1960, he was assigned to the Staff of the Commander in Chief, Pacific, in Hawaii. He was promoted to brigadier general in July 1960. On Feb. 1, 1963, he became CG of the 1st MAW in Iwakuni, Japan.

BOWSER, Alpha Lyons. Major General. Assistant Chief of Staff, G-1, HQMC, Washington, D.C.: b. Crofton, Pa., Aug. 21, 1910. After graduation from high school at Crafton, Alpha Bowser entered the U. S. Naval Academy and was commissioned a Marine second lieutenant upon graduation, June 2, 1932. He completed basic school at the Philadelphia Navy Yard in June 1933, and later saw duty aboard the USS *Texas*. In July 1934, he was assigned to the 1st Mar. Brig., Quantico, Va. He served there until July 1935, when he was promoted to first lieutenant. Bowser then entered the Army Field Artillery School, Fort Sill, Okla., and upon completing the course in June 1936, returned to Quantico. In June 1937, he joined the Marine Detachment aboard the USS *Nevada*. He was promoted to captain in Oct. 1938. Detached from the *Nevada* in Jan. 1939, he was transferred to San Diego, Calif. He commanded artillery batteries there until June 1940, when he returned to Quantico to serve as an artillery instructor for two years. He was promoted to major in May 1942. In July 1942, he joined the 3rd Mar. Div. at Camp Lejeune, N.C., moved with it to San Diego

that Oct., and sailed for the Pacific area in Jan. 1943. He was promoted to lieutenant colonel in Mar. 1943. Lt. Col. Bowser served as an observer during the New Georgia operation in Aug. 1943, and as Assistant Operations Officer of the 3rd Mar. Div. during the Bougainville operation in Nov. and Dec. 1943. For heroic achievement in the latter assignment, he was awarded his first Bronze Star Medal. In Feb. 1944, he was given command of the 3rd 105mm Howitzer Bn., 12th Marines, 3rd Mar. Div. He was awarded a second Bronze Star Medal for outstanding service in this capacity during the recapture of Guam, and his first Legion of Merit with Combat "V" during the Iwo Jima campaign. Following his return to the States in Apr. 1945, he was stationed at HQMC as Chief, Records Branch, Personnel Department, until May 1946. Following this, he served for three years on the Staff of the MCS at Quantico. He was promoted to colonel in Aug. 1949. That Sept. he joined the Staff of FMF, Pacific, in Honolulu, Hawaii, as Naval Gunfire Officer. He served in this capacity until July 1950 when he was ordered to Korea. There he served as Assistant Chief of Staff, G-3, 1st Mar. Div. For outstanding service during the Inchon-Seoul and Chosin Reservoir actions, respectively, he was awarded a second and third Legion of Merit with Combat "V." After his return from Korea in May 1951, Col. Bowser served at Camp Pendleton, Calif., as Assistant Chief of Staff, G-3, of the MCB, until Feb. 1952, when he became Chief of Staff of the 3rd Mar. Div. In July 1952, he was ordered to Paris, France, where he served until July 1954 as Staff Officer, Plans Branch, and Senior Marine Officer, Supreme HQ, Allied Powers, Europe (SHAPE). On his return to Washington, he entered the National War College in

Aug. 1954, completing the course in June 1955. Transferred to San Diego that July, Col. Bowser began a year's duty on the Staff of Commander, Amphibious Force, U.S. Pacific Fleet, as Assistant Chief of Staff for Troop Operations and Training, and Force Marine Officer. In Aug. 1956, he assumed command of the Recruit Training Command, Marine Corps Recruit Depot, San Diego. He was promoted to brigadier general in Sept. 1956. Gen. Bowser served in San Diego until June 1958, when he became Assistant Division Commander, 1st Mar. Div., Camp Pendleton. Subsequently, in Jan. 1959, he was assigned as Commanding General, Force Troops, FMF, Pacific, and CG, MCB, Twentynine Palms, Calif. While serving in this capacity, he was promoted to major general in July 1960. Gen. Bowser departed Twentynine Palms for Washington in Oct. 1960, and that same month assumed his current assignment as Assistant Chief of Staff, G-1, HQMC.

BOYDSTON, Erwin Jay. Private. Medal of Honor: b. Deer Creek, Col., Apr. 22, 1875. Pvt. Boydston's citation reads, in part: "... in the presence of the enemy at Peking, China, July 21 to Aug. 17, 1900. Under heavy fire from the enemy during this period, Pvt. Boydston assisted in the erection of barricades...."

BOYINGTON, Gregory. "Pappy." Colonel. Marine Corps ace, credited with the destruction of 28 Japanese aircraft. Medal of Honor: b. Coeur d'Alene, Idaho, Dec. 4, 1912. After graduation from Lincoln High School in Tacoma, Wash., Gregory Boyington majored in aeronautical engineering at the University of Washington, graduating in 1934 with a Bachelor of Science degree. Always an athlete, he was a member of the college

Boyington

wrestling and swimming teams, and is a one-time holder of the Pacific Northwest Intercollegiate middleweight wrestling title. Boyington started his military career while still attending college. As a member of the ROTC for four years, he became a cadet captain. He was commissioned a second lieutenant in the Coast Artillery Reserve in June 1934, and served two months of active duty with the 630th Coast Artillery at Fort Worden, Wash. On June 13, 1936, he enlisted in the Volunteer Marine Corps Reserve. On that date, he went on active duty and returned to inactive duty on July 16. In the meantime, he had become a draftsman and engineer for the Boeing Aircraft Co. of Seattle. On Feb. 18, 1937, Boyington accepted an appointment as an aviation cadet in the Marine Corps Reserve. He was assigned to the NAS, Pensacola, Fla. for flight training. He was designated a Naval Aviator on Mar. 11, 1937, and was transferred to Quantico, Va. for duty with Aircraft One, FMF. He was discharged from the Marine Corps Reserve on July 1, 1937, in order to accept a commission as second lieutenant in the regular Marine Corps. Detached to the Basic School, Philadelphia, in July, 1938, Lt. Boyington was transferred to the 2nd MAG at the San Diego NAS upon completion of his studies. With that unit he took part in fleet problems aboard the aircraft carriers USS *Lexington* and USS *Yorktown*. Promoted to first lieutenant on Nov. 4, 1940, he went back to Pensacola as an instructor. Boyington resigned his commission in the Marine Corps on Aug. 26, 1941, to accept a position with the Central Aircraft Manufacturing Co. (CAMCO). CAMCO was a civilian organization formed for the protection of the Burma Road. The unit later became known as the American Volunter Group (AVG), the famed "Flying Tigers" of China. During his months with the "Tigers" Boyington became a squadron commander and shot down six Japanese planes to secure an appreciable lead over other American aces who didn't get into the fight until after Dec. 7, 1941. He flew 300 combat hours before the AVG was disbanded. Boyington returned to the States in July 1942, and accepted a commission as a first lieutenant in the Marine Corps Reserve on Sept. 29 of that year. He reported for active duty at the NAS, San Diego, on Nov. 23, 1942, and was assigned to MAW, Pacific. The following day he was temporarily promoted to major in the Reserve. Within two months, he was on his way overseas again. Maj. Boyington joined MAG 11 of the 1st MAW and became CO of Marine Fighting Squadron 214 after a short tour in

the Solomon Is. with another squadron. The new squadron was made up of a group of casuals, replacements, and green pilots and was dubbed the "Black Sheep" Squadron. Before organizing the "Black Sheep," Boyington had done some combat flying at Guadalcanal in Apr. 1943, as Executive Officer of Marine Fighting Squadron 122, but he had added no enemy planes to his score there. However, during those two periods of intense activity in the Russell Is.-New Georgia and Bougainville-New Britain-New Ireland areas, "Pappy," so named because of his age (31) as compared to that of his men, added to his total almost daily. During his squadron's first tour of combat duty, Boyington personally shot down 14 enemy planes in 32 days. On Dec. 17, 1943, he headed the first Allied fighter sweep over impregnable Rabaul. By Dec. 27, his record had climbed to 25. He tied the then-existing American record of 26 planes on Jan. 3 when he shot down another fighter over Rabaul. Typical of Maj. Boyington's daring feats was his attack on Kahili airdrome at the southern tip of Bougainville on Oct. 17, 1943. He and 24 other fighter pilots circled the field persistently where 60 hostile aircraft were grounded, goading the Japanese into sending up a large numerically superior force. In the fierce battle that followed, 20 of the enemy planes were shot out of the skies. The Black Sheep roared back to their base without the loss of a single ship. On Jan. 3, 1944, 48 American planes including one division (4 planes) from the Black Sheep Squadron took off from Bougainville for a fighter sweep over Rabaul. Pappy was the tactical commander of the flight and arrived over Rabaul at 8 o'clock in the morning. In the ensuing action the major was seen to shoot down his 26th plane. He then became embroiled in the general melee of diving, swooping planes and was not seen or heard from again. Following a determined search which proved futile, the major was declared missing in action. Actually he had been picked up by the Japanese. While a prisoner of the enemy he was selected for temporary promotion to the rank of lieutenant colonel. Then came mid-Aug. 1945, the atom bombs, and the Japanese capitulation. Maj. Boyington was liberated from Japanese custody at Omori Prison Camp in the Tokyo area on Aug. 29 and arrived in the States shortly afterward. On Sept. 6, the top ace who had been a prisoner of the Japanese for 20 months accepted his temporary commission as a lieutenant colonel in the Marine Corps. At the time of his release it was confirmed that Col. Boyington had actually accounted for three Japanese planes on Jan. 3, the day he himself was shot down. That set his total at 28 planes. Shortly after his return home, Col. Boyington was ordered to Washington to receive the nation's highest award, the Medal of Honor. Col. Boyington was retired from the Marine Corps on Aug. 1, 1947, and, for his performance of duty in actual combat, he was advanced to his present rank.

BROWN, Charles. Corporal. Medal of Honor: b. New York, N.Y. Charles Brown enlisted in the Marine Corps at Hong Kong, China. He was awarded the Nation's highest military honor for bravery while serving aboard the USS *Colorado* in action against a Korean fort, June 11, 1871. Cpl. Brown assisted in capturing the Korean standard in the center of the citadel of the fort.

BUCKLEY, Howard Major. Private. Medal of Honor: b. Croton Falls, N.Y., Jan. 23, 1868. Pvt. Buckley was awarded the nation's highest military honor for dis-

tinguished conduct during the Philippine Insurrection (1899-1906). He was cited for courageous action in the presence of the enemy in battle while with the 8th Army Corps on Mar. 25, 26, 27 and Apr. 4, 1899.

BURNES, James. Private. Medal of Honor: b. Worcester, Mass., Jan. 14, 1870. James Burnes enlisted in the Marine Corps at Mare Island, Calif., on June 9, 1898. He received the Medal of Honor on Apr. 21, 1902. His citation reads, in part: "... for bravery in crossing the river at Tientsin, China, June 20, 1900, in a small boat with three other men under heavy fire. He assisted in destroying buildings occupied by the enemy...." Pvt. Burnes was discharged from the Corps at Bremerton, Wash., on June 8, 1903.

BURROWS, William Ward. Lieutenant Colonel. 2nd Commandant of the Marine Corps: b. Charleston, S.C., Jan. 16, 1758; d. Washington, D.C., 1805. William Burrows studied law first in Charleston, S.C., then in London, England. He returned to the States in 1775 in time to fight in the Revolution as a militiaman. After the war he moved to Philadelphia where he again practiced law until July 12, 1798, when President John Adams commissioned him as Major Commandant of the newly established U.S. Marine Corps. Burrows realized immediately that the country was in desperate need of a force such as his Corps represented. With the prospect of war with France, the United States was hurriedly recreating its fleet. Burrows plunged into the task of recruiting and training the detachments for the ships. By early 1799, his 881-man Marine Corps was thinly spread over 25 ships and several shore stations. The quasi war with France continued until Sept. 1800, when the States finally settled their differences with Napoleon. On the crest of the economy wave which followed, Congress sold many of the Navy's ships and drastically reduced the Marine Corps. This move proved unwise, for the war with the Barbary States followed and Burrows was again faced with the task of obtaining another 500 Marines to reinforce the Mediterranean squadron. In 1804, having nurtured the Corps through two wars, established headquarters at Eighth and Eye Streets in the nation's capital, and formed the Marine Band, he asked to be retired for reasons of health. He died one year later and now lies in Arlington National Cemetery.

Buse

BUSE, Henry William. Major General: b. Ridley Park, Pa., Apr. 10, 1912. After graduation from high school, Henry Buse

attended the Severn Preparatory School, Md., for one year. He then entered the U.S. Naval Academy and was commissioned a Marine second lieutenant upon graduation on May 31, 1934. After completing Basic School at the Philadelphia Navy Yard in Apr. 1935, Lt. Buse went aboard the USS *Oklahoma* for a year's duty at sea. In June 1936, he was ordered to Quantico, Va., for duty with the 1st Mar. Brig., FMF. He was transferred in Mar. 1937, to the Marine Barracks at Pearl Harbor and, while there, was promoted to first lieutenant in July 1937. In Sept. 1939, he entered the Army Infantry School at Fort Benning, Ga., completing the course the following Feb. He joined the 5th Marines, 1st Mar. Brig. at Quantico in March 1940, serving as a company officer and later company commander. He was promoted to captain in July 1940. That Sept. Capt. Buse embarked with the brigade for Guantanamo Bay, Cuba. With the redesignation of the brigade as the 1st Mar. Div. in March 1941, he was made commander of the division's 1st Scout Co., and continued to command the company at Quantico and New River (later Camp Lejeune), N.C. He was serving in this capacity when WWII broke out. In Apr. 1942, he was assigned to the 1st Tank Bn, 1st Mar. Div., as Bn. Executive Officer. He was promoted to major in May 1942. In June 1942, he embarked for the Pacific area. Arriving in Wellington, New Zealand, he was named Assistant Operations Officer of the 1st Mar. Div., and shortly thereafter took part in the Guadalcanal landing, and the capture and defense of Guadalcanal. He was promoted to lieutenant colonel in Apr. 1943. In Dec. 1943, while serving as Assistant Operations Officer of the 1st Div., Lt. Col. Buse landed on Cape Gloucester, and the following month, was assigned as CO, 3rd Bn., 7th Marines. He later joined the 5th Marines, serving successively as Regimental Executive Officer and CO, during the Talasea (New Britain) operation. Returning to the States in July 1944, he was assigned to HQMC where he served as Executive Officer, G-3 Section. In July 1946, he departed Washington for duty with Troop Training Unit, Amphibious Training Command, and served as Regimental Combat Team Instructor in Japan in connection with training 8th Army troops. Lt. Col. Buse returned to Pearl Harbor in Feb. 1947, to serve as Assistant Chief of Staff, G-4 (Supply), FMF, Pacific until Feb. 1949. After his return to the continental United States, he completed the Armed Forces Staff College at Norfolk, Va., in June 1949 and, the following month, was ordered to Marine Corps Schools, Quantico. There he commanded the 22nd Marines (reinforced), FMF, until Sept. 1949, then became CO of the Schools troops. He was promoted to colonel in Oct. 1949. In May 1950, he became CO of the Special Training Regiment, Marine Corps Schools, Quantico. In Sept. he was transferred to Camp Lejeune, where he commanded the 6th Marines, 2nd Mar. Div. until Dec. 1951, then served as the division's Assistant Chief of Staff, G-3 (Operations and Training). Ordered to Korea in Sept. 1952, he saw combat as Chief of Staff of the 1st Mar. Div. Returning from Korea in July 1953, Col. Buse became Assistant G-3 at HQMC. In July 1954, he began a two-year assignment as Chief of Staff of the Marine Corps Recruit Depot, Parris Is., S.C. He embarked again for Pearl Harbor in July 1956, and served there for a year and a half as Chief of Staff, FMF, Pacific. In Dec. 1957, he reported to Norfolk, Va., as Chief of Staff, FMF, Atlantic. While serving in this capacity, he was promoted to brigadier general in Aug.

1958. The following month, Gen. Buse began a three-year assignment as Marine Corps Liaison Officer to the Vice Chief of Naval Operations. Following this, he served as Assistant Chief of Staff, G-3, HQMC, from Sept. 1961, to May 1962. Ordered overseas, Gen. Buse assumed command of the 3rd Mar. Div. on Okinawa in June 1962. In addition, as the senior Marine commander in the western Pacific area, he was designated Commander of Task Force 79, the amphibious striking arm of the 7th Fleet. He was promoted to his present rank of major general July 1, 1962.

BUSH, Richard Earl. Corporal. Medal of Honor: b. Glasgow, Ky., Dec. 23, 1924. Richard Bush enlisted in the Marine Corps at Bowling Green, Ky., on Sept. 22, 1942, and received his recruit training at San Diego, Calif. He was later transferred to a replacement battalion at Camp Elliot, Calif. for further training as an armorer. He was awarded the Medal of Honor for leading a squad in the final assault against Mt. Yaetake on Okinawa on Apr. 16, 1945. His citation reads, in part: "For rallying his men forward with indomitable determination, Cpl. Bush boldly defied the slashing fury of concentrated Japanese artillery fire pouring down from the gun-studded mountain fortress to lead his squad up the face of the rocky precipice, sweep over the ridge and drive the defending troops from their deeply entrenched position. He fought relentlessly until seriously wounded and evacuated with others under protecting rocks. Although prostrate under medical treatment when a Japanese hand grenade landed in the midst of the group, Cpl. Bush, alert and courageous in extremity as in battle, unhesitatingly pulled the deadly missile to himself and absorbed the shattering violence of the exploding charge in his own body, thereby saving his fellow Marines from severe injury or death despite the certain peril to his own life."

BUTCHER, Joseph Orville. Brigadier General: b. Bloomington, Ind., Sept. 16, 1912. Joseph Butcher attended Indiana University and, upon graduation in 1936, he received a Bachelor of Arts degree. While at the university, he completed advanced training with the Army ROTC unit, and was commissioned in the Army Infantry Reserve in June 1935. He resigned his Army Reserve commission to accept appointment as a Marine second lieutenant July 7, 1936. Upon completing Basic School at the Philadelphia Navy Yard in Apr. 1937, Lt. Butcher was transferred to the USS *Arkansas* as a member of the Marine Detachment. He completed his tour of sea duty in Sept. 1938, and, the following month, was assigned to Marine Barracks, Washington, D.C., where he was stationed for almost three years. He served there as Editor and Publisher of *Leatherneck Magazine;* CO of the Marine Corps Institute Detachment; Post Exchange Officer; and saw temporary duty as a member of the Marine guard detachment at the "Little White House" at Warm Spring, Ga. He was promoted to first lieutenant in July 1939. In June 1941, he was ordered to the Marine Corps Air Station, Quantico, Va., where he served as Station Quartermaster. While at Quantico he was promoted· to captain in June 1942, and to major in August 1942. In Oct. 1942, Maj. Butcher was assigned to New River (later Camp Lejeune), N.C., and served as First School Adjutant and Executive Officer, Quartermaster School, School Bn., FMF Training Center. He also served for an interim period from Jan. to Sept. 1943, as Bn. Commander and, subsequently, as

Bn. Executive Officer. He was promoted to lieutenant colonel in Mar. 1944. He was ordered overseas in Oct. 1944, for duty with Service Command, FMF, Pearl Harbor, Hawaii, as Assistant Officer in Charge, and subsequently Officer in Charge, General Supply Section, Supply Div. A Letter of Commendation with Commendation Ribbon was awarded him for meritorious performance while on the Staff of the CG, Supply Service, from Oct. 9, 1944, to May 31, 1945, in the Iwo Jima and Okinawa operations. In June 1945, Lt. Col. Butcher was transferred to the U.S. Army Forces, western Pacific, Manila, Philippines, for duty as Marine Logistics Officer with the Marine Detachment (Provisional), at Gen. Douglas MacArthur's headquarters, in preparation for the invasion of Japan. In Oct. 1945, he returned to Service Command, FMF, Pearl Harbor, and served as Assistant G-3 until his return to the States in Feb. 1946. Arriving in Washington, D.C., Lt. Col. Butcher was assigned as Editor-in-Chief of *Leatherneck* Magazine from Mar. through July 1946; as Executive Officer, Division of Public Information, HQMC, Aug. 1946, through Aug. 1947; and as a student in the Industrial College of the Armed Forces, from Sept. 1947, through June 1948. He returned to HQMC to serve as Supply Officer and Assistant Head, Materiel Section, Div. of Aviation from July 1948, through June 1951. In July 1951, he was transferred to the Marine Corps Recruit Depot, San Diego, Calif., as Depot G-4/Supply Officer. He was promoted to colonel in Nov. 1951, and remained in San Diego until May 1954, when he was assigned overseas duty. That month he joined the 1st MAW in Korea, and served as Wing Supply Officer through May 1955. In July 1955, he assumed duty at the Marine Corps Supply Center, Barstow, Calif., serving concurrently as Director, Materiel Div. and CO, 3rd Bn., until Aug. 1957, when he became Chief of Staff of the Supply Center. In Sept. 1958, he was transferred from Barstow to become CO, Marine Corps Supply Schools, Camp Lejeune, N.C. He served there for 18 months. In Mar. 1960, Col. Butcher was assigned to the Pentagon and completed a tour of duty in the Office of Supply Management Policy, Office of the Assistant Secretary of Defense (Supply and Logistics). In July 1961, he was promoted to his present rank of brigadier general and appointed Assistant Quartermaster General of the Marine Corps. Gen. Butcher served as Assistant Quartermaster General until Sept. 1962, when he departed HQMC, and assumed the post of CG, Marine Corps Supply Center, Albany, Ga.

BUTLER, Smedley Darlington. Major General. "Old Gimlet Eye." One of the most colorful officers in the history of the Corps: b. West Chester, Pa., July 30, 1881; d. Naval Hospital, Philadelphia, Pa., June 21, 1940. One of the two Marines who received the Medal of Honor for separate acts of heroism, Butler was appointed a Marine second lieutenant May 20, 1898, during the War with Spain. He was commissioned a first lieutenant on Apr. 8, 1899, and ordered to Manila, P.I. Butler served with distinction in China from June 14, 1900, to Oct. 1900. He was promoted to captain by brevet for distinguished conduct in the presence of the enemy near Tientsin. In that battle, Butler was wounded on July 13, 1900. From 1901 to 1912, he served at various Stateside posts and in Puerto Rico and Panama. On Aug. 11, 1912, he commanded an expeditionary battalion in Nicaragua. From Oct. 12 to

Butler

31, 1912, he participated in the bombardment, assault, and capture of Coyotepe. He returned to Panama in Nov. 1912. His first medal of honor was presented following action at Vera Cruz, Mexico, Apr. 21 and 22, 1914, when he commanded the Marines who landed and occupied the city. His citation reads, in part, "... was eminent and conspicuous in command of his battalion. He exhibited courage and skill in leading his men through the action of the 22nd and in the final occupation of the city." The following year he was awarded his second Medal of Honor for bravery and forceful leadership as CO of detachments of Marines and seamen of the USS *Connecticut* in repulsing Caco resistance on Fort Riviere, Haiti, on Nov. 17, 1915. During WWI, he commanded the 13th Regt. of Marines in France. For exceptionally meritorious service, he was awarded the Army Distinguished Service Medal, the Navy Distinguished Service Medal, and the French Order of the Black Star. On his return to the States in 1919, he became CG of the Marine Barracks, Quantico, Va. He served in this capacity until Jan. 1924, when he was granted a leave of absence to accept the post of Director of Public Safety in Philadelphia, Pa. In Feb. 1926, he returned to the Corps and assumed command of the Marine Corps Base, San Diego, Calif. From Mar. 1927, to Apr. 1931, he served again in China with the 3rd Mar. Brig. His last tour of duty, from Apr. to Oct. 1931, was spent as CG of the Marine Barracks at Quantico. On Oct. 1, 1931, he was retired upon his own application after 33 years of service in the Marine Corps. Two years after his death in 1940, the USS *Butler,* a destroyer, later converted to a high-speed mine sweeper, was named for Gen. Butler.

BUTTON, William Robert. Corporal. Medal of Honor: b. St. Louis, Mo., Dec. 3, 1895. While serving as a lieutenant in the Haitian Gendarmerie, Cpl. Button accompanied 2nd Lt. Herman Hanneken on a mission to capture or destroy Charlemagne Peralte, the reigning chieftain of the Cacos who had been terrorizing the countryside. Disguised as natives, Button and Hanneken found the bandit encampment and, in the face of one-hundred-to-one odds, they made an aggressive stand. Charlemagne Peralte was killed, thus breaking the back of the Caco bandit scourge. Cpl. Button's citation reads, in part: "... near Grande Riviere, Republic of Haiti, on the night of Oct. 31-Nov. 1, 1919 ... he distinguished himself by his excellent judgment and leadership ... unhesitatingly exposed himself to great personal danger when the slightest error would have forfeited not only his life, but the lives of the detachments of Gendarmerie under his command...." Cpl. Button lies buried in Haiti, the country of his memorable exploits.

C

CADDY, William Robert. Private First Class. Medal of Honor: b. Quincy, Mass., Aug. 8, 1925; d. KIA, Iwo Jima, Mar. 3, 1945. William Caddy was inducted into the Marine Corps through Selective Service on Oct. 27, 1943. He received recruit training at Parris Is., S.C., where he fired a score of 305 with the service rifle to qualify as a sharpshooter. After extensive training at Camp Lejeune, N.C. and Hilo, Hawaii, he embarked aboard the USS *Drake* for Iwo Jima. Landing against the fanatic opposition which had charac-

terized the Japanese forces since Tarawa, Caddy fought on Iwo for 12 days. On Mar. 3, he, his platoon leader, and his acting platoon sergeant, were advancing against shattering Japanese machine-gun and small arms fire in an isolated sector. Seeking temporary refuge, the three Marines dropped into a shell hole where they were immediately pinned down by a well concealed enemy sniper. After several unsuccessful attempts to advance further, the 19-year-old Marine and his lieutenant engaged in a furious hand grenade battle with the defending Japanese. When an enemy grenade landed in their hole, P.F.C. Caddy immediately covered it with his body and absorbed the deadly impact. For his act of heroism he was posthumously awarded the nation's highest award on Sept. 8, 1946.

CAFFERATA, Hector Albert, Jr. Private First Class. Medal of Honor: b. New York, N.Y., Nov. 4, 1929. Hector Cafferata enlisted in the MCR on Feb. 15, 1948, and was a member of the 21st Reserve Inf. Bn. at Dover, N.J., until he was called to active duty on Sept. 6, 1950. After training at Camp Pendleton, Calif., he embarked for Korea in Oct. 1950. He earned the nation's highest military award for his heroic stand against an enemy attack at the Chosin Reservoir. His citation reads, in part: "... as a rifleman with Co. F, 2nd Bn., 7th Marines, 1st Mar. Div., in action against enemy aggressor forces in Korea on Nov. 28, 1950. When all other members of his fire team became casualties, creating a gap in the lines during the initial phase of a vicious attack against his company's hill position, Pvt. Cafferata waged a lone battle with hand grenades and rifle fire as the attack gained momentum and the enemy threatened penetration through the gap.... Making a target of himself under the devastating fire from automatic weapons, rifles, grenades, and mortars he maneuvered up and down the line and delivered accurate and effective fire against the onrushing force, killing 15, wounding many more, and forcing the others to withdraw so that reinforcements could move up and consolidate the position. Again, fighting desperately against a renewed onslaught later that same morning when a hostile grenade landed in a shallow entrenchment occupied by wounded Marines, Pvt. Cafferata

rushed into the gully under heavy fire, seized the deadly missile in his left hand and hurled it free of his comrades ... severing part of one finger and seriously wounding him in the left hand and arm. Courageously ignoring the intense pain, he staunchly fought on until he was struck by a sniper's bullet and forced to submit to evacuation...." He was sent to Japan in Dec. 1950, and returned to the States the following month for treatment. He was placed on the retired list on Sept. 1, 1951.

CAMPBELL, Albert Ralph. Corporal. Medal of Honor: b. Williamsport, Pa., Apr. 8, 1875. Albert Campbell enlisted in the Marine Corps on Oct. 7, 1897. He was awarded the Medal of Honor on Mar. 24, 1902, "... for distinguished conduct in the presence of the enemy in the advance on Tientsin, China, June 21, 1900...."

CAMPBELL, Daniel. Private. Medal of Honor: b. Prince Edward Is., Oct. 26, 1874. Pvt. Campbell's citation reads, in part: "... On board the USS *Marblehead* during the cutting of the cable leading from Cienfuegos, Cuba, May 11, 1898. Facing the heavy fire of the enemy, Campbell set an example of extraordinary bravery and coolness throughout this action...."

CANNON, George Ham. First Lieutenant. Medal of Honor: b. Webster Groves, Mo.; d. KIA, Midway Is., Dec. 7, 1941. George Cannon attended the Culver Military Academy in Culver, Ind., prior to entering the University of Michigan at Ann Arbor. While attending that university he was a member of the ROTC and graduated with a Bachelor of Science degree in Mechanical Engineering in June 1938. He was commissioned a second lieutenant in the Engineer Reserve, U.S. Army, during his last year at the University of Michigan. Upon graduation, he resigned to accept a commission as a Marine second lieutenant. Commissioned on June 25, 1938, he was ordered to duty on July 5, 1938, at the Philadelphia Navy Yard to await assignment to the next class of Basic School. He began studies on July 18 of that year. His first tour of duty was aboard the USS *Boise*, following the completion of his schooling May 20, 1939. He was assigned to the Post Service Battalion at the Marine Barracks, Quantico, Va., on July 10, 1940, and two weeks later entered the Base Defense Weapons Course at the Marine Corps Schools. Ordered to the MCB, San Diego, Calif. in Dec. 1940, he joined Battery H, 2nd Defense Bn. on Feb. 16, 1941. In Mar. 1941, the battery joined the 6th Defense Bn. and in July the unit sailed for Pearl Harbor. In Aug. 1941, Cannon was promoted to first lieutenant, to rank from June 25, 1941. On Sept. 7, 1941, he reported to Midway Is. as a platoon leader and member of the Bn. Coding Board. He was killed in action on the first day of WWII, Dec. 7, 1941, during the sneak attack by Japanese forces. His citation reads, in part: "Lt. Cannon was at his Command Post when he was mortally wounded by enemy shell fire. He refused to be evacuated from his post until after his men who had been wounded by the same shell, were evacuated, and directed the reorganization of his Command Post until forcibly removed and as a result of his utter disregard of his own condition, he died from loss of blood." On May 25, 1943, a destroyer was named for Lt. George Cannon.

CARLSON, Evans Fordyce. Brigadier General. Leader of the famed "Carlson's Raiders": b. Sidney, N.Y., Feb. 26, 1896;

Carlson

d. Emmanuel Hospital, Portland, Ore., May 27, 1947. Evans Carlson's military career began in 1912 when at the age of 16 he left high school and enlisted in the U.S. Army. When he finished his four-year enlistment he was a "top sergeant." He had served in the Philippines and in Hawaii. Carlson stayed out of uniform less than one year and returned to the army in time for the Mexican punitive expedition. During WWI he saw action in France, and was awarded the Purple Heart for wounds received in action. He was commissioned a second lieutenant in May 1917, and made captain of field artillery in Dec. 1917. Later he served in Germany with the Army of Occupation. Carlson's spectacular career as a Marine started in 1922 when he enlisted as a private. In 1923, he was commissioned a second lieutenant. After duty at Quantico, Va., he sailed for Culebra, Puerto Rico in 1924 and remained there five months before being ordered to the west coast for duty with the Pacific Fleet. Applying for aviation training in 1925, he went to Pensacola, Fla., for instruction, but subsequently returned to duty with ground units. He served another tour of foreign shore duty from 1927 to 1929 at Shanghai, China. Next, he was ordered to Nicaragua in 1930 as an officer in the Guardia Nacional. A first lieutenant at the time, he won his first Navy Cross for leading 12 Marines against 100 bandits. He was also commended for his actions following the earthquake at Managua in 1931, and for performance of duties as Chief of Police in 1932 and 1933. Returning to the States in 1933, he was sent almost immediately to Shanghai again. Shortly afterward he was transferred to the Marine Detachment, American Legation, Peiping, China, where he served as Adjutant and began study of the Chinese language. In 1936 he returned to the States via Japan. Carlson then served at Quantico while attending MCS and studying International Law and Politics at George Washington University in Washington, D.C. He went back to China for the third time in 1937 as an official student of the Chinese language and as a military observer with Chinese forces. There he was afforded the opportunity to learn the tactics of the Japanese soldier. Traveling thousands of miles through the interior of China, often on foot and horseback over the most hazardous terrain, he lived under the primitive conditions of native troops. When he left China in 1938, he was commended by the Commander in Chief of the Asiatic Fleet for his services. Carlson was

now so impressed with the danger of Japanese aggression in the Far East that in 1939 he resigned his commission as a captain in order to be free to write and lecture on that subject. When the danger he foresaw neared reality in 1941, he requested to be recommissioned in the Marine Corps and was accepted with the rank of major. A year later he was placed in command of the 2nd Mar. Raider Bn. with the rank of lieutenant colonel. His leadership of that unit in the raid on Makin Island, Aug. 17, 1942, won him a Gold Star in lieu of a second Navy Cross. A second Gold Star was awarded him for heroism and distinguished leadership on Guadalcanal in Nov. and Dec. of that year. Col. Carlson was ordered back to the States for medical treatment in the spring of 1943, and subsequently returned to Tarawa as an observer. In that engagement he was cited for volunteering to carry vital information through enemy fire from an advanced post to div. HQ. He was wounded during the Saipan operation while attempting to rescue a wounded enlisted man from a front line observation post, and was awarded a Gold Star in lieu of a second Purple Heart. Physical disability resulting from the wounds received on Saipan caused Carlson's retirement on July 1, 1946. He was advanced to the rank of brigadier general on the retired list at that time for having been specially commended for the performance of duty in actual combat. On May 27, 1947, the 51-year-old veteran succumbed to a heart illness at Emmanuel Hospital, Portland, Ore.

CARR, William Louis. Corporal. Medal of Honor: b. Peabody, Mass., Apr. 1, 1875. William Carr enlisted in the Marine Corps at Boston, Mass., on June 7, 1898. He was presented with the Medal of Honor on Dec. 11, 1901. His citation reads, in part: ". . . for distinguished conduct in the presence of the enemy at Peking, China, July 21, 1900 to Aug. 17, 1900." Carr was discharged as a corporal at Boston, Mass., on June 10, 1903.

Cates

CATES, Clifton Bledsoe. General. 19th Commandant of the Marine Corps: b. Tiptonville, Tenn., Aug. 31, 1893. After completing his elementary education in country schools, Clifton Cates was sent to the Missouri Military Academy where he became an honor student and a four-letter man in sports. His Bachelor of Laws degree was obtained at the University of Tennessee in 1916. On June 13, 1917, as a reserve second lieutenant, he reported for active duty at Marine Barracks, Port Royal, S.C., and sailed for France the following Jan. As a young lieutenant with the 6th Mar. Regt. in WWI, Cates fought in the Verdun de-

fensive sector; at Bouresches and Belleau Wood in the Aisne defensive; at Soissons in the Aisne-Marne offensive; in the Marbache sector of the St.-Mihiel offensive; and in the Mont Blanc and Argonne-Forest engagements of the Meuse-Argonne offensive. He won the Navy Cross, Army Distinguished Service Cross, and an Oak Leaf Cluster in lieu of a second Distinguished Service Cross for heroism in the Bouresches and Belleau Wood fighting, where he was both gassed and wounded. He won the Silver Star Medal at Soissons, where he was wounded a second time, and an Oak Leaf Cluster in lieu of a second Silver Star Medal in the Mont Blanc fighting. Apart from those decorations, the French government recognized his heroism with the Legion of Honor and the Crois de Guerre with Gilt Star and two palms. After participating in the occupation of Germany, Cates returned to the States in Sept. 1919, and during the next year served in Washington, D.C., as a White House aide and Aide-de-Camp to the Commandant of the Marine Corps. He then served at San Francisco, Calif., as Aide-de-Camp to the CG, Department of the Pacific, from Oct. 1920 until June 1923, when he began a tour of sea duty as commander of the Marine Detachment aboard the USS *California*. That assignment was completed in Apr. 1925. A month later he began a year of service with the 4th Mar. Regt. at San Diego, Calif. In Mar. 1928, after serving on recruiting duty at Spokane, Wash., and Omaha, Neb., he was named a member of the American Battle Monuments Commission at Washington. He served in that capacity until May 1929, then was ordered to Shanghai, China, where he rejoined the 4th Marines. Three years later he was detached from that regiment to return to Washington for study in the Army Industrial

College. Completing his course in June 1933, he reported the following month to Quantico, where he served with the 7th Marines and completed the Senior Course in the MCS. He returned again to Washington in Sept. 1935, and was assigned to the War Plans Section of the Division of Operations and Training at HQMC. In Aug. 1937, Cates sailed for Shanghai as a bn. commander with the 6th Mar. Regt., serving with that unit until he rejoined the 4th Marines in Mar. 1938. Again the following year he was brought back to Washington for instruction in the Army War College. That course was completed in June 1940, and he reported the next month to the Philadelphia Navy Yard as director of the Marine Officers' Basic School. By the time the United States entered WWII, he had been promoted to colonel. In May 1942, Col. Cates took command of the 1st Mar. Regt. which, as part of the 1st Mar. Div., he led at Guadalcanal. With the invaluable experience obtained in that campaign, he was returned to the States the following Mar. for his first tour of duty as Commandant of the MCS at Quantico. He continued in that capacity until June 1944. The following month he took command of the 4th Mar. Div., leading that organization in the Pacific theater until the end of the war. Meanwhile, he had been promoted to major general. Ordered back to the States in Dec. 1945, the general became President of the Marine Corps Equipment Board at Quantico, holding that position for six months before he was named CG of the Marine Barracks, Quantico. He held that command until Jan. 1, 1948, when he was advanced to the rank of general and sworn in as Commandant of the Marine Corps, succeeding Gen. Alexander A. Vandegrift. When he completed his four-year term as Commandant, he reverted to the rank of lieutenant general and began his second tour as Commandant of the MCS. He was again promoted to general upon his retirement on June 30, 1954.

CATLIN, Albertus W. Brigadier General. Medal of Honor: b. Gowanda, N.Y., Dec. 1, 1868; d. Culpeper, Va., May 31, 1933. Albertus Catlin was commissioned a second lieutenant in the Marine Corps on July 1, 1892. After serving at various stations in the States and on board ships of the navy, Catlin saw action in the Spanish-American War as CO of the Marine detachment aboard the USS *Maine*, when the ship was destroyed in Havana Harbor in Feb. 1898. On duty in Cuba in 1911, Catlin commanded a battalion of the 1st Marines at Guantanamo Bay. At Vera Cruz, Mex. in 1914, Catlin led the 3rd Marines and was awarded the Medal of Honor for bravery in action. Soon after the outbreak of WWI Catlin, now a lieutenant colonel, was placed in charge of the Marine training camp at Quantico. In Oct. 1917, he went to France as CO of the 6th Marines. From June 1 to 6, 1918, Col. Catlin's 6th Marines saw action in the front lines from Paris-Metz Road through Lucy le Bocage to Hill 142. For gallantry in action against the enemy at Belleau Wood, Catlin was awarded two Croix de Guerre, one with palms and one with gilt star. At Belleau Wood, he was wounded by a bullet which went through his shoulder and lung. Upon his return to the States, Col. Catlin for a time was on duty at HQMC, and then was appointed a brigadier general on Aug. 30, 1918. His next tour of duty was at the MB, Quantico, and in Nov. 1918, he sailed for Haiti where he assumed command of the 1st Brig. of Marines until Sept. 1919. As a result of his WWI wound, Gen. Catlin was in ill health from the time of his retirement in Dec. 1919 until he died at Culpeper, Va., on May 31, 1933.

CHAMBERS, Justice Marion. Colonel. Medal of Honor: b. Huntington, W.Va., Feb. 8, 1908. Justice Chambers completed three years at Marshall College in Huntington, then attended George Washington University and National University, both in Washington, D.C., where he obtained his law degree. Following the completion of two years enlistment in the naval reserve in 1930, he joined the Marine Corps Reserve as a private. He was commissioned in 1932 and continued his studies toward promotion. He was a major, attending summer camp, when Washington's 5th Bn. was called up in 1940. On Tulagi, Chambers received the Silver Star Medal for evacuating the wounded and directing the night defense of a battalion aid station, where he himself was a patient already seriously wounded. He commanded the 3rd Bn., 25th Marines, in the Roi-Namur campaign. On Saipan he suffered blast concussion, but returned to lead his command there and on Tinian. On Iwo Jima, Chambers, now a lieutenant colonel, commanded the 3rd Bn., 25th Mar. Regt., in the landing on Feb. 19, 1945. His sector was beneath high ground from which heavy enemy fire raked the whole landing beach. Capture of the high ground was essential to the success of the D-Day operations. Had this not been accomplished, there would have been a most serious threat to the subsequent operations of the 5th Amphibious Corps. The 3rd Bn. lost more than half its officers and nearly one-half its enlisted strength on D-Day. But by fearless disregard for his own life and leading his depleted battalion by example rather than command, Lt. Col. Chambers won the key

heights and anchored the right flank of the Marines' position. On the fourth day, directing the Marines' first rocket barrage and exposed to the enemy's main line of resistance, Chambers fell under enemy machine gun fire. His wounds were so serious that he was medically retired and, because he had been specially commended for performance of duty in combat, he was promoted to colonel. His Medal of Honor citation reads, in part: "... as Commanding Officer of the 3rd Assault Bn. Landing Team, 25th Marines, 4th Mar. Div., in action against enemy Japanese forces on Iwo Jima, Volcano Islands, from 19 to 22 Feb. 1945. Under a furious barrage of enemy machine gun and small arms fire from the commanding cliffs on the right, Col. Chambers, then Lt. Col., landed immediately after the initial assault waves of his battalion on D-Day to find the momentum of the assault threatened by heavy casualties from withering Japanese artillery, mortar, rocket, machine gun and rifle fire. Exposed to relentless hostile fire, he coolly reorganized his battle-weary men, inspiring them to heroic efforts by his own valor and leading them in an attack on the critical, impregnable high ground from which the enemy was pouring an increasing volume of fire directly onto troops ashore, as well as amphibious craft in succeeding waves. Constantly in the front lines, encouraging his men to push forward against the enemy's savage resistance, Col. Chambers led the 8-hour battle to carry the flanking ridge top and reduce the enemy's fields of aimed fire, thus protecting the vital foothold gained. His zealous fighting spirit undiminished, despite terrific casualties and the loss of most of his key officers, he again reorganized his troops for renewed attack against the enemy's main line of resistance and was directing the fire of the rocket platoon when he fell, critically wounded."

CHAMPAGNE, David Bernard. Corporal. Medal of Honor: b. Wakefield, R.I., Nov. 13, 1932; d. KIA, Korea, May 28, 1952. Cpl. Champagne's citation reads, in part: "... while serving as a Fire Team Leader of Co. A, 1st Bn., 7th Marines, 1st Mar. Div. (Reinf.), in action against the enemy aggressor forces in Korea on May 28, 1952. Advancing with his platoon in the initial assault of the company against a strongly fortified and heavily defended hill position, Cpl. Champagne skillfully led his fire team through a veritable hail of intense enemy machine gun, small arms, and grenade fire, overrunning trenches and a series of almost impregnable bunker positions before reaching the crest of the hill and placing his men in defensive positions. Suffering a painful leg wound while assisting in repelling the ensuing hostile counterattack, which was launched under cover of a murderous hail of mortar fire, he steadfastly refused evacuation and fearlessly continued to control his fire team. When the enemy counterattack increased in intensity, and a hostile grenade landed in the midst of the fire team, Cpl. Champagne unhesitatingly seized the deadly missile and hurled it in the direction of the approaching enemy. As the grenade left his hand, it exploded, blowing off his hand and throwing him out of the trench. Mortally wounded by enemy mortar fire while in this exposed position, Cpl. Champagne, by his valiant leadership, fortitude, and gallant spirit of self-sacrifice in the face of almost certain death, undoubtedly saved the lives of several of his fellow Marines. ..."

CHAPMAN, Leonard Fielding, Jr. Major General. Assistant Chief of Staff, G-4,

HQMC, Washington, D.C.: b. Key West, Fla., Nov. 3, 1913. After graduation from high school at Deland, Fla., Leonard Chapman entered the University of Florida where he was a member of the ROTC unit for four years. Upon graduation in June 1935, he was commissioned in the Army Field Artillery Reserve. He resigned that commission to accept appointment as a Marine second lieutenant, July 8, 1935. After completing Basic School at the Philadelphia Navy Yard, he served with the 1st Bn., 10th Marines, at Quantico, Va., from Apr. 1936 until Aug. 1937. In June 1938, after completing Field Artillery School at Fort Sill, Okla., he was assigned to the 10th Marines at the MCB, San Diego, Calif. He was promoted to first lieutenant in Sept. 1938. In June 1940, Chapman departed San Diego for Honolulu. There he completed Gunnery School aboard the USS *New Orleans* prior to reporting on board the USS *Astoria* in July 1940 for a two-year assignment as CO of the Marine Detachment. He was promoted to captain in Apr. 1941. Aboard the *Astoria* following the outbreak of WWII, Capt. Chapman took part in the early Pacific raids culminating in the battles of the Coral Sea and Midway. He was promoted to major in May 1942, and returned to the States late that June. He was assigned to MCS, Quantico, in Aug. 1942 as an instructor in the Artillery Course. Promoted to lieutenant colonel in May 1943, he was named Executive Officer of the Artillery Section at MCS. In June 1944, Lt. Col. Chapman again departed for combat duty. Joining the 1st Mar. Div. in the Pacific area, he earned the Legion of Merit with Combat "V" for meritorious service as R-3, Eleventh Marine Artillery Regiment, and CO, 4th Bn., 11th Marines, respectively, during combat at Peleliu in Sept. and Oct. 1944;

and the Bronze Star Medal with Combat "V" as 4th Bn. Commander at Okinawa, Apr. to July 1945. Following the war he served as Secretary of the General Staff, FMF, Pacific, from Sept. 1945 to July 1946, when he returned to the continental United States. From Aug. 1946 until May 1949, he was stationed at HQMC, Washington, D.C., serving as Executive Officer, G-3 Section, Division of Plans and Policies. Ordered to MCS, Quantico, Lt. Col. Chapman served as Coordinator, Reserve Artillery Training Unit; completed the Amphibious Warfare School, Senior Course, in June 1950; then served as Chief of the Supporting Arms Group, Marine Corps Development Center. While at Quantico, he was promoted to colonel in July 1950. In July 1952, he departed Quantico for Camp Pendleton, Calif., where he joined the 3rd Mar. Div. as Regimental Commander, 12th Marines. He sailed with the division in Aug. 1953 for Japan, where he continued to command the 12th Marines. In Aug. 1954, he was named CO, Marine Barracks, U.S. Fleet Activities, Yokosuka, Japan, serving in this capacity until May 1956. In July 1956, Col. Chapman assumed duties in Washington, D.C., as CO, Marine Barracks, and Director of the Marine Corps Institute. Two years after assuming these duties, he was promoted to brigadier general, July 1, 1958. Following his promotion, Gen. Chapman was assigned to Camp Lejeune, N.C., serving as CG, Force Troops, FMF, Atlantic, until Aug. 1961. He reported to HQMC in Sept. 1961 as Deputy Assistant Chief of Staff, G-4. Gen. Chapman was promoted to major general on Nov. 1, 1961, and on the same date assumed his current duties as Assistant Chief of Staff, G-4.

CHRISTIANSON, Stanley Reuben. Private First Class. Medal of Honor: b. Mindoro, Wis., Jan. 24, 1925; d. KIA, Seoul, Korea, Sept. 29, 1950. Stanley Christianson enlisted in the Marine Corps on Oct. 2, 1942 at the age of 17. Following recruit training at San Diego, Calif., he took advanced training with the 2nd Mar. Div. and went overseas with that unit. He fought at Tarawa, Saipan, Tinian, Iheya, Aguni, and Okinawa, and served with the occupation forces in Japan. Discharged in Dec. 1945, Christianson reenlisted in the regular Marine Corps three months later. He served at the NAS in Pensacola, Fla., as a Drill Instructor at Parris Is., S.C.; at the Naval Ammunition Depot, Hastings, Neb.; at the Brooklyn Navy Yard, Brooklyn, N.Y.; and at Camp Lejeune, N.C., before going overseas to Korea with the 1st Mar. Div. in Aug. 1950. Eleven days later he earned the Medal of Honor. His citation reads, in part: "... while serving with Co. E, 2nd Bn., 1st Marines, 1st Mar. Div. (Reinf.) in action against enemy aggressor forces at Hill 132, Seoul, Korea, in the early morning hours of Sept. 29, 1950. Manning one of the several listening posts covering approaches to the platoon area when the enemy commenced the attack, P.F.C. Christianson quickly sent another Marine to alert the rest of the platoon. Without orders, he remained in his position and, with full knowledge that he would have slight chance of escape, fired relentlessly at oncoming hostile troops attacking furiously with rifles, automatic weapons, and incendiary grenades. Accounting for seven enemy dead in the immediate vicinity before his position was overrun and he himself fatally struck down, P.F.C. Christianson, by his superb courage, valiant fighting spirit, and devotion to duty, was responsible for allowing the rest of the platoon time to man positions, build up a stronger defense on that flank, and repel the attack with 41 of the enemy destroyed, many more wounded, and three taken prisoner. . . ."

CLOUD, George Harlon. Major General. Commanding General, Marine Corps Supply Center, Barstow, Calif.: b. Goldthwaite, Tex., Sept. 27, 1904. Following graduation from high school in 1922, George Cloud attended the University of Texas. He began his Marine Corps career as an enlisted man in May 1927. Shortly afterward, he embarked for China duty with the 4th Marines under the late Maj. Gen. Smedley D. Butler, and returned in June 1929. Commissioned a Marine second lieutenant Mar. 12, 1930, he later entered the Basic School at the Philadelphia Navy Yard, completing the course in June 1931. That month he joined the 1st Marines at Quantico, Va., and participated with them in the early experimental joint fleet amphibious exercises in Hawaii, which laid the ground work for amphibious techniques used successfully by Marines during their island-jumping operations of WWII. Going aboard the USS *New York* in July 1932, he served a tour of sea duty as Marine Detachment Officer. On his return to Quantico in July 1934, he served with the 5th Marines in the newly formed FMF. He was promoted to first lieutenant in Dec. 1934, and in Oct. 1935 was assigned duty at the MB, Washington, D.C. In Jan. 1937, he returned to Shanghai where he commanded the Machine Gun Co., 2nd Bn., 4th Marine Regt. That Sept. he was promoted to captain. Ordered to the States in July 1939, Capt. Cloud began his first tour at Parris Is., S.C., as a battalion supply officer. Embarking for the Pacific area with the 4th Defense Bn. in Feb. 1941, he was stationed at Guantanamo Bay, Cuba, then moved to Pearl Harbor in Oct.

where he subsequently witnessed the Japanese attack, and later served in the New Hebrides. Cloud was promoted to major in Feb. 1942, and to lieutenant colonel in Aug. 1942. In Feb. 1943, Lt. Col. Cloud was assigned to the First Base Depot, Noumea, Caledonia, returning to the States in June 1943 to become Post Quartermaster at Parris Is. He returned to the Pacific area in July 1944, and served as Assistant Supply Officer with the 1st Mar. Div., then preparing for the Peleliu invasion. While serving in that capacity, he joined the 25th Div., Sixth Army, as an observer during the Luzon invasion, before returning to the 1st Mar. Div. for the Okinawa campaign. Shortly thereafter, he rejoined the Sixth Army Staff to aid in the advance planning for the Japanese mainland invasion and subsequent occupation. Returning to the States in Dec. 1945, he served as Assistant Post Supply Officer at Parris Is. until Feb. 1947, when he assumed command of the Supply School at Camp Lejeune, N.C. While at Camp Lejeune, he was promoted to colonel in Feb. 1948. Assigned to HQMC, Washington, D.C., in Nov. 1949, Col. Cloud saw duty there as Chief, Administrative Branch, Supply Department. In June 1952, he reported to the Marine Corps Supply Center, Albany, Ga., where he served four years as Chief of Staff. He was then transferred to the MCRD, Parris Is., in June 1956, and served there as Assistant Chief of Staff, G-4/Depot Supply Officer, for two years. Col. Cloud was promoted to brigadier general in July 1958, upon assuming command of the MCSC, Barstow, Calif. Four years later, while serving in this capacity, he was promoted to major general in Aug. 1962.

COLE, Darrell Samuel. Sergeant. Medal of Honor: b. Flat River, Mo., July 20,

1920; d. KIA, Iwo Jima, D-Day, Feb. 19, 1945. After graduation from high school, Darrell Cole joined the Civilian Conservation Corps, where he became an assistant forestry clerk and assistant educational advisor for his company. On Aug. 25, 1941, he enlisted in the Marine Corps and was sent to Parris Is., S.C., for training, where his proficiency with the French horn marked him as a logical candidate for Field Music School. Completing Field Music School, he was transferred to the 1st Marines, 1st Mar. Div. On Aug. 7, 1942, he found himself wading ashore with his buddies of Company H of the 2nd Bn. on the beaches of Guadalcanal. When a regular machine gunner of his unit fell wounded, Cole assumed the role of gunner, and acquitted himself in such a manner as to win the praise of his CO. He returned to the States on Feb. 2, 1943, and joined the 1st Bn., 23rd Marines, which was then forming at Camp Lejeune, N.C., as part of the new 4th Mar. Div. During the first engagement of the division, at Roi-Namur in the Kwajalein Atoll, Cole again went into action as a machine gunner. Four months later the 4th Mar. Div. stormed ashore at Saipan, and Cole was designated as a machine gun section leader. During the battle when his squad leader was killed, Cole, although wounded himself, assumed command of the entire squad. A few days after the battle of Saipan, Cole led his squad ashore in the invasion of the neighboring island of Tinian. In Jan. 1945, Sgt. Cole, who had been promoted the previous Nov., sailed with his company for Iwo Jima. On D-Day, Feb. 19, Cole led his machine gun section ashore in the assault on Iwo's shifting beaches. One of his squads had hardly reached dry land before their advance was halted by a deadly hail of fire from two enemy positions. Taking stock of the situation, Cole crawled forward and wiped out the two positions with hand grenades. His unit continued the advance until they were again halted by fire from three Japanese pillboxes. One of Cole's machine guns silenced the most threatening position, then jammed. Armed with only a pistol and one hand grenade, Sgt. Cole made a one-man attack against the two remaining positions. Twice he returned to his own lines for additional grenades and continued the attack under the fierce enemy fire until he had succeeded in destroying the Japanese strong point. Returning to his own squad, he was instantly killed by an enemy grenade. By his one-man attack and heroic self-sacrifice, Sgt. Cole enabled his company to move forward against the remaining fortifications and attain their ultimate objective. For his unselfish act of heroism he was awarded the nation's highest military award, the Medal of Honor.

COLEMAN, John. Private. Medal of Honor: b. County of Cork, Ireland, Oct. 9, 1847. Pvt. Coleman was cited for bravery "... on board the USS *Colorado* in action at Korea on June 11, 1871. Fighting hand-to-hand with the enemy, he succeeded in saving the life of Alexander McKenzie...."

COLLINS, William Robert. Brigadier General. Chief of Staff, Joint Task Force — 4, Fort Monroe, Va.: b. Washington, D.C., Feb. 5, 1913. William Collins completed Western High School in 1931 and entered Georgetown University from which he graduated in 1935 with a Bachelor of Foreign Service degree. While at the university he was a member of the ROTC unit. He resigned his Army Reserve commission to accept appointment as a Marine second lieutenant,

Sept. 1935. After completing Marine Officers' Basic School at the Philadelphia Navy Yard the following spring, he was assigned to the 5th Marines, FMF, at Quantico, Va. While there he was promoted to first lieutenant in Sept. 1938. That month Collins entered the Infantry School at Fort Benning, Ga., and on completing the Tank Course in June 1939, served as Platoon Leader and Executive Officer in the 1st Tank Co., Quantico. In May 1940, after attending Fleet Gunnery School in Hawaii, he became CO of the Marine Detachment aboard the USS *New Orleans*. He was promoted to captain in Oct. 1941. He was serving aboard the *New Orleans* when Pearl Harbor was attacked on Dec. 7, 1941, and took part in the Pearl Harbor-Midway operation. Later he participated in the Coral Sea and Midway raids in 1942. He was promoted to major in May 1942, and a month later was detached from the *New Orleans*. In July 1942, Maj. Collins was assigned to Camp Elliott, San Diego, Calif., as CO of the Tank School at the Training Center. He was promoted to lieutenant colonel in June 1943. In Feb. 1944, he moved to Camp Pendleton, Calif., as CO of the 5th Tank Bn., 5th Mar. Div. With his battalion he was ordered overseas in Sept. 1944. For conspicuous gallantry in action on Iwo Jima from Feb. 19 to Mar. 26, 1945, he was awarded the Silver Star Medal. He moved with the division into Japan in Sept. 1945, and in Dec. joined the 6th Marines, 2nd Mar. Div., as Regimental Military Governor, Fukuoka, Japan, and later served as Regimental Executive Officer. In Sept. 1946, Lt. Col. Collins was ordered to San Diego, where he served as Inspector-Instructor of the 11th Tank Bn., USMCR. Transferred in Aug. 1948 to Quantico, he completed the Senior Course, MCS, in May 1949; then he

served as Operations Officer and Instructor, Combined Arms Section, Marine Corps Educational Center; and as Chief of the Landing Assault Section, Landing Force Development Center, respectively. He was promoted to colonel in Feb. 1951. He entered the National War College in Aug. 1951 and graduated in June 1952. He arrived in London, England, in July 1952 for duty with the Joint American Military Advisory Group. Shortly afterward, he moved to Frankfurt, Germany, as Staff Operations Officer, Policy Branch, J-3 Division, HQ, U.S. European Command, concurrent with the establishment of that Command. He served in that post for two years. On his return to the States in Aug. 1954, he served as a Member of the Advance Research Group, Marine Corps Educational Center, Quantico. Col. Collins was assigned to the 2nd Mar. Div., Camp Lejeune, N.C., from Aug. 1955, to May 1958. During that time he served as Regimental Commander of the 2nd Marines until July 1956; then as Assistant Chief of Staff, G-3, of the division; and as Chief of Staff during Operation Deep-Water in Turkey. Following a brief assignment on the Personnel Board at HQMC, Col. Collins returned to MCS, Quantico, from June 1958 through Feb. 1961. There he served as President of the Tactics and Techniques Board, Marine Corps Landing Force Development Center, until Oct. 1959 when he was named Director of the Development Center. His rank of brigadier general dates from Nov. 1, 1959. Upon his detachment from Quantico, Gen. Collins assumed his current duties at Fort Monroe, Va., in Feb. 1961.

COMMISKEY, Henry Alfred. "Hank." Major. Medal of Honor: b. Hattiesburg, Miss., Jan. 10, 1927. Hank Commiskey, the first Marine to be awarded the Medal

Commiskey

of Honor for extraordinary heroism in the Korean War, served more than five years as an enlisted man, including 21 months overseas. Following recruit training at San Diego, Calif., he served at Camp Pendleton, Calif., Hawaii and Japan, in addition to the combat operations at Iwo Jima. While serving as a drill instructor at Parris Is., S.C., as a staff sergeant, he was accepted for officer training and commissioned a second lieutenant, Sept. 10, 1949. He completed training in June 1950, and taught in the tactics section at the MCS, Quantico, before going to Korea with the 1st Mar. Regt. in Aug. 1950. The action for which Commiskey received the Medal of Honor came a few days after the Inchon landing, in which he participated. His citation reads, in part: " . . . as a Platoon Leader in Co. C,

1st Bn., 1st Marines, 1st Mar. Div. (Reinf.), in action against enemy aggressor forces near Yongdungpo, Korea, on Sept. 20, 1950. Directed to attack hostile forces well dug in on Hill 85, 1st Lt. Commiskey, spearheaded the assault, charging up the steep slopes on the run. Coolly disregarding the heavy enemy machine gun and small arms fire, he plunged on well forward of the rest of his platoon and was the first man to reach the crest of the objective. Armed only with a pistol, he jumped into a hostile machine gun emplacement occupied by five enemy troops and quickly disposed of four of the soldiers with his automatic pistol. Grappling with the fifth, Commiskey knocked him to the ground and held him until he could obtain a weapon from another member of his platoon and kill the last of the enemy gun crew. Continuing his bold assault, he moved to the next emplacement, killed two more of the enemy and then led his platoon toward the rear nose of the hill to rout the remainder of the hostile troops and destroy them as they fled from their positions." Following hospitalization at the Naval Hospital in Pensacola, he served at the Naval Air Rocket Test Station, Lake Denmark, Dover, N.J. In Sept. 1951, he became a student naval aviator at the NAS, Pensacola. He received his wings at Corpus Christi in June 1953, and later completed jet training at El Toro, Calif. In Apr. 1954, he returned to Korea as a pilot with Marine Attack Squadron 212, MAG 12, 1st MAW. He returned to the States in Sept. 1954, and at his own request was assigned line duty. He joined the 1st Mar. Div. in Dec. 1954, and served consecutively as a company commander, Assistant S-3 of the 1st Service Regt., and Division Reenlistment Officer. From Sept. 1956 until July 1959, he served as Officer in Charge of the Marine Corps Recruiting Station, 6th Marine Corps Reserve and Recruitment District, Jackson, Miss. Commiskey completed the Junior Course at MCS, Quantico, from Aug. 1959 to June 1960, where he is an instructor and student company commander at the Basic School.

CONOLEY, Odell Maurice. Brigadier General. Deputy G-3, HQ, U.S. European Command, Paris, France: b. Amarillo, Tex., Nov. 9, 1913. Odell Conoley completed high school at Amarillo in 1931. Upon graduation from Texas A & M College in June 1935, he was commissioned in the Army Inf. Reserve. Shortly afterward, he resigned this commission to accept appointment as a Marine second lieutenant on Sept. 11, 1935. After completing Basic School at the Philadelphia Navy Yard in May 1936, Lt. Conoley was stationed at the MCB, San Diego, Calif. In Sept. 1937, he embarked for China. While there he saw duty in Shanghai; at the American Embassy in Peiping; and with the Marine Detachment in Tientsin. He returned to San Diego in Nov. 1938 as a first lieutenant. Six months later, he was assigned sea duty as commander of the Marine Detachment aboard the USS *Henderson,* serving in this capacity from May 1939 through Aug. 1940. In Sept. 1940, he joined the 1st Mar. Brig., serving at Parris Is., S.C.; Guantanamo Bay, Cuba; and Camp Lejeune, N.C. Three days after the United States entered WWII, he received his promotion to captain. In Apr. 1942, Conoley embarked with the 2nd Bn., 7th Marines, for the Pacific area. Later, with his unit as part of the 1st Mar. Div., he took part in the Guadalcanal campaign where he earned the Navy Cross, and in the Cape Gloucester and Bismarck Archipelago operations, advancing from major in May 1942, to

lieutenant colonel in July 1943. For gallantry in action in Dec. 1943, while commanding the 2nd Bn., 7th Marines, at Cape Gloucester, Lt. Col. Conoley was awarded the Silver Star Medal. After his return to the States in June 1944, he entered the Infantry Course at the Command and Staff School, Fort Leavenworth, Kan., prior to brief assignments at Camp Pendleton and San Diego. He left the States in July 1945, for duty with 6th U.S. Army HQ in the Philippines, later moving with the headquarters to Kyoto, Japan. In Jan. 1946, he began a year's assignment with 8th U.S. Army HQ in Yokohama, serving as Assistant G-3 and Liaison Officer. For service in this capacity, he received the Army Letter of Commendation with Commendation Ribbon. Upon reporting to San Diego in Jan. 1947, Lt. Col. Conoley was attached to Troop Training Unit, Amphibious Forces, Pacific Fleet, as an instructor. That May he began a three-year tour of duty at HQMC, Washington, D.C., as Operations Officer, G-3 Section, Division of Plans and Policies. In July 1950, he enrolled at the Army War College, Fort Leavenworth, and was promoted to colonel in Feb. 1951. On completing the course in July 1951, Col. Conoley served as an instructor at MCS, Quantico, for six months, and as Assistant Chief of Staff, G-4, from Dec. 1951, to July 1954. He then joined the 1st Mar. Div. in Korea in Aug. 1954, as Deputy Chief of Staff. In Oct., he was named CO of the 7th Marines. With the 1st Mar. Div. he returned to Camp Pendleton in June 1955, at which time he became the 1st Div.'s Chief of Staff. In May 1956, he was again ordered to MCS, Quantico, where he served consecutively as Member, FMF, Organization and Composition Board; Member, Advance Research Group; and Chief of Staff, Marine Corps Educational

Center. In Sept. 1957, he became Deputy Director of the Marine Corps Educational Center. Following this assignment, Col. Conoley was transferred in July 1959, to Camp Lejeune, N.C., where he served for 20 months as Assistant Division Commander, 2nd Mar. Div. He was promoted to brigadier general in Nov. 1959.

COONEY, James. Private. Medal of Honor: b. Limerick, Ireland, July 27, 1860; d. Mar. 14, 1903. James Cooney enlisted in the Marine Corps on Aug. 19, 1889. He was awarded the Medal of Honor on Jan. 24, 1902 for distinguishing himself by meritorious conduct in the presence of the enemy during the battle near Tientsin, China, July 13, 1900.

COURSEY, John P. Brigadier General: b. Lyons, Ga., Dec. 20, 1914. John Coursey entered the University of Michigan at Ann Arbor, and was graduated in 1937 with a Bachelor of Science degree in chemistry. While in college he was a member of the ROTC unit for four years. He was commissioned a second lieutenant in the Army Infantry Reserve in Feb. 1937, and resigned that commission to accept appointment as a Marine second lieutenant, Aug. 5, 1937. After completion of Basic School at the Philadelphia Navy Yard, and Secondary Battery Gunnery School aboard the USS *Nevada,* he joined the USS *Arizona.* In July 1939, after one year of sea duty, he reported to the 2nd Mar. Brig. as a communications officer. He was promoted to first lieutenant in Sept. 1940. In May 1941, he embarked for Honolulu, Hawaii, where he again joined the Marine Detachment aboard the USS *Arizona.* After the Pearl Harbor attack, during which the *Arizona* was sunk, Lt. Coursey served as a company commander at the Marine Barracks, Pearl

Harbor. While there he was promoted to captain in Feb. 1942, and to major in Aug. 1942. From Pearl Harbor — and following a short tour on Midway Island — he reported for flight training in Nov. 1942 at the U.S. Naval Air Station, Dallas, Texas. He was designated a Naval Aviator at the Naval Air Training Center, Pensacola, Fla. in May 1943, then completed operational training at the Naval Air Station, Jacksonville, Fla. He was next assigned to Marine Fleet Air, West Coast, for duty with Marine Utility Squadron 953 and MAG 15 at Camp Kearney, San Diego, and Corvalis, Ore. He was promoted to lieutenant colonel in May 1944. Ordered overseas again in Oct. 1944, he served as Executive Officer of MAG 25 and CO of Marine Transport Squadron 152, respectively, during the Northern Solomons campaign. Following WWII, he returned to the States and completed the Marine Command and Staff School at MCS, Quantico, Va., in Feb. 1946. The following month he became CO of the Marine Air Detachment, Marine Air Reserve Training Command, Naval Air Station, Atlanta, Ga. In Jan. 1950, he completed the Armed Forces Staff College, Norfolk, Va. He was then assigned to the Marine Corps Educational Center, Quantico, where he served as an instructor in the Aviation Section until Dec. 1951, and as Officer in Charge of the Aviation Section until July 1952. While at Quantico, he was promoted to colonel in Nov. 1951. During the Korean War, he served in Korea from Aug. 1952 until April 1953 as Executive Officer of MAG 33. In May 1953, he was assigned to Maxwell Air Force Base, Ala., where he served as Instructor and Marine Corps Representative, Naval Advisory Group, Air University, until Aug. 1955; and was graduated from the Air War College in June 1956. He returned to Hawaii in Aug.

1956, to assume duties as Deputy G-3, FMF, Pacific. On his return to the States in May 1958, he became CO of MCAS, Quantico. In Dec. 1959, he was named Military Secretary to the Commandant of the Marine Corps. During this assignment, he was promoted to his present grade of brigadier general in Aug. 1962. In Oct. 1962, Gen. Coursey became Assistant Wing Commander, 2nd MAW, at Cherry Point.

COURTNEY, Henry Alexius, Jr. Major. Medal of Honor: b. Duluth, Minn., Jan. 6, 1916; d. KIA, Okinawa, May 15, 1945. Before entering the service, Henry Courtney had been admitted to the bar in Minnesota and Illinois, having received his bachelor's degree from the University of Minnesota and his doctor's degree from Loyola University in Chicago, Ill. He received his commission as a second lieutenant in the Marine Corps Reserve in Feb. 1940, and in Mar. of that year was placed in command of the Duluth unit of the Marine Corps Reserve which was mobilized and sent to San Diego, Calif., for training. He later went to Iceland where he served for 10 months. At Guadalcanal, Solomons Is., he participated in the first United States offensive of WWII, commanding a company of the 1st Mar. Div. His next combat action was Okinawa, where his gallantry won for him the Medal of Honor. His citation reads, in part: "Ordered to hold for the night in static defense behind Sugar Loaf Hill, Maj. Courtney weighed the effect of a hostile night counterattack against the tactical value of an immediate Marine assault. He resolved to initiate the assault and obtained permission to seize the forward slope of the hill. He declared his personal intention of moving forward, then proceeded on his way, boldly blasting nearby cave positions and neutralizing

enemy guns as he went. . . . Subsequently, reinforced by 26 men and an LVT load of grenades, he determined to storm the crest of the hill. . . . Upon reaching the crest and observing large numbers of Japanese forming for action less than 100 yards away he instantly attacked, waged a furious battle and succeeded in killing many of the enemy and forcing the remainder to take cover in the caves. . . ." Maj. Courtney was killed instantly by a hostile mortar burst while moving among his men.

CROWE, Henry P. Colonel (Retired): b. Boston, Ky., Mar. 7, 1899. After attending high school at Mt. Pulaski, Ill., Henry Crowe enlisted in the Marine Corps on Oct. 28, 1918. As an enlisted man, he served in the Dominican Republic from 1921 to 1923, in Nicaragua in 1928, and at various other posts and stations. He was also a frequent participant in local and national shooting competition, winning the coveted Distinguished Marksman Medal. Commissioned a marine gunner (a warrant officer rank) in Sept. 1934, he served on Pacific maneuvers and at several stations in the States during the next two years. He embarked for China in Oct. 1936, and after three years with the Marine Detachment at the American Embassy, Peiping, he returned to the States in Oct. 1939, to join the 6th Mar. Regt. at San Diego, Calif. He was transferred to the 8th Mar. Regt. in Apr. 1940, and was promoted to chief marine gunner in Feb. 1941. Crowe embarked with the 8th Marines for Samoa in Jan. 1942, and the following month was promoted from chief gunner to captain. He was promoted to major in Mar. 1943, and to lieutenant colonel in Jan. 1944. He fought as commander of the regimental weapons company at Guadalcanal and as commander of the

2nd Bn. at Tarawa and Saipan. He also served with that regiment in New Zealand and Hawaii before he returned to the States in Sept. 1944 for treatment of the wounds he received at Saipan. He was released from the U.S. Naval Hospital at San Diego in Mar. 1945, and the following month was named Training Officer of FMF, Pacific, at Pearl Harbor. After WWII, Lt. Col. Crowe served briefly with the 29th Marines in China and with Marine garrison forces, 14th Naval District, at Pearl Harbor. He returned to the States in Mar. 1946, and after duty at San Diego and Quantico, entered the Senior Course in the Amphibious Warfare School at Quantico in Sept. 1947. He completed the course in May 1948, and reported to the 1st Mar. Div. at Camp Pendleton, Calif. the following month. There he served as a battalion executive officer, as division special service officer, and as executive officer of the 1st Shore Party Bn. before taking command of that unit in July 1950. He arrived in Japan the following month to help prepare for the Inchon landing. After fighting in Korea, he returned to the States in May 1951. Lt. Col. Crowe was promoted to colonel in Dec. 1951, while serving as Chief of the Tactical School Section with the Troop Training Unit, Amphibious Training Command, at Coronado, Calif. He later served there as Chief of the Administrative Schools Section before assuming command of the Headquarters and Service Bn. at the Recruit Depot, San Diego, in Jan. 1953. Following his detachment from San Diego, he completed his final tour of duty June 1957 to Mar. 1960, as CO, MB, Norfolk Naval Shipyard, Portsmouth, Va.

CUKELA, Louis. Major. Navy Medal of Honor, Army Medal of Honor: b. Spalato, Serbia, May 1, 1888; d. U.S. Naval

Cukela

Hospital, Bethesda, Md., Mar. 19, 1956. Louis Cukela was educated in the grade schools of Spalato; then he attended the Merchant Academy, and later the Royal Gymnasium, both for two-year courses. In 1913, he emigrated to the United States and he and his brother settled in Minneapolis, Minn. On Sept. 21, 1914, he enlisted in the U.S. Army. He was serving as a corporal in Company H, 13th Inf. when he was honorably discharged by purchase on June 12, 1916. Seven months later, on Jan. 31, 1917, with WWI raging in Europe, he enlisted in the Marine Corps. Following the United States' entry into the conflict, he went to France and took part in all the engagements in which the 5th Marines fought. He was awarded both Medals of Honor for the same action near Villers-Cotterets, France, on the morning of July 18, 1918, during the Soissons engagement. The 66th Co., 5th Marines, in which Cukela was a gunnery sergeant, was advancing through the Forest de Retz when it was held up by an enemy strong point. Despite the warnings of his men, Sgt. Cukela crawled out from the flank and advanced alone toward the German lines. Getting beyond the strong point despite heavy fire, "Gunny" Cukela captured one gun by bayoneting its crew. Picking up their hand grenades, he then demolished the remaining portion of the strong point from the shelter of a nearby gunpit. He took four prisoners and captured two undamaged machine guns. This famous Marine was wounded in action twice, but since there is no record of either wound at the Navy's Bureau of Medicine and Surgery, he was never awarded the Purple Heart. The first wound was suffered at Jaulny, France, on Sept. 16, 1918, during the St.-Mihiel engagement. Sgt. Cukela was wounded again during the fighting in the Champagne sector. Neither wound was serious. Cukela received a field appointment to the rank of second lieutenant in the Marine Corps Reserve on Sept. 26, 1918, and was selected for a commission in the regular Marine Corps on Mar. 31, 1919. Promoted to first lieutenant on July 17, 1919, he was advanced to the rank of captain on Sept. 15, 1921. After WWI, Cukela served at various overseas bases in Haiti, Santo Domingo, the Philippines, and China; and at stations in Quantico, Va.; Philadelphia, Pa.; Norfolk, Va.; Hampton Roads, Va.; Mare Island, Calif.; Washington, D.C.; Nashville, Ind.; and Fort Knox, Ky. From June 1933, to Jan. 1934, he served as a company commander with the Civilian Conservation Corps. His last years in the Marine Corps were spent at

Norfolk, where he served as the post quartermaster. Retired as a major on June 30, 1940, he was recalled to active duty on July 30 of the same year. During WWII the major served at Norfolk and Philadelphia. He finally returned to the inactive retired list on May 17, 1946. Maj. Cukela served a few days less than 32 years of active duty in the Army and Marines. On Mar. 19, 1956, Major Cukela died at the U.S. Naval Hospital, Bethesda, Md. He was buried with full military honors in Arlington National Cemetery, Mar. 22, 1956.

CUNNINGHAM, Alfred Austell. Lieutenant Colonel. First Marine Aviator: b. Atlanta, Ga., 1882; d. Sarasota, Fla., May 27, 1939. Shortly after he was commissioned a second lieutenant in the Marine Corps, Alfred Cunningham developed a strong interest in flying. Stationed at Philadelphia at the time, he managed to rent a forlorn contraption which had been built as a flying machine. Permission was granted Cunningham to make take-off attempts at the Philadelphia Navy Yard, but the "plane" never got off the ground. Named the "Noisy Nan" by his fellow officers, it was capable of little more than a bumpy ride down the runway. Eventually, however, the Corps took pity on the young aviation enthusiast and sent him to the Navy Aviation Camp at Annapolis, Md. on July 9, 1912. In early 1913, he went to Guantanamo Bay, Cuba, where he participated in naval exercises. Duty at the Washington Navy Yard followed on Sept. 26, 1913. Several months later he was appointed to a board which was planning the organization of a Naval Aeronautic Service. In Feb. 1914, he became a test pilot. Duty and further instruction at Pensacola, Fla. during the next two years left Cunningham with a broken back suffered in an experimental catapult hop. Fully recovered in Apr. 1916, he requested instruction in "land flying" — an innovation for the Navy. When he reported to San Diego, Calif., he was the first Marine or Naval officer to take up land flying. With the advent of WWI, Cunningham was sent to France on observation duty. On his return to the States in Jan. 1918, he recommended the organization of a Marine aviation force to participate in the European hostilities. The project was approved and Cunningham, then a major, was in command of the Marine flying units until the end of the war. He was the first officer-in-charge of Marine Corps aviation and held the position until Nov., 1920, when he was detailed to command the 1st Marine Air Squadron in Santo Domingo. When his tour of aviation duty ended in July 1922, he was sent to Quantico for instruction. From then till June 1926, he was Assistant Adjutant and Inspector, after which he was ordered as Division Marine Officer and as aide on the Staff of Commander, Battleship Division 3. In June 1928, he was detailed to temporary detached duty at Nicaragua and served with the 2nd Brig. Marines as Executive Officer of the Western Area at Leon, Nicaragua. When that tour of duty expired, he became executive officer and registrar of the Marine Corps Institute from 1929 to 1931, and then was detailed as an Assistant Quartermaster at the MB, Philadelphia, where he served from Apr. 1931 to Mar. 1935. About this time, Maj. Cunningham's health began to fail and he spent several months in the hospital. On May 10, 1935, he appeared before a Naval Retiring Board at MB, Washington, D.C., which found him to be incapacitated for active service and 10 days later he was ordered home to await retirement on the first of Aug. of that year.

While on the retired list, he was appointed a lieutenant colonel with rank from Jan. 16, 1936.

CUSHMAN, Robert Everton, Jr. Major General. Assistant Chief of Staff, G-2 (Intelligence) and Assistant Chief of Staff, G-3 (Plans, Operations and Training) HQMC, Washington, D.C.: b. St. Paul, Minn., Dec. 24, 1914. After graduation from St. Paul Central High School at the age of sixteen, Robert Cushman was appointed to the U.S. Naval Academy. Upon graduation, he was commissioned a Marine second lieutenant, June 6, 1935. Lt. Cushman completed Marine Officers' Basic School at the Philadelphia Navy Yard, then served briefly at the Marine Corps Base, San Diego, Calif. In Feb. 1936, he arrived in Shanghai, China, serving with the 4th Marines, and later the 2nd Mar. Brig., as a platoon commander. On his return to the States in Mar. 1938, he served at Naval shipyards in Brooklyn, N.Y., and Portsmouth, Va. He was promoted to first lieutenant in Aug. 1938. In Apr. 1939, he was assigned to the Marine Detachment at the New York World's Fair, and was subsequently stationed at the Marine Barracks, Quantico, Va. He was promoted to captain in Mar. 1941. In June 1941, Capt. Cushman went aboard the USS *Pennsylvania* at San Diego, enroute to Pearl Harbor, as CO of the ship's Marine Detachment. He was serving in this capacity when the Japanese attacked the ship and other Naval installations at Pearl Harbor on Dec. 7, 1941. Upon his transfer from the *Pennsylvania*, he joined the 9th Marines at San Diego as a battalion executive officer in May 1942 and, that same month, was promoted to major. With his unit he moved to Camp Pendleton in Sept. 1942 and embarked for the Pacific area in Jan. 1943. He was promoted to lieutenant colonel in May 1943. That month Lt. Col. Cushman was appointed CO of the 2nd Bn., 9th Marines. During the two years he held that post, he led his battalion repeatedly into combat, earning the Bronze Star Medal with Combat "V" on Bougainville, the Navy Cross during the recapture of Guam, and the Legion of Merit with Combat "V" during the Iwo Jima campaign. On his return to the States in May 1945, he was stationed at MCS, Quantico, for three years. During that period he completed the Senior School, served as an instructor in the Command and Staff School, and during his last two years there was Supervisory Instructor, Amphibious Warfare School. In June 1948, he was named Head of the Amphibious Warfare Branch, Office of Naval Research, Navy Department, Washington, D.C. From Oct. 1949, until May 1951, he served at HQMC. While there he was promoted to colonel in May 1950. In June, 1951, he joined the Staff of Commander in Chief, U.S. Naval Forces, Eastern Atlantic and Mediterranean Fleet, in London, England, serving

as Amphibious Plans Officer until June 1953. Following his return to the States, he was transferred to Norfolk, Va., as a member of the faculty of the Armed Forces Staff College, and in July 1954, became Director of the Plans and Operations Division there. In July 1956, he assumed command of the 2nd Mar. Regt., 2nd Mar. Div., at Camp Lejeune, N.C. Assigned to Washington, D.C., in Feb. 1957, he served four years on the staff of former Vice President Richard Nixon, as Assistant to the Vice President of the United States for National Security Affairs. While serving in this capacity, he was promoted to brigadier general in July 1958. Gen. Cushman became Assistant Division Commander, 3rd Mar. Div. on Okinawa in Mar. 1961. He was promoted to his present rank of major general in Aug. 1961, and in Sept. assumed command of the 3rd Mar. Div. In July 1962, he returned to HQMC where he assumed his current assignment as Assistant Chief of Staff, G-2 (Intelligence) and Assistant Chief of Staff, G-3 (Plans, Operations and Training).

D

DAHLGREN, John Olof. Corporal. Medal of Honor: b. Kahliwar, Sweden, Sept. 14, 1872. Cpl. Dahlgren's citation reads, in part: " . . . for distinguished conduct in the presence of the enemy at the battle of Peking, China, June 20 to July 16, 1900 . . ."

DALY, Daniel. "Dan." Sergeant Major. Called by Gen. Smedley D. Butler, "The fightin'est Marine I ever knew": b. Glen Cove, Long Island, N.Y., Nov. 11, 1873;

d. Glendale, Long Island, N.Y., Apr. 28, 1937. Only other Marine, in addition to Butler, to be awarded two Medals of Honor for separate acts of heroism. A small man — 5 feet, 6 inches, 132 pounds — Daly was nevertheless a fine military figure, erect and well-proportioned. He was also a strict disciplinarian, yet always fair-minded and very popular among both officers and enlisted men. He joined the Marine Corps on Jan. 10, 1899, and was sent to the Asiatic Fleet. In May

Daly

1900, he shipped aboard the USS *Newark* for Taku Bay, China, where he landed with other Marines and entrained for Peking. The American Marines, together with the Germans, had been stationed on Tartar Wall, south of the American Legation, but intense enemy fire had driven them from the position. With Capt. Hall, Daly manned the wall bastion, bayoneted rifle in hand. On Aug. 14, Capt. Hall left to bring up reinforcements and Daly remained to defend the position singlehanded. Chinese snipers fired at him and stormed the bastion, but he fought them off until reinforcements arrived. For this gallantry Daly was awarded his first Medal of Honor. Fifteen years later, in action against Haitian bandits, Daly earned a second Medal of Honor. The citation accompanying the award states: "... on the night of Oct. 24, 1915, three officers and 35 enlisted men were attacked by 400 Cacos while crossing a river in a deep ravine concealed in bushes about 100 yards from a fort. The Marine detachment fought its way forward to a good position which it maintained during the night, although subjected to a continuous fire from the Cacos. At daybreak the Marines in three squads under the command of Capt. Upshur, Lt. Osterman and Gy. Sgt. Daly advanced in three different directions surprising and scattering the enemy in all directions. Had one squad failed, not one man of the party would have lived to tell the tale. Gy. Sgt. Daly, 15th Co., during the operations was the most conspicuous figure among the enlisted men." In the years that followed, Dan Daly's service included sea duty aboard the USS *Newark, Panther, Cleveland, Marietta, Mississippi, Ohio,* and *Machias.* In addition, he saw combat in China and Haiti. During WWI, Daly served in combat in the Toulon sector (Mar.-May 1918); the Aisne Operations (June 1918); and the Chateau-Thierry sector (Belleau Wood, June 1918). On June 5, at the risk of his life, he extinguished a fire in the ammunition dump at Lucy le Bocage. Two days later, while the same sector was under one of its heaviest bombardments, Daly visited all machine gun crews of his company, which were over a wide section of the front, to cheer on his men. On June 10, singlehanded, he attacked an enemy machine gun emplacement, capturing it with hand grenades and an automatic pistol. On the same date, during an enemy attack on the village of Bouresches, he brought in wounded under heavy fire. Daly is perhaps best remembered for a famous battle cry delivered during the bloody fighting at Belleau

Wood in June 1918. The Marines were taking a terrific pounding on the outskirts of Lucy le Bocage on the fringe of Belleau Wood. They were outnumbered, outgunned, and pinned down. Then Daly made history. He ordered an attack. Leaping forward, he allegedly yelled to his tired men, "Come on, you sons of bitches, do you want to live forever?" Daly also served in the St.-Mihiel offensive (Sept. 1918). He was wounded in action on June 21 and twice on Oct. 8, 1918. He then served with the American Army of Occupation in Germany following the Armistice. In 1919, he was placed on the retainer list of the Fleet Marine Corps Reserve, awaiting retirement. He took a job as a bank guard on Wall Street, New York City, and held the position for 17 years. Daly was retired officially on Feb. 6, 1929. After his death in 1937, a destroyer was named for him. His record as a fighting man remains unequalled in the annals of Marine Corps history.

DAMATO, Anthony Peter. Corporal. Medal of Honor: b. Shenandoah, Pa., Mar. 28, 1922; d. KIA, Engebi Island, Eniwetok Atoll. Anthony Damato enlisted in the Marine Corps on Jan. 8, 1942. He distinguished himself during the first year of his enlistment, and was advanced in rate for especially meritorious conduct in action while serving aboard ship at Arzeau, Algeria, Nov. 8, 1942; he landed with an assault wave entering the port from seaward and assisted in boarding and seizing vessels in the harbor as well as the seizure of the port. He returned to the States in Mar. 1943, and three months later sailed for Pacific duty. As a member of the 22nd Mar. Regt., on the night of Feb. 19, 1944, on Engebi Island, he was crouched in a foxhole with two comrades when a Japanese threw in a

grenade. His citation reads in part: "Realizing the imminent peril to all three and fully aware of the consequences of his act, he unhesitatingly flung himself on the grenade and, although instantly killed as his body absorbed the explosion, saved the lives of his two companions."

DAVENPORT, Jack Arden. Corporal. Medal of Honor: b. Kansas City, Mo., Sept. 7, 1931; d. KIA, Songnae-Dong, Korea, Sept. 21, 1951. Cpl. Davenport's citation reads, in part: " . . . while serving as a Squad Leader in Co. G, 3rd Bn., 5th Marines, 1st Mar. Div. (Reinf.), in action against enemy aggressor forces in the vicinity of Songnae-Dong, Korea...while expertly directing the defense of his position during a probing attack by hostile forces attempting to infiltrate the area, Cpl. Davenport, acting quickly when an enemy grenade fell into the foxhole which he was occupying with another Marine, skillfully located the deadly projectile in the dark and, undeterred by the personal risk involved, heroically threw himself over the live missile, thereby saving his companion from serious injury or possible death. . . ."

DAVIS, Henry W. Private. See Murray, William H.

DAVIS, Raymond Gilbert. Colonel. Medal of Honor: b. Fitzgerald, Ga., Jan. 13, 1915. Raymond Davis graduated in 1933 from Atlanta Technical High School, Atlanta, Ga. He then entered the Georgia School of Technology, graduating in 1938 with a Bachelor of Science degree in chemical engineering. While in college he was a member of the ROTC unit. After graduation, he resigned his commission in the U.S. Army Infantry Reserve to accept appointment as a Marine second lieutenant on June 27, 1938. In

May 1939, Lt. Davis completed the Marine Officers' Basic School at the Philadelphia Navy Yard, and began a year of service with the Marine Detachment on board the USS *Portland* in the Pacific. He returned to shore duty in July 1940 for weapons and artillery instruction at Quantico, Va., and Aberdeen, Md. Completing the training in Feb. 1941, Davis was assigned to the 1st Antiaircraft Machine Gun Battery of the 1st Mar. Div. at Guantanamo Bay, Cuba. He returned to the States with the unit in Apr., and the following month was appointed Battery Executive Officer, serving in that capacity at Parris Is., S.C., and Quantico. He was promoted to first lieutenant in Aug. 1941. In Sept. 1941, he moved with the battery to the Marine Barracks, New River (later Camp Lejeune), N.C. Upon his promotion to captain in Feb. 1942, he was named Battery Commander. During WW II, he participated in the Guadalcanal-Tulagi landings, the capture and defense of Guadalcanal, the Eastern New Guinea and Cape Gloucester campaigns, and the Peleliu operation. Embarking for the Pacific area with his unit in June 1942, he took part in combat on Guadalcanal from Aug. 1942, to Feb. 1943. Following that campaign, he was appointed Executive Officer of the 1st Special Weapons Bn., 1st Mar. Div. He was promoted to major in Mar. 1943. In Oct. 1943, he became commander of the 1st Special Weapons Bn., and served in that capacity at New Guinea and Cape Gloucester. In Apr. 1944, while on Cape Gloucester, he was named CO, 1st Bn., 1st Marines, 1st Mar. Div. Maj. Davis' action while commanding the 1st Bn. at Peleliu in Sept. 1944 earned him the Navy Cross and the Purple Heart. Although wounded during the first hour of the Peleliu landing, he refused evacuation to remain with his men; and, on one occa-

sion, when heavy Marine casualties and the enemy's point-blank cannon fire had enabled the Japanese to break through, he personally rallied and led his men in fighting to re-establish defensive positions. In Oct. 1944, he returned to Pavuvu and was promoted to lieutenant colonel. Returning to the States in Nov. 1944, Davis was assigned to Quantico, as Technical Inspector, MCS. He was named Chief of the Infantry Section, Marine Air-Infantry School, Quantico, in May 1945, and served in that post for two years before returning to the Pacific area in July 1947 to serve with the 1st Prov. Mar. Brig. on Guam. Lt. Col. Davis was the 1st Brigade's Assistant Chief of Staff, G-3 (Operations and Training), until Aug. 1948, and from then until May 1949 was Assistant Chief of Staff, G-4 (Supply). Upon his return from Guam in May 1949, he was named Inspector-Instructor of the 9th MCR Inf. Bn. at Chicago, Ill. He served there until Aug. 1950, when he embarked for Korea. In Korea, he commanded the 1st Bn., 7th Marines, from Aug. to Dec. 1950. In addition to receiving the Medal of Honor for action during that period, he twice earned the Silver Star Medal by exposing himself to heavy enemy fire while leading and encouraging his men in the face of strong enemy opposition. He also received the Legion of Merit with Combat "V" for exceptionally meritorious conduct and professional skill in welding the 1st Bn. into a highly effective combat team. Later, as Executive Officer of the 7th Marines, from Dec. 1950 to June 1951, Lt. Col. Davis earned the Bronze Star Medal with Combat "V" for his part in rebuilding the regiment after the Chosin Reservoir campaign. He returned from Korea in June 1951. Ordered to HQMC, Washington, D.C., he served as Assistant Officer in Charge of the Operations Subsection, G-3, Division of Plans and Policies, until Feb. 1952, when he took charge of the subsection. In Apr. 1953, he became Head of the Operations and Training Branch, G-3 Division. While serving in this capacity, he was promoted to colonel in Oct. 1953. The following July, Col. Davis entered the Special Weapons Employment Course, Fleet Training Center, Norfolk, under instruction. In Sept. 1954, he entered the Senior Course, MCS, Quantico. On completing the course in June 1955, he served consecutively as Assistant Director and, later, Director, of the Senior School. In Oct. 1957, Col. Davis was again transferred to Washington, D.C., and served as Assistant G-2, HQMC, until Aug. 1959. The following June he completed the course at the National War College in Washington, prior to embarking for Europe. In July 1960, he assumed duty in Paris, France, on the Staff of the Commander in Chief, Europe, HQ, United States European Command. In July 1962, he was selected for promotion to brigadier general by the Selection Board at HQMC.

DAY, George L. Served under the name of ADAMS, John M. (*q.v.*)

DE BLANC, Jefferson Joseph. Captain. Medal of Honor: b. Lockport, La., Feb. 15, 1921. Jefferson De Blanc enlisted in the Naval Reserve as a seaman second class on July 29, 1941, and received elimination flight training at the Naval Reserve Aviation Base in New Orleans for two weeks before going to the NAS at Corpus Christi, Tex., to continue his training. His Naval enlistment was terminated on Oct. 15, 1941, and he was appointed an aviation cadet, USNR, on the following day. Commissioned a second lieutenant in the Marine Corps

Reserve on May 4, 1942, Lt. De Blanc moved to San Diego to join Headquarters Squadron, 2nd MAW. In July, he was assigned to the Advance Carrier Training Group, where he remained under instruction until Aug. 6. He was placed in the new pilot's pool until he joined Marine Fighting Squadron 112, MAG 11, of the 1st MAW in Oct. Two weeks later he left for overseas and arrived at Guadalcanal on Nov. 1. On Jan. 31, 1943, he was flying over enemy-held Kolombangara Is. in the Solomons as a section leader of six fighter planes of Marine Fighting Squadron 112. Their mission was to escort a strike force of dive bombers and torpedo planes out to attack Japanese surface vessels. Leading his section directly to the target area, the lieutenant and the strike force encountered a large number of Japanese Zeros protecting the enemy's surface craft. Immediately engaging the Zeros at 14,000 feet, Lt. De Blanc aggressively countered their repeated attempts to drive off the Marine bombers and waged fierce combat until he received a call for assistance from the dive bombers which were under attack at 1000 feet. Diving to that altitude, he plunged into the formation of enemy float planes and single-handedly disrupted their attack, thus enabling the Marine dive bombers to complete their runs on the enemy ships and to escape. His escort mission thus completed, Lt. De Blanc nevertheless remained on the scene, despite his rapidly diminishing fuel supply, and challenged the superior number of float planes. His aggressiveness against these tremendous odds paid off as he destroyed three of the enemy planes and dispersed the remainder. Preparing to maneuver his damaged plane back to Guadalcanal, the lieutenant had climbed aloft and set his course before he noticed two more Zeros closing in upon him from behind. In a short, bitterly fought contest, Lt. De Blanc sent two more Japanese planes crashing into the sea. However, his own plane was so badly damaged in the encounter that the new Marine ace was forced to bail out at a perilously low altitude atop the trees of Japanese-held Kolombangara. Landing in the sea, Lt. De Blanc discovered that he was badly wounded in the back, arms, and legs and that he was a long way from shore. Supported only by his life jacket, he headed for the beach. After six hours in the water he crawled up on the enemy beach, and for more than two days subsisted on coconuts while his wounds went unattended. He was found by a party of friendly natives who hid him and cared for him. The coast-watcher in that locality was notified and immediately started trying to contact the Allied authorities by clandestine radio. After 15 days on Kolombangara, one of the Navy PBYs landed on the surf off the island and the natives paddled Lt. De Blanc out to it in a canoe. He was flown back to his base and to the hospital. Lt. De Blanc had been promoted to first lieutenant on Dec. 19, 1942, and he was further advanced to captain on June 1, 1943. He was transferred to Marine Fighting Squadron 122, also of MAG 11, in July, and his return to the States followed about six weeks later. Assigned to Headquarters Squadron 41, Marine Base Defense Air Group 41, MCAS, El Toro, Santa Ana, Calif., he remained in that unit until Dec. 1943, when he was transferred to HQ Squadron of MAG 32. Two months later he rejoined Marine Base Defense Air Group 41. After one month with them, the captain was assigned to Marine Fighting Squadron 461, Marine Base Defense Air Group 43, at El Centro, Calif. In Nov. 1944, Capt. De Blanc embarked upon his

second tour of overseas service. He joined Marine Fighting Squadron 422 in the Marshall Is. and remained in that area until May 1945, when he flew northward to participate in the Okinawa campaign with Marine Fighting Squadron 212. He continued operating in the Ryukyus until the end of the war, bagging one more Japanese plane to raise his total to nine. He returned to the States again in Oct. and was detached to the NAS at Seattle, Wash. Capt. De Blanc's relief from active duty occurred on Dec. 31, 1945. On Dec. 6, 1946, Capt. De Blanc was awarded the Medal of Honor at the White House.

Del Valle

DEL VALLE, Pedro A. Lieutenant General (Retired). CG, 1st Mar. Div. during the attack and occupation of Okinawa,

Apr. 1 to July 21, 1945: b. San Juan, Puerto Rico, Aug. 28, 1893. Upon graduation from the U.S. Naval Academy in June 1915, Pedro Del Valle was commissioned a Marine second lieutenant on June 5, 1915. After finishing a course of instruction at the Marine Officers' School, Norfolk, Va., he went on foreign shore duty with the 1st Prov. Mar. Brig. in the Republic of Haiti. In May 1916, he landed from the USS *Prairie* and participated in the capture of Santo Domingo City and the subsequent campaign in the Republic of Santo Domingo. A tour of sea duty followed as CO, Marine Detachment, USS *Texas*, serving with the British Grand Fleet under Admiral Beatty during the surrender of the German High Seas Fleet. In Feb. 1919, he was detached to the MB, Quantico, Va. After another tour of sea duty, on this occasion aboard the USS *Wyoming*, he was assigned as Aide-de-Camp to Maj. Gen. J. H. Pendleton and accompanied the general in an inspection tour of the West Indies. In 1924, he went to HQMC, Washington, D.C. While stationed there he was Marine Corps Representative on the Federal Traffic Board. In 1926, he was ordered to foreign shore duty with the Gendarmerie d' Haiti for three years and upon his return to the States in 1928, attended the Field Officers' Course at the MCS, Quantico, Va. Upon graduation he became an instructor, then served on temporary duty with the U.S. Electoral Mission in Nicaragua. After a tour of sea duty as Squadron Marine Officer on board the USS *Richmond*, during which tour he participated in the operations resulting from the Cuban Revolution in 1933, he was ordered to HQMC. From Oct. 1935, to June 1937, he was Assistant Naval Attaché, attached to the American Embassy at Rome, Italy, and on duty as an observer with the Italian Forces during the

Ethiopian War. He returned to the States to attend the Army War College, Washington, D.C., and, following graduation, was assigned to HQMC where he was Executive Officer, Division of Plans and Policies. He became CO, 11th Marines (Artillery) in Mar. 1941. He was serving in this capacity when the U.S. entered WWII. He remained as the regiment's CO, and led it overseas in 1942, participating in the seizure and defense of Guadalcanal as part of the 1st Mar. Div. (Reinforced) from Aug. 7 to Dec. 9, of that year. From May to July 1943, he served as Commander of Marine Forces (less aviation), on Guadalcanal, Tulagi, Russell, and Florida Is. He returned to the States to become President of the Marine Corps Equipment Board. He went again to the Pacific in Apr. 1944, this time as CG, 3rd Corps Artillery, 3rd Amphibious Corps, and took part in the Guam operation in July and Aug. of 1944. He became CG, 1st Mar. Div. and was awarded a Distinguished Service Medal for his leadership of that organization on Okinawa from Apr. 1 to July 1945. At war's end, he was ordered back to HQMC to become Inspector General and was assigned duties as the Director of Personnel, Oct. 1, 1946, a post which he held until his retirement. He was transferred to the retired list on Jan. 1, 1948. Having been specially commended for the performance of duty in combat, he was advanced to lieutenant general on the retired list. His retirement climaxed more than 30 years of active service.

DENIG, J. Henry. Sergeant. Medal of Honor: b. York, Pa., 1839. Sgt. Denig's citation reads, in part: "... on board the USS *Brooklyn*, during action against rebel forts and gunboats and with the ram *Tennessee*, in Mobile Bay, Aug. 5, 1864. Despite severe damage to his ship and the loss of several men on board as enemy fire raked her decks, Sgt. Denig fought his gun with skill and courage throughout the furious two-hour battle which resulted in the surrender of the rebel ram *Tennessee* and in the damaging and destruction of batteries at Fort Morgan. . . ."

Devereux

DEVEREUX, James P. S. Brigadier General (Retired). CO of the Wake Detachment, 1st Defense Bn., during the heroic but futile defense of Wake Island from Dec. 8 to 23, 1941: b. Cabana, Cuba, Feb. 20, 1903. James Devereux attended the Army and Navy Preparatory School in Washington, D.C. and, later, La Villa at Lausanne, Switzerland. He enlisted in the Marine Corps in July 1923, was commissioned a second lieutenant in Feb.

1925, then was assigned to duty in Norfolk; Philadelphia; the MB, Quantico, Va.; and at Guantanamo Bay, Cuba. In 1926, he was detailed to the mail guard detachment in New York, and later was transferred to the force of Marines in Nicaragua as a company officer. Returning to the States early in 1927, he was assigned to the USS *Utah* and subsequently was transferred ashore again to Nicaragua. Shortly thereafter he was ordered to the Orient, and while in China was promoted to first lieutenant. Other duty in China included command of the Mounted Detachment of the Legation Guard at Peking. An expert horseman, Devereux has always been associated with mounted activities at stations where he had been assigned. In 1933, following a year's tour of duty at Quantico, he was assigned to the Coast Artillery School at Fort Monroe, Va. Following his promotion to captain in Dec. 1935, he was ordered back to Quantico where, until 1936, he instructed in the Base Defense Weapons School and aided in the preparation of a Marine Corps manual on Base Defense Weapons. This knowledge was most useful later on the wind-swept coral atoll known as Wake Island. Following a tour of duty with the Marine Detachment on board the USS *Utah*, Devereux was transferred to the MCB, San Diego, Calif., in 1938. In Jan. 1941, he was ordered to Pearl Harbor and later assumed command of the 449 Marines on Wake Island who, after a bitter struggle, surrendered to the Japanese on Dec. 23, 1941. While a prisoner of the Japanese, he was selected for promotion to lieutenant colonel, but it was announced that men who were listed as prisoners of war would not be able to assume their new rank. Thus, it was not until shortly after his repatriation that his new rank became effective. He was promoted to colonel in Jan. 1946, to rank from Nov. 10, 1942, in order to assume his rightful place on the lineal list together with his contemporaries. Upon returning to the States following his release from prison camp in Hokkaido, Col. Devereux was ordered to HQMC in Washington to narrate his personal account of the defense of Wake for the CMC. He was given a rehabilitation leave, and late in 1945 he was ordered to the MCS, Quantico, Va. Later, from Sept. 1946 to May 1947, he was assigned as a student in the Senior Course, Amphibious Warfare School at Quantico. Upon completion of his studies he was detached to the 1st Mar. Div. at Camp Pendleton, Oceanside, Calif., and was serving with that organization when he concluded his brilliant 25-year career on Aug. 1, 1948. Devereux was advanced to his present rank of brigadier general upon retirement in accordance with law, having been specially commended for the performance of duty in actual combat.

DEWEY, Duane Edgar. Corporal. Medal of Honor: b. Grand Rapids, Mich., Nov. 16, 1931. Cpl. Dewey's citation reads, in part: " . . . as a Gunner in a machine gun platoon of Co. E, 2nd Bn., 5th Marines, 1st Mar. Div. (Reinf.), in action against enemy aggressor forces near Panmunjom, Korea, on Apr. 16, 1952. When an enemy grenade landed close to his position while he and his assistant gunner were receiving medical attention for their wounds during a fierce night attack by numerically superior hostile forces, Cpl. Dewey, although suffering intense pain, immediately pulled the corpsman to the ground and, shouting a warning to the other Marines around him, bravely smothered the deadly missile with his body, personally absorbing the full force of the explosion to save his comrades from possible injury or death . . . ." He was hos-

pitalized for 50 days after the action and was released from active duty on Aug. 19, 1952.

Diamond

DIAMOND, Leland. "Lou." Master Gunnery Sergeant. One of the most famous of all "Old Breed" Marines, Lou Diamond represents the legend of a colorful chapter of Marine Corps tradition and history: b. Bedford, Ohio, May 30, 1890; d. Great Lakes Naval Training Center Hospital, Sept. 20, 1951. Although Diamond first enlisted in the Marine Corps at the age of 27 — somewhat older than most recruits — the difference never was noticeable. His salty, hard-driving personality soon expressed itself in both word and deed. Because of the incredible voice which matched his 5-foot, 11-inch, 200-pound frame, Lou was once dubbed "The

Honker." Though cool in training and battle, he was rarely quiet. According to his WWI buddies, "The tougher the action, the louder Lou would yell." Many of his comrades at Guadalcanal considered him "a human air-raid warning system." Although in the military service, Diamond lived informally, going hatless and wearing dungarees practically everywhere. He even accepted one of his decorations in dungarees. When receiving the citation awarded him in Australia by Gen. A. A. Vandegrift, Lou looked the general in the eye and said, "I made my landing in dungarees — guess they're good enough to get my commendation in." Self-confidence, even cockiness, was one of the sergeant's outstanding characteristics. He considered anybody with less than ten years in the Corps a "boot." While he bawled out recruits who sometimes instinctively saluted him, he himself frequently failed to salute less than a field grade officer. Opportunities to apply for a commission were rejected by the grizzled campaigner, who explained that "nobody can make a gentleman out of me." Though not a "spit-and-polish" Marine, Diamond proved himself an expert with both 60- and 81-mm. mortars, his accurate fire being credited as the turning point of many an engagement in the Pacific during WWII. Diamond enlisted in the Marine Corps at Detroit, Mich., July 25, 1917, listing as his former occupation "railroad switchman." As a corporal in Jan. 1918, he shipped out from Philadelphia aboard the USS *Von Stuben* bound for Brest, France. He saw action with the 6th Marines in the battles at Chateau-Thierry, Belleau Wood, the Aisne-Marne, St.-Mihiel and the Meuse-Argonne. Promoted to the grade of sergeant, he marched to the Rhine with the Army of Occupation. At war's end, he returned to the States,

disembarked at Hoboken, N.J., and on Aug. 13, 1919, received an honorable discharge from the Corps. But railroading and civilian life in general did not suit Lou's fancy, and on Sept. 23, 1921, Lou again walked into a Marine recruiting office. Promotions were rapid for him and while serving as Assistant Armorer at Parris Is., S.C., in Feb. 1925, he regained his sergeant's stripes. But Lou itched for more action and he soon got it — in Shanghai with Company M, 3rd Bn., 4th Mar. Regt. However, the Sino-Japanese controversy, in Lou's opinion, was "not much of a war," and on June 10, 1933, he returned to the States, disembarking from the USS *Henderson* at Mare Island, Calif. By then a gunnery sergeant, Diamond returned to Shanghai with his old outfit, the 4th Marines, ten months later; was transferred to the 2nd Marines in Dec. 1934; and returned to the States in Feb. 1937. Two years after his promotion to master gunnery sergeant, July 10, 1939, he was assigned to the Depot of Supplies at Philadelphia to help design a new infantry pack. Following the Japanese attack at Pearl Harbor, Lou shipped out to Guadalcanal with H Co., 2nd Bn., 5th Marines, 1st Mar. Div., arriving at the beaches Aug. 7, 1942. He was then 52 years old. Among the many fables concerning his "'Canal" service is the tale that he lobbed a mortar shell down the smoke stack of an off-shore Japanese cruiser. It is considered possible, however, that he actually drove the cruiser from the bay with his harassing "near-misses." An indication of Sgt. Diamond's value to the Corps is found in a letter of commendation for "outstanding performance of duty on Tulagi and Guadalcanal," from Gen. A. A. Vandegrift, Commander of the 1st Mar. Div., and later CMC. The letter states in part: "To every man in your company you were a counselor, an arbiter of disputes, and an ideal Marine. Your matchless loyalty and love of the Marine Corps and all it stands for, are known to hundreds of officers and men of this Division, and will serve as an inspiration to them on all the battlefields on which this Division may in the future be engaged." After two months on Guadalcanal, physical disabilities dictated Lou's evacuation by air against his wishes. He was moved to the New Hebrides and later to a hospital in New Zealand, where he proved to be a somewhat obstreperous patient. Somehow, he acquired orders to board a supply ship for New Caledonia, where a friend ordered him back to Guadalcanal — the supposed location of his old outfit. Upon his arrival, however, Diamond discovered that the 1st Mar. Div. had shipped out to Australia, a distance of over 1,500 miles. Lou made the trip, without orders, by "bumming" rides on planes, ships and trains. But Diamond was destined to see no more combat. On July 1, 1943, he disembarked from the USS *Hermitage* at San Pedro, Calif., and 12 days later was made an instructor at the Recruit Depot, Parris Is., S.C. He was transferred to Camp Lejeune on June 15, 1945, and joined the 5th Training Bn. with the same duties. A familiar sight in the early morning on the company street thereafter was "Old Lou," standing with watch in hand and whistle in mouth, awaiting the first note of reveille to break the men out. M. Gy. Sgt. Leland Diamond retired on Nov. 23, 1945, and returned to his home in Toledo, Ohio. His death at the Great Lakes Naval Training Center Hospital, Sept. 20, 1951, was followed by a funeral, with full military honors, at Sylvania, Ohio.

DICKSON, Donald Lester. Colonel. Marine Corps artist: b. Cambridge, Mass., Jan. 28, 1906. While attending the art school of the Worcester, Mass. Museum, Donald Dickson enlisted in the Army Reserve on Dec. 17, 1924. Before his first enlistment was completed, he transferred to an organized MCR unit in Boston in 1927. He continued to serve with this unit, going through all the ranks from private to first lieutenant, until the unit was mobilized on Nov. 8, 1940. He remained with the unit until it arrived in Cuba and was then transferred to the 1st Mar. Div. With the division he went ashore on Guadalcanal on Aug. 7, 1942 as R-1 with the staff of the 5th Marines. He was ordered back to the States on Nov. 28, 1942, after the national release of his drawings and paintings made on Guadalcanal which had appeared in *Life* Magazine and other publications. Prior to WWII, Dickson's "Stony Craig" had become a familiar and widely read, internationally syndicated adventure strip. In June 1942, he sailed for Pearl Harbor and was assigned to work with CINPaC as Public Relations Officer and on the preparation of coverage of Marine operations in the central Pacific. He participated in landings on the Marshalls, Saipan, and Tinian. He returned to the States on Nov. 5, 1944, and was assigned to the Northeastern Procurement Division as Public Relations Officer. He remained with this organization until Feb. 1945, when he was released from active duty as a lieutenant colonel. He returned to civilian life and accepted a position with the Curtis Publishing Company. On June 23, 1951, he was recalled to active duty, promoted to colonel, and assigned as Editor-Publisher of *Leatherneck* Magazine.

DOBBIN, John Francis. Brigadier General. Assistant Wing Commander, 1st MAW, Iwakuni, Japan (1963): b. Boston, Mass., May 1, 1912. After completing high school in Boston in 1929, John Dobbin entered Boston College from which he was graduated with a Bachelor of Arts degree in 1933. In June 1934, he enlisted in the Naval Reserve and, after serving as a seaman second class, was an aviation cadet for one year. He was discharged from the Naval Reserve to accept a commission in the Marine Corps on July 8, 1936. In Sept. 1936, after a period as a student aviator at Pensacola, Fla., Lt. Dobbin was designated a naval aviator and transferred to Marine Barracks, Quantico, Va., as Assistant Squadron Operations Officer. He attended Basic School at the Philadelphia Navy Yard from July 1937 to June 1938, then joined Scouting Squadron 3 in the Virgin Islands. He was promoted to first lieutenant in Aug. 1939. He departed from the Virgin Islands in May 1940. The following month he joined a Marine fighter squadron at San Diego, Calif., later moving with it to Ewa, Oahu, Hawaii. After the outbreak of WWII, he served as a squadron executive officer in the Hawaiian Islands and at Midway. He was promoted to captain in Jan. 1942, and to major in Aug. 1942. Maj. Dobbin flew with Marine Fighting Squadron 224, 1st MAW, at Guadalcanal and elsewhere in the Solomon Is. He was declared a Marine Corps "ace" in Oct. 1942. In Jan. 1943, he returned to the States for duty as a flight instructor at the Naval Air Station, Jacksonville, Fla. He was promoted to lieutenant colonel in Dec. 1943. In June 1944, Lt. Col. Dobbin was assigned to Cherry Point, N.C., as Operations Officer of the 9th MAW. That Oct. he became CO of Marine Carrier Air Group 1 attached to the aircraft carrier USS *Block Island* in the Pacific and on Saipan and Okinawa. He came back to the States in Nov. 1945. He was stationed briefly at the MCAS, Santa Barbara, Calif., and in Jan. 1946, was transferred to MCAS, Cherry Point, as a squadron

officer and, later, Assistant Chief of Staff, G-4. He left there in Nov. 1947, to serve for almost three years as Aviation Materiel Officer and Assistant Logistics Officer, G-4 Section, Division of Plans and Policies at HQMC, Washington, D.C. In July 1950, with the outbreak of hostilities in Korea, Lt. Col. Dobbin was ordered to the MCAS, El Toro, Calif. He served there as CO of Marine Training Squadron 2, Aircraft, FMF, Pacific, from Aug. 1950 until Mar. 1951, and briefly as CO, MAG 13. In Nov. 1951, he reported to London, England, for duty under instruction in the United Kingdom Joint Services Staff College. He was promoted to colonel in Dec. 1951. On completing the course in May 1952, Col. Dobbin returned to the States and was assigned duty at the MCAS, Quantico, as CO, Marine Corps Aviation Technical School, and Executive Officer, MCAS respectively. The following Sept. he entered the Senior Course, MCS, Quantico, completing the course in June 1954. From July 1954 to June 1955, he served in the Far East as commander of MWSG 17, 1st MAW, Japan. Following his return to the States, he was assigned in Aug. 1955, as a student in the National War College, Washington, D.C. Upon graduation in June 1956, he served with the Joint Operations Analysis Group for two months and in Aug. 1956 joined the Weapons Systems Evaluation Group, Institute of Defense Analysis, Office of the Assistant Secretary of Defense (Research and Development). He remained in Washington until June 1958, when he was assigned as a student in the Helicopter Training Group at Pensacola. After completing the course in Aug. 1958, Col. Dobbin served as Assistant to the Commanding General, and later as CO, MAG 36, 3rd MAW, Marine Corps Air Facility, Santa Ana, Calif. In Nov. 1959, he assumed duties as Assistant

MEDAL OF HONOR

Continental Marine Private, 1775   Marine Private, 1812   Marine Private, Indian Wars, 1836

Marine Sergeant, Mexican War, 1846, full dress uniform   Marine Musician, Mexican War, 1846   Marine Second Lieutenant, undress uniform, 1859-1868

Marine Private, undress uniform, 1859-1868

Marine Private, full dress uniform, 1875

Marine Private, field service uniform, 1900

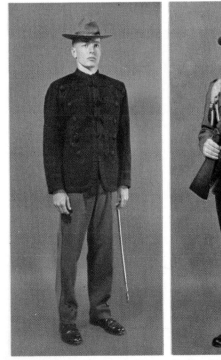

Marine Second Lieutenant, fatigue uniform, 1900

Marine Private, field service uniform, 1917

Marine Corps Officer in dress blue uniform

Ribbons of Decorations and Medals Authorized for Wear by U.S. Marine Corps Personnel

Row 1
Row 2
Row 3
Row 4
Row 5
Row 6
Row 7
Row 8
Row 9
Row 10
Row 11
Row 12
Row 13
Row 14
Row 15
Row 16
Row 17

Row 1   Navy and/or Army Medal of Honor. Marine Corps Brevet Medal. Navy Cross. Army Distinguished Service Cross. Navy Distinguished Service Medal.

Row 2   Army Distinguished Service Medal. Silver Star Medal. Legion of Merit. Distinguished Flying Cross. Navy and Marine Corps Medal.

Row 3   Army Soldiers Medal. Bronze Star Medal. Air Medal. Navy Commendation Ribbon. Army Commendation Medal.

Row 4   Navy Commendation for Achievement. Purple Heart. Specially Meritorious Medal. Presidential Unit Citation. Army Distinguished Unit Emblem.

Row 5   Navy Unit Commendation Ribbon. Gold Life Saving Medal. Silver Life Saving Medal. Reserve Special Commendation Ribbon. Marine Corps Good Conduct Medal.

Row 6   Navy Good Conduct Medal. Army Good Conduct Medal. Coast Guard Good Conduct Medal. Organized Marine Corps Reserve Medal. Naval Reserve Medal.

Row 7   Dewey Medal. Sampson Medal. Peary Polar Expedition Medal. NC-4 Medal. Byrd Antarctic Expedition Medal (1928-30).

Row 8   Byrd Antarctic Expedition Medal (1933-35). U. S. Antarctic Expedition Medal (1939-41). Civil War Campaign Medal. Expeditionary Medal. Spanish Campaign Medal.

Row 9   Spanish War Service Medal. Army of Cuban Occupation Medal. Army of Puerto Rican Occupation Medal. Philippine Campaign Medal. Philippine Congressional Medal.

Row 10   China Relief Expedition Medal. Cuban Pacification Medal. Nicaraguan Campaign Medal (1912). Haitian Campaign Medal (1915 & 1919-20). Mexican Border Service Medal.

Row 11   Dominican Campaign Medal. Victory Medal World War I. Army-Navy Occupation of Germany Medal (1918-23). Second Nicaraguan Campaign Medal. Mexican Service Medal.

Row 12   Yangtze Service Medal. China Service Medal (1937-39 & Sept. 1945-). American Defense Service Medal. American Campaign Medal. European-African Middle Eastern Campaign Medal.

Row 13   Asiatic-Pacific Campaign Medal. Victory Medal World War II. Army-Navy Occupation Service Medal. National Defense Service Medal. Korean Service Medal.

Row 14   Antarctica Service Medal. Armed Forces Expeditionary Medal. Marine Corps Reserve Ribbon. Armed Forces Reserve Medal. United Nations Ribbon.

Row 15:   Merchant Marine Distinguished Service Medal. Merchant Marine Meritorious Service Medal. Merchant Marine Gallant Ship Unit Citation. Merchant Marine Mariners Medal. Merchant Combay Bar.

Row 16   Merchant Marine Defense Bar. Merchant Marine Atlantic War Zone. Merchant Marine Mediterranean Middle East War Zone. Merchant Marine Pacific War Zone. Philippine Defense Ribbon.

Row 17   Philippine Liberation Ribbon. Philippine Independence Ribbon. Philippine Presidential Unit Citation. Korean Presidential Unit Citation. Viet-Nam Presidential Unit Citation.

Ribbons Courtesy of Hilborn-Hamberger, New York, N. Y.

Wing Commander, 3rd MAW, MCAS, El Toro. While serving in this capacity, he also saw temporary duty as Chief of Staff, 3rd Prov. Mar. Brig., Camp Pendleton, from Feb. through May 1960, at which time he returned to El Toro. Subsequently, he served as Chief of Staff, 3rd Wing, until Apr. 1961, when he again assumed duties as Assistant Wing Commander. While serving in this capacity, he was promoted to his present rank of brigadier general in July 1961. Following his detachment from the 3rd MAW, Gen. Dobbin assumed his current duties as Assistant Wing Commander, 1st MAW, Iwakuni, Japan, in Jan. 1962.

DOUGHERTY, James. Private. Medal of Honor: b. Langhash, Ireland, Nov. 16, 1839. James Dougherty enlisted in the Marine Corps at Philadelphia, Pa. on July 30, 1869. His citation reads, in part: "... on board the USS *Benecia* ... attack on and capture of the Korean forts, June 11, 1871 ... for seeking out and killing the commanding officer of the Korean forces. ..."

DUNLAP, Robert Hugo. Major. Medal of Honor: b. Abingdon, Ill., Oct. 20, 1920. Following graduation from high school Robert Dunlap entered Monmouth College at Monmouth, Ill., where he was a prominent football player and trackman. He was graduated in May 1942, with a Bachelor of Arts degree. He enlisted in the Marine Corps on Mar. 5, 1942, while still a student at Monmouth, and was promoted to private first class at that time. He was placed on the inactive list with the Platoon Leaders' Unit of the 9th Reserve District until his graduation. Called to active duty in May 1942, he was transferred to the Candidate's Class at Quantico, Va. He was discharged as an enlisted man on July 17, and received

his second lieutenancy the next day. Following Reserve Officers Class at Quantico, Dunlap requested parachute training and was ordered to the Parachute Training School at Camp Gillespie, San Diego, Calif. He was designated a parachutist on Nov. 23, 1942, and in Dec. was assigned to the 3rd Parachute Bn. Advanced to first lieutenant in Apr. 1943, he took part in the invasions of Vella La Vella and Bougainville in the Solomon Is. during the latter part of 1943. During the Iwo campaign, Dunlap led his company through a hail of artillery, mortar, rifle, and machine gun fire in a determined advance from low ground uphill toward the steep cliffs from which the enemy poured a devastating rain of bullets and shrapnel. It was the day following the original landing on Feb. 19, 1945. Finally, when the volume of enemy fire became too intense to advance any farther toward the caves located high to the front, Dunlap held up his company and crawled alone approximately 200 yards forward of his front lines. From his position at the base of the cliff, about 50 yards from the Japanese lines, the major spotted the enemy gun positions and, returning to his own lines, relayed the vital information to the supporting artillery and naval gunfire units. Persistently disregarding his own safety, he then placed himself in an exposed vantage point to direct more accurate supporting fire. He worked without respite for two days and two nights under constant enemy fire, skillfully directing a smashing bombardment against the almost impregnable enemy positions. He returned to the States in Mar. 1944, to join the 5th Mar. Div. then being formed at Camp Pendleton, Oceanside, Calif. The veteran officer became a machine gun platoon leader in G Co. of the 3rd Bn., 26th Marines. He departed for overseas for the second time in the summer of 1944, and on Oct. 2, 1944, was promoted to captain. With his new rank he became CO, C Co., 1st Bn., 26th Marines, in which capacity he was serving when he won the Medal of Honor at Iwo Jima. On Feb. 26, 1945, Maj. Dunlap caught a bullet in the left hip. He was evacuated from Iwo Jima and subsequently became a patient at the U. S. Naval Hospitals at Guam, Pearl Harbor, San Francisco, and Great Lakes, Ill. Hospitalized for nearly 14 months, Maj. Dunlap was discharged from the Great Lakes Naval Hospital on Apr. 20, 1946. He went on inactive duty in Sept. 1946, and was then retired.

DYER, Jesse Farley. Brigadier General. Medal of Honor: b. St. Paul, Minn., Dec. 2, 1877; d. U.S. Naval Hospital, Corona, Calif., Mar. 31, 1955. Jesse Dyer served with the 13th Minnesota Inf. during the Spanish-American War. He was commissioned a Marine second lieutenant in 1903. Before action at Vera Cruz, for which he was awarded the Medal of Honor, he served at sea and in the Philippines, Cuba, and Panama. During WWI he was Aide to the Governor of the Virgin Islands. After that he served on expeditionary duty in Haiti and China during the 1920s and early '30s. Before he retired in 1937, he was stationed at Parris Is., S.C. He won the Nation's highest decoration on April 21-22, 1914, when a Marine and Naval landing force occupied Vera Cruz, after the arrest of some American sailors had touched off a crisis between the United States and Mexico. His citation states, in part, that Capt. Dyer "...was, in both days' fighting, at the head of his company, and was eminent

and conspicuous in his conduct, leading his men with skill and courage." He was advanced to brigadier general on the retired list in 1942, when Congress passed the law providing for promotion of retired officers who had been specially commended in combat.

DYESS, Aquilla James. Lieutenant Colonel. Medal of Honor: b. Augusta, Ga., Jan. 11, 1909; d. KIA, Namur Island, Kwajalein Atoll, Marshall Is., Feb. 2, 1944. Aquilla Dyess graduated from Clemson College, Clemson, S.C. in 1932 with a Bachelor of Science degree in architecture. At Clemson, he served as a cadet major in the ROTC, and was appointed a second lieutenant in the Army Infantry Reserve in 1931. He was appointed a first lieutenant in the Marine Corps Reserve in Nov. 1936. He was awarded the Medal of Honor posthumously for "conspicuous gallantry and intrepidity at the risk of his life" at the head of his troops on Namur Island, Kwajalein Atoll, Marshall Is. Dyess was killed by a burst of enemy machine gun fire while standing on the parapet of an antitank trench directing a group of infantry in a flanking attack against the last Japanese position in the northern part of the island. In this final assault, Dyess posted himself between the opposing lines and, exposed to fire from heavy automatic weapons, led his troops in the advance. Wherever the attack was slowed by heavier enemy fire, he quickly appeared and placed himself at the head of his men and inspired them to push forward and gain ground. The airfield at Roi, Namur Island, has been named in his honor.

E

Edson

EDSON, Merritt Austin. "Red Mike." Major General. Medal of Honor: b. Rutland, Vt., Apr. 25, 1897; d. Washington, D.C., Aug. 14, 1955. Merritt Edson attended the University of Vermont before enlisting in the MCR at the outbreak of WWI. He was commissioned a second lieutenant in the regular Marine Corps on Oct. 9, 1917. He served in France from Sept. 1918 to Dec. 1919. Throughout his Marine Corps career, Edson was closely associated with the development of small arms marksmanship. In 1921, he was a firing member of the winning Marine Corps National Match Rifle Team at Camp Perry, Ohio. In 1927, 1930, and 1931, he was attached to the Marine Corps National Rifle and Pistol Teams as Assistant Team Coach. During the Regional Match years of 1932 and 1933, he acted as Team Coach and Team Captain respectively. Upon the resumption of the National Matches in 1935, he was captain of the Marine Corps National Rifle and Pistol Teams of 1935 and 1936, successfully winning the national trophies in both years. In June 1941, Edson was assigned as CO, 1st Bn., 5th Mar. Regt. For the next six months, he was engaged in conducting experimental operations and training in close conjunction with destroyer transports, which led to the organization of the 1st Mar. Raider Bn. one month after the United States' entry into WWII. This battalion was a prototype of every Mar. Raider Bn. and Army Ranger Bn. formed throughout the war. On Aug. 7, 1942, the 1st Mar. Raider Bn., commanded by Edson — now a colonel — landed on Tulagi in the Solomon Is., and captured that island after two days of severe fighting. After the airfield on Guadalcanal had been seized from the enemy, Col. Edson, with a force of 800 men, was assigned to the occupation and defense of a ridge dominating the jungle on either side of the airfield. He was awarded the Medal of Honor for this action, his citation reading in part: "... as CO of the 1st Mar. Raider Bn., with Parachute Bn. attached, during action against Japanese forces in the Solomon Is. on the night of 13-14 Sept. 1942... Col. Edson, although continuously exposed to hostile fire throughout the night, personally directed the defense of the reserve position against a fanatical foe of greatly superior numbers. By his astute leadership and gallant devotion to duty, he enabled his men, despite severe losses to cling tenaciously to their position on the vital ridge, thereby retaining command not only of the Guadalcanal airfield, but also of the 1st Division's entire offensive installations in the surrounding area." In Nov. 1943, he participated as Chief of Staff of the 2nd Mar. Div. in the battle of Tarawa. Shortly thereafter, he was promoted to the rank of brigadier general. In 1944, he was appointed Chief of Staff, FMF, Pacific. After his return to the States, having completed 44 months of continuous duty in the Pacific area, he was assigned to the Office of the Chief of Naval Operations, and later to HQMC. Upon his retirement from the Corps, Gen. Edson returned to his native state of Vermont, where he was appointed Commissioner of Public Safety. He also became President of the National Rifle Association. He returned to active duty for a short period in order to serve on a special commission to recommend standards of action for prisoners of war.

ELLIOTT, George Frank. Major General. 10th Commandant of the Marine Corps — Oct. 3, 1903 to Nov. 30, 1910: b. Utah, Ala., Nov. 30, 1846; d. Washington, D.C., Nov. 4, 1931. After attending the U.S. Military Academy for two years, George Elliott was appointed a second lieutenant in the Marine Corps Oct. 12, 1870. During his early career he performed the usual round of sea and shore duty, was on field duty with the naval expedition to Panama in 1885, and guarded the legation at Seoul, Korea, after a precarious march to that city during the war between China and Japan in 1894. During the Spanish-American War, he won considerable distinction in command of a detachment of Marines and Cubans fighting the Spaniards near Guantanamo Bay, Cuba. Later, Elliott commanded a battalion of Marines in the Battle of Novaleta during the Philippine Insurrection. He was made Brigadier General Commandant of the Marine Corps on Oct. 3, 1903, but left his headquarters shortly afterward and took personal command of a brigade of Marines maintaining order in Panama shortly after that country gained its independence. During his tenure as Commandant he raised the educational requirements for officers, instituted an improved system of rifle firing and, by his untiring efforts, obtained stronger support of Congress for the Corps. By his skillful maneuvering of a delicate situation he succeeded in having Marines replaced on board vessels of the Navy from which they had been removed by order of President Theodore Roosevelt. He retired from the Corps with the rank of major general on Nov. 30, 1910.

ELROD, Henry Talmage. Major. Medal of Honor: b. Rebecca, Ga., Sept. 27, 1905; d. KIA, Wake Island, Dec. 23, 1941. Henry Elrod enlisted in the Marine Corps in Dec. 1927, and was appointed a second lieutenant in Feb. 1931. He attended the University of Georgia and Yale University prior to his entry into the Marine Corps. Following more than a year at the Marine Corps Basic School in Philadelphia and at the MB there as a student aviator, Lt. Elrod was ordered to the NAS, at Pensacola. Here he served as a company officer and as student aviator. In Feb. 1935, he won his wings and, as a Marine aviator, was transferred to Quantico, where he served with a Marine Aircraft unit until Jan. 1938. In addition to his other duties, he was Squadron School, Personnel, and Welfare Officer. In July 1938, Elrod went to San Diego for duty at the NAS and served as squadron materiel, parachute, and personnel officer until Jan. 1941, when he was detached to the Hawaiian area. He arrived at Wake a short time before the hostilities commenced and was one of the 12 pilots who flew the Marine planes onto the island. During the defense of Wake, Maj. Elrod repeatedly displayed conspicuous gallantry and intrepidity at the risk of his life, above and beyond the call of duty. On Dec. 12, he singlehandedly attacked a flight of 22 enemy planes and shot down two. On several flights he executed low altitude bombing and strafing runs on enemy ships, and became the first man to sink a major warship with small caliber bombs delivered from a fighter-type aircraft. When his plane was destroyed by hostile fire, he organized a unit of ground troops into a beach defense and repulsed repeated Japanese attacks until he fell mortally wounded. The citation reads, in part, "His superb skill as a pilot, daring leadership, and unswerving devotion to duty distinguished him among the defenders of Wake Island. . . ."

ELWOOD, Hugh McJunkin. Brigadier General. WWII Marine Corps ace. Service Plans Analysis and Review Officer, Office of the Deputy Chief of Staff (Plans and Programs), HQMC, Washington, D.C.: b. Pittsburgh, Pa., Nov. 14, 1915. Hugh Elwood graduated from high school at Oakmont, Pa., and at the age of 16, he enlisted in the Marine Corps on Aug. 1, 1932, for duty as a field musician. He was immediately assigned to active duty. Requesting sea duty, he served aboard the USS *Chicago*, and attended the Naval Academy Preparatory Class at Norfolk, Va. He was appointed to the U.S. Naval Academy in July 1934, and was commissioned a Marine second lieutenant upon graduation, June 2, 1938.

Following Basic School at the Philadelphia Navy Yard, Lt. Elwood commanded the Marine Corps Institute Detachment at the MB, Washington, D.C., and in 1940 was assigned to flight training at NAS, Pensacola, Fla. He was designated a naval aviator, Feb. 21, 1941. Remaining at Pensacola as an instructor, he was promoted to first lieutenant in July 1941, and to captain in Feb. 1942. Shortly after the outbreak of WWII, he completed the Naval School of Photography and was assigned as a communications officer with a Marine photographic squadron, and later served as Aide-de-Camp to the CG, MAW, Pacific. He was transferred overseas in Mar. 1943, and a month later was promoted to major. He served as Executive Officer and later CO of Marine Fighting Squadron 212 in the Solomon Is. area. During this assignment, he shot down six enemy aircraft and was designated a Marine Corps ace. For heroism in aerial combat from Oct. 1943 to Apr. 1944, he received the Distinguished Flying Cross and the Air Medal. In May 1944, he was assigned as Operations Officer, Air Defense Command, Marianas. He returned to the States in Oct. 1944, and two months later was promoted to lieutenant colonel. Elwood subsequently completed the Command and Staff School at Quantico, Va. From Apr. 1945 until Oct. 1946, he was attached to the Naval Aviation Mission to Peru as Operations Officer and, later Chief of the Mission and Inspector General of the Peruvian Air Force. On his return to the States, he commanded the Marine Air Det., Marine Air Reserve Training Command, St. Louis, Mo., until July 1949. He was next assigned to the Naval Academy where he was an instructor in the Aviation Department for two years. Ordered to Korea in Aug. 1951, he took part in combat as Executive Officer and

Tactical Officer, MAG 12, 1st MAW. He earned a second Distinguished Flying Cross for heroism in this capacity on Jan. 26, 1952, when he led his division on a 12-plane interdiction mission against 15 hostile tanks, executed a series of devastating bombing and strafing attacks in the face of enemy antiaircraft fire, then escorted the damaged plane of his wingman safely back to the base. He also earned a Bronze Star Medal and a second Air Medal in Korea. Returning to the States in the summer of 1952, he completed the Strategy and Tactics Course at the Naval War College, Newport, R.I. in June 1953, then returned to Quantico where he served for three years as Chief, Air Section, Marine Corps Educational Center. While at Quantico, he was promoted to colonel in Nov. 1953. In the summer of 1956, Col. Elwood was assigned briefly as Chief of Staff, Amphibious Troops, Naval Forces, Eastern Atlantic and Mediterranean. He then served as Assistant Chief of Staff, G-4, 2nd MAW, Cherry Point, N.C., and from May 1957 to Jan. 1959, commanded MAG 32, 2nd Wing, at Beaufort, S.C. Ordered to the Far East, he joined the 1st MAW at Iwakuni, Japan, in Mar. 1959 as Assistant Chief of Staff, G-3. In June 1960, he began a two-year assignment in the Plans and Policy Directorate, Joint Staff, Office of the Joint Chiefs of Staff, serving as a member of the Basic War Plans Branch, J-5, and later as Chief of the Branch. In July 1962, he was transferred to the Office of the Deputy Chief of Staff (Plans and Programs), HQMC, as Service Plans Analysis and Review Officer. In Feb. 1963, he was promoted to brigadier general.

EPPERSON, Harold Glenn. Private First Class. Medal of Honor: b. Akron, Ohio, July 14, 1923; d. KIA, Saipan, June 25,

1944. P.F.C. Epperson's citation reads, in part: " . . . while serving with the 1st Bn., 6th Marines, 2nd Mar. Div., in action against enemy Japanese forces on the island of Saipan. . . . With his machine gun emplacement bearing the full brunt of a fanatic assault initiated by the Japanese under cover of pre-dawn darkness, P.F.C. Epperson manned his weapon with determined aggressiveness, fighting furiously in defense of his battalion's position and maintaining a steady stream of devastating fire against rapidly infiltrating hostile troops to aid materially in annihilating several of the enemy and in breaking the abortive attack. Suddenly a Japanese soldier, assumed to be dead, sprang up and hurled a powerful hand grenade into the emplacement. Determined to save his comrades, P.F.C. Epperson unhesitatingly chose to sacrifice himself and, diving upon the deadly missile, absorbed the shattering violence of the exploding charge in his own body. . . . P.F.C. Epperson fearlessly yielded his own life that his able comrades might carry on the relentless battle against a ruthless enemy. . . ."

ERSKINE, Graves Blanchard. General (Retired): b. Columbia, La., June 28, 1897. Graves Erskine graduated from Louisiana State University in 1917, then reported for active duty with the Marine Corps as a second lieutenant on July 5, 1917. He sailed for France in Jan. 1918 and as a member of the 6th Mar. Regt., participated in the Aisne-Marne defensive (Chateau-Thierry) where he was wounded in action and the St.-Mihiel offensive where he was again wounded, this time so severely that he was evacuated for hospitalization to the States and sailed for home in Oct. 1918. Foreign shore duty with the 1st Prov. Mar. Brig. in Santo Domingo followed. After a pe-

Erskine

riod aboard the USS *Olympia*, Erskine again went on foreign shore duty, on this occasion with the 2nd Mar. Brig. in Santo Domingo. During this time he was detached for a short period to San Juan, Puerto Rico. In Sept. 1924, he became Depot Quartermaster, MB, Quantico, and two years later was assigned as a student at the Army Infantry School, Fort Benning, Ga. Upon completion of the school, he was ordered to the MCS, Quantico, where he assumed duties as an instructor in the Department of Tactics. In Mar. 1928, he was ordered to foreign shore duty in Nicaragua where he was a member of the 2nd Mar. Brig. for three months before being detached to the Nicaragua National Guard Detachment. Upon return to the States he became successively an instructor at Basic School,

MB, Navy Yard, Philadelphia; a student at the Command and General Staff School, Fort Leavenworth, Kans.; and an instructor in the 1 and 2 Sections, MCS, Quantico. In Jan. 1935, he went to China to join the Marine Detachment at the American Embassy in Peiping, where he remained until returning to the MCS to become Chief of the 1 and 2 Sections. After a short period as Executive Officer of the 5th Mar. Regt., Erskine became Chief of Staff, Amphibious Force, Atlantic Fleet, the position he held at the time of the United States' entry into WWII. From Sept. 1942, to Oct. 1944, he was Chief of Staff, Amphibious Training Staff; Amphibious Corps, Pacific Fleet; FMF, San Diego Area; 5th Amphibious Corps and the FMF, Pacific. During this period he received a Legion of Merit and a Gold Star in lieu of a second Legion of Merit for exceptionally meritorious service. His second award came as a direct result of his outstanding work in the Saipan and Tinian Operations. He became CG of the 3rd Mar. Div. in Oct. of 1944 and led that division in the battle for Iwo Jima for which he was awarded the Distinguished Service Medal. He continued as CG until Oct. 1945, when he returned to Washington where, as a result of a special Congressional Act, he was appointed Administrator of the Retraining and Reemployment Administration (RRA). This Administration had "general supervision and direction of the activities of all existing executive agencies (except the Veterans' Administration) in the fields of retraining, reemployment, vocational education and vocational rehabilitation for the purpose of coordinating such activities and eliminating overlapping functions of such agencies." In June 1947 Gen. Erskine, upon his release from the RRA, assumed command of Camp Pendleton in California and later assumed command of the 1st Mar. Div. which returned to Camp Pendleton from China. The welding together of the Marine Air Units at nearby El Toro Air Station with the 1st Mar. Div. troops at Camp Pendleton became a reality in all respects. It was this combination, after three years of training together over the hills of Camp Pendleton, that boarded ships for the combat area in Korea and which later made such an enviable record in combat against the North Koreans and Chinese Communist troops. During the period of service at Camp Pendleton, Gen. Erskine was also assigned additional duties of Deputy Commander, FMF, Pacific, with headquarters in Hawaii and for a period of time commuted between the two headquarters to exercise this dual command. In June 1950 the Secretary of Defense appointed Gen. Erskine Chief of Military Group, Joint State-Defense Mutual Defense Assistance Program Survey Mission to Southeast Asia. In carrying out his assigned duties, the Mission visited the Philippines, French Indochina, Malaya, Thailand, and Indonesia. During the three and one-half months of this survey

Gen. Erskine inspected troops and training schools of the countries mentioned and held many conferences with military and civilian leaders in each area. Upon reporting back to HQMC, Gen. Erskine received orders to assume duties as CG, Department of the Pacific, San Francisco, Calif., where he not only exercised command responsibilities in this assignment but also was charged with the responsibility of being CG, Marine Corps Emergency Forces, Western Sea Frontier. In July 1951, Gen. Erskine was assigned as the CG, FMF, Atlantic, which included two MAWs, one Mar. Div. and an assortment of force and special troops with a total personnel of some 50,000 which were engaged in continuous, strenuous training to maintain the capability of immediate embarkation for foreign shores for assault operations on orders. Gen. Erskine was authorized to retire from active service by a Special Act of Congress in June 1953 for the purpose of accepting a position as Assistant to the Secretary of Defense as Director of Special Operations of the Department of Defense.

F

FAIRBOURN, William Taro. Brigadier General. Assistant Division Commander, 1st Mar. Div. (Reinf.), Fleet Marine Force, Camp Pendleton, Calif.: b. Sandy, Utah, June 28, 1914. William Fairbourn completed high school in 1931, then entered the University of Utah from which he was graduated in 1935. He was commissioned a Marine second lieutenant on July 10, 1935. He completed Basic School

at the Philadelphia Navy Yard in Mar. 1936. The following month he joined the 2nd Bn., 10th Marines, 2nd Mar. Brig., at the MCB (later Marine Corps Recruit Depot), San Diego, Calif. From there he was assigned to the Field Artillery School, Fort Sill, Okla., in Aug. 1937, completing the regular course in June 1938, prior to returning to San Diego. He was promoted to first lieutenant in Oct.

1938. He was assigned a two-year tour of sea duty aboard the USS *Chester* in June 1940, as Commander of the Marine Detachment. He was promoted to captain in Apr. 1941. Following the United States' entry into WWII, he participated in the Pacific raids on the Marshalls and Tulagi, and in the Coral Sea and Midway operations. He was promoted to major in June 1942. Returning to San Diego the following month, Fairbourn served in the States until Mar. 1943, when he again embarked for combat duty in the Pacific area. He was promoted to lieutenant colonel in July 1943. As Operations Officer, 12th Marines, 3rd Mar. Div., he participated in the action on Bougainville and Guam, twice earning the Bronze Star Medal with Combat "V" during these campaigns. Later he saw combat on Iwo Jima as CO, 2nd Bn., 12th Marines. In May 1945, Lt. Col. Fairbourn was ordered to Camp Lejeune, N.C., where he served as G-3 of the Marine Training Command. Early in 1946, he was assigned briefly to Commander Task Force 100. He began a three-year assignment in the Office of the Chief of Naval Operations, Washington, D.C., in June 1946, becoming Assistant to OP-09M in Sept. 1947. After leaving Washington, he entered the Command and General Staff College, Fort Leavenworth, Kans. in Aug. 1949, and graduated in June 1950. Ordered to HQ, FMF, Atlantic, Norfolk, Va., he served as Assistant Chief of Staff, G-2, until Oct. 1950, when he became Assistant Chief of Staff, G-3. He was promoted to colonel in Jan. 1951. Detached from Norfolk in July 1952, he was assigned to the Naval War College, Newport, R.I., where he completed the Strategy and Tactics Course in June 1953, and served on the staff until June 1955. The following month he was ordered to Camp Pendleton, Calif., to become Regi-

mental Commander, 11th Marines, 1st Mar. Div. (Reinf.). Col. Fairbourn was transferred to the Far East in Oct. 1956 and served consecutively as Chief of Staff of the 3rd Mar. Div. through Nov. 1957, and Chief of Staff of the 1st Marine Expeditionary Force through Mar. 1958. He returned to the States the following month. In May 1958, he became Director, 1st MCR and Recruitment District, Garden City, Long Island, N.Y. He was promoted to brigadier general in Nov. 1959. In Dec. 1959, Gen. Fairbourn was assigned to HQMC as Deputy Director of the MCR. He then served as Director of the Reserve from Jan. 1960, to June 1962. Transferred to Camp Pendleton, he assumed his current duties as Assistant Division Commander, 1st Mar. Div. (Reinf.), in July 1962.

FARDY, John Peter. Corporal. Medal of Honor: b. Chicago, Ill., Aug. 8, 1922; d. KIA, Okinawa, May 7, 1945. John Fardy was inducted into the Marine Corps on May 8, 1943, and received recruit training at San Diego, Calif. After attending Japanese Language School, he joined the 29th Replacement Bn. and sailed for New Caledonia. There he was reassigned to the 27th Replacement Bn. He made the Dec. 26th landing on Cape Gloucester, and later the Peleliu landing. On Okinawa, he earned the nation's highest award. His citation reads, in part: "...on May 7, 1945, when his squad was suddenly assailed by extremely heavy small arms fire from the front during a determined advance against strongly fortified, fiercely defended Japanese positions, Cpl. Fardy temporarily deployed his men along a nearby drainage ditch. Shortly thereafter, an enemy grenade fell among the Marines in the ditch. Instantly throwing himself upon the deadly missile, Cpl. Fardy absorbed the exploding blast in his own body, thereby protecting his comrades from certain and perhaps fatal injuries. . . ."

FIELD, Oscar Wadsworth. Private. Medal of Honor: b. Jersey City, N.J., Oct. 6, 1873. Oscar Field enlisted in the Marine Corps at Brooklyn, N.Y. on Aug. 10, 1896. He was awarded the Medal of Honor on Aug. 19, 1899. His citation reads, in part: ". . . while serving on board the USS *Nashville,* for extraordinary bravery and coolness while cutting the cables leading from Cienfuegos, Cuba, May 11, 1898, under heavy fire from the enemy. . . ." Pvt. Field was discharged from the Corps on Nov. 6, 1905.

FIELDS, Lewis Jefferson. Major General. Director of Personnel, HQMC, Washington, D.C.: b. Delmar, Md., Oct. 1, 1909. Lewis Fields graduated from high school at Crisfield, Md. in 1927. He received his Bachelor of Arts degree in mathematics upon graduation from St. John's College, Annapolis, Md., on June 3, 1931. He was a member of the Maryland National Guard from Mar. 1925, until Jan. 1932, when he enlisted in the Marine Corps. After three and a half years as an enlisted man, he was commissioned a Marine second lieutenant on June 25, 1935. He completed Basic School at the Philadelphia Navy Yard in Oct. 1935, then served with the Sea School Detachment at Portsmouth, Va. In July 1936, he was assigned duty aboard the USS *Quincy* upon that vessel's commissioning, and later participated in the evacuation of U.S. nationals during the Spanish Revolution. The following July, he entered the Base Defense Weapons Course at the MCS, Quantico, Va. He was promoted to first lieutenant in July 1938. In Sept. 1939, Lt. Fields began serving as Aide-de-Camp to the CG, FMF, and CG,

MCB, San Diego. While serving in this capacity, he was promoted to captain in Mar. 1941. He remained in San Diego until Nov. 1941, and the following month entered the Field Artillery School, Fort Sill, Okla. On completing the Battery Officers' Course in Mar. 1942, he was transferred to MCB, Camp Lejeune, N.C., for duty with the 3rd Bn., 11th Marines, 1st Mar. Div. He was promoted to major in May 1942. Maj. Fields embarked with the 3rd Bn. for the Pacific area that May, and in Aug. saw action on Guadalcanal. He was named CO, 1st Bn., 11th Marines, 1st Mar. Div. in Nov. 1942 on Guadalcanal. In Jan. 1943, he moved with the 1st Bn. to Australia for training. He was promoted to lieutenant colonel in May 1943. He led the 1st Bn. in action in Dec. 1943 at Cape Gloucester, where he earned his first Bronze Star Medal. In May 1944, he was named Assistant Chief, G-3, 1st Mar. Div. Subsequently, he was awarded the Legion of Merit with Combat "V" for outstanding service as the 1st Division's Operations Officer, during the preparation for and seizure of Peleliu and Ngesebus. He departed for the States in Dec. 1944. In Jan. 1945, Lt. Col. Fields became Aide to CMC, Gen. A. A. Vandegrift. He continued as Aide until June 1947, when he was ordered to Quantico. Upon completing the Senior Course, MCS, in June 1948, he was assigned to the Staff of the Commander in Chief, Atlantic Command, and U.S. Atlantic Fleet, Norfolk, Va. He also saw duty with NATO as Assistant to the U.S. Representative to the North Atlantic Ocean Regional Planning Group, serving as principal advisor on ground matters and defense of land areas in the Atlantic Command; and as military advisor to the Joint Department of State/Department of Defense team sent to Portugal. He was promoted to colonel in May 1950. In early 1951, he was designated the Assistant Chief of Staff, Personnel and Administration, for the Supreme Allied Command, Atlantic (SACLANT). His initial task was to establish the present SACLANT headquarters in Norfolk. Upon being detached from Norfolk in Aug. 1951, he began two years' duty at HQMC, Washington, D.C., as Head of the Plans Branch, G-3 Division; and as Marine Corps Member of the Joint Strategic Plans Committee, Joint Chiefs of Staff. Ordered to Korea in Sept. 1953, Col. Fields served as Assistant Chief of Staff, G-2, 1st Mar. Div., and later as CO, 11th Marines (artillery), until Apr. 1954. He then returned briefly to HQMC and, in June 1954, was assigned to the Supreme Headquarters, Allied Powers, Europe, in Paris, France, as Chief of the Plans Section. He served there two years. Returning to the States, Col. Fields became Assistant Chief of Staff, G-3, at HQ, FMF, Atlantic, in Norfolk, serving in this capacity from Sept. 1956 to Sept. 1957 and, subsequently, as Chief of Staff. Transferred to Washington, D.C., in Nov. 1957, he served almost a year as Marine Corps Liaison Officer to the Vice Chief of Naval Operations. He was promoted to the rank of brigadier general in July 1958. In Sept. 1958, Gen. Fields began a two-year assignment on the Joint Staff, Office of the JCS, as Deputy Director, J-5 Plans and Policy Directorate. On completing this assignment, he served for two years as CG, Force Troops, FMF, Pacific, and CG, MCB, Twentynine Palms, Calif. Reporting to HQMC in Sept. 1962, he assumed duty as Assistant Director of Personnel, and the following month was promoted to major general. In Nov. 1962, he became Director of Personnel.

FISHER, Harry. Private. Medal of Honor: b. McKeesport, Pa., Oct. 20, 1874; d. KIA, Peking, China, July 16, 1900. Pvt. Fisher enlisted in the Marine Corps on May 19, 1899. After serving at Cavite, P.I., he was transferred to the battleship *Oregon* on Dec. 7, 1899 for service with the Marine Guard. In May 1900, Fisher went ashore with the Marine Guard of his ship under the command of Capt. John T. Myers, and proceeded from Tientsin to Peking. At Peking, in view of the threatening attitude of the Chinese, they formed an American Legation Guard. In defense of the Legation against the Chinese Boxers and Imperial Troops, Fisher lost his life assisting in the erection of barricades under the heavy fire of the enemy.

FISHER, Morris. "Bud." Chief Warrant Officer (Retired). World famous Marine marksman: b. Youngstown, Ohio, May 4, 1890. Morris Fisher enlisted in the Marine Corps in 1911. He distinguished himself as a marksman in 1915 at Winthrop, Md., when he won a gold medal and distinguished marksmanship badge. In Sept. 1918, he broke two world's records in the International Free Rifle Team Match fired at Camp Perry, Ohio, in Sept. 1918. The match was fired at 300 meters, each rifleman firing 40 shots from the standing, kneeling, and prone positions, a total of 120 shots. Fisher's score was 1090, a total of 17 points over the former world's record. His score for the prone position was 385, or 10 points over the former world's record. The American team won the match with a score of 5301, breaking the former world's record of 5172 made by the Swiss team in 1912. In France, Fisher continued his marksmanship record with the American Expeditionary Force team. In 1920 he was on the Olympic team and won the individual Olympic championship in Belgium. He again shot on

Fisher

the winning team in Lyons, France, in 1921 and in Milan, Italy, in 1922. The following year, he won the individual world's championship, and later at Chalons, France, won the Olympic championship. In 1927, Sgt. Fisher represented the Marine Corps in eight consecutive International matches. The report of the Commandant of the Marine Corps for that year, summarizing the results of the Marine Corps shooting competitions, stated that the Marines had participated in 96 rifle and pistol matches and had won 81 of them. They were awarded a total of 49 trophies. In 1930, Fisher represented the United States in Europe in the last big-bore international rifle match. Gy. Sgt. Fisher retired from the Corps in June 1941, after 30 years' service. His expert marksmanship in matches all over

the world had brought him more medals than his broad chest could ever hold. With the advent of WWII, Fisher returned to active duty with the Marines in Mar. 1942, as boss of the Rifle Range at Parris Is., S.C. Drawing from a lifetime of marksmanship experience, he was able to coach and train young men who had never fired a rifle until they came to boot camp. At Parris Is., the legendary Fisher is said to have put every shot into the bull's eye, while a playful Marine boot dangled from his shooting arm! He was promoted to chief warrant officer on Sept. 30, 1943, and returned to inactive status at the end of the war.

FITZGERALD, John. Private. Medal of Honor: b. Limerick, Ireland, Mar. 17, 1873. Pvt. Fitzgerald received the nation's highest military award for " . . . heroism and gallantry in action at Cuzco, Cuba, on June 14, 1898. . . ." Along with Sgt. Maj. John Quick, Fitzgerald stood on the crest of a hill, under enemy fire, and signaled the USS *Dolphin*, asking her to throw shells into a valley below in order to force the enemy from concealment. Quick was also awarded the Medal of Honor for this same courageous exploit.

FLEMING, Richard Eugene. Captain. Medal of Honor: b. St. Paul, Minn., Nov. 2, 1917; MIA June 5, 1942; d. June 6, 1942. Richard Fleming enlisted in the MCR in 1939 and applied for flight training. He was commissioned a second lieutenant in the Reserve on Sept. 10, 1940, and was designated a naval aviator on Nov. 13 of the same year. On Dec. 17, 1941, he participated in a flight from Oahu, T.H. to Midway, a distance of 1137 nautical miles overwater with no surface vessels assigned as plane guards. From that day until June 5, 1942, he made many flights against enemy forces in the Midway area. Capt. Fleming was officially listed as missing in action on June 5, 1942, when he and his radio-gunner failed to return to base from an attack mission against two enemy battleships about 140 miles from Midway. He was officially declared dead on June 6, 1942. For his heroism in action, he was posthumously awarded the Medal of Honor. His citation reads, in part: "... as Flight Officer, Marine Scout-Bombing Squadron 241, during action against enemy Japanese forces in the battle of Midway on 4 and 5 June 1942. When his Squadron Commander was shot down ... Capt. Fleming led the remainder of the division with such fearless determination that he dived his own plane to the perilously low altitude of 400 feet before releasing his bomb. ..."

FOLEY, Alexander Joseph. Sergeant. Medal of Honor: b. Heckersville, Pa., Feb. 19, 1866. In a battle near Tientsin, China on July 13, 1900, Foley distinguished himself during the bitterest period of fighting. With complete disregard for himself, he organized and led a rescue party to evacuate the American wounded who lay helpless under direct enemy fire. For his gallantry in combat he was awarded the nation's highest military honor.

FONTANA, Paul John. Brigadier General. WWII ace and Korea combat aviator. Commander, Marine Corps Air Bases, Eastern Area, and CG, MCAS, Cherry Point, N.C. (1963): b. Lucca, Italy, Nov. 27, 1911. Paul Fontana grew up in Sparks, Nev., and after completing high school there, entered the University of Nevada at Reno. He graduated in 1934 with a Bachelor of Science degree in electrical engineering. A member of the ROTC unit at the university, he re-signed his Army Reserve commission to accept appointment as a Marine second lieutenant, July 6, 1936. After Basic School at the Philadelphia Navy Yard, a sea duty assignment aboard the USS *Salt Lake City,* and duty at the MB, Mare Island, Calif., Lt. Fontana was ordered to Pensacola, Fla., for flight training in Jan. 1939. He was promoted to first lieutenant in July 1939. Lt. Fontana was designated a naval aviator on Jan. 25, 1940. In Mar. 1940, he was assigned to the NAS, San Diego, Calif. He returned to Pensacola in Nov. 1940, and served as a flight instructor until July 1941, when he joined Marine Fighting Squadron 111, MAG 11, at Quantico, Va. He also completed the aviation course at the Chemical Warfare School, U.S. Army, Edgewood Arsenal, Md. He was promoted to captain in Oct. 1941. When the United States entered WWII, Capt. Fontana was ordered to aviation duty in San Diego. In Mar. 1942, he joined Marine Fighting Squadron 112, becoming CO in May 1942. He was promoted to major in Aug. 1942. In Oct. 1942, Maj. Fontana embarked with his squadron for the Pacific area. As CO, Squadron 112, MAG 14, he took part in combat against the Japanese in the capture and defense of Guadalcanal. Downing five enemy aircraft in four days over Guadalcanal in Nov. 1942, he was awarded the Navy Cross and designated a Marine Corps ace. Remaining with the 1st MAW, he was named Assistant Operations Officer of the Strike Command, Solomon Is., in Apr. 1943. After taking part in the consolidation of the southern Solomons, he returned to the States in Oct. 1943. He was promoted to lieutenant colonel in Dec. 1943. He was then assigned to Marine Fleet Air, West Coast, in San Diego, as Assistant Operations Officer, having served briefly as commander of the Flight

Training Unit, MCAS, El Toro, Calif. In Dec. 1944, he was ordered to Hawaii for duty with the 2nd MAW as Assistant Operations Officer. He also served in this capacity with the Army's 10th Tactical Air Force for the Okinawa campaign and was awarded the Bronze Star Medal with Combat "V" for heroic action against the Japanese prior to and during the amphibious assault of Okinawa, from Jan. 9 to June 30, 1945. The Distinguished Flying Cross was awarded him for heroism as a fighter plane pilot in the Ryukyu Islands area from May to July 1945. He remained on Okinawa until Jan. 1946. Following WWII, Lt. Col. Fontana served in Washington, D.C., as Assistant Plans, Operations, and Training Officer, Division of Aviation, HQMC, from Mar. 1946 to July 1948. The following month he entered the Air War College, Maxwell Air Force Base, Maxwell Field, Ala. After graduation in the summer of 1949, he returned to the MCAS, El Toro, in July as commander of Marine Fighting Squadron 311, MAG 12, 1st MAW. At the outbreak of the Korean War, Fontana was serving as Deputy Commander of MAG 12, 1st MAW, FMF, having assumed this assignment in May 1950. For conspicuous gallantry in action, Sept. 21, 1950, while serving briefly as Deputy Group Commander, MAG 33, executing close air support of the Army's 10th Corps during an attack on enemy installations at Yongdongpo, Korea, he was awarded the Silver Star Medal (Army). Rejoining his group on its arrival in the Wonsan area, he earned the Legion of Merit with Combat "V" for exceptionally meritorious conduct from Oct. 10 to Nov. 8, 1950, prior to and during operations at Wonsan. In Jan. 1951, Lt. Col. Fontana was named CO of MAG 33, 1st MAW, and in this capacity continued combat operations against the Communist forces.

He was promoted to colonel in Mar. 1951, and the following month returned to the States. He reported at El Toro in Apr. 1951, and in May became Assistant Chief of Staff, G-3, Aircraft, FMF, Pacific. He served there until July 1952. The following month, he entered the National War College, Washington, D.C. After graduation in June 1953, he served at HQMC as Head, Operations and Training Branch, Division of Aviation. In June 1955, following his detachment from HQMC, Col. Fontana took command of the Overhaul and Repair Facility, MCAS, Cherry Point, N.C. He served in this capacity two years. In Aug. 1957, he assumed command of MAG 13, 1st Mar. Brig., MCAS, Kaneohe Bay, Hawaii, and in addition was assigned with his group to the 1st MAW in Japan from Oct. 1958 through Feb. 1959. Following this assignment, he became Chief of Staff of the 1st Mar. Brig. in June 1959. While serving in Hawaii, he was promoted to brigadier general in July 1960. In Aug. 1960, Gen. Fontana began a two-year tour of duty at the Pentagon as Deputy Director for Operations, J-3 Directorate, Joint Staff, Office of the JCS. Following this assignment, he became Commander, Marine Corps Air Bases, Eastern Area, and CG, MCAS, Cherry Point.

FORD, Patrick F., Jr. Private. (Name changed to Ford from James Meredith on June 6, 1900.) Medal of Honor: b. Omaha, Neb., Apr. 11, 1872. Patrick Ford enlisted in the Marine Corps at Boston, Mass. on July 23, 1896. He was awarded the Medal of Honor on Aug. 15, 1899 for extraordinary bravery and coolness while cutting the cables leading from Cienfuegos, Cuba, May 11, 1898. He was serving aboard the USS *Marblehead*. Ford was discharged from the Corps on Sept. 9, 1901.

FORSTERER, Bruno Albert. Gunnery Sergeant. Medal of Honor: b. Königsberg, Germany, July 14, 1869; d. June 14, 1957. Bruno Forsterer enlisted in the Marine Corps in 1896. Several years later, on Apr. 1, 1899, near Tagalli, Samoa, American and British Marines and sailors were set ashore to protect their countries' interests on that small South Pacific island chain during a native uprising. The islands had been recognized as a quasi-independency under the combined political control of the U.S. and Great Britain, and the naval forces of both nations were actively drawn into a dispute between two Samoan chiefs. The American and British forces (which included some 110 friendly natives, missionaries, and interpreters) were ambushed as they made their way inland. Sgt. Forsterer and two other Marines rallied the U.S. Marines at a wire fence in front of a ravine, where they fought a delaying action until the wounded could be evacuated and the entire landing force could be withdrawn to the shore line. Forsterer and the other two Marines remained at the fence and contained the enemy, then fought their way back across the ravine and rejoined their unit. After the landing force had reached the beach and were awaiting reinforcements from the ships Sgt. Forsterer volunteered to lead more friendly natives to safety. For his heroism in combat he was awarded the Medal of Honor. Sgt. Forsterer was discharged in 1909 as a gunnery sergeant.

FOSS, Joseph Jacob. Major. WWII ace. Medal of Honor: b. near Sioux Falls, S.D., Apr. 17, 1915. Following graduation from high school, Joseph Foss attended Augustana College for one year

Foss

and Sioux Falls College for three semesters. He then enrolled at the University of South Dakota, Vermillion, and graduated in 1940 with a degree in business administration. In college he was a member of the boxing, track, and football teams. He became interested in flying when a squadron of Marine flyers staged an air show at Sioux Falls in 1932. Three years later he had his first airplane ride, paying five dollars to go up with a barnstormer. In 1937, he paid $65 on the installment plan for his first course in flying. In 1939, he took a Civil Aeronautics Authority flying course at the University of South Dakota and, by the time he graduated from college, he had 100 hours of flying time to his credit. On June 14, 1940, he enlisted in the MCR and was assigned to inactive duty. Honorably discharged from the Reserve on Aug. 8, 1940, he accepted an appointment as an aviation cadet in the MCR the following day. He was called to active duty Aug. 23, and sent to Pensacola, Fla., for training. He completed further training at Miami, won his Marine wings and was commissioned a second lieutenant in the MCR on Mar. 31, 1941. He was advanced to first lieutenant Apr. 10, 1942, while serving as an instructor at Pensacola and was promoted to captain Aug. 11, 1942, at Camp Kearney, Calif. Capt. Foss arrived at Guadalcanal in Sept. 1942, and became a Marine Corps ace on Oct. 29. Flying almost daily for one month, he shot down 23 enemy planes during that period, for which he was awarded the Medal of Honor. Bagging three more later raised his total to 26, which tied the WWI record of the noted Capt. Eddie Rickenbacker, and set a new record for WWII. His 26 planes included 20 Zero fighters, four bombers, and two bi-planes. His citation reads, in part: " . . . as Executive Officer of a Marine Fighting Squadron at Guadalcanal, Solomon Is. Engaging in almost daily combat with the enemy from Oct. 9 to Nov. 19, 1942, Capt. Foss personally shot down 23 Japanese planes and damaged others so severely that their destruction was extremely probable. In addition, during this period, he successfully led a large number of escort missions, skillfully covering reconnaissance, bombing, and photographic planes as well as surface craft. On Jan. 15, 1943, he added three more enemy planes to his already brilliant successes for a record of aerial combat achievement unsurpassed in this war. Boldly searching out an approaching enemy force on Jan. 25, Capt. Foss led his eight Marine planes and four Army planes into action and,

undaunted by tremendously superior numbers, intercepted and struck with such force that four Japanese fighters were shot down and the bombers were turned back without releasing a single bomb." While at Guadalcanal, Capt. Foss was forced to make three dead-stick landings on Henderson Field as a result of enemy bullets crippling his engine. In Nov., he was shot down over the island of Malaita after accounting for three Zeros. He was picked out of the water by natives in a small boat. Returning to the States in Apr. 1943, he reported at HQMC, Washington, D.C., and the following month was sent on a tour of Navy preflight schools and Naval Air Stations where Marines were in training. He was promoted to major on June 1, 1943. Back in the Pacific in Feb. 1944, Foss became squadron commander of Marine Fighting Squadron 115. He served in the combat zone around Emirau, St. Mathias Group, but failed to better his "shootdown" record. He returned to the States in Sept. 1944, and was ordered to Klamath Falls, Ore. In Feb. 1945, he became operations and training officer at the MCAS, Santa Barbara, Calif. At the end of the war in Aug. 1945, he requested to be released to inactive duty. Finally relieved from active duty on Dec. 8, 1945, he was retained in the MCR on inactive duty. In 1948, Foss went into politics and won an election to the State (South Dakota) House of Representatives. Two years later he made an unsuccessful bid in the Republican gubernatorial primary. He returned to the State Legislature and in June 1954, won an overwhelming victory for the gubernatorial nomination. He was elected Governor of South Dakota the following Nov., and two years later was re-elected.

FOSTER, William Adelbert. Private First

Class. Medal of Honor: b. Cleveland, Ohio, Feb. 17, 1915; d. KIA, Okinawa, May 2, 1945. William Foster was enlisted in the Marine Corps Reserve through Selective Service on Apr. 1, 1944. He received recruit training at the MCB at San Diego, Calif. In Sept. 1944, after combat training at Camp Pendleton, Calif., he embarked for overseas duty on board the USS *General C. G. Morton*, bound for the Russell Is. in the Solomon group. There he joined his regular unit — Co. K, 3rd Bn., 1st Marines, 1st Mar. Div. He landed with his organization on Okinawa on Apr. 1, 1945, the first anniversary of his enlistment in the Marine Corps. On May 2, he earned the nation's most coveted decoration. Dug in with another Marine, he and his comrade engaged in a fierce hand grenade duel with infiltrating enemy soldiers. When a Japanese grenade landed beyond reach in their foxhole, P.F.C. Foster, with complete disregard for his personal safety, dove on it and absorbed its full explosion with his own body, thus protecting the other Marine from serious injury. Mortally wounded, he handed his two remaining grenades to his comrade and said, "Make them count . . ." His citation states: ". . . he had unhesitatingly relinquished his own chance of survival that his fellow Marine might carry on the relentless fight against a fanatic enemy. . . ."

FRANCIS, Charles Robert. Sergeant Major. Medal of Honor: b. Doylestown, Pa., May 19, 1875. Charles Francis enlisted in the Marine Corps at Philadelphia, Pa., on Apr. 21, 1898. He received the Medal of Honor ". . . for distinguished conduct in the presence of the enemy in the advance on Tientsin, China, June 21, 1900." He was retired as a sergeant major on Apr. 30, 1923.

FRANKLIN, Joseph John. Marine Gunner. Medal of Honor: b. Buffalo, N.Y., June 18, 1870; d. U.S. Naval Home, Philadelphia, Pa., Apr. 28, 1940. Gunner Franklin received the nation's highest military award " . . . while serving on board the USS *Nashville,* for extraordinary bravery and coolness while cutting the cables leading from Cienfuegos, Cuba, May 11, 1898, under a heavy fire of the enemy. . . ."

FREEMAN, Orville Lothrop. Lieutenant Colonel (USMCR): b. Minneapolis, Minn., May 9, 1918. Orville Freeman attended Minneapolis Central High School, where he competed in track and football. In 1940, he was awarded a Bachelor of Arts degree with high honor from the University of Minnesota and was selected a Phi Beta Kappa. He continued his studies at the University of Minnesota Law School until shortly after the start of WWII when he began his active Marine Corps service. He enlisted in the MCR at Minneapolis, Minnesota, Aug. 7, 1941, and was appointed a private first class upon enlistment. He was assigned active duty on Jan. 30, 1942, and joined the Feb. Officer Candidates' Class at MCS, Quantico, Va. Upon completing the course he was commissioned a second lieutenant in the MCR, Apr. 4, 1942. He then completed the Reserve Officers' Class at MCS in June 1942. Assigned to Company K, 3rd Bn., 9th Marine (Reinf.), Lt. Freeman served as a platoon leader and company officer at Camp Elliott, Calif., from June until Sept. 1942, then moved with his company to Camp Pendleton, Calif. In Jan. 1943, he was promoted to first lieutenant and later that month sailed with his company aboard the USS *Mt. Vernon* for the Pacific area. Lt. Freeman was stationed in New Zealand from Feb. until July 1943. With the company he was then transferred to Guadalcanal, and from there moved to Bougainville action, and upon his release from hospitalization and treatment, he was transferred to Washington, D.C. He served as Staff Officer in the Rehabilitation Division, Special Services Branch, Personnel Department, HQMC until Dec. 1945. Returning to Minneapolis on terminal leave, he was subsequently relieved from active duty on Feb. 13, 1946, and assigned to the 9th Mar. Reserve Dist. He was promoted to major in the MCR in Mar. 1951, and to lieutenant colonel in Oct. 1959. Admitted to the Minnesota bar in 1947, he was a member of a Minneapolis law firm until Jan. 1955, when he was inaugurated Governor of Minnesota. He served six years (three terms) in that office and in Jan. 1961 became Secretary of Agriculture in President John F. Kennedy's Cabinet.

FRY, Isaac N. Orderly Sergeant. Medal of Honor: Sgt. Fry was cited for bravery while serving aboard the USS *Ticonderoga* during attacks on Fort Fisher, Jan. 13-15, 1865. As a member of the Marine Guard and captain of a gun, he performed his duties with skill and courage as the *Ticonderoga* maintained a well placed fire upon the batteries to the left of the palisades during the initial phases of the three-day battle.

FRYER, Eli Thompson. Brigadier General (Retired). Medal of Honor: b. Hightstown, N.J., Aug. 22, 1878. Eli Fryer was appointed a Marine second lieutenant on Mar. 21, 1900, and after a course of instruction at MB, New York, N.Y., he served at the MB, Newport, R.I., from Aug. 1901 to June 1903, except for a period of detached duty with the Marine Bn. in Panama from Sept. 13 to Dec. 8, 1902. From June 5, 1903, to Mar. 14, 1905, he served with the Marine Expedi-

tionary Bn. on board the USS *Panther* and at Camp Roosevelt, Culebra, Puerto Rico, and commanded the Marines at Dry Tortugas, Fla. Following a one-year tour at the MB, New York, Fryer joined a battalion organized for service in the Philippines. From Apr. 1906 to Nov. 1908, he served at Olongapo, Polloc, and Cavite. During the next five years Fryer worked as Post Quartermaster for the MB and the School of Application at Annapolis, Md., and commanding the Marine Detachments on the USS *Louisiana, New Hampshire,* and *Alabama.* Assigned to the 2nd Advance Base Regt. in Nov. 1913 Fryer, now a captain, served at Pensacola, Culebra, and Vera Cruz, where he was awarded the Medal of Honor "For distinguished conduct in battle, engagements of Vera Cruz, Apr. 21 and 22, 1914. . . ." He returned with the 2nd Regt. to the States in Nov. 1914 and was assigned duty as Regimental Adjutant. Shortly after the arrival of the 2nd Regt. in Haiti, Aug. 4, 1915, Capt. Fryer was relieved of duty as Adjutant and was assigned to command the 20th Co. One year later, he was detached from Haiti and assigned to the MB, New Orleans, La., as Post Quartermaster with additional duty as Inspector-Instructor of the Marine Co., Louisiana Naval Militia. From June 1918, to Nov. 1919, Fryer served on the USS *Brooklyn* as Fleet Marine Officer and as aide to the Commander in Chief, Asiatic Fleet. As a result of Allied intervention in Siberia, the *Brooklyn* remained in the vicinity of Vladivostok during most of this period. After WWI, Fryer served at Charleston, S.C., Quantico, Va., and with the Marine Corps Expeditionary Force in Panama, and on Culebra. In Aug. 1925, he again joined the Mar. Brig. in Haiti until July 26, 1927, when he was detached to Quantico, Va., as a student in the Field

Officers' Course. After completing this instruction Fryer was assigned duty as Chief of Staff, MB, Quantico, and CO of the 1st Regt. Fryer joined MB, Parris Is., S.C., July 15, 1929, and served as Post Commander to Oct. 1, 1929, when he assumed command of the Naval Prison. Detached from Parris Is. in Sept. 1933, he served some two months as CO of the MB at the Philadelphia Navy Yard before he assumed command of the 2nd Regt. in Haiti. He continued in command of the 2nd Regt., with brief periods as Brig. Commander until July 1934, when he was ordered to the MB, New York, to await retirement. Col. Fryer was placed on the retired list on Oct. 1, 1934, and was appointed a brigadier general on the retired list from Feb. 23, 1942.

FULLER, Ben Hebard. Major General. 15th Commandant of the Marine Corps: b. Big Rapids, Mich., Feb. 27, 1870; d. Washington, D.C., June 8, 1937. Ben Fuller, whose active service in the Corps totaled 48 years, 9 months, and 8 days, entered the U.S. Naval Academy in May 1885. After finishing the four-year course of instruction, he was assigned to the prescribed two-year cruise as a naval cadet on various vessels of the Pacific Squadron. He was commissioned a second lieutenant in the Marine Corps on July 1, 1891 with six other members of his graduating class. Together with his Marine classmates, he took the first course ever given for Marine officers in the School of Application at the MB, Washington, D.C., from which he graduated in Mar. of the following year. His military education continued in the following years with courses of instruction at the Army School at Fort Leavenworth, the Army War College, and the Navy War College. Fuller's first three years of service in the Marine Corps were spent ashore at different posts in the eastern part of the States. On Sept. 7, 1893, he was promoted to first lieutenant and then went to sea for the first time as a Marine officer on the USS *Atlanta* in Apr. of the next year. During his active career he spent nearly seven years at sea on a dozen different naval vessels. During the Spanish-American War he was in command of the Marine detachment of the USS *Columbia* and served in West Indian waters. Shortly after that war he was promoted to captain and transferred to the Philippines for duty, where he participated in the Battle of Novaleta. At the outbreak of the Boxer Rebellion in 1900, he was placed in command of a company of artillery in an expeditionary Marine force. He participated in the siege and capture of Tientsin and was commended in Navy General Orders for his "gallant, meritorious and courageous conduct" in battle. He joined in the march of the relief column to Peking and was in command of an independent detachment at Fong Chow, China. Capt. Fuller returned to the Philippines in Oct. 1900, and went to the States the following year. During the next three years he was given several peacetime shore assignments, and also spent a few months at sea. He was promoted to major in Mar. 1904. Shortly afterward he was transferred to the command of MB, Honolulu, T.H., where he served for about two years, then went to New York for duty. After a brief tour of duty in the States, a part of which was spent as instructor in the School of Application at Annapolis, he again went to foreign duty — this time to the Canal Zone where he served as CO of the battalion of Marines from Aug. 1908 until Feb. 1910. His next regular station of duty was in command of the MB at Charleston, S.C. He was promoted to lieutenant colonel Mar. 8,

1911. While serving at Charleston he commanded a regiment of an expeditionary Brigade of Marines that went to Guantanamo Bay, Cuba in May 1911. Since the show of force alone was sufficient to quiet the Cuban political situation, the expedition was withdrawn and Col. Fuller resumed his duties at Charleston. He spent most of the next two years in service schools. Fuller joined the 5th Regt. of Marines as second in command in July 1914, and spent several months with that organization on the *Hancock,* cruising around Haiti-Santo Domingo and in camp at Guantanamo Bay. Some two years later, after a short cruise as Fleet Marine Officer, Atlantic Fleet, and while attending the Navy War College he was promoted to colonel in Mar. 1917. He commanded the MB, Philadelphia, Pa. for about one year, beginning early in Sept. 1917, and was then assigned to the command of the 2nd Prov. Brig. of Marines engaged in a military occupation of Santo Domingo. He was promoted to temporary brigadier general in Aug. 1918, but reverted to his regular rank of colonel about one year later. While serving in Santo Domingo he had extensive experience in administering several cabinet positions in the military government of that country. He joined the staff of the Naval War College as an instructor in Nov. 1920, and in July 1922 took command of the MCS at Quantico, which position he held for the next year and a half. Next Fuller was assigned to command the 1st Brig. of Marines occupying Haiti in Jan. 1924 until Dec. 1925. He was promoted to the regular rank of brigadier general as of Feb. 8, 1924. During the next two and a half years he spent most of the time serving on various boards and on court-martial duty in Washington, D.C. He was made assistant Commandant of the Corps in July 1928

under Maj. Gen. Lejeune, and continued to serve in that capacity not only during the remainder of Lejeune's tenure of office but also throughout that of Gen. Neville. During Gen. Neville's brief period as Major General Commandant in 1929-1930, Gen. Fuller frequently acted as Commandant when the Commandant was ill. After the death of Gen. Neville, Fuller was selected as Major General Commandant on Aug. 6, 1930. Gen. Fuller's tenure as Commandant of the Marine Corps, which continued until his retirement for age on Mar. 1, 1934, was one of general retrenchment due to the world-wide depression, the initiation of the good-neighbor policy in dealing with Latin American countries, and other reasons. The depression brought about sharp reduction in the federal revenue and in an effort to offset this, appropriations for the Marine Corps were reduced and the curtailments were offset by reductions in the enlisted strength, and a flat reduction in pay. Plans for the ultimate withdrawal of the Marine Brigades from both Haiti and Nicaragua developed from the beginning of Fuller's commandantcy, and the last contingent of Marines was withdrawn from Nicaragua early in Jan. 1933. The same process of curtailing the activities of the Marines in Haiti had been continuing for a number of years, and by 1934 and some time previously they were serving only in Cape Haitien and Port-au-Prince and as officers in the Garde d'Haiti. The 4th Regt. of Marines continued on duty in China throughout this period. With the gradual release of Marines on foreign duty, greater progress was made in the education of officers and in the more advanced technical training of enlisted men. Sweeping changes in foreign policy caused the Marines Corps to redefine its mission in the scheme of national defense. The necessity for a substantial expeditionary force of Marines to be in readiness to accompany the Fleet was an idea that had taken form not long after the turn of the century, but it was not until 1933 when personnel became available as a result of withdrawal of Marines from foreign countries that the idea was fully developed and such a force as the Fleet Marine Force was organized. That organization came into being in Dec. of that year with part of its force at Quan-

tico, Va., and part at San Diego, Calif. The gradual expansion of the Navy during Fuller's tenure of office demanded more and more Marines for sea duty. This, together with the further development of the Fleet Marine Force, influenced the development of the Corps' amphibious doctrines. General Fuller was transferred to the retired list of the Marine Corps on Mar. 1, 1934, after having attained the statutory age limit of 64 years.

G

GAIENNIE, Louis Rene. Private. Medal of Honor: b. St. Louis, Mo., June 9, 1878; d. during WWII, exact date not known. Louis Gaiennie enlisted in the Marine Corps at Mare Island, Calif., on July 11, 1899. He received the Medal of Honor on Dec. 11, 1901 "... for distinguished conduct in the presence of the enemy at Peking, China, July 21, to Aug. 17, 1900...."

GALE, Anthony. Lieutenant Colonel. 4th Commandant of the Marine Corps — Mar. 3, 1819 to Oct. 8, 1820: b. Dublin, Ireland, Sept. 17, 1782; d. Lincoln County, Ky., 1843. Fewer records survive concerning Anthony Gale than of any other Commandant of the Corps. For six months following the death of Commandant Lieutenant Colonel Franklin Wharton, the Corps was officially without a leader. However, Archibald Henderson was temporarily at the helm. By Mar. of 1819, the Secretary of the Navy had made his decision and the post of Commandant went to Gale. The few records which remain indicate that Gale was neither

effective nor efficient as the head of the Corps. He was finally removed from office and the Corps on Oct. 8, 1820. The government, however, awarded him a pension which continued until his death in 1843.

GALER, Robert Edward. Brigadier General (Retired). Medal of Honor: b. Seattle, Wash., Oct. 23, 1913. Robert Galer was commissioned a second lieutenant in the Marine Corps July 1, 1936. Following his designation as a naval aviator in Apr. 1937, he was transferred to the 1st Mar. Brig. at Quantico for duty with Aircraft 1. In July of the same year he was assigned to a course of instruction at the Basic School at Philadelphia, Pa. Following the completion of his studies in June 1938, he was ordered to the New York Navy Yard, but shortly thereafter was transferred to the Virgin Is. where he served with Marine Scouting Squadron 3 at St. Thomas. He was advanced to first lieutenant in July 1939. He returned to the States in June 1940, and in July reported to the 2nd MAW in

San Diego, Calif. In Jan. 1941, he was ordered to Hawaii and was appointed a captain in Mar. 1941. He was serving at MCAS, Ewa, when the Japanese attacked Pearl Harbor on Dec. 7, 1941. In May 1942, Galer assumed command of Marine Fighting Squadron 224. It was while in command of this unit that he received the nation's highest award, shortly after his promotion to the rank of major. His citation reads, in part: ". . . as leader of a Marine Fighting Squadron in aerial combat with enemy Japanese forces in the Solomon Is. area, Aug.-Sept. 1942. Leading his squadron repeatedly in daring and aggressive raids against Japanese aerial forces, vastly superior in numbers, Maj. Galer availed himself of every favorable attack opportunity, individually shooting down 11 enemy bomber and fighter aircraft over a period of 29 days. Though suffering the extreme physical strain attendant upon protracted fighter operations at an altitude above 25,000 feet, the squadron, under his zealous and inspiring leadership, shot down a total of 27 Japanese planes. . . ." Following the presentation of the Medal of Honor, he was ordered to Marine Forces, Air, West Coast, Miramar, Calif., where he served as Assistant Operations Officer. Shortly after advancement to the rank of lieutenant colonel in Nov. 1943, he was ordered to return to the Hawaiian Is., where he became Chief of Staff, Marine Air, Hawaiian Area. In May 1944, he was named as Operations Officer, 3rd MAW. He served as an observer during the Palau Is. campaign while on temporary duty from the 3rd MAW. His next assignment found him as Training Officer of Provisional Air Support Command, FMF, Pacific. Galer again returned to the States in June 1945, and in July he reported to the MB, Naval Air Training

Base, Corpus Christi, Tex. as officer in charge of a cadet regiment. He remained in that capacity until Aug. 1947, at which time he was assigned as a student at the Armed Forces Staff College in Norfolk, Va. In June 1948, Col. Galer reported to MAG-14, 2nd MAW, at the MCAS, Cherry Point, N.C. where he served as Operations and Training Officer. He joined HQ Squadron 2 at that station in Apr. 1949, and was transferred Apr. 26, 1950, to the NAS, San Diego, Calif. He served there as Marine Planning Officer and, later, as Assistant Chief of Staff for Plans on the Staff of the Commander, Air Force, U.S. Pacific Fleet. Col. Galer sailed in Mar. 1952 for Korea, where he saw duty as Assistant Chief of Staff, G-4 (Supply) of the 1st MAW until the following May. He was then named CO of MAG 12, 1st MAW there. Col. Galer was also awarded the Legion of Merit with Combat "V" for his service in Korea from May 24 to Aug. 5, 1952, when he was shot down behind enemy lines by anti-aircraft fire and later rescued by helicopter. After a period of hospitalization, he returned to duty at El Toro, Calif. in Oct. 1952 as Assistant Chief of Staff, G-1 (Personnel), and later, G-3 (Operations), of Aircraft, FMF, Pacific. He was enrolled as a student in the Air War College, Maxwell Air Force Base, Montgomery, Ala. in July 1953. Upon his graduation from the College the following June, he was transferred to HQMC, Washington, D.C., where he became Assistant Director, Guided Missiles Division, Bureau of Aeronautics, Department of the Navy. He served in that capacity until Jan. 1956, when he assumed duties as Acting Director. On July 31, 1957 he was retired and advanced to brigadier general.

GARCIA, Fernando Luis. Private First

Class. Medal of Honor: b. Utuado, Puerto Rico, Oct. 14, 1929; d. KIA, Korea, Sept. 5, 1952. P.F.C. Garcia's citation reads, in part: ". . . while serving as a member of Co. I, 3rd Bn., 5th Marines, 1st Mar. Div. (Reinf.) in action against enemy aggressor forces in Korea on Sept. 5, 1952. While participating in the defense of a combat outpost located more than one mile forward of the main line of resistance during a savage night attack by a fanatical enemy force employing grenades, mortars, and artillery, P.F.C. Garcia, although suffering painful wounds, moved through the intense hail of hostile fire to a supply point to secure more hand grenades. Quick to act when a hostile grenade landed nearby, endangering the life of another Marine as well as his own, he unhesitatingly chose to sacrifice himself and immediately threw his body upon the deadly missile, receiving the full impact of the explosion. . . ."

GAUGHAN, Philip. Sergeant. Medal of Honor: b. Belmullet, Ireland, Mar. 17, 1865; d. U.S. Naval Hospital, Philadelphia, Pa. Dec. 30, 1913. Philip Gaughan enlisted in the Marine Corps at Philadelphia, Pa. on July 19, 1887. His citation reads, in part: ". . . while serving on board the USS *Nashville* . . . for extraordinary heroism and coolness while cutting the cables leading from Cienfuegos, Cuba, May 11, 1898, under heavy fire of the enemy. . . ." He was discharged from the Corps on July 18, 1899.

GEIGER, Roy Stanley. General. Commander of both air and grounds units during WWII: b. Middleburg, Fla., Jan. 25, 1885; d. National Naval Medical Center, Bethesda, Md., Jan. 23, 1947. Roy Geiger attended Florida State Normal School and received an LLB degree from Stetson University, following which he

Geiger

enlisted in the Marine Corps on Nov. 2, 1907. He was commissioned a second lieutenant on Feb. 5, 1909. Following attendance at the Marine Officers' School at Port Royal, S.C., he served as a member of the Marine Detachments aboard the USS *Wisconsin* and the USS *Delaware*. In Aug. 1912, he went to foreign shore duty in Nicaragua and while in that country participated in the bombardment, assault, and capture of Coyotepe and Barranca. Further foreign shore duty followed in the Philippines and China with the 1st Mar. Brig. and with the Marine Detachment, American Legation, Peking, China, from 1913 to 1916. In Mar. 1916, he joined the Naval Aeronautic Station at Pensacola, Fla., as a student naval aviator. He successfully completed the course and was designated a naval aviator in June 1917. Further training followed and in July 1918 he arrived in France. Geiger served with Group Number Five, Royal Air Forces at Dunkerque. He commanded a squadron of the 1st Mar. Aviation Force and was attached to the Day Wing, Northern Bombing Group. He was detached to the States in Jan. 1919. For distinguished service in leading bombing raids against the enemy, he was awarded the Navy Cross. From Dec. 1919, to Jan. 1921, he was a squadron commander with the Mar. Aviation Force attached to the 1st Prov. Brig. in Haiti. Upon return to the States and after duty at the Marine Flying Field, Marine Barracks, Quantico, Va., he attended Command and General Staff School at Fort Leavenworth, Kans. He graduated in June 1925. Again he went to foreign shore duty, commanding Observation Squadron Two with the 1st Mar. Brig. in Haiti. In Aug. 1927, he returned to Quantico as a squadron officer and instructor at the MCS, and in May 1928, was assigned to duty in the Aviation Section, Div. of Operations and Training at HQMC. After attending Army War College and graduating in June 1929, he was ordered to Quantico, where he was assigned duty as CO, Aircraft Squadrons, East Coast Expeditionary Force. He returned to Washington for duty with Aeronautics, Navy Department as Officer in Charge, Marine Corps Aviation. In June 1935, he returned to Quantico as CO, Aircraft One, FMF. From June 1939, to Mar. 1941, he was a student at the Senior and the Advanced Courses, Naval War College, Newport, R.I. This was followed by a brief tour of duty in the Office of the Naval Attaché, London, England. In Aug. 1941, he became CG, 1st MAW, FMF, in which capacity he was serving upon this country's entry into WWII. He led the 1st

MAW from Sept. 3 to Nov. 4, 1942, while stationed at Guadalcanal. For extraordinary heroism in this capacity as well as commander of all aircraft, he was awarded a Gold Star in lieu of a second Navy Cross. His citation reads in part, "Despite almost continuous bombardment by enemy aircraft, hostile naval gunfire and shore based artillery, the combined total of Army, Navy and Marine Corps units stationed at Guadalcanal under Maj. Gen. Geiger's efficiently coordinated command succeeded in shooting down 268 Japanese planes in aerial combat and inflicting damage on a number estimated to be as great. . . . Sank six enemy vessels, including one heavy cruiser, possibly sank three destroyers and one heavy cruiser, and damaged 18 other ships, including one heavy cruiser and five light cruisers." He was recalled to HQMC in May 1943, to become Director of Aviation. In Nov. 1943, he returned to the field, this time as CG of the 1st Mar. Amphibious Corps and led the Corps from Nov. 9 to Dec. 15, 1943, in the Bougainville Operation, for which he was awarded the Distinguished Service Medal. Redesignated 3rd Amphibious Corps in Apr. 1944, Geiger led this organization in the invasion and subsequent recapture of Guam during July and Aug. 1944, and in the assault and capture of the southern Palau Islands in Sept. and Oct. of the same year. For these operations he was awarded two Gold Stars in lieu of a second and third Distinguished Service Medal. Gen. Geiger led this Corps into action for the fourth time as part of the Tenth Army in the invasion and capture of Okinawa. In July 1945, he assumed duties as CG of the FMF, Pacific, which position he held until called back to HQMC in Nov. 1946. On Jan. 23, 1947, Gen. Geiger died at the National Naval Medical Center, Bethesda, Md. Gen. Geiger was promoted to the rank of general posthumously by the 80th Congress to be effective from Jan. 23, 1947.

Glenn

GLENN, John Herschel, Jr. Lieutenant Colonel. National Aeronautics and Space Administration Mercury Astronaut, Marine Corps test pilot, and first American to orbit the earth: b. Cambridge, Ohio, July 18, 1921. John Glenn graduated from high school in New Concord, Ohio, in 1939, and while attending Muskingum College enlisted in the U.S. Naval Reserve in Mar. 1942. He was assigned active duty May 28, 1942 and transferred to the Naval Aviation Pre-Flight School, Iowa City, Iowa, and while there was designated an aviation cadet, Aug. 4, 1942. Following pre-flight instruction, he

completed the primary flight training course at the U.S.N.R. Aviation Base, Kansas City, Olathe, Kans., from Aug. 1942 to Nov. 1942. He then joined the Naval Air Training Center, Corpus Christi, Tex., where, on completing flight training, Mar. 31, 1943, he was commissioned a second lieutenant in the MCR, and designated a naval aviator. He was promoted to first lieutenant in Oct. 1943, and sailed for the Pacific area in Feb. 1944. During WWII, he flew 59 missions in the Marshall Is. campaign, earning two Distinguished Flying Crosses and ten Air Medals as a pilot in Marine Fighter Squadron (VMF) 155, MAG 31, 4th MAW. Returning to the States in Feb. 1945, he was subsequently assigned to the 9th MAW, MCAS, Cherry Point, N.C., and NAS, Patuxent River, Md. He was promoted to captain in July 1945, and integrated in the regular Marine Corps in Mar. 1946. Glenn next served at the MCAS, El Toro, Calif., from Mar. until Dec. 1946. He then departed the States for two years' duty with MAG 24, 1st MAW, and during this time was a member of Marine Fighter Squadron 218 on North China patrol and on Guam. From Jan. 1949 to June 1951, he served as Flight Instructor, Instructors' Advanced Training Unit, Naval Auxiliary Air Station, Cabaniss Field, Corpus Christi; and as Instrument Flight Instructor, NAS, Corpus Christi. In July 1951, he was transferred to MCS, Quantico, Va., where he completed the Junior Course in Nov. 1951, then served as Assistant G-2/G-3. He was promoted to major in July 1952. Glenn departed Quantico in Nov. 1952 and completed the Jet Refresher Course at MCAS, Cherry Point. In Feb. 1953, he arrived in Korea for duty as a jet pilot with Marine Fighter Squadron 311, MAG 33. During the Korean War, he flew a total of 90 combat missions. Flying 63 missions with VMF-311 from Feb. through May 1953, he was awarded a third Distinguished Flying Cross and six Air Medals. As an exchange pilot with the 5th U.S. Air Force from June to Sept. 1953, he flew 27 missions with the 25th Fighter Squadron, 51st Fighter Interceptor Wing. While serving with the 25th Squadron, he destroyed three MIGs in nine days. For this outstanding performance, the U.S. Air Force awarded him a Distinguished Flying Cross, his fourth such award; and two Air Medals, his 17th and 18th. He remained in Korea through Dec. 1953. Early in 1954, Maj. Glenn entered the Navy Test Pilot Training School at the NAS, Patuxent River, completing the course in July 1954. After graduation, he was Project Officer on a number of aircraft, including the F8U, F8U-1, and F8U-P, at the Armament Test Division of the Naval Air Test Center, Patuxent River. In Nov. 1956, he was assigned as Project Officer, Fighter Design Branch, Bureau of Aeronautics, Navy Dept., in Washington, D.C. On July 16, 1957, Maj. Glenn completed the first non-stop supersonic coast-to-coast flight in an F8U-1 Crusader. This flight, from Los Alamitos NAS, Calif., to Floyd Bennett Field, N.Y., took 3 hours 23 minutes and 8.1 seconds. He was awarded another Distinguished Flying Cross for this feat, his fifth such award. His rank as lieutenant colonel dates from Apr. 1, 1959. With the advent of Project Mercury John Glenn was one of the original 69 selectees brought to the Nation's Capital for interviews to determine their qualifications to become America's first astronauts. Of the 69 men, all military test pilots or former test pilots, 32 were chosen for further screening under grueling physical and mental stresses. Glenn was among the 32. On Apr. 9, 1959, NASA introduced the

seven best qualified men; John Glenn had become one of the nation's first seven astronauts. Less than two years later, on Feb. 20, 1962, in his *Friendship 7* Mercury Spacecraft, Glenn orbited the earth three times in four hours, 56 minutes — four and three-fourths hours of which he was weightless in space. In his Mercury craft, he was rocketed into space by a modified Atlas missile from Cape Canaveral, Fla., at 9:47 A.M. (EST) and landed in the Atlantic Ocean, 166 miles east of Grand Turk Island in the Bahamas at 2:43 P.M. During the second and third orbits, he controlled the capsule himself through the autopilot after the automatic controls broke down just at the end of the first orbit. During his 83,000-mile ride through space, he had achieved an orbital speed of 17,530 miles an hour at a high point of 162.5 statute miles and a low point of 98.9 statute miles. Following re-entry, Col. Glenn landed with his spacecraft in the Atlantic, five miles from the destroyer USS *Noa*. He was picked up still inside his spacecraft and lowered to the deck of the destroyer at 3:04 P.M. Later, he was lifted from the *Noa* by helicopter and transferred to the carrier USS *Randolph* for transport to Grand Turk Island for examination by a team of doctors and technicians. He was pronounced in excellent condition. Although new astronauts have been added to the original seven, Col. Glenn has continued in his assignment with the NASA program.

GLOWIN, Joseph Anthony. Corporal. Medal of Honor: b. Detroit, Mich., Mar. 14, 1892. Joseph Glowin enlisted in the Marine Corps at Norfolk, Va. on Dec. 9, 1913. His citation reads, in part: "... for extraordinary heroism in the line of his profession and for eminent and conspicuous courage in the presence of the enemy at the action at Guayacanes,

Dominican Republic, July 3, 1916. . . ."

GOMEZ, Edward. Private First Class. Medal of Honor: b. Omaha, Neb., Aug. 10, 1932; d. KIA, Korea, Sept. 14, 1951. P.F.C. Gomez' citation reads, in part: ". . . while serving as an ammunition bearer in Co. E, 2nd Bn., 1st Marines, 1st Mar. Div. (Reinf.), in action against enemy aggressor forces in Korea on Sept. 14, 1951. Boldly advancing with his squad in support of a group of riflemen assaulting a series of strongly fortified and bitterly defended hostile positions on Hill 749, P.F.C. Gomez consistently exposed himself to the withering barrage to keep his machine gun supplied with ammunition during the drive forward to seize the objective. As his squad deployed to meet an imminent counterattack, he voluntarily moved down an abandoned trench to search for a new location for the gun and, when a hostile grenade landed between himself and his weapon, shouted a warning to those around him as he grasped the activated charge in his hand. Determined to save his comrades, he unhesitatingly chose to sacrifice himself and, diving into the ditch with the deadly missile, absorbed the shattering violence of the explosion in his own body. . . ."

GONSALVES, Harold. Private First Class. Medal of Honor: b. Alameda, Calif., Jan. 28, 1926; d. KIA, Okinawa, Apr. 15, 1945. P.F.C. Gonsalves' citation reads, in part " . . . as Acting Scout Sgt. of a Forward Observer Team, serving with Battery L, 4th Bn., 15th Marines, 6th Mar. Div., during action against enemy Japanese forces on Okinawa Shima in the Ryukyu Chain, Apr. 15, 1945 . . . when his CO determined to move into the front lines in order to register a more effective bombardment in the enemy's defensive position, he unhesitatingly advanced uphill with the officer and another Marine despite a slashing barrage of enemy mortar and rifle fire. As they reached the front, a Japanese grenade fell close within the group. Instantly P.F.C. Gonsalves dived on the deadly missile, absorbing the exploding charge in his own body and thereby protecting the others from serious and perhaps fatal wounds. . . ."

GRAY, Ross Franklin. Sergeant. Medal of Honor: b. Marvel Valley, Ala., Aug. 1, 1920; d. KIA, Iwo Jima, Feb. 27, 1945. Two days after D-day on Iwo Jima, Sgt. Gray was acting platoon sergeant of one of A Company's platoons which had been held up by a sudden barrage of Japanese hand grenades in the area northeast of Airfield No. 1. Promptly withdrawing his platoon out of range of the grenades, the sergeant moved forward to reconnoiter. He ascertained that the advance was held up by a series of enemy emplacements connected by covered communication trenches and fronted by a mine field. Despite enemy small arms fire, the sergeant cleared a path through the mine field up to the mouth of one of the fortifications, then returned to his own lines where, with three volunteers, he went back to the battalion dump and acquired 12 satchel charges. Placing these in a defiladed area within his platoon he took one weighing 24 pounds and, covered by the three volunteers, advanced up the path he had cleared and threw the charge into the enemy position, sealing it. Immediately brought under fire from a machine gun in another opening of the same position, Sgt. Gray returned to the defiladed spot, obtained another charge, returned to the position, and completely destroyed it. Spotting another emplacement, he went through the mine field for the seventh and eighth time to get another charge and destroy another enemy stronghold. He continued this one-man attack, all the time under heavy small arms fire and grenade barrage, until he had destroyed six enemy positions. Throughout the action, he went unarmed so that he could more easily carry the charges and accessories. When he had eliminated the six positions, Sgt. Gray disarmed the whole mine field before returning to his platoon. He emerged from the entire courageous undertaking, which undoubtedly saved the lives of many Marines, without a scratch. A recapitulation of the day's work revealed that he had killed over 25 of the enemy, destroyed one machine gun, one small field piece, and an ammunition dump containing small arms ammunition and mines. Although he remained unscratched through his 12 trips back and forth among enemy mines, constantly under heavy fire, Sgt. Gray was killed six days later on Feb. 27, by an enemy shell.

Greene

GREENE, Wallace Martin, Jr. Lieutenant General. Chief of Staff, HQMC, Washington, D.C.: b. Burlington, Vt., Dec. 27, 1907. Gen. Greene graduated from high school in 1925 and attended the University of Vermont for a year before entering Annapolis. Upon graduation from the Naval Academy, June 5, 1930, he was commissioned a Marine second lieutenant and ordered to Marine Officers' Basic School at the Philadelphia Navy Yard. He completed that school in June 1931, then served for a year at the MB, Navy Yard, Portsmouth, N.H. In July 1932, he completed Sea School at San Diego, Calif., and joined the Marine Detachment aboard the USS *Tennessee.* Returning from sea duty in Mar. 1934, the general served briefly at Pensacola, Fla., and Quantico, Va., before reporting to

the MB, NAS, Lakehurst, N.J., that Nov. Except for a temporary assignment at Edgewood Arsenal, Md., where he completed a course in the Chemical Warfare School, he remained at Lakehurst until Mar. 1936. After that he served at the MCRD, San Diego, until he sailed for Guam in Oct. 1936. He was stationed there until June 1937, when he embarked for Shanghai to join the 4th Marines. Upon his return from China in Aug. 1939, he entered the Junior Course, MCS, Quantico. He completed the course in May 1940, then took command of the 1st Chemical Co., 1st Mar. Brig., sailing with it that Oct. for Guantanamo Bay, Cuba. While there, the Brigade was redesignated the 1st Mar. Div. Returning with the unit in Apr. 1941, he served at Quantico and New River (later Camp Lejeune), N.C., as Assistant Operations Officer, 1st Mar. Div. In Nov. 1941, Greene was ordered to London, England, as a Special Naval Observer. During that assignment, he attended the British Amphibious Warfare School at Inverary, Scotland, and the Royal Engineer Demolitions School at Ripon, York, England, returning to the States in Feb. 1942. Named Assistant Chief of Staff, G-3, 3rd Mar. Brig. that Mar., Greene sailed with the brigade for Upolu, Western Samoa, the following month. He remained on that island until Nov. 1943, when he joined the 5th Amphibious Corps in Hawaii as Assistant Chief of Staff, G-3, Tactical Group 1. For outstanding service in this capacity during the planning and execution of the Marshall Is. invasion, he was awarded his first Legion of Merit with Combat "V." Following the disbanding of the group in Mar. 1944, he joined the 2nd Mar. Div. as G-3, earning a second Legion of Merit for outstanding service in this capacity on Saipan and Tinian. He remained with the 2nd Div. until his return to the States in Sept. In Oct. 1944, he was appointed Officer in Charge, G-3, Operations, Division of Plans and Policies, HQMC, Washington, D.C. He held that post until July 1945, then served as Executive Officer, Special Services Branch, Personnel Department. In Apr. 1946, he was ordered to Little Creek, Va., as G-3, Troop Training Unit, Amphibious Training Command, U.S. Atlantic Fleet. Leaving Little Creek in June 1948, he reported to Pearl Harbor that Aug. as G-3, FMF, Pacific. Col. Greene returned from that assignment in June 1950, and for the next two years was Chief of the Combined Arms Section, MCS, Quantico. He also served briefly

as Chief of the Coordination and Evaluation Section there, before entering the National War College, Washington, in Aug. 1952. He graduated in June 1953, and the next month became Staff Special Assistant to the JCS for National Security Council Affairs. In Sept. 1955, he was promoted to brigadier general and became Assistant Commander, 2nd Mar. Div., Camp Lejeune. Transferred to the MCRD, Parris Is., S.C., in May 1956, he served as CG, Recruit Training Command, until Mar. 1957; and, subsequently, as CG of the Recruit Depot. In July 1957, Gen. Greene became CG of the MCB, Camp Lejeune. Ordered to HQMC, Washington, in Jan. 1958, he served for over a year as Assistant Chief of Staff, G-3. He was promoted to major general in Aug. 1958. In Mar. 1959, he was named Deputy Chief of Staff (Plans), serving in this capacity through Dec. of that year. On Jan. 1, 1960, he was promoted to lieutenant general on assuming his current assignment as Chief of Staff.

GROSS, Samuel. Private. (Real name was Samuel Margulies.) Medal of Honor: b. Philadelphia, Pa., May 9, 1891; d. Sept. 13, 1934. In an attack on Fort Riviere, Haiti on Nov. 17, 1915, Pvt. Gross was the second man to charge through a breach in the wall under heavy fire from the enemy. A hand-to-hand battle within the fort followed, with the Cacos waging a desperate defense with rifles, clubs, and stones. After the ten minute bloody conflict the fort was captured. Gross was discharged from the Corps as an epileptic on Sept. 10, 1918.

GUILLEN, Ambrosio. Staff Sergeant. Medal of Honor: b. La Junta, Calif., Dec. 7, 1929; d. KIA, Korea, July 25, 1953. S. Sgt. Guillen's citation reads, in part: ". . . while serving as a platoon sergeant of Co. F, 2nd Bn., 7th Marines, 1st Mar. Div. (Reinf.), in action against enemy aggressor forces in Korea on July 25, 1953. Participating in the defense of an outpost forward of the main line of resistance, S. Sgt. Guillen maneuvered his platoon over unfamiliar terrain in the face of hostile fire and placed his men in fighting positions. With his unit pinned down when the outpost was attacked under cover of darkness by an estimated force of two enemy battalions supported by mortar and artillery fire, he deliberately exposed himself to the heavy barrage and attacks to direct his men in defending their positions and personally supervise the treatment and evacuation of the wounded. Inspired by his leadership, the platoon quickly rallied and engaged the enemy in fierce hand-to-hand combat. Although critically wounded during the course of the battle, S. Sgt. Guillen refused medical aid and continued to direct his men throughout the remainder

of the engagement until the enemy was defeated and thrown into disorderly retreat. Succumbing to his wounds within a few hours, S. Sgt. Guillen, by his outstanding courage and indomitable fighting spirit, was directly responsible for the success of his platoon's repelling a numerically superior enemy force. . . ."

GURKE, Henry. Private First Class. Medal of Honor: b. Neche, N.D., Nov. 6, 1922; d. KIA, Bougainville, Nov. 9, 1943. P.F.C. Gurke's citation reads, in part: " . . . while attached to the 3rd Mar. Raider Bn . . . while his platoon was engaged in the defense of a vital road block, P.F.C. Gurke, in company with another Marine, was delivering a fierce stream of fire against the main vanguard of the Japanese. When a Japanese grenade dropped squarely into their foxhole, P.F.C. Gurke thrust his companion aside and flung his own body over the missile to smother the explosion. . . ."

H

HAMBLET, Julia E. Lieutenant Colonel. Former Director of Women Marines: b. Winchester, Mass., May 12, 1916. Julia Hamblet attended the Hartridge School, Plainfield, N.J., and graduated from Vassar in 1937 with a Bachelor of Arts degree. She obtained a Master of Science degree in public administration at Ohio State University in 1951. After serving with the U.S. Information Service, Washington, D.C. from 1937 until 1943, she entered the Marine Corps that spring. Upon graduation from the first Marine Corps Women's Reserve Officer Training Class at Mt. Holyoke, Mass., she was commis-

sioned a first lieutenant in the Reserve on May 4, 1943. During WWII, Lt. Hamblet commanded Aviation Women Reserve Group 1, numbering some 2600 women, at the MCAS, Cherry Point, N.C. After her release from active duty in 1946, she spent two months in London, then was called back to HQMC in Washington to serve as Director of Women Reserves. When women were accepted into the regular components of the armed forces in 1948, she accepted a regular commission. She was promoted to lieutenant colonel in Aug. 1949. In 1951, after completing graduate work at Ohio State

University, Col. Hamblet was assigned to the Staff of the Commander, FMF, Pacific, in Hawaii. The following year she was named Officer in Charge of the Women Marine Officers' Training Detachment, MCS, Quantico, Va. Col. Hamblet became Director of Women Marines on May 1, 1953. The post carried the rank of colonel, and she continued to serve in that capacity when her four year tour was extended by the Commandant of the Marine Corps. In Mar. 1959, she reverted to her permanent rank of lieutenant colonel when she became Military Secretary to the Commander in Chief, Allied Forces, Southern Europe. Since the latter part of 1962, she has been CO of the Women Marine Detachment at MCRD, Parris Is.

HANNEKEN, Herman Henry. Brigadier General (Retired). Medal of Honor: b. St. Louis, Mo., June 23, 1893. While on duty in Haiti in 1919, Herman Hanneken suppressed the activities of the bandit leader, Charlemagne Peralte, by killing the notorious outlaw in a daring raid on his camp in northern Haiti. For this outstanding feat, he was awarded the Medal of Honor. In another daring exploit, just five months following the execution of Charlemagne, he shot and killed Osiris Joseph, another Haitian bandit chieftain who had succeeded Charlemagne. Hanneken was awarded the Navy Cross for this act of heroism. His Marine Corps career, which was to endure for 34 years, began when he enlisted as a private in July 1914. He served for five years as an enlisted man, rising to the rank of sergeant. He was appointed a second lieutenant in Dec. 1919. Upon receipt of his commission he was assigned to duty with the Haitian Gendarmerie. He was ordered to return to the States in Apr. 1920, and following his arrival at the MB,

Hanneken

Quantico, he was assigned to a special course at the MCS. As a member of the 6th Mar. Regt., Hanneken, now a first lieutenant, sailed for Brazil to participate in the Brazilian Exposition. The unit returned to Quantico in the latter part of 1922. Several months later, he was transferred to the Marine Detachment, USS *Antares,* where he assumed duties as CO. In Jan. 1925, Hanneken was transferred to the MB, NAS, Lakehurst, N.J., and in Apr. 1927, was detached to the MB at the Philadelphia Navy Yard. Again ordered to foreign duty in Dec. 1928, he arrived in Corinto, Nicaragua, in Jan. of the following year. Upon his arrival in Nicaragua he was assigned to duty with the 2nd Brig. Marines. It was in that Central American country, less than a month after his arrival, that Hanneken captured another notorious bandit leader. He was awarded his second Navy Cross for "bringing in" bandit chieftain Sandino's Chief of Staff, Gen. Jiron. In July 1930, he returned to Quantico to attend the Company Officers' Course, MCS. Upon graduation in Jan. of the next year, he was transferred to the MCB at San Diego, Calif., and later to the Naval Base at San Pedro, Calif. His next assignment found Hanneken at the MB, Marine Island, Calif., in Aug. 1936 where, during his tour of duty, he was appointed a major. He was ordered to Quantico in June 1938, and two months later, reported for a course of instruction at that base in the Senior Course, MCS. From June 1939 to Dec. 1940, he was CO, MB, NAD, Hingham, Mass. He was next ordered to New York to assume command of the Marine Detachment aboard the USS *Harry Lee* with additional duties as Transport Quartermaster. The major served with the 1st Mar. Div. from June 1941 until Nov. 1944, when he returned to the States to command the 2nd Inf. Training Regt. and the HQ Bn. at Camp Pendleton, Calif. While with the 1st Mar. Div. his duties were varied. While CO of the 7th Marines during the Guadalcanal campaign he was awarded the Silver Star Medal for conspicuous gallantry and intrepidity in action against the enemy. Again, during the Peleliu action, he won the Legion of Merit for meritorious conduct in action and, during the Cape Gloucester operation, was decorated with the Bronze Star Medal. In Sept. 1945, he was assigned as CO of the Staging Regiment at the Marine Training and Replacement Command, San Diego Area, prior to his transfer to the Troop Training Unit, Amphibious Forces, Pacific Fleet. Gen. Hanneken was serving as Chief of Staff of that organization when he was transferred to the retired list for

Marine Corps officers. Following his retirement on July 1, 1948, he was advanced to his present rank for having been especially commended for his performance of duty in combat.

HANSEN, Dale Merlin. Private First Class. Medal of Honor: b. Wisner, Neb., Dec. 13, 1922; d. KIA, Okinawa, May 11, 1945. Private Hansen's citation reads, in part: " . . . while serving with Co. E, 2nd Bn., 1st Marines, 1st Mar. Div. in action against enemy Japanese forces on Okinawa Shima, May 7, 1945. Cool and courageous in combat, Pvt. Hansen unhesitatingly took the initiative during a critical state of the action and, armed with a rocket launcher, crawled to an exposed position where he attacked and destroyed a strategically located hostile pillbox. With his weapon subsequently destroyed by enemy fire, he seized a rifle and continued his one-man assault. Reaching the crest of a ridge, he leaped across, opened fire on six Japanese and killed four before his rifle jammed. Attacked by the remaining two Japanese, he beat them off with the butt of his rifle and then climbed back to cover. Promptly returning with another weapon and supply of grenades, he fearlessly advanced, destroyed a strong mortar position and annihilated eight more of the enemy." P.F.C. Dale Hansen was killed by a Japanese sniper four days after his valiant exploits for which he earned the nation's highest award.

HANSON, Robert Murray. First Lieutenant. Medal of Honor: b. Lucknow, India, Feb. 4, 1920; d. MIA, last seen Feb. 3, 1944, when his plane crashed into the sea over Rabaul, New Britain. Famous for one killing spree in which he downed 20 enemy planes in six consecutive flying days, 1st Lt. Hanson was commended in the citation accompanying the Medal of Honor for his bold attack against six enemy torpedo bombers Nov. 1, 1943, over Bougainville Is., and for bringing down four Zeros while fighting them alone over New Britain on Jan. 24, 1944. His citation reads, in part: "A master of individual air combat, Lt. Hanson dauntlessly attacked six enemy torpedo bombers, forcing them to jettison their bombs and destroying one Japanese plane," in the Bougainville action, which occurred over Empress Augusta Bay during the landing operations. In the New Britain action, over Simpson Harbor, "he waged a lone and gallant battle against hostile interceptors as they were orbiting to attack our bombers and, striking with devastating fury, brought down four Zeros and probably a fifth." Lt. Hanson arrived in the South Pacific in June 1943, and his daring tactics and total disregard for death soon became well known. His fatal crash occurred just one day before his twenty-fourth birthday.

HARRELL, William George. Platoon Sergeant. Medal of Honor: b. Rio Grande City, Tex., June 26, 1922. William Harrell enlisted in the Marine Corps on July 3, 1942, at Harlington, Tex. Completing his basic training at the MCB, San Diego, Calif., he was temporarily in the First Guard Co. at that base prior to his transfer to H&S Co., 2nd Antitank Bn., Camp Elliott, San Diego, Calif., in Sept. 1942. He was promoted to private first class upon his arrival at Camp Elliott, and while there was later advanced to corporal. Following completion of the Basic Rocket Course, Harrell departed for overseas in Feb. 1943 with A Co., 1st Bn., 28th Marines, 5th Mar. Div. as an armorer. He first served at Hawaii, went on to Saipan then to Iwo Jima. On Mar. 3, 1945 Harrell, now a sergeant, and an-

other man dug in for the night in a long narrow two-man foxhole on a little ridge 20 yards forward of the depression where the company CP was established. Beyond the foxhole the ridge fell off into a ravine which was in Japanese territory. Because of their nearness to the enemy, the two men took turns standing one-hour watches throughout the night. An attack by the Japanese was repulsed, but the other Marine's weapon jammed and he returned to the CP to obtain another. While he was gone, the enemy managed to explode a grenade in the foxhole, blowing off Sgt. Harrell's left hand. The second Marine returned just as the Japanese were swarming up to the foxhole and, together, he and Harrell drove them off. Thinking he was dying due to the severity of his wounds and saber cuts suffered in the last repulse, Sgt. Harrell ordered his companion to retire to safety. His friend left, but only to get another rifle. During his absence, two Japanese charged the foxhole, setting off another grenade. As Sgt. Harrell attempted to push it out of the hole it exploded, tearing off his right hand. He was evacuated and treated at various field hospitals prior to his arrival in the States. Sgt. Harrell was discharged from the Marine Corps in Feb. 1946 because of disability from his wounds.

HARRIS, Field. Lieutenant General (Retired): b. Versailles, Ky., Sept. 18, 1895. Field Harris graduated from the U.S. Naval Academy in Mar. 1917, and was appointed a second lieutenant in the Marine Corps on Mar. 30 of that year. Following a short tour of duty aboard the USS *Nevada*, he joined the 3rd Prov. Brig. at Guantanamo Bay, Cuba, where he remained until Apr. 1919. He again saw foreign shore duty in Dec. of the same year when he was assigned to the

Harris

MB, Naval Station, Cavite, P.I. Returning to the States in June 1922, he served
three years in the Office of the Judge
Advocate General, Navy Department,
Washington, D.C. A tour of sea duty followed as CO of the Marine Detachment,
USS *Wyoming*. In Aug. 1927, he attended
a one-year course at the MCS, Quantico,
and then began flight training at NAS,
Pensacola, Fla. On Apr. 13, 1929 he was
designated a naval aviator. His first flying duties were at NAS, San Diego, Calif.,
where he was CO and Executive Officer
of an Aircraft Squadron, West Coast Expeditionary Force. A course of instruction
at the Air Corps Tactical School, Langley
Field, Va., was followed by foreign shore
duty in Haiti and sea duty aboard the
aircraft carrier USS *Lexington*. In June

1935, Harris joined the Aviation Section
at HQMC, Washington, D.C., following
which he attended the Naval War College at Newport, R.I., where he graduated from the Senior Course in May
1939. In the following two years he was
stationed in Quantico, and at Guantanamo Bay, Cuba, and in Aug. 1941, went
to Cairo, Egypt as Assistant Naval Attaché, and Assistant Naval Attaché for
Air. During WWII, Gen. Harris served
as Chief of Staff to the Commander, Aircraft, at Guadalcanal from Apr. to July
1943, and was awarded the Legion of
Merit for his outstanding services. He
won a second Legion of Merit while Commander, Aircraft, Northern Solomons, in
the autumn of 1943. From Feb. to Apr.
1944, he was Commander of Air for the
Green Island Operation, where he was
awarded a Gold Star in lieu of his third
Legion of Merit. For his services as Director of Marine Aviation during the latter years of WWII, the general received
a Gold Star in lieu of his fourth Legion
of Merit. He remained as Director of
Marine Aviation until Feb. 1948, at which
time he was ordered to duty as CG, Aircraft, FMF, Atlantic, and the 2nd MAW
at Cherry Point, N.C. He became CG,
Aircraft, FMF, Pacific, and the 1st MAW
at El Toro, Santa Ana, Calif., in July
1949. In Aug. 1950, he sailed for Korea
as CG, 1st MAW. Returning to the States
in June 1951, he was assigned duties at
HQMC, Washington, D.C. In Sept. 1951,
he became CG, Air, FMF, Atlantic, at
Norfolk, Va. He was retired and advanced
to lieutenant general on July 1, 1953.

HARRIS, John. Colonel. 6th Commandant of the Marine Corps — Jan. 7, 1859
to May 2, 1864: d. Washington, D.C.,
May 12, 1864. Col. John Harris became
the leader of his Corps in old age and
after 45 years of commissioned service.

He entered the Corps as a second lieutenant on Apr. 14, 1814, and there are no records which indicate that he rendered any outstanding services during the War of 1812. In the years following that war, he was assigned as commander of Marine guards on a number of the larger naval vessels and at various times was stationed at Erie, Philadelphia, Norfolk, New York, and Boston. He rendered conspicuous service with Gen. Archibald Henderson in the Florida Indian wars in 1836-37, in command of a mounted detachment of Marines. For this service he was later awarded the brevet rank of major. He returned to Washington in Mar. 1837, as the bearer of a treaty which had been made by the CG with the Seminole chiefs. From that time until the Mexican War, he was assigned to routine post duties and recruiting. During the Mexican War his services were limited. He did not go to the theater of operations until the closing month of the war when he took a battalion of Marines to Mexico, but arrived after the armistice had been concluded. He was sent with his battalion to Alvarado, Mex. as part of an occupying force, pending negotiations to determine whether or not the Isthmus of Tehuantepec would be placed under American control. The project failed shortly thereafter and Harris returned to the States and resumed his round of peace-time duties, spending the remainder of the time until he was made commandant in command of the MB at Philadelphia and New York. He was promoted to lieutenant colonel on Dec. 10, 1855, and appointed to the office of Colonel Commandant of the Corps on Jan. 7, 1859 — the day following the death of Gen. Archibald Henderson. Although Harris had succeeded a vigorous, aggressive commandant, he conducted the peace-time affairs of the Corps satisfac-

torily until the approach of the Civil War. After the election of Abraham Lincoln as President, the Marine Corps, together with the other military services of the U.S., began to distintegrate when a large proportion of the commissioned personnel resigned to offer their services to their native southern states. This divided loyalty in the Corps seems to have affected Harris somewhat, although he himself was not a southerner. When, for example, one of the Marine officers resigned during the crisis with the obvious intention of joining the Confederacy, Harris gave him a letter of recommendation commending him highly to any military organization in need of the services of an experienced officer. With the actual outbreak of the war, however, Harris doubtless saw his obligations more clearly. His position grew more difficult as nearly half of the officers of the Corps resigned, many of them younger officers with particularly distinguished records. The older officers of the Corps, nearly all of whom remained with the Union, were well on in years and had lost most of their zest for combat. Official records fail to disclose any recommendations by Harris for the expansion of the Marine Corps to sufficiently meet the great national emergency. He seemed to have been content with supplying Marines to guard shore establishments of the navy and supplying Marine detachments for the larger vessels. There is no evidence that he appreciated the value of an expeditionary force of Marines of sufficient strength to assist the fleet in its operations along the Confederate coast. The record of the Marine Corps in the Civil War and during the remainder of Harris' tour as Commandant was brilliantly successful concerning men serving on naval vessels but negligible when fighting on shore. Harris' tour as Commandant and his long career of 50 years as a Marine officer came to its close when he died in Washington on May 12, 1864.

HARVEY, Harry. Sergeant. Medal of Honor: b. New York, N.Y., June 4, 1873; d. Apr. 5, 1929. Harry Harvey enlisted in the Marine Corps on Feb. 5, 1895, at Brooklyn, N.Y. He was awarded the Medal of Honor on Jan. 24, 1902. His citation reads, in part: " . . . For distinguished conduct in the presence of the enemy in battle at Benefictican, Philippine Is., Feb. 16, 1900." Sgt. Harvey was discharged from the Marine Corps Feb. 4, 1903.

HAUGE, Louis James, Jr. Corporal. Medal of Honor: b. Ada, Minn., Dec. 12, 1924; d. KIA, Okinawa, May 14, 1945. Cpl. Hauge's citation reads, in part: " . . . Although painfully wounded as he charged the first machine gun, he launched a vigorous singlehanded grenade attack, destroyed the entire hostile gun position and moved relentlessly forward. . . ." At the time of his death, Cpl. Hauge was squad leader of a machine gun squad in southern Okinawa engaged in an assault against a heavily fortified Japanese hill. It was during the evening that the left flank of Co. C, 1st Bn., 1st Marines, was pinned down by a barrage of mortar and machine gun fire. The enemy was pouring enfilade fire into the ranks of the Marines. Quickly spotting the two guns responsible for the damage, the corporal boldly rushed across an open area, heaving hand grenades as he ran. Wounded before he reached the first gun, he nevertheless continued his one-man assault and completely destroyed the position. Without stopping, he pushed forward and attacked the second gun with grenades and demolished it before falling from the deadly fire of the Japanese snipers.

HAWKINS, William Dean. First Lieutenant. Medal of Honor: b. Fort Scott, Neb., Apr. 18, 1914; d. KIA, Betio Is., Nov. 21, 1943. William Hawkins enlisted in the Marine Corps on Jan. 5, 1942 and was assigned to the 7th Recruit Bn., Recruit Depot, San Diego. He then joined the 2nd Marines, 2nd Mar. Div., completed Scout-Snipers' School at Camp Elliott, San Diego, and on July 1, 1942 embarked on board the USS *Crescent City* for the Pacific area. A private first class when he went overseas, he was quickly promoted to corporal and then to sergeant. On Nov. 17, 1942, he was commissioned a second lieutenant while taking part in the Guadalcanal campaign in the battle for the Solomons. On June 1, 1943, he was promoted to first lieutenant. Less than six months later, he was killed in action leading a scout-sniper platoon in the attack on Betio Is. during the assault on Tarawa. During the two-day assault, Lt. Hawkins led attacks on pill boxes and installations, personally initiated an assault on a hostile position fortified by five enemy machine guns, refused to withdraw after being seriously wounded, and destroyed three more pill boxes before he was mortally wounded on Nov. 21, 1943. In recognition of his leadership and daring action against enemy positions, the air strip on Betio Is. was named Hawkins Field in his honor. With his unit Lt. Hawkins also shared in the two Presidential Unit Citations awarded the 1st Mar. Div. (Reinf.) for heroic action during the Guadalcanal and Tarawa campaigns. His citation accompanying the Medal of Honor reads, in part: " . . . as CO of a Scout-Sniper Platoon attached to the 2nd Marines, 2nd Mar. Div., in action against Japanese-held Tarawa in the Gilbert Is., Nov. 20 and 21, 1943. The first to disembark from the jeep lighter, Lt. Hawkins unhesitatingly moved forward under heavy enemy fire at the end of the Betio pier, neutralizing emplacements in coverage of troops assaulting the main beach positions. Fearlessly leading his men on to join the forces fighting desperately to gain a beachhead, he repeatedly risked his life throughout the day and night to direct and lead attacks on pill boxes and installations with grenades and demolitions. At dawn on the following day, Lt. Hawkins returned to the dangerous mission of clearing the limited beachhead of Japanese resistance, personally initiating an assault on a hostile position fortified by five enemy machine guns and, crawling forward in the face of withering fire, boldly fired point-blank into the loopholes and completed the destruction with grenades. Refusing to withdraw after being seriously wounded in the chest during this skirmish, Lt. Hawkins steadfastly carried the fight to the enemy, destroying three more pill boxes before he was caught in a burst of Japanese shell fire and mortally wounded. . . ."

HAYDEN, Sterling Walter. Captain. Served with the Office of Strategic Services (OSS) during WWII: b. Montclair, N.J., Mar. 26, 1916. At the age of 17, Sterling Hayden shipped out of New London, Conn., as a seaman aboard the schooner *Puritan.* For the next nine years he followed the sea as a seaman, navigator, first officer and finally as master. By 1941 Sterling Hayden was fast becoming known to millions of American movie-goers. In Oct. of that year Hayden decided that he wanted an active part in the conflict which was sweeping Europe and was soon to engulf America. He spent the next six months in Scotland and England, training with commando and parachute units. In Oct. 1942, Hayden enlisted in the MCR as a private and was sent to Parris Is., S.C., for recruit training. Upon completion of his training in Dec. of the same year, he was recommended for assignment to Officers' School, and was transferred to Quantico, to attend OCS and Reserve Officers' Class. He graduated on Apr. 21, 1943, and received a commission as second lieutenant in the MCR on the same day. The following month, the CMC received a request from the Director of Strategic Services that Lt. Hayden be transferred to OSS for duty. The transfer was accomplished on June 25, 1943, and two days later Hayden legally changed his name to John Hamilton. After a short period of indoctrination into the OSS, "John Hamilton" boarded a plane and reported to the Strategic Services Officer at Cairo, Egypt, for duty. The next two years of Hamilton's career are shrouded in the veil of mystery which surrounded the activities of all who were connected with the OSS. The official records indicate that he was promoted to first lieutenant on Sept. 13, 1944, and that he received his captaincy on Feb. 14, 1945. He participated in the Naples-Foggia campaign and received a commendation for establishing Air Crew Rescue Unit Teams in enemy-occupied territory. He was also awarded a Bronze Arrowhead which is given for parachuting into enemy-held territory. Hayden was also authorized to wear a bronze combat star for participation in action against the enemy in the Balkan countries, and was awarded the Silver Star Medal for gallantry in action in the Mediterranean Theater. The accompanying citation simply states: "Lt. Hamilton (Hayden) displayed great courage in making hazardous sea voyages in enemy-infested waters and reconnaissance through enemy-held areas." Capt. "John Hamilton" was relieved from active duty on Dec. 24, 1945.

HAYES, Charles Harold. Major General. Assistant Commandant of the Marine Corps, HQMC, Washington, D.C.: b. San Marcial, N.M., Sept. 18, 1906. Charles Hayes graduated from high school in Albuquerque and, a year later, attended Colorado A&M College for a year before entering the U.S. Naval Academy in 1926. Graduating from the Academy on June 5, 1930, he was commissioned a Marine second lieutenant. The following June, he completed Marine Officers' Basic School at the Philadelphia Navy Yard. In July 1931, he reported to the MB, Quantico, where, during the next three years, he served with the Barracks Detachment and the 1st and 10th Marines. In addition, he served with the 1st Bn., 1st Marines, aboard the battleships *Wyoming* and *Arkansas* from Jan. to May 1932, and with the U.S. Electoral Mission in Nicaragua from July to Dec. of that same year. He also completed the Battalion Officers' Artillery School at Quantico before leaving in June 1934 to join the Marine Detachment aboard the aircraft carrier *Lexington*. Returning from sea duty in Nov. 1934, he was promoted to first lieutenant and entered aviation training at Pensacola, Fla., the following month. He was designated a naval aviator in Apr. 1936. That June he returned to Quantico to serve with Scouting Squadron 7-M, Bombing Squadron 1-M, and Utility Squadron 1-M. He was promoted to captain in July 1937. Leaving Quantico in June 1940, he reported the following month to the NAS, San Diego, Calif., where he was assigned to Marine Utility Squadron 2 (later redesignated Utility Squadron 252). He departed for Pearl Harbor in Jan. 1941, and with the squadron helped set up a new MCAS

at Ewa, Oahu, Hawaii. Just four days before the Pearl Harbor attack, he sailed for San Diego to become Executive Officer of Marine Fighter Squadron 251. He was promoted to major in Jan. 1942. In June 1942, Hayes sailed with the squadron for Noumea, New Caledonia, and several weeks later moved to Espiritu Santo in the New Hebrides Islands. He was awarded the Navy Distinguished Service Medal for his accomplishments in the crucial early days of the Guadalcanal campaign when he was sent to that island by Vice Admiral John S. McCain, Commander, Aircraft, South Pacific, to expedite the completion of vital Henderson Field. Now a major, he landed there on Aug. 15, 1942, with a Navy construction unit and four shiploads of hard-to-get aviation supplies and, despite daily Japanese air raids, had the field ready for operation within four days. The first planes arrived on Aug. 20 and he remained on the island as operations officer of the airstrip until Sept. 5, 1942, shortly after his promotion to lieutenant colonel. Later in the campaign he served as Assistant Operations Officer of the 1st MAW. Returning to the States in Mar. 1943, Lt. Col. Hayes saw duty as Executive Officer of Air Operational Training Squadron 8 at Cherry Point, N.C. In Dec. 1943, he returned to the Pacific area to become Air Officer on the Staff of the Commander, 3rd Amphibious Corps. He was promoted to colonel in Jan. 1944. Awarded the Legion of Merit in that assignment, Col. Hayes took part in the planning and execution of the Green Island, Emirau, Leyte, and Luzon invasions and the planning phase of the Palau operation. He arrived in Tokyo Bay with the initial occupation forces on the day of the surrender, and in Oct. 1945 returned to the States. Ordered to Cherry Point, Col. Hayes served as Chief of

Staff of the MCAS until Dec. 1947, and as commander of MAG 11 for the next six months. He left Cherry Point in June 1948, to enter the Senior Course at the Naval War College, Newport, R.I. Completing the course in May 1949, he was assigned to the Office of the Chief of Naval Operations in Washington as Assistant Head of the Aviation Liaison and Special Projects Section, Strategic Plans Division. He became the head of the section in Oct. 1950, and held that post until he was ordered to Korea in Aug. 1952. For outstanding service in the Korean War from Sept. 1952 to June 1953, as Assistant Chief of Staff, G-3 (Operations), 1st MAW, Col. Hayes was awarded a second Legion of Merit with Combat "V." He left Korea for Hawaii in June 1953 to become Deputy Chief of Staff, FMF, Pacific. In Aug. 1954, he was named CO of MCAS, Kaneohe Bay, Oahu. He was promoted to brigadier general in Oct. 1955, following his return to Washington, and assumed duty that month as Marine Corps Liaison Officer to the Office of the Vice Chief of Naval Operations. In July 1956, Hayes was appointed a member of the Cordiner Advisory Committee on Professional and Technical Compensation in the Armed Forces by Secretary of Defense Charles E. Wilson. On completing his assignment in Washington, he was transferred to Japan where he assumed command of the 1st MAW in Dec. 1957. Following his return from the Far East in May 1959, Gen. Hayes was assigned to MCAS, El Toro, Calif., as CG of the 3rd MAW. He was promoted to major general in June 1959. In Jan. 1960, Hayes became Deputy Commander, FMF, Pacific, at Camp H. M. Smith, Oahu, and served there until Sept. 1961. Assigned to HQMC the following month, he assumed the post of Deputy Chief of Staff (Plans), later re-

designated Deputy Chief of Staff (Plans and Programs). He is now Assistant Commandant of the Marine Corps.

HEISCH, Henry William. Private. Medal of Honor: b. Latendorf, Germany, June 10, 1872; d. July 10, 1941. Pvt. Heisch's citation reads, in part: " . . . for bravery in crossing the river at Tientsin, China, June 20, 1900, in a small boat with three other men under a heavy fire, Heisch assisted in destroying buildings occupied by the enemy. . . ."

HELMS, John Henry. Sergeant. Medal of Honor: b. Chicago, Ill., Mar. 16, 1874; d. Feb. 17, 1919. John Helms enlisted in the Marine Corps on July 6, 1897, at HQMC, Washington, D.C. His citation reads, in part: " . . . while serving on board the USS *Chicago*, for heroism in rescuing Ishi Tomizi, ship's cook, from drowning at Montevideo, Uruguay, Jan. 10, 1901."

HENDERSON, Archibald. Brigadier General. 5th Commandant of the Marine Corps — Oct. 17, 1820, to Jan. 6, 1859: b. Colchester, Fairfax County Va., Jan. 21, 1783; d. Washington, D.C., Jan. 6, 1859. Archibald Henderson was appointed a second lieutenant in the Marine Corps on June 4, 1806; was promoted to first lieutenant Mar. 6, 1807; to captain Apr. 1, 1811; and appointed a major, by brevet, in the year 1814. As a captain he served during the War of 1812 on board the U.S. Frigate *Constitution*, and participated in the engagement between that vessel and the *Java* on Dec. 29, 1812. He was also in the engagements with the *Cyane* and *Levant* on Feb. 20, 1812. During the years between the second war with Great Britain, and the year he was appointed commandant, Henderson was on duty at such posts and stations as Bos-

Henderson

ton, Mass.; Portsmouth, N.H.; HQMC; and New Orleans, La. The years from 1820 to 1835 were marked by neither unusual nor outstanding activities on the part of the Marine Corps other than its part in the suppression of piracy in the West Indies, and the operations in the early 1830s against the pirates of Quallah Battoo. During the war with the Seminole and Creek Indians in Georgia and Florida in 1836-37, in which the Marine Corps took an active part, Commandant Henderson tacked a famous sign on his door which read:

HAVE GONE TO FLORIDA TO FIGHT INDIANS. WILL BE BACK WHEN THE WAR IS OVER.

A. Henderson
Col. Commandant

He then went into the field with his command, sharing in the dangers and expo-

sures of that campaign. For his services in checking Indian hostilities, he was advanced in rank to brigadier general. During the Mexican War, which was preceded by much military activity on the part of the Marine Corps during the years 1845-46 on the west coast, Henderson ably administered the affairs of the Marine Corps. The success attained by the Corps during war operations and other activities, including its expansion and development from a small fighting force into a well-organized and very formidable arm of the nation's military forces, was due in no small measure to the leadership and ability of its commandant. During the years between the Mexican war and the Civil War, the Marine Corps, under the ever watchful eye and direction of Commandant Henderson, was by no means an idle organization. In 1852-53, the Marines took part in the famous expeditions of Commodore Perry to Japan. In 1855 they participated in an expedition to Uruguay as a result of an insurrection at Montevideo, and in 1856 fought an engagement with the hostile Indians at Seattle in the Washington Territory. Also, during the same year, Marines took part in the capture of the Barrier Forte in China. In the year 1857, during the "Know Nothing" political excitement, the Marines were ordered upon the request of the mayor of Washington, D.C., to suppress an armed mob of "hired roughs and bullies." These men had been imported from Baltimore to take possession of the election booths, and the situation had gotten beyond the control of the civil authorities. During the serious riot, a cannon was put into position by a large crowd of "Plug Uglies" and others who threatened that unless the Marines were instantly withdrawn the piece would be discharged into their ranks. "General Henderson deliberately went up to the piece and placed his body against the muzzle, thereby preventing it from being aimed at the Marines, just at the moment when it was about to be discharged." This act of heroism brought an abrupt end to the riot, and the Marines restored order. For more than 38 years Henderson had guided the destiny of the Corps, battling for its position as a strong armed force in the American military structure and, at the same time, attending religiously to every minute administrative detail. When the "grand old man of the Marine Corps," who had served as Commandant under eleven presidents, died in office at the age of 76, he left his beloved Marine Corps with a heritage of tradition and an *esprit de corps* that less vigorous commandants and trying days could never dispel.

HENDERSON, Margaret Monroe. Colonel. Director of Women Marines: b. Cameron, Tex., Feb. 6, 1911. Margaret Henderson graduated from high school at Kenedy, Tex. in 1928, and received her BBA degree upon graduation from the University of Texas in 1932. She then taught in secondary schools of Lubbock, Tex. until 1943 when she entered the Marine Corps. After completing the Marine Corps Women's Reserve Officer Training School at Mt. Holyoke, Mass., she was commissioned a second lieutenant in the Reserve on June 30, 1943. During WWII, she served as an instructor at Women Marine Schools, Camp Lejeune, N.C., and as Officer in Charge of the Business School, Marine Corps Institute, Washington. Returning to Camp Lejeune in Sept. 1945, she became Executive Officer of the Women's Reserve Bn. Detached from active duty in May 1946, Margaret Henderson returned to Lubbock, where she served as an instructor

at Texas Technological College for two years. In Nov. 1948, she was integrated into the Regular Marine Corps and returned to active duty. During subsequent tours of duty, she served consecutively as Commander of the Women's Recruit Training Bn., Marine Corps Recruit Depot, Parris Is., S.C.; as Head, Women's Affairs Section, Division of Plans and Policies, HQMC; and as Commander of the Women Officers' Training Detachment, MCS, Quantico. She also saw duty on the west coast from Jan. 1955 to Mar. 1957 as Assistant G-1, at the Marine Corps Base, Camp Pendleton, Calif. In Apr. 1957, Lt. Col. Henderson was reassigned to HQMC as Head, Women's Affairs Section, G-1 Division. On Feb. 13, 1959, she succeeded Col. Julia Hamblet as Director of Women Marines.

HEYWOOD, Charles. Major General. 9th Commandant of the Marine Corps — June 30, 1891, to Oct. 2, 1903. b. in Maine, Oct. 3, 1839; d. Washington, D.C., Feb. 26, 1915. Charles Heywood was appointed a second lieutenant in the Marine Corps on Apr. 5, 1858. During that year he was stationed at the MB, Washington, D.C., and at Brooklyn, N.Y. While on duty in Brooklyn he served in the Quarantine riots at Staten Island, N.Y. He performed special duty on the *Niagara*, and later on board the *St. Louis* of the Home Squadron, the ship seeking filibusters in Central America. He was invalided from Aspinwall (Colon) in Jan. 1860, and later was ordered to the sloop of war *Cumberland*, flagship of the Squadron of Observation at Vera Cruz, Mex. In Mar. 1861, he returned to duty on board the *Cumberland*, and with that vessel took part in the destruction of the Norfolk Navy Yard during the Civil War. In May 1861, Heywood was promoted to first lieutenant and as such landed

Heywood

with the Marines at Hatteras Inlet, where he was present at the capture of Forts Clark and Hatteras. He was advanced to captain in Nov. of that year, and during the winter of 1861-62 participated actively in a number of boat expeditions in the James River. In the fight between the *Cumberland* and the *Merrimac* in Mar. 1862, his conduct was particularly noteworthy while commanding the after gun deck division, firing the last gun in the fight and saving himself by jumping overboard as the *Cumberland* went down with her flag flying. He was favorably mentioned for his gallant conduct and received the brevet rank of major for his services during the engagement. For some time afterward, both on shore and at sea, he was actively engaged in the search for the notorious raider *Alabama*,

until he applied for duty on board the flagship *Hartford*. He was ordered to that vessel as Fleet Marine Officer of the West Gulf Squadron. He served on shore at Pensacola and was on board the *Hartford* in the battle of Mobile Bay, where he received the brevet rank of lieutenant colonel for gallant and meritorious services. During that engagement he had charge of two 9-inch guns. His services during the Civil War thus secured for him two brevet ranks for distinguished gallantry in the presence of the enemy. From 1865 to 1867 he performed duty on board various ships, serving as Admiral Farragut's Fleet Marine Officer on the European Station and later in the same capacity in the North Atlantic Squadron. During this period he also served for a time at Washington, Norfolk, and Brooklyn. In Nov. 1876, he attained the regular rank of major to which he had been brevetted more than ten years before, and was ordered to command the MB, Washington, D.C. During the serious labor riots of the summer of 1877 Heywood commanded a battalion of Marines at Baltimore, Philadelphia, and Reading, Pa. He was honorably mentioned by Gen. Hancock, U.S. Army, who was in general command, and received thanks from the Navy Department for his services. His next two years of duty carried him to widely separated posts — Mare Island, Calif., and Brooklyn, N.Y. In Apr. 1885, he organized, within 24 hours from the time of the order, a battalion of 250 Marines for duty on the Isthmus of Panama to open the transit. Subsequently under his command on the Isthmus were 800 Marines in addition to a strong detachment of the U.S. Navy and the artillery. For his arduous services the admiral commanding asked Heywood to "receive his grateful acknowledgments." He was promoted to lieutenant colonel on Mar. 9, 1888, and on June 30, 1891 was appointed Colonel Commandant of the Marine Corps. By special acts of Congress he was promoted to brigadier general in Mar. 1899, and to major general in July 1902. The energy, experience, and training which he had shown and obtained in his early days in the Marine Corps were fully brought into play from the moment he assumed command of the Corps. At that time the Marine Corps consisted of 75 officers and 2,100 enlisted men; but the number gradually rose during Gen. Heywood's tenure of office until, at the time of his retirement in 1903, it had reached the total of 278 officers and 7,532 enlisted personnel. He was always aware of the problem of more closely associating the Corps with the Navy so that the work of the two could be in closest harmony. He was the first to establish a regular system of examinations for officers for promotion, and set up the system of officers' schools, which has continued with slight interruption since then. By increasing the efficiency of the Corps he tried to demonstrate to the Navy how absolutely essential it was as an auxiliary to the naval service. Under his administration the number of Marine Corps posts were increased from 12 to 21. There was scarcely a regular post at which Gen. Heywood was not able to provide new barracks or officers' quarters. He caused the regular system of target practice to be established and adopted good conduct medals for the betterment of the discipline in the Marine Corps. The declaration of war with Spain found the Marine Corps prepared. Gen. Heywood closed a most distinguished career of more than 45 years as a commissioned officer in the Marine Corps, when on Oct. 3, 1903, in accordance with law, having attained the age of 64 years, he was placed on the retired list. His death occurred in Washington, D.C. on Feb. 26, 1915, and his remains were interred in the Arlington National Cemetery.

HILL, Frank. Private. Medal of Honor: b. Hartford, Conn., Aug. 13, 1864. Frank Hill enlisted in the Marine Corps on Sept. 14, 1896, at Portsmouth, Va. He received the nation's highest military award on Aug. 15, 1899. His citation reads, in part: " . . . while serving aboard the USS *Nashville,* for extraordinary heroism and coolness while cutting the cables leading from Cienfuegos, Cuba, May 11, 1898, under heavy fire of the enemy. . . ." Hill was discharged from the Corps on Oct. 12, 1901.

HILL, Walter Newell. Brigadier General. Medal of Honor: b. Haverhill, Mass., Sept. 29, 1881; d. St. Albans Naval Hospital, N.Y., June 29, 1955. While a captain, Hill was awarded the Medal of Honor for bravery on Apr. 21-22, 1914, when a Marine and Naval landing force occupied Vera Cruz during a crisis between the United States and Mexico. His citation states in part: " . . . Captain Hill was in both days' fighting at the head of his company, and was eminent and conspicuous in his conduct, leading his men with skill and courage." Walter Hill was a student at Harvard University prior to his appointment as a Marine second lieutenant Feb. 1, 1904. He served at sea, at various posts and stations in the United States and in Cuba, China, and the Philippines. He went on to serve in France during WWI, and in the Virgin Islands, Haiti, and the Dominican Republic. He was awarded the Haitian Medaille Militare for service in that country during operations against rebel bandits. Upon retirement in Sept. 1938, he was advanced to brigadier general on the retired list for having been specially commended in combat. Returning to active duty in Jan. 1942, he served at HQMC, Washington, D.C., until the end of the war.

HOCHMUTH, Bruno Arthur. Brigadier General. Deputy Chief of Staff Research and Development, HQMC, Washington, D.C.: b. Houston, Tex., May 10, 1911. Bruno Hochmuth completed high school in Houston in 1930. In June 1935, he graduated from Texas A&M College, receiving a Bachelor of Science degree in industrial education. He was commissioned a Marine second lieutenant in July 1935. After completing Basic School at the Philadelphia Navy Yard, he joined the Marine Detachment, Texas Centennial, Dallas, Tex, in June 1936. In Dec. 1936, he was transferred to the 2nd Bn., 6th Marines in San Diego. Departing for Shanghai, China in Aug. 1937, he served briefly with the 6th Marines then saw two and one-half years' duty with the 4th Marines. On his return to the States, he was detached to the 7th Defense Bn. in Sept. 1940. The following Feb., he embarked with the battalion for American and British Samoa. In Mar. 1943, after two years overseas, he was assigned briefly to the Antiaircraft Artillery School, Camp Lejeune, N.C. From June 1943 to May 1944, he served as Assistant Director, Command and Staff School, Quantico, prior to embarking again for the Pacific area. He participated in the campaigns at Saipan and Tinian as Assistant Operations Officer with the 3rd Amphibious Corps, and later served as CO of the 3rd Bn., 4th Marines, in the Okinawa campaign. As Executive Officer of the 4th Marines, he made the initial landing on Japan on Aug. 29, 1945, and on Sept. 2 of the same year attended the formal surrender ceremony at Yokosuka. Return-

ing to the States in Aug. 1947, he saw three years' duty at HQMC, then entered the Industrial College, Fort McNair, Washington, D.C. He graduated in June 1951, and returned to Camp Lejeune as CO, 2nd Marines, 2nd Mar. Div. In July 1952, he was named G-1, 2nd Mar. Div., Camp Lejeune. Ordered to Kingston, Ont. in Sept. 1953, he served as Instructor, Canadian Army Staff College, for two years. He again went to the Far East in Aug. 1955 to serve as G-4, 3rd Mar. Div., Japan and Okinawa. On Aug. 1956, he was assigned to Quantico as a Member of the Advanced Research Group, Marine Corps Educational Center. In July 1957, he was transferred to the Marine Corps Recruit Depot, San Diego, serving as Chief of Staff through Oct. 1959. On Nov. 1, 1959, he was promoted to brigadier general and became CG of the Marine Corps Recruit Depot, San Diego. He assumed duties as CG, Recruit Training Command, Dec. 1, 1959. On Jan. 1, 1960, he became Deputy Chief of Staff, Research and Development, HQMC, Washington, D.C.

HOFFMAN, Charles. Gunnery Sergeant. Real name of JANSON, Ernest A. (*q.v.*).

HOLCOMB, Thomas. General. 17th Commandant of the Marine Corps—Dec. 1, 1936, to Dec. 31, 1943: b. New Castle, Del., Aug. 5, 1879. Thomas Holcomb was educated in Delaware and in Washington, D.C. He was appointed a second lieutenant from civil life on Apr. 13, 1900. Holcomb was on detached duty with a company of Marines, organized for service with a Marine Bn. attached to the North Atlantic Fleet, from Sept. 1902 to Apr. 1903. He was promoted to first lieutenant Mar. 3, 1903. He served in the Philippine Is. from Apr. 1904 to Aug. 1905, and from Oct. to Nov. 1906.

Holcomb

Lt. Holcomb was on duty with the Legation Guard, Peking, China, from Sept. 1905 to Sept. 1906, and again from Dec. 1908 to July 1910, being then detached from the Legation Guard. On May 13, 1908, he was promoted to captain. He continued on duty in Peking as Attaché on the staff of the American Minister for study of the Chinese language and remained on that duty until May 1911. In Dec. 1911 he was again ordered to the Legation at Peking to continue his study of the Chinese language, and remained there until May 1914. Thomas Holcomb has been prominently identified with the development of rifle shooting, and served as Inspector of Target Practice, in the Marine Corps from Oct. 1914 to Aug. 1917. In addition, he was a member of the Marine Corps Rifle Teams of 1901,

1902, 1903, 1907, 1908, and 1911, and of teams representing the United States in the Palma Trophy Match in 1902 and 1903. On Aug. 29, 1916, he was promoted to major. From Aug. 1917 to Jan. 1918, he commanded the 2nd Bn., 6th Regt., at MB, Quantico, in preparation for overseas service. From Feb. 1918 to July 1919, he served with the AEF in France, in command of the 2nd Bn. until Aug. 1918, and thereafter as second in command of the 6th Regt. He participated in all engagements in which the Regiment took part — the Aisne defensive (Chateau-Thierry); the Aisne-Marne offensive (Soissons); the Marbache sector; the St.-Mihiel offensive; the Meuse-Argonne (Champagne) offensive; the Meuse-Argonne (Argonne Forest) offensive; and the march to the Rhine in Germany following the Armistice. He was promoted to lieutenant colonel on June 4, 1920. In recognition of his distinguished services he was awarded the Navy Cross, the Silver Star with three Oak Leaf Clusters, a Meritorious Service Citation by the Commander-in-Chief, AEF, the Purple Heart, and was three times cited in General Orders of the 2nd Div., AEF. The French government conferred on him the Cross of the Legion of Honor, and three times awarded him the Croix de Guerre with Palm. From Sept. 1922 to June 1924, he commanded the MB, Naval Station, Guantanamo Bay, Cuba, and on his return to the States, was ordered to the Command and General Staff School of the Army at Fort Leavenworth, completing the course as a Distinguished Graduate in June 1925. He was then ordered to HQMC, for duty in the Division of Operations and Training, where he remained until June 1927. On Dec. 22, 1928 he was promoted to colonel. From Aug. 1927 to Feb. 1930, Col. Holcomb commanded the Marine Detachment,

American Legation, Peiping, China. In June 1930, he went to the Naval War College as a student, Senior Course, from which he graduated in June 1931. He was then ordered to the Army War College, from which course he graduated in June 1932. From June 1932 to Jan. 1935, Holcomb served in the Office of Naval Operations, Navy Department. He was promoted to brigadier general on Feb. 1, 1935. He then served as Commandant of the MCS in Quantico until Nov. 1936, when he was ordered to HQMC to assume the office of Major General Commandant on Dec. 1, 1936. During his tenure he expanded the organization from 15,000 to 305,000 fighting men. Not only did he show "superlative ability" in directing this expansion, but he also inculcated the greater Marine Corps with the *esprit de corps* of the smaller organization, as typified in the invasion of Tarawa. On Dec. 1, 1940, he was reappointed Major General Commandant for four years by the President. With his advancement to lieutenant general on Jan. 20, 1942, Gen. Holcomb became the highest ranking officer ever to command the Corps. Upon retiring as Marine Corps Commandant on Jan. 1, 1944, Gen. Holcomb was placed on the retired list, raised to full general, and then ordered to active duty. After more than 40 years of service, he went off the active rolls of the Marine Corps on Apr. 10, 1944 to take over his new job as Minister to South Africa. He served in that capacity for four years before retiring on a farm near St. Mary's City, Maryland.

HORTON, William Charlie. Private. Medal of Honor: b. Chicago, Ill., July 21, 1876. William Horton enlisted in the Marine Corps on Apr. 22, 1898, at Philadelphia, Pa. He was awarded the Medal of Honor on Jan. 5, 1902. His citation reads, in part: "...for distinguished conduct in the presence of the enemy at Peking, China, July 21 to Aug. 17, 1900. Horton assisted in erecting barricades under heavy fire...." He was discharged from the Corps on Apr. 21, 1903.

HUDSON, Michael. Sergeant. Medal of Honor: b. Sligo County, Ireland, 1834. Michael Hudson enlisted in the Marine Corps at Brooklyn, N.Y. on Sept. 12, 1861. His citation reads, in part: "...on board the USS *Brooklyn* during action against rebel forts and gunboats and with the ram *Tennessee* in Mobile Bay, Aug. 5, 1864. Despite severe damage to his ship and the loss of several men on board as enemy fire raked the decks, Sgt. Hudson fought his gun with skill and courage throughout the furious 2-hour battle which resulted in the surrender of the rebel ram *Tennessee*."

HUGHES, John Arthur. "Johnny the Hard." Lieutenant Colonel. Medal of Honor: b. New York, N.Y., Nov. 2, 1880; d. Veterans Administration Hospital, St. Petersburg, Fla. John Hughes served as an enlisted man in the Marine Corps from Nov. 1900 to Dec. 1901. He was commissioned a second lieutenant on Dec. 17, 1901. During his career he saw service in the Philippines, Cuba, Panama, Santo Domingo, Mexico, and at various posts throughout the States. He served in WWI in France and was wounded on two occasions. He was also wounded in Santo Domingo in 1916. He was awarded the Medal of Honor for his gallantry in action around Vera Cruz, Mexico, "...for distinguished conduct in battle engagements of Vera Cruz, Apr. 21 and 22, 1914; was in both days' fighting at the head of his company and was eminent and conspicuous in his conduct, leading his men with skill and courage...." He was retired from the Corps on July 3, 1919.

HULBERT, Henry Lewis. First Lieutenant. Medal of Honor: b. Kingston-upon-Hull, England, Jan. 12, 1867; d. KIA, France, near Mont Blanc, Oct. 4, 1918. Henry Hulbert enlisted in the Marine Corps on Mar. 28, 1898. On Apr. 1, 1899, he distinguished himself in the face of the enemy at Samoa when he refused to desert disabled comrades, although his own life was endangered. For his exceptional bravery, he was awarded the Medal of Honor. At the outbreak of WWI, he was appointed a marine gunner, and joined the 5th Regt. of Marines and sailed for France. Gunner Hulbert was cited for bravery at Chateau-Thierry by Gen. John J. Pershing in the following: "On June 6, 1918, displayed coolness and extraordinary heroism throughout the attack. During the counterattack of the enemy, he, armed with a rifle, charged and routed a group of machine gunners." Death in action in the Battle of Mont Blanc Ridge came to this heroic officer shortly after he had been promoted to the rank of first lieutenant.

HUNT, Leroy Philip. General (Retired): b. Newark, N.J., Mar. 17, 1892. Leroy Hunt was commissioned a second lieutenant in the Marine Corps on Mar. 16, 1917, and joined the MB, Norfolk, Va. as a student at the Marine Officers' School. He sailed for France in Aug. 1917, and as a member of the 5th Mar. Regt. participated in the Verdun Defensive sector, and in the Aisne-Marne defensive (Chateau-Thierry) in June, 1918, where he was gassed in action. He took part in the Aisne-Marne offensive (Soissons) where he was wounded in action, the St.-Mihiel offensive, the Meuse-Argonne offensive (Champagne) and the Meuse-Argonne

offensive (Argonne Forest). He was a member of the Army of Occupation in Germany and sailed for home on July 25, 1919. For repeated acts of heroism in action near St.-Etienne, France, in Oct. 1918, Hunt was awarded the Distinguished Service Cross. Upon return to the States, he was assigned recruiting duty at Portland, Ore., and then to the staff of MCS, Quantico, and later to the MB, Quantico, again becoming a member of the 5th Mar. Regt. In June 1924, he went to sea as CO of the Marine Detachment aboard the USS *Maryland*. Following sea duty he was attached to the MCB at San Diego and for a short time acted as a CO of the Western Mail Guard Detachment. Duty overseas with the 3rd Mar. Brig. in Shanghai, China, as a battalion commander was followed by duty at the MB, Quantico, where he was successively Post Adjutant and a student at the Field Officers' Course, MCS, graduating in June 1930. Foreign shore duty with the Nicaragua National Guard Detachment as CO Northern Area and Intelligence and Operations Officer followed. Upon return to the States, Hunt was successively assigned to the Naval Training Station, Great Lakes, Ill.; HQMC; and the MB, Quantico, where he joined the 5th Mar. Regt. In 1935, he went on temporary duty to Alaska with the Matanuska Colonization project. A tour of duty as Registrar of the Marine Corps Institute in Washington and Executive Officer and CO, MB, Washington, D.C., was followed by an assignment as a student at the Senior Course, Naval War College, Newport, R.I. After graduation in May 1939, he became Force Marine Officer aboard the USS *California*, where he remained until ordered to the 2nd Mar. Div. in Feb. 1941 as CO of Special and Service Troops. For a short period in June 1941, he was on temporary duty in Iceland, and from then until Sept. 1942, he was a member of the 1st Mar. Div., first as Chief of Staff, and secondly as CO of the 5th Mar. Regt. In the latter capacity he led the regiment in the seizure and defense of Guadalcanal. Upon return to the States he became Area and Corps Inspector of the Amphibious Command, Pacific Fleet, which position he held until ordered to the Pacific to assume command of the Marine Garrison Forces, 14th Naval District. He was next ordered to the 2nd Mar. Div. as Assistant Division Commander and participated in operations involving the mopping-up of Saipan and Tinian and the capture of Okinawa. Appointed Division Commander, he led the division in the occupation of the Japanese homeland. For a period he was CG, 1st Army Corps. In Feb. 1946, Gen. Hunt returned to the States and assumed duties as CG, Troop Training Unit, Training Command, Amphibious Forces, Pacific Fleet. In Jan. 1947, he became CG, Department of Pacific, San Francisco, and in July, two years later, became CG, FMF, Atlantic, at Norfolk, Va. He was retired from the Corps on July 1, 1951.

HUNT, Martin. Private. Medal of Honor: b. County of Mayo, Ireland, July 9, 1873; d. July 22, 1938. Martin Hunt enlisted in the Marine Corps in Boston, Mass., on Aug. 27, 1896. He received the Medal of Honor on July 2, 1915. His citation reads, in part: "... for distinguished conduct in the presence of the enemy at the battle of Peking, China, June 20 to July 16, 1900. ..." Pvt. Hunt was discharged from the Corps at Cavite, P.I. on Aug. 26, 1901.

HUNTINGTON, Robert W. Colonel: b. Connecticut, Dec. 3, 1840; d. Charlottesville, Va., Nov. 3, 1917. Robert Huntington accepted a commission as second

lieutenant in the Marine Corps on June 5, 1861, shortly after the Civil War began. In the War between the States he fought at the First Battle of Bull Run, and later served with the south Atlantic blockading squadron. After the Civil War he served the normal peacetime tours of sea and shore duty. In 1885 he was on an expedition to Panama. Four years later he was commanding the Marine detachment on board the USS *Trenton* in Samoa when his ship was caught in a hurricane and totally wrecked. When the United States went to war with Spain, he commanded a battalion of Marines and made a landing at Guantanamo Bay, Cuba, on June 10, 1889. His battalion drove off the Spanish troops, and secured Guantanamo Bay as a base of operations for the American navy. After a long, active career, he retired on Jan. 15, 1900.

HURST, Edward Hunter. Colonel. Selected for promotion to brigadier general by the July 1962 Selection Board at HQMC: b. Fort Valley, Ga., Dec. 18, 1916. Edward Hurst graduated from Mercer University at Macon, Ga., in June 1938, with a Bachelor of Arts degree in journalism. While in college, he enlisted in the MCR, Apr. 13, 1936, and completed the Platoon Leaders' Class at Quantico, in the summers of 1936 and 1937. Designated an honor graduate of the PLC, he was commissioned a second lieutenant on June 27, 1938, and assigned to active duty. On completing Basic School in May 1939, Lt. Hurst served consecutively with the Marine Detachment aboard the USS *New Mexico;* at the Rifle Range, Parris Is., S.C.; and as commander of the Aviation Detachment at the MB, NAS, Pensacola, Fla. He was promoted to first lieutenant in Aug. 1941; to captain in Feb. 1942; and to major in Mar. 1943. Shortly after his last promotion, he became CO of the Marine Training Detachment, U.S. Naval Reserve Midshipmen's School (Women's Reserve), Northampton, Mass. In July 1943, he moved to Camp Lejeune, N.C., as CO of the Officers' Training School, Marine Corps Women's Reserve Schools. He later completed the Command and Staff Course at MCS, Quantico. In Apr. 1944, Maj. Hurst sailed for the Pacific area as CO, 3rd Bn., 7th Marines, 1st Mar. Div. The Silver Star Medal was awarded him for conspicuous gallantry in action during the seizure and occupation of Peleliu in Sept. 1944. Forced to land his assault battalion of amphibious tanks in single file because of the heavily barricaded beach, he personally reconnoitered the front lines and directed his battalion's attack on Japanese caves and blockhouses, annihilating one enemy reinforced battalion of approximately 1600 men. The following month, he was promoted to lieutenant colonel. In Apr. 1945, Lt. Col. Hurst participated in the action which earned him the Navy Cross on Okinawa. He was wounded in action on June 19 and subsequently evacuated to the States for hospitalization. Following the war, he served in the Division of Plans and Policies at HQMC until May 1947. In addition, he served as Marine Corps Liaison Officer, Secretary's Committee of Research on Reorganization, Office of the Secretary of the Navy. In June 1947, he returned to MCS, Quantico, where he

completed the Instructors' Orientation Course, then served as Leadership Section Chief and Officer in Charge of the Student Battalion at the Basic School, until Dec. 1949. In July 1950, on completing the Swedish Language School at the U.S. Naval School in Anacostia, he assumed duty at the American Embassy, Stockholm, Sweden, as Assistant Naval Attaché and Assistant Naval Attaché for Air. He returned to the States in Nov. 1952, and the following month joined the 2nd Mar. Div. at Camp Lejeune. He served consecutively as Regimental Executive Officer of the 8th Marines, and Assistant Chief of Staff, G-3, of the 2nd Div. until June 1954. During the latter assignment, he was promoted to colonel. In July 1954, Col. Hurst was assigned to HQMC, serving in the G-3 Division for three years, as Head, JCS and Plans Review Section, and Head, Plans Branch, respectively. He completed the National War College, Washington, D.C. in June 1958. From July 1958 until Mar. 1960, he served in Hawaii on the Joint Staff of the Commander in Chief, Pacific, as Head, Southeast Asia Plans and Policy Section. In May 1960, he became CO of the Schools Bn., Camp Pendleton, and Camp Commander of Camp Del Mar. He assumed command of the 3rd Mar. Regt., 3rd Mar. Div. (Reinf.), on Okinawa, in Mar. 1962, and in addition serves as Camp Commander of Camp Schwab.

I

IAMS, Ross Lindsey. Major (Retired). Medal of Honor: b. May 5, 1879, Graysville, Pa. Under various temporary appointments as marine gunner, first and second lieutenant, and captain, Iams served with the Corps until he was placed on the retired list on Nov. 1, 1932. His foreign service record includes eleven month in France in 1918-19, and assignments in Haiti, Mexico, China, the Philippines, and Nicaragua. He was awarded the Medal of Honor for conspicuous gallantry during the Haitian Campaign. His citation states that while in company with members of the 5th, 13th, and 23rd Companies and a Marine and sailor detachment from the USS *Connecticut*, he participated in the attack on Fort Riviere, Haiti, on Nov. 17, 1915. Following a concentrated drive, several different detachments of Marines gradually closed in on the old French bastion fort in an effort to cut off all avenues of retreat for the Caco bandits. Approaching a breach in the wall which was the only entrance to the fort, Iams unhesitatingly jumped through the breach, despite constant fire from the Cacos, and engaged the enemy in desperate hand-to-hand combat until the bastion was captured and Caco resistance neutralized.

J

JACKSON, Arthur J. Captain. Medal of Honor: b. Cleveland, Ohio, Oct. 18, 1924. Arthur Jackson was inducted into the Marine Corps at Portland, Ore., on Jan. 11, 1943. He received his basic training at the Recruit Depot, San Diego, Calif. and soon thereafter joined the 1st Mar. Div. Jackson received a letter of commendation on Cape Gloucester for carrying a wounded Marine to safety in the face of well-entrenched Japanese troops on the slope of a steep hill, thus saving the wounded man's life. His feat, for which he was awarded the Medal of Honor, took place on Peleliu, Palau Islands, when he was a P.F.C. His citation reads, in part: "... while serving with the 3rd Bn., 7th Marines, 1st Mar. Div., in action against enemy Japanese forces on the Is. of Peleliu, Sept. 18, 1944. Boldly taking the initiative when his platoon's left-flank advance was held up by the fire of Japanese troops concealed in strongly fortified positions, P.F.C. Jackson unhesitatingly proceeded forward of our lines, and, courageously defying the heavy barrages, charged a large pillbox housing approximately 35 enemy soldiers. Pouring his automatic fire into the opening of the fixed installation to trap the occupying troops, he hurled white phosphorus grenades and explosive charges brought up by a fellow Marine, demolishing the pillbox and killing all of the enemy. Advancing alone under the continuous fire from other hostile emplacements, he employed similar means to smash two smaller positions in the immediate vicinity. Determined to crush the entire pocket of resistance although harassed on all sides by the shattering blasts of Japanese weapons and covered only by small rifle parties, he stormed one gun position after another, dealing death and destruction to the savagely fighting enemy in his ... drive against the remaining defenses and succeeded in wiping out a total of 12 pillboxes and 50 Japanese soldiers...."

JACOBSON, Douglas Thomas. Captain.

Medal of Honor: b. Rochester, N.Y., Nov. 25, 1925. Capt. Jacobson won the nation's highest award at Iwo Jima. His citation reads, in part: "Promptly destroying a stubborn 20-mm. antiaircraft gun and its crew.... Jacobson waged a relentless battle as his unit fought desperately ... he first destroyed two hostile machine gun positions, then attacked a large block-house, completely neutralizing the forti-fication before dispatching the five-man crew of a second pillbox.... He wiped out an earth-covered rifle emplacement and, confronted by a cluster of similar em-placements...fearlessly advanced, quick-ly reduced all six positions...killed 10 of the enemy, opened fire on a Japanese tank...and smashed the enemy tank's gun turret...." It was reported that Capt. Jacobson destroyed a total of 16 enemy positions and annihilated approximately 75 Japanese.

JANSON, Ernest August. Sergeant Major. Medal of Honor: b. New York, N.Y., Aug. 17, 1878; d. Long Island, N.Y., May 14, 1930. Following nearly ten years of service with the U.S. Army, Ernest Janson en-listed in the Marine Corps on June 14, 1910, at the MB, Bremerton, Wash. He was appointed a corporal on Mar. 14, 1911, and honorably discharged June 13, 1914. He re-enlisted on June 17, 1914, and was appointed a sergeant on Aug. 24, 1914. During this second enlistment, he served on the USS *Nebraska* from July 13, 1914, until Jan. 30, 1915; on detached duty on the USS *Montana* from Jan. 30, 1915 until Feb. 6, 1915; on the USS *Nebraska* again from Feb. 6, 1915 until Oct. 22, 1916; and at Norfolk, Va., from Oct. 22, 1916 until May 25, 1917. Sgt. Janson sailed for France on the USS *De Kalb* on June 14, 1917, and disem-barked at St. Nazaire, France, June 27, 1917. Appointed a gunnery sergeant, a

Janson

temporary warrant for the duration of the war, on July 1, 1917, he served honorably with the 49th Co., 5th Regt., in its vari-ous activities and on June 6, 1918, was severely wounded in action. For his con-spicuous services on that date, Sgt. Jan-son was awarded the Congressional (Army) Medal of Honor and the Navy Medal of Honor. His citation reads, in part: "... in action with the enemy near Chateau-Thierry, France, June 6, 1918. Immediately after his company had reached its objective on Hill 142, several hostile counterattacks were launched against the line before the new position had been consolidated. Gy. Sgt. Janson was attempting to organize a position on the north slope of the hill when he saw 12 of the enemy, armed with five light machine guns, crawling toward his group. Giving the alarm, he rushed the hostile detachment, bayoneted the two leaders, and forced the others to flee, thus abandoning their guns. His quick action, initiative, and courage drove the enemy from a position from which they could have swept the hill with machine gun fire and forced the withdrawal of our troops." The French Medaille Militaire which carries the Croix de Guerre with Palm, the Montenegran Silver Medal, the Portuguese Cruz de Guerra, and the Italian Croce di Guerra were also awarded him for this same act of bravery. In Nov. 1918, Sgt. Janson returned to the States and was admitted to the Naval Hospital, N.Y., for treatment of the wounds received in action on June 6. At the expiration of his second enlistment, April 25, 1919, he was honorably discharged. He re-enlisted May 7, 1919, and served the full term of this enlistment as a recruiter at New York City. He was honorably discharged on May 6, 1923. His 4th enlistment took place May 7, 1923, and he remained on recruiting duty until July 20, 1926, when he was transferred to MB, Quantico. On his return to Quantico, he was reinstated to his wartime rank of gunnery sergeant. He requested retirement the following month. He was advanced one grade to sergeant major on Aug. 31, 1926, and placed on the retired list, Sept. 30, 1926. Janson returned to New York and during his last years lived on Long Island. He died after a brief illness, May 14, 1930, and was buried in Evergreen Cemetery, Brooklyn, N.Y.

JOHN, Philip William. Brigadier General. Member of the Staff of the Commander in Chief, Allied Forces, Southern Europe, Naples, Italy: b. Seattle, Wash., Oct. 6, 1907. After graduation from high school, Philip John attended Whitman College and Oregon State College. He enlisted in the Organized MCR in Feb. 1930, and was commissioned a second lieutenant on Oct. 15, 1935. He was promoted to first lieutenant in Dec. 1938. In Nov. 1940, Lt. John was called to active duty with the 6th Marines in San Diego, Calif. The following May, he joined the 1st Mar. Brig. (Prov.) and embarked for duty in Iceland. While there, he was promoted to captain in Jan. 1942. He was assigned to the 2nd Mar. Div. in Apr. 1942, and served with the division until the end of the war. He was promoted to major in Aug. 1942, and to lieutenant colonel in Dec. 1943. During this period, John commanded the Div. Service Bn., and later saw action in the Saipan, Tinian, and Okinawa operations as Div. Quartermaster until Aug. 1945. On his return to the States in Sept. 1945, Lt. Col. John was named Officer in Charge of the Marine Corps Forwarding Depot, Seattle, Wash. He was integrated into the Regular Marine Corps in July 1946. Reporting to Fairbanks, Alaska, in Nov. 1946, he was an observer with Task Force Frigid, an Army extreme cold weather test force. In June 1947, he began two years' duty as Executive Officer, Barstow Annex, Marine Corps Depot of Supplies, San Francisco, Calif. Following this assignment, he entered the Command and General Staff School at Fort Leavenworth, Kans., in Aug. 1949, and upon graduation in June 1950 was assigned to the Marine Corps Supply Depot, Camp Lejeune, N.C., as Executive Officer. He was promoted to colonel in Feb. 1951. In July 1951, he became CO, Marine Corps Supply Depot, Camp Lejeune, and served in that capacity until Oct. 1953. That month he was transferred to the MCAS, El Toro, Calif., where he served as Staff Supply Officer, Aircraft, FMF, Pacific, until July 1956.

He then joined MCS, Quantico, as a member of the Advanced Research Group, Marine Corps Educational Center. Transferred to Washington, D.C. in June 1957, Col. John was assigned to the Staff of the Quartermaster General, HQMC. He was promoted to brigadier general Jan. 1, 1960, at which time he was designated Director, Materiel Division, Supply Department. Shortly after, he was detached from HQMC to assume his current assignment in Naples, Italy, in Apr. 1960.

JOHNSON, James Edmund. Sergeant. Medal of Honor: b. Pocatello, Idaho, Jan. 1, 1926; d. MIA, Yudam-ni, Korea, Dec. 2, 1950. Sgt. Johnson's citation reads, in part: . . . "while serving as a squad leader in a provisional rifle platoon composed of artillerymen and attached to Co. J, 3rd Bn., 7th Marines, 1st Mar. Div. (Reinf.), in action against enemy aggressor forces at Yudam-ni, Korea on Dec. 2, 1950. Vastly outnumbered by a well-entrenched and cleverly concealed enemy force wearing the uniforms of friendly troops and attacking his platoon's open and unconcealed positions, Sgt. Johnson unhesitatingly took charge of his platoon in the absence of the leader and exhibiting great personal valor in the face of a heavy barrage of hostile fire, coolly proceeded to move about among his men, shouting words of encouragement and inspiration and skillfully directing their fire. Ordered to displace his platoon during the fire fight, he immediately placed himself in an extremely hazardous position from which he could provide covering fire for his men. Fully aware that his voluntary action meant either certain death or capture, he courageously continued to provide effective cover for his men and was last observed in a wounded condition singlehandedly

engaging enemy troops in close hand grenade and hand-to-hand fighting. . . ."

JONES, William Kenefick. Brigadier General. Legislative Assistant to the Commandant of the Marine Corps, HQMC, Washington, D.C.: b. Joplin, Mo., Oct. 23, 1916. William Jones attended Southwest High School in Kansas City, Mo., graduating in 1933. In 1937, he was graduated from the University of Kansas with a Bachelor of Arts degree. While in college, Jones enlisted in the MCR Apr. 25, 1936, and attended summer training courses in the Platoon Leaders' Class at San Diego, Calif. He was commissioned a Marine Reserve second lieutenant on Jan. 31, 1938, and was assigned to active duty on Sept. 29, 1939. After completing the Reserve Officers' Course at Quantico, in Nov. 1939, he joined the 1st Bn., 6th Marines, at San Diego. The following Nov. he was integrated into the regular Marine Corps. He remained with the 1st Bn. for almost six years, including the entirety of WWII. In May 1941, he embarked with the 6th Marines for Iceland as part of the 1st Mar. Brig. He returned to the States in Mar. 1942, when the regiment was attached to the 2nd Mar. Div. at San Diego. In the spring of 1942, he was promoted to first lieutenant and, shortly after, to captain. With his unit, he was ordered to the Pacific area in Oct. 1942. He took part in the Guadalcanal campaign as a company executive officer, and later served as a company commander, and battalion executive officer. He was promoted to major in May 1943. In Sept. 1943, he became CO of the 1st Bn., and in this capacity took part in four more campaigns: Tarawa, where he earned the Silver Star Medal and a field promotion to lieutenant colonel; Saipan, where he earned the Navy Cross; Tinian; and Okinawa. The Silver Star

Medal was awarded him for gallantry in action at Tarawa on the night of Nov. 22-23, 1943 when, his citation states, he exposed himself to withering shellfire to organize and direct a mortar platoon and elements of his HQ company in a brilliantly executed counterattack against Japanese troops who had broken through his battalion's lines. Returning to the States in July 1945, Lt. Col. Jones was stationed at MCS, Quantico, as Head, Tactics and Techniques Section, Basic School, until May 1947; then as Chief of the Infantry Section, Junior School, until June 1948. Following brief duties in Washington, D.C., he sailed in Aug. 1948 for Sweden, where he served for two years as Assistant Naval Attaché and Assistant Naval Attaché for Air at the American Embassy in Stockholm. In Aug. 1950, he reported for duty in the G-3 Section, Division of Plans and Policies, HQMC. He served there as Head of the Operations Subsection until Feb. 1952, when he became Head of the Operations and Training Branch. During the latter assignment, he was promoted to colonel in Aug. 1952. In Sept. 1953, after serving for three months as Assistant G-3 at HQMC, he arrived in Korea where he served as Assistant Chief of Staff, G-3, 1st Mar. Div. for five months. He then commanded the 1st Mar. Regt. until his return to the States in July 1954. During the next four years, he was again stationed at MCS, Quantico, where he served as Assistant Chief of Staff, G-2/G-3, for two years, with additional duty as a member of the Fleet Marine Force Organization and Composition Board, from June 1956 to Jan. 1957; and in Aug. 1956 became CO of the Basic School. Leaving Quantico in July 1958, he assumed command of the Recruit Training Regiment, MCRD, Parris Is., S.C. He held this command until July 1960, when

he entered the Naval War College, Newport, R.I. Upon completing the course in Naval Warfare, he was assigned to the Pentagon as Chief, General Operations Division, J-3, Operations Directorate, Joint Staff, Office of the Joint Chiefs of Staff, in July 1961. He served in this capacity until Sept. 1962, when he was assigned to HQMC.

JULIAN, Joseph Rudolph. Platoon Sergeant. Medal of Honor: b. Worcester, Mass., Apr. 3, 1918; d. KIA, Iwo Jima, Mar. 9, 1945. Joseph Julian enlisted in the MCR after graduation from high school. He served as a drill instructor at Parris Is., and later was assigned to the 5th Mar. Div. His citation reads, in part: " . . . as a platoon sergeant, serving with the 1st Bn., 27th Marines, 5th Mar. Div., in action against enemy Japanese forces during the seizure of Iwo Jima in the Volcano Islands, Mar. 9, 1945. Determined to force a breakthrough when Japanese troops occupying trenches and fortified positions on the left front laid down a terrific machine gun and mortar barrage in a desperate effort to halt his company's advance, Pl. Sgt. Julian quickly established his platoon's guns in strategic supporting positions and then, acting on his own initiative, fearlessly moved forward to execute a one-man assault on the nearest pillbox. Advancing alone, he hurled deadly demolitions and white phosphorus grenades into the emplacement, killing two of the enemy and driving the remaining five out into the adjoining trench system. Seizing a discarded rifle, he jumped into the trench and dispatched the five before they could make an escape. Intent on wiping out all resistance, he obtained more explosives and, accompanied by another Marine, again charged the hostile fortifications and knocked out two more cave positions.

Immediately thereafter, he launched a bazooka attack unassisted, firing four rounds into the one remaining pillbox and completely destroying it before he fell, mortally wounded by a vicious burst of enemy fire."

K

KATES, Thomas Wilber. Private. Medal of Honor: b. Shelby Center, N.Y., May 7, 1865. Thomas Kates enlisted in the Marine Corps at Marine Barracks, N.Y. on July 21, 1899. He was awarded the Medal of Honor " . . . for distinguished conduct in the presence of the enemy in the advance on Tientsin, China, June 21, 1900. . . ." He was discharged from the Corps at Brooklyn, N.Y. on May 19, 1903.

KEARNEY, Michael. Captain. Medal of Honor: b. Newmarket, Ireland, Oct. 4, 1874; d. Oct. 1937. Michael Kearney enlisted in the Marine Corps at Boston, Mass. on Apr. 21, 1896. He earned the nation's highest military award " . . . while serving aboard the USS *Nashville,* for extraordinary bravery and coolness while cutting the cables leading from Cienfuegos, Cuba, May 11, 1898. . . ." Kearney was discharged from the Corps on June 1, 1901 at Brooklyn, but reenlisted and served until Dec. 22, 1926 when he was retired as a captain.

KELLY, John Doran. Private First Class. Medal of Honor: b. Youngstown, Ohio, July 8, 1928; d. KIA, Korea, May 28, 1952. P.F.C. Kelly's citation reads, in part: " . . . while serving as a radio operator of Co. C, 1st Bn., 7th Marines, 1st Mar. Div. (Reinf.), in action against enemy aggressor forces in Korea on May 28, 1952. With his platoon pinned down by a numerically superior enemy force employ-ing intense mortar, artillery, small arms and grenade fire, P.F.C. Kelly requested permission to leave his radio in the care of another man and to participate in an assault on enemy key positions. Fearlessly charging forward in the face of a murderous hail of machine gun fire and hand grenades, he initiated a daring attack against a hostile strongpoint and personally neutralized the position, killing two of the enemy. Unyielding in the face of heavy odds, he continued forward and singlehandedly assaulted a machine gun bunker. Although painfully wounded, he bravely charged the bunker and destroyed it, killing three of the enemy. Courageously continuing his one-man assault, he again stormed forward in a valiant attempt to wipe out a third bunker and boldly delivered point-blank fire into the aperture of the hostile emplacement. Mortally wounded by enemy fire while carrying out this heroic action, P.F.C. Kelly, by his great personal valor and aggressive fighting spirit, inspired his comrades to sweep on, overrun, and secure the objective. . . ."

KELLY, John Joseph. Private. Medal of Honor: b. Chicago, Ill., June 24, 1898. John Kelly enlisted in the Marine Corps in May 1917. In France, he saw action in the engagements at Chateau-Thierry, St.-Mihiel, Mont Blanc, the Argonne, the advance to the Meuse, and the march to the Rhine for the occupation of the Coblenz Bridgehead. At Mont Blanc Ridge, Pvt. Kelly was credited with having run "through our own barrage 100 yards in advance of the front line and attacking an enemy machine gun nest, killing the gunner with a grenade, shooting another member of the crew with his pistol, and returning through the barrage with eight prisoners."

KELSO, Jack William. Private. Medal of Honor: b. Madera, Calif., Jan. 23, 1934; d. KIA, Korea, Oct. 2, 1952. Pvt. Kelso's citation reads, in part: ". . . while serving as a rifleman of Co. I, 3rd Bn., 7th Marines, 1st Mar. Div. (Reinf.), in action against enemy aggressor forces in Korea on Oct. 2, 1952. When both the platoon commander and the platoon sergeant became casualties during the defense of a vital outpost against a numerically superior enemy force attacking at night under cover of intense small arms, grenade, and mortar fire, Pvt. Kelso bravely exposed himself to the hail of enemy fire in a determined effort to reorganize the unit and to repel the onrushing attackers. Forced to seek cover, along with four other Marines, in a nearby bunker which immediately came under attack, he unhesitatingly picked up an enemy grenade which landed in the shelter, rushed out into the open and hurled it back at the enemy. Although painfully wounded when the grenade exploded as it left his hand, and again forced to seek the protection of the bunker when the hostile fire became more intensified, Pvt. Kelso refused to remain in his position of comparative safety and moved out into the fire-swept area to return the enemy fire, thereby permitting the pinned-down Marines in the bunker to escape. Mortally wounded while providing covering fire for his comrades, Pvt. Kelso, by his valiant fighting spirit, aggressive determination, and self-sacrificing efforts in behalf of others, served to inspire all who observed him. . . ."

KENNEMORE, Robert Sidney. Technical Sergeant. Medal of Honor: b. Greenville, S.C., June 21, 1920. Sgt. Kennemore's citation reads, in part: ". . . as leader of a machine gun section in Co. E, 2nd Bn., 7th Marines, 1st Mar. Div. (Reinf.), in action against enemy aggressor forces in Korea on Nov. 27 and 28, 1950. With the company's defensive perimeter overrun by a numerically superior hostile force during a savage night attack north of Yudam-ni — and with his platoon commander seriously wounded — Sgt. Kennemore unhesitatingly assumed command, quickly reorganized the unit, and directed the men in consolidating their position. When an enemy grenade landed in the midst of a machine gun squad, he bravely placed his foot on the missile and, in the face of almost certain death, personally absorbed the full force of the explosion to prevent injury to his fellow Marines. . . ."

KIER, Avery Raymond. Major General. CG, Aircraft, Fleet Marine Force, Pacific, El Toro, Calif. Also, CG, Marine Corps Air Station, El Toro, and Commander, Marine Corps Air Bases, Western Area: b. Gentry, Mo., Feb. 11, 1905. Avery Kier attended Argentine High School in Kansas City, Kans., and received his Bachelor of Laws degree upon graduation from the Kansas City School of Law in June 1927. He then completed two years of study in aeronautical engineering at the University of Minnesota. On June 4, 1929, he enlisted in the MCR at St. Paul, Minn., and was assigned to Flight School at the NAS, Pensacola, Fla. He was commissioned a Marine Reserve second lieutenant and graduated from flight training in June 1930, then saw six months' duty with the Aircraft Squadrons, West Coast Expeditionary Forces, at North Is., San Diego, Calif. Relieved from active duty in Jan. 1931, Lt. Kier joined the Administrative staff of the University of Minnesota, Minneapolis, Minn., working there until May 1938. During this time he served brief tours of active duty with the Marine Air Reserve Detachment at the Naval Reserve Aviation Base, Minneapolis, and was Executive Officer of the Marine Reserve Aviation Squadron. He was promoted to captain in Aug. 1937. During the summer of 1938, he served on active duty as a flight instructor at Minneapolis in connection with the Naval Aviation Cadet Training program. Following a brief tour at the Naval Reserve Aviation Base, Kansas City, Kans., he reported to the NAS, Pensacola in Mar. 1939 for active duty and training as an instructor. On his detachment from Pensacola in May 1940, he returned to the Naval Reserve Aviation Base, Minneapolis, for duty as Inspector-Instructor of Marine Reserve Aviation activities at that station, and as CO of the Marine Reserve Aviation Unit. He was integrated into the Regular Marine Corps in Feb. 1941, and that month joined Marine Scout Bombing Squadron 2, 2nd MAG, at the NAS, San Diego as a naval aviator and squadron gunnery officer. In Apr. 1941, he moved with the squadron to Ewa, Oahu, Hawaii. On Dec. 7, 1941, when Pearl Harbor was attacked, Capt. Kier was aboard the USS *Lexington* en route with the bomber squadron to Midway Is. The *Lexington* returned to Pearl Harbor where the squadron disembarked Dec. 10. On Dec. 17, ten days after the originally scheduled fly-off, Capt. Kier was among the 17 pilots who flew 1137 miles from Oahu to Midway to bolster that island's defense. This was then the

longest mass overwater, single-engined flight on record. Six months later, in May 1942, he was promoted to major. Returning to the States in Dec. 1942, Maj. Kier served on the staff of the CG, Marine Air West Coast, as Assistant Chief of Staff, G-3, located at the NAS, San Diego. He was promoted to lieutenant colonel in Apr. 1943. A year later, he was again ordered overseas, arriving in the Marshalls in May 1944 for duty as Operations Officer, and later Executive Officer of MAG 13, 4th Marine Air Base Defense Wing. In Nov. 1944, he joined HQ, Provisional Air Support Command, FMF, Pacific, as Operations Officer, during the formation and training of the Landing Force Air Support Control Units, which were later assigned to Amphibious Forces, Pacific Fleet. He was promoted to colonel in Dec. 1944. Next he served ashore on Iwo Jima and Okinawa with the Marine Air Support Control Units. Following his return to this country in Aug. 1945, Col. Kier commanded Marine Air Support Group 51 at MCAS, Santa Barbara, Calif, until Jan. 1946; then he commanded MAGs 46 and 33 at MCAS, El Toro, Calif. until July. In Sept. 1946, he entered MCS, Quantico, completing the Senior Course in June 1947. He was next assigned to Norfolk, Va., serving as Force Air Officer and Assistant Chief of Staff, G-2, FMF, Atlantic. In July 1948, he joined the Staff of the Commander in Chief, Atlantic Fleet, as Fleet Marine Officer. Transferred to the American Embassy, London, England, in Aug. 1950, Col. Kier began a two-year tour of duty as Assistant Naval Attaché for Air. Returning to the States in Aug. 1952, he was attached to the 3rd MAW, MCAS, Miami, Fla., serving consecutively as Assistant Chief of Staff and Chief of Staff of the Wing. In Aug. 1954, he became CO, MCAS, Quantico. After two years at Quantico, he was ordered to the MCAS, El Toro, in Aug. 1956, for a brief tour of duty as Assistant Chief of Staff, G-3, Aircraft, FMF, Pacific, prior to his detachment to the Far East in Dec. 1956. The following month he assumed duties in Japan as Assistant Commander, 1st MAW. While serving in this capacity, he was promoted to brigadier general in April 1957. That same month, Gen. Kier was transferred to Kaneohe Bay, Hawaii, as CG, 1st Mar. Brig., FMF. He served 25 months in this capacity prior to his return to the continental United States. In July 1959, he became Director of Information, HQMC, Washington, D.C. Following this assignment, he returned to Japan in Apr. 1960 as CG, 1st MAW. He was promoted to his present rank of major general in July 1960, and remained in Japan until June of the following year. From July 1961 through June 1962, Gen. Kier commanded the 3rd MAW at El Toro. He then remained at El Toro where he assumed his present commands as CG, Aircraft, FMF, Pacific in June 1962, and CG, MCAS, El Toro and Commander, Marine Corps Air Bases, Western Area in July 1962.

KINSER, Elbert Luther. Sergeant. Medal of Honor: b. Greeneville, Tenn., Oct. 21, 1922; d. KIA, Okinawa, May 4, 1945. Elbert Kinser enlisted in the Marine Corps in Dec. 1942, and received recruit training at Parris Is., S.C. He sailed from the States in Mar. 1943, and joined the 7th Replacement Bn. in Pago Pago, Tutuila, American Samoa. Later, that battalion joined the 1st Mar. Div. in Melbourne, Australia and Sgt. Kinser was assigned to I Co., 1st Marines. Action with the 1st Marines followed at Cape Gloucester, New Britain, and later at Peleliu, Palau Is. On Easter Sunday, Apr. 1, 1945, Sgt. Kinser landed with his unit at Okinawa

where he was subsequently killed in action on May 4. He won the nation's highest military decoration while acting as a leader of a rifle platoon, serving with Co. I, 3rd Bn., 1st Marines, 1st Mar. Div., in action on Okinawa. Taken under sudden and close attack by hostile troops entrenched on the reverse slope while moving up a strategic ridge along which his platoon was holding newly won positions, Sgt. Kinser engaged the enemy in a fierce hand grenade battle. Quick to act when a Japanese grenade landed in the immediate vicinity, Sgt. Kinser unhesitatingly threw himself on the deadly missile, absorbing the full charge of the shattering explosion in his own body and thereby protecting his men from serious injury and possible death.

KLINE, Roy Lewis. Brigadier General. Deputy Director, J-5 (Plans and Policy) Directorate, Joint Staff, Office of the Joint Chiefs of Staff: b. Sept. 10, 1914. After graduation from high school, Roy Kline received his Bachelor of Science degree in mechanical engineering from Iowa State College, Ames, Iowa. While attending college he was a member of the Army Engineers ROTC. Upon graduation he entered the Marine Corps and was commissioned a Marine second lieutenant Sept. 10, 1935. He completed Basic School at the Philadelphia Navy Yard in June 1936, then served with the Marine Detachment aboard the USS *Saratoga* for one year. Following this duty, he was enrolled in the Flight Training Course at the NAS, Pensacola, Fla. He was designated a naval aviator in Apr. 1938. That June he joined the 2nd MAG, FMF, at the NAS, San Diego, Calif. He was promoted to first lieutenant in Sept. 1938. He remained in San Diego until Nov. 1940 when he became a flight instructor at the Pensacola NAS. In May

1941, he was assigned to the 1st MAG, MB, Quantico, Va. He was promoted to captain in Nov. 1941. In Dec. 1941, Capt. Kline began a two-year assignment with the Bureau of Aeronautics, Navy Department, Washington, D.C. While there, he was promoted to major in May 1942, and to lieutenant colonel in Sept. 1943. Ordered overseas, Lt. Col. Kline joined MAG 23 on Midway in Feb. 1944, and served initially as Group Operations Officer and later as Group Executive Officer. In Aug. 1944, he was transferred to Schofield Barracks, Honolulu, Hawaii, to become Assistant Air Officer for the 10th Army. He accompanied that organization to Okinawa. In Aug. 1945, he joined the Staff of the Commander in Chief, Pacific, as Assistant Fleet Aviation Officer. The following Apr., after his return to the States, he was named CO of the MAD, MARTC, NAS, Grosse Ile, Mich. He returned to Quantico in Aug. 1947 as a student in the Amphibious Warfare School, Senior Course. After completing the Senior School in May 1948, Lt. Col. Kline became a Resident Member of the Marine Corps Board at MCS, Quantico. In Aug. 1950, he was transferred to the MCAS, Cherry Point, N.C., for two years' duty with MAG 14, 2nd MAW. He served consecutively as Executive Officer, Deputy Group Commander, and CO. During this period he also served for four months in the Pacific area and the Far East as a member of the Pacific Fleet Evaluation Group. Later he served in the Caribbean area for five months as Chief of Staff of TRAEX-1, the first exercise of its kind in FMF, Atlantic. He was promoted to colonel in Feb. 1951. From Aug. 1952 to June 1953, he was a student in the Strategy and Tactics Course at the Naval War College, Newport, R.I. In July 1953, he rejoined the 2nd MAW, serving in various capacities

including Chief of Staff for "Weldfast," the landing force for the NATO Mediterranean maneuvers. He also served briefly as CO, Marine Air Control Group 1, 2nd MAW, prior to becoming Assistant Chief of Staff, G-3, in Dec. 1953. Departing Cherry Point in Aug. 1954, Col. Kline was assigned to the 1st MAW in Korea as Assistant Chief of Staff, G-2, and later, Assistant Chief of Staff, G-1. In June 1955, upon returning to the States, he was ordered to MCS, Quantico. He served there as Director of the Junior School, Chief of Staff of the Marine Corps Educational Center, and Chief of Staff of MCS, respectively. In June 1958, he was ordered to HQMC, Washington, D.C. He served there for 18 months as Military Secretary to the CMC. He was promoted to his present rank of brigadier general in Nov. 1959. Detached from HQMC in Jan. 1960, Gen. Kline served consecutively as Assistant Wing Commander, 2nd MAW, Cherry Point, until Feb. 1961; and Assistant Wing Commander, 1st MAW, Iwakuni, Japan, until Jan. 1962. He then returned to the States and in Feb. 1962 became Marine Corps Liaison Officer to the Vice Chief of Naval Operations. In Nov. 1962, he was assigned as Deputy Director, J-5 (Plans and Policy) Directorate, Joint Staff, Office of the Joint Chiefs of Staff.

KOCAK, Matej. Sergeant. Medal of Honor: b. Egbell, Hungary, Dec. 31, 1882. Matej Kocak enlisted in the Marine Corps at Pittsburgh, Pa. on Oct. 16, 1907. For his part in the action on July 18, 1918, in the Villers Cotterets Forest, south of Soissons, France, he was cited for extraordinary heroism. His citation reads, in part, " . . . he advanced ahead of the American line and captured a machine gun and its crew. Later the same day, he took command of several squads of

Allied troops and led them forward in the advance...." For his bravery he was awarded the Medal of Honor (Army) on Feb. 18, 1919, and the Medal of Honor (Navy) on Nov. 11, 1920.

KRAUS, Richard Edward. Private First Class. Medal of Honor: b. Chicago, Ill., Nov. 24, 1925; d. KIA, Peleliu, Oct. 3, 1944. P.F.C. Kraus won the Medal of Honor while serving as an amphibious tractor driver with the 8th Amphibious Tractor Bn., FMF, which participated in the D-Day landings on Peleliu. He and three companions had accepted a volunteer mission to evacuate a wounded fellow Marine from the front lines. As the group made their way forward, they were met by an intense barrage of hand grenade fire which forced them to take cover. While returning to the rear, the stretcher party observed two men approaching whom they believed to be Marines. Upon challenging the pair, they proved to be Japanese, and one of the enemy responded by throwing a hand grenade into the midst of the group. Pvt. Kraus unhesitatingly hurled himself on top of it, and by his prompt action and personal valor in the face of certain death, saved the lives of his three comrades.

KRULAK, Victor Harold. Major General. Special Assistant to the Director for Counter Insurgency and Special Activities, Joint Staff, Joint Chiefs of Staff: b. Denver, Col., Jan. 7, 1913. Victor Krulak was commissioned a Marine second lieutenant upon graduation from the U.S. Naval Academy, May 31, 1934. His first assignment after completing Basic School at the Philadelphia Navy Yard was with the Marine Detachment aboard the USS *Arizona*, followed by an assignment at the U.S. Naval Academy. In July 1936, he joined the 6th Marines at the MCB, San Diego, Calif. The following Mar. he sailed with his unit for Shanghai, China, where he served with the 4th Marines for two years as a company commander. While there, he was promoted to first lieutenant in July 1937. Lt. Krulak left China in May 1939. On his return to the States, he completed the Junior Course at MCS, Quantico, in June 1940, and was appointed Assistant to the Brigade Quartermaster, 1st Mar. Brig., FMF. He was promoted to captain in Aug. 1940. With the 1st Mar. Brig. (later the 1st Mar. Div.), Capt. Krulak embarked for Guantanamo Bay, Cuba, in Oct. 1940. Returning to Quantico in Apr. 1941, he served on the staff of Gen. Holland M. Smith, then CG of Amphibious Corps, Atlantic Fleet. He was serving in this capacity when WWII broke out. In May 1942, he was promoted to major. He moved with the staff of the Amphibious Corps to San Diego in Sept. 1942, and continued as Aide to the CG and as Assistant G-4 until Jan. 1943, when he volunteered for parachute training. He completed training and was designated a parachutist on Feb. 15, 1943. The following month he sailed for the Pacific area and at New Caledonia took command of the 2nd Parachute Bn., 1st Mar. Amphibious Corps. He was promoted to lieutenant colonel in Apr. 1943, and went into action that Sept. at Vella, Lavella. That Oct., Lt. Col. Krulak commanded the diversionary landing on Choiseul to cover the Bougainville invasion, during which action he earned the Navy Cross for extraordinary heroism and the Purple Heart for wounds received in combat. He returned to the States in Nov. 1943, served in the Division of Plans and Policies, HQMC, until Oct. 1944, then went overseas again. He joined the newly formed 6th Mar. Div. as Assistant Chief of Staff, G-3 (Operations). For outstanding service in the planning and execution of the Okinawa campaign, he was awarded the Legion of Merit with Combat "V." He also received the Bronze Star Medal at the war's end for his part in negotiating the surrender of Japanese forces in the Tsingtao, China area. Returning to the States in Oct. 1945, Lt. Col. Krulak reported to Quantico as Officer in Charge of the Research Section, and subsequently became Assistant Director of the Senior School. He left Quantico in June 1949 for Camp Pendleton, where he served as Regimental Commander of the 5th Marines, 1st Mar. Div. He was promoted to colonel in Aug. 1949. Ordered to Pearl Harbor in June 1950, Col. Krulak was serving as Assistant Chief of Staff, G-3, FMF, Pacific, when the Korean War began. In the ensuing year, his duties took him to the battle front many times and, during the latter half of 1951, he remained in Korea as Chief of Staff of the 1st Mar. Div. He earned a second Legion of Merit with Combat "V" in that capacity, and was awarded the Air Medal for reconnaissance and other flights in Korea between Aug. 1950 and July 1951. Col. Krulak remained in Korea until Nov. 1951, then returned to Washington for duty at HQMC as Secretary of the General Staff until June 1955. In Aug. 1955, he rejoined FMF, Pacific, at Pearl Harbor, serving as Chief of Staff. He was promoted to brigadier general in July 1956, and at the same time assumed duties as Assistant Division Commander, 3rd Mar. Div., on Okinawa. On his return to the States in July 1957, Gen. Krulak became Director of the Marine Corps Educational Center, Quantico. While at Quantico, he was promoted to his present rank of major general in Nov. 1959. The following month, Gen. Krulak assumed command of the MCRD, San Diego. In Feb. 1962, he relinquished his

command in San Diego, and assumed his current assignment as Special Assistant to the Director for Counter Insurgency and Special Activities, Joint Staff, Joint Chiefs of Staff.

KUCHNEISTER, Herman William. Private. Medal of Honor: b. Hamburg, Germany, Oct. 15, 1875. Herman Kuchneister enlisted in the Marine Corps at Brooklyn, N.Y. on Aug. 19, 1897. He was awarded the Medal of Honor on July 7, 1899. His citation reads, in part: ". . . while serving aboard the USS *Marblehead*, for extraordinary bravery and coolness while cutting the cables leading from Cienfuegos, Cuba, May 11, 1898. . . ." He was discharged from the Corps at Boston, Mass. on Mar. 28, 1900.

KYLE, Wood Barbee. Brigadier General. CG, Force Troops, Fleet Marine Force, Atlantic, at Camp Lejeune, N.C.: b. Pecos, Tex., Mar. 3, 1915. Wood Kyle entered Texas A&M College in 1932 where he was a member of the ROTC unit, and graduated with Military Department honors in June 1936. He resigned his commission in the U.S. Army Infantry Reserve to accept appointment as a Marine second lieutenant July 11, 1936. After short tours of duty at San Diego, Calif., and the Philadelphia Navy Yard, Lt. Kyle served with the 2nd Mar. Brig. at Shanghai, China, from Oct. 1937 to Apr. 1938. Returning to San Diego with the brigade, he was promoted to first lieutenant in July 1939. He remained in San Diego until May 1940, when he was assigned to the Marine Detachment on board the USS *Lexington*. Detached from the *Lexington* in Dec. 1941, he joined the 1st Bn., 2nd Marines, 2nd Mar. Div., in San Diego, and that same month was promoted to captain. He embarked for the Pacific area in July 1942, and in

Aug. 1942 was promoted to major. Later, when the CO of the 1st Bn., 2nd Marines, was seriously wounded at Guadalcanal, Maj. Kyle, then Executive Officer, assumed command of the battalion, refusing evacuation for his own wounds, and continued to head the battalion from Nov. 1942 to Jan. 1943. The Silver Star Medal was awarded him for heroism during this campaign. A second Silver Star Medal was awarded Maj. Kyle for courageous leadership during combat on Tarawa in Nov. 1943, when he personally led his men in an attack on the heavily defended central sector of the island. He was promoted to lieutenant colonel in Jan. 1944. After participating in campaigns at Saipan and Tinian, Lt. Col. Kyle returned to San Diego in Oct. 1944. In Jan. 1945, he was assigned to the Command and General Staff School, Fort Leavenworth, Kans. for instruction. On completing the course in Mar. 1945, he was assigned to the school's faculty. For outstanding performance during the final months of the war, he was awarded the Army Commendation Ribbon. He remained at the school until Aug. 1947. From Sept. 1947 to May 1949, he was Assistant G-3, FMF, Pacific. During this period he served at Tsingtao, China, Guam, Hawaii, and on the United States west coast. In June 1949, Lt. Col. Kyle assumed duty as Executive Officer, Division of Reserve, HQMC. Two years later,

he was also designated liaison officer between HWMC and the Reserve Forces Policy Board. In July 1951, he became Assistant Director of the Division of Reserve, and continued as liaison officer. He was promoted to colonel in Nov. 1951. In June 1952, Col. Kyle was assigned to Little Creek, Va., where he served as Assistant G-3 and G-3, respectively, of Troop Training Unit, Atlantic, until Aug. 1954. Departing the States, he assumed duty in Sept. 1954 as Regimental Commander of the 4th Marines (Reinf.), 3rd Mar. Div., in Japan. In Feb. 1955, he moved with the regiment to Kaneohe Bay, Hawaii, where he helped establish the 4th Marines, and continued as Regimental Commander until his return to the States in June 1955. In July 1956, he completed the course at the Army War College, Carlisle Barracks, Pa. He then became Chief, Tactics and Technique Board, Marine Corps Landing Force Development Center, Quantico, Va., in Aug. 1956. In June 1958, he was again ordered overseas and, that same month, assumed duties in Paris, France, as Chief, Plans Branch, J-3, HQ, U.S. European Command. While serving in this post, he was promoted to his present rank of brigadier general Apr. 1, 1961. Gen. Kyle completed a three-year tour of duty in Paris prior to reporting to his present post as CG, Force Troops, FMF, Atlantic, in Aug. 1961.

L

LaBELLE, James Dennis. Private First Class. Medal of Honor: b. Columbia Heights, Minn., Nov. 22, 1925; d. KIA, Iwo Jima, Feb. 8, 1945. P.F.C. LaBelle's

citation reads, in part: "... filling a gap in the front lines during a critical phase of the battle, P.F.C. LaBelle had dug into a foxhole with two other Marines and, grimly aware of the enemy's persistent attempts to blast a way through our lines with hand grenades, applied himself with steady concentration to maintaining a sharply vigilant watch during the hazardous night hours. Suddenly a hostile grenade landed beyond reach in his foxhole. Quickly estimating the situation, he determined to save the others if possible, shouted a warning, and instantly dived on the deadly missile, absorbing the exploding charge in his own body and thereby protecting his comrades from serious injury. . . ."

LARSON, August. Major General (Retired): b. Sherburn, Minn., July 2, 1904. August Larson graduated from high school in Sherburn, then attended the University of Minnesota for three years. He enlisted in the Marine Corps on Jan. 13, 1928 and served as an enlisted man until Feb. 26, 1931, when he was commissioned a Marine second lieutenant after completing Basic School at the Philadelphia Navy Yard. He embarked for China in Dec. 1932, and saw duty with the 4th Marines until Sept. 1934. Subsequently, while attached to the USS *Augusta*, he studied the Russian language in Shanghai, and returned to the States in Nov. 1935. In Jan. 1936, he reported to Quantico, and for the next six weeks helped train the Marine Detachment which served at the late President Franklin D. Roosevelt's residence at Warm Springs, Ga. In May 1936, Larson began a three-year tour at Quantico, where he served with the 5th Marines, and completed the Junior Course at the MCS. An outstanding rifle and pistol shot, he was a member of the Marine Corps Rifle and Pistol Team in 1931, 1932, 1936, and 1937, and coached the team in 1938 and 1939. He entered the Ordnance Field Service School at the Raritan Arsenal,

Metuchen, N.J. in Sept. 1939 and completed the course that Dec. He then joined the Sea School Detachment at the Norfolk, Va. Navy Yard the following month, and in Apr. 1940 took command of the Marine Detachment aboard the USS *Wasp*. Returning to Quantico in Feb. 1942, he served on the Staff at the MCS, and completed the Command and Staff Course prior to his detachment in Mar. 1944. That Apr. he embarked for the Pacific area. As Assistant Chief of Staff, G-4 (Supply), 1st Prov. Mar. Brig., he participated in the initial landing against the Japanese on Guam in July 1944, earning the Legion of Merit with Combat "V." After the brigade was reorganized in Sept. 1944, he held the same post with the 6th Mar. Div. and, in this capacity, won the Bronze Star Medal with Combat "V" on Okinawa during the period Apr. 1 to May 17, 1945. As Executive Officer, 22nd Marines, and later Regimental Commander, during the latter part of the Okinawa campaign, he was awarded the Silver Star Medal for gallantry in action, May 17 to June 21, 1945. Resuming his duties as Executive Officer, he moved with the regiment to Tsingtao, China, at the end of the war. In Mar. 1946, he was transferred to Peiping to command the 5th Marines, 1st Mar. Div. On his return to the States in Aug. 1946, he served as Assistant Chief of Staff, G-4, of the Troop Training Unit, Amphibious Training Command, U.S. Atlantic Fleet, Little Creek, Va., until Mar. 1949. Subsequently, he completed the Logistics Course at the Command and General Staff College, Fort Leavenworth, Kans., in June 1949, and at the U.S. Naval War College, Newport, R.I., in June 1950. The following month, he was named Marine Corps Liaison Officer with the Logistics Plans Division, Office of the Chief of Naval Operations, Navy

Department, serving in this capacity until Apr. 1952. Shortly afterward, in July 1952, he became Marine Corps Liaison Officer in the Office of the Secretary, Joint Chiefs of Staff. He left Washington in Aug. 1953 to become a member of the Advanced Research Group at Quantico. In July 1955, he was transferred to the west coast for a two-year tour of duty as Deputy Base Commander, MCB, Camp Pendleton, Calif. While serving there, he was promoted to brigadier general in July 1956. Upon his detachment, he departed for Okinawa where he assumed duty as Assistant Division Commander, 3rd Mar. Div., in July 1957. He returned to the States in June 1958. Assigned to HQMC, he served briefly as Deputy Chief of Staff, Research and Development, prior to becoming Director of Personnel in Aug. 1958. In Aug. 1959, he was promoted to his present rank of major general. At the time of his retirement on Feb. 1, 1963, Gen. Larson was assigned to the Office of the Chief of Staff, HQMC.

LEE, Harry. "Light Horse." Major General: b. Washington, D.C., June 4, 1872; d. Quantico, Va., May 13, 1935. Harry Lee was appointed a second lieutenant in the Marine Corps (for the war with Spain) on Aug. 2, 1898, and after a brief period of instruction was ordered to the USS *Resolute*. Sailing for Havana, Cuba, he served there until Feb. 9, 1899, on which date he was ordered home, being honorably discharged Feb. 14, 1899. He was commissioned a first lieutenant in the Marine Corps on Apr. 17, 1899 and was promoted to captain July 23, 1900. From Mar. 4, 1904 to Aug. 24, 1905, Capt. Lee served in the Philippine Is., and from Sept. 12, 1905 to Apr. 11, 1906, he commanded the Marine Guard, U.S. Legation, Peking, China. From Apr. 27,

1906 to Jan. 9, 1907, he again served in the Philippines. He served at various posts and stations in the States and on several vessels of the Navy until Aug. 23, 1912, when he sailed from Philadelphia on the *Prairie* as Adjutant of the 1st Prov. Regt. for service in Panama. He served in Nicaragua from Sept. 5 to Nov. 21, 1912, and participated in the bombardment, assault, and capture of the fortifications of Coyotepe and Barranca. From Feb. 18, 1913 to May 27, 1913, he was absent on temporary expeditionary service at Guantanamo Bay, Cuba. He also served for short periods in Haiti and Santo Domingo during 1914, 1915, and 1916. On Aug. 1, 1917, Lt. Col. Lee joined the MB, Quantico, for duty with the 6th Regt., arriving with it in France on Feb. 8, 1918. There he was detached to the U.S. Army for duty. He participated in the battles in the Chateau-Thierry sector June 1 to July 5, 1918 as second in command of the 6th Regt. until June 6, and as its CO from that date on, after the evacuation of Col. Catlin, who was wounded in action. Under Lee's command, the regiment participated with distinction in the Aisne-Marne offensive (Soissons), July 17 to July 21, 1918; the Marbache sector, Aug. 7 to 16, 1918; the St.-Mihiel offensive, Sept. 12 to 16, 1918; Mont Blanc Ridge, Champagne Sector, Oct. 2 to 10, 1918; the Meuse-Argonne offensive (Argonne Forest), Nov. 1 to 11, 1918; and in the march of the Allies to the Rhine. He returned to the States Aug. 6, 1919. He commanded the 1st Regt. of Marines at the MB, Navy Yard, Philadelphia, Pa. from Sept 25, 1919 to May 20, 1920, then served at Quantico from Oct. 2, 1920 to July 23, 1921. From Aug. 1921 to July 18, 1924, Gen. Lee served as Brig. Commander of the 2nd Brig. in Santo Domingo, and later served in the additional capacity as Military

Governor of that country. From there he was ordered to the MB, Parris Is., S.C. as CG of that post, which duty he performed until Aug. 12, 1927 when he was detached to the MB, Quantico, for duty as Executive Officer. On Oct. 1, 1929, he returned to Parris Is. for a second tour as CG of the post. On Mar. 1, 1933, he assumed command of the MB, Quantico, the post he was holding at the time of his death.

Leek

LEEK, Frederick Everett. Major General. CG, 1st Marine Aircraft Wing, Iwakuni, Japan: b. Stockton, Calif., Oct. 12, 1914.

Frederick Leek completed high school in 1931; then he attended the University of California, from which he graduated in May 1935 with a Bachelor of Arts degree. After four years with the ROTC unit at the University of California, he was commissioned an ensign in the U.S. Naval Reserve in May 1935. He resigned his naval commission to accept appointment as a Marine second lieutenant on Sept. 10, 1935. After completing Basic School at the Philadelphia Navy Yard in May 1936, he saw a year of sea duty aboard the USS *Tennessee*. Following a brief assignment in San Diego, he embarked in Sept. 1937 for duty in China with the 1st Bn., 6th Marines, 2nd Mar. Brig. The following Apr., he returned with the brigade to San Diego. He was promoted to first lieutenant in Oct. 1938. Lt. Leek remained in San Diego until June 1939. That month he reported to the U.S. Embassy in Mexico City, and was assigned advanced instruction at the University of Mexico. After earning his Master of Arts degree in Spanish, he continued at the university until Mar. 1941, and served subsequently as Assistant Naval Attaché to the American Embassy in Mexico. He was promoted to captain in Dec. 1941, and to major in May 1942, shortly before his departure from Mexico. Following his return to the States, he entered flight school in July 1942 at the NAS, New Orleans, La. In Apr. 1943, he was designated a naval aviator at the Naval Air Training Center, NAS, Pensacola, Fla. He then served briefly at the NAS, Sanford, Fla. He was promoted to lieutenant colonel in Aug. 1943. That month, Lt. Col. Leek joined HQ Squadron, MAG 15, Camp Kearney, Calif., as Squadron Commander. Ordered overseas in Dec. 1943, he reported to Marine Utility Squadron, MAG 25, Tontouta Air Base, New Caledonia, as Squadron Executive Officer, and in Jan. 1944 became Squadron CO. During this assignment, his group, as part of South Pacific Combat Air Transport (SCAT), performed flight missions in the Solomon Is. area, New Georgia, and Emirau. In June 1944, he was assigned as Operations Officer, MAG 25, operating between Tontouta and Espiritu Santo in the New Hebrides. Transferred to MAG 12 in Aug. 1944, Leek served as Group Operations Officer at Emirau Island, prior to moving to Leyte in the Philippines in Jan. 1945. From there he took part in the assault landings on Mindanao Province, Philippines, until May 1945, when he returned to the States. His flights in the Solomons and Philippines area merited him three Distinguished Flying Crosses, and nine Air Medals. The Legion of Merit with Combat "V" was awarded him for exceptionally meritorious service as Group Operations Officer, MAG 12, in the Bismarck Archipelago area, Sept. 1944 to Jan. 1945; and in the central and southern Philippines area, Jan. to May 1945. In July 1945, Lt. Col. Leek reported as Executive Officer, MCAS, Santa Barbara, Calif. After deactivation of the station, he departed in Apr. 1946 for duty as Executive Officer of MCAS, Ewa, Hawaii. On his return to the continental U.S. in Jan. 1948, he was assigned to HQMC, Washington, D.C. as Assistant Head, Reserve Branch, Division of Aviation. Transferred to Norfolk, Va., in July 1950, he served as Assistant G-3 (Air), and Deputy Chief of Staff, respectively, at HQ, FMF, Atlantic. He was promoted to colonel in Jan. 1951. Following his detachment from Norfolk in July 1952, he entered the Naval War College, Newport, R.I. On completing the course in June 1953, he reported to HQ, 2nd MAW, Cherry Point, N.C., as Assistant Chief of Staff, G-1. Following this as-

signment, he moved to NAS, Pensacola, in Oct. 1954, and completed the course in helicopter training. He was then assigned to the Marine Corps Air Facility, New River, N.C., in Jan. 1955, as Commander of Marine Helicopter Group 26. He remained at that station until late Feb. 1956. The following month, Col. Leek joined the 1st MAW in the Far East as CO, Marine Helicopter Group 16, in Oppama, Japan. He returned to the States in Apr. 1957, and that June became Chief of Staff, Marine Air Reserve Training Command, Glenview, Ill. In July 1959, he was promoted to brigadier general and named Commander of Marine Air Reserve Training, Glenview. Gen. Leek remained at Glenview until Dec. 1960, and the following month assumed duty at Camp Pendleton as Assistant Division Commander, 1st Mar. Div., a billet usually held by a ground officer. He also served as Division CG during June and July 1961, then resumed his post as Assistant Division Commander until May 1962. Ordered overseas, he assumed command of the 1st MAW, Iwakuni, Japan, in June 1962. In Aug. 1962, he was promoted to major general while serving in his present post.

LEIMS, John Harold. First Lieutenant. Medal of Honor: b. Chicago, Ill., June 8, 1921. Lt. Leims' citation reads, in part: " . . . as commanding officer of Co. B, 1st Bn., 9th Marines, 3rd Div., in action against the enemy Japanese forces on Iwo Jima in the Volcano Islands, Mar. 7, 1945. Launching a surprise attack against the rock-imbedded fortifications of a dominating Japanese hill position, Lt. Leims spurred his company forward with indomitable determination and, skillfully directing his assault platoons against the cave-emplaced enemy troops and heavily fortified pillboxes, succeeded in capturing the objective late in the afternoon. When it became apparent that his assault platoons were cut off in this newly won position, approximately 400 yards forward of adjacent units, and that he lacked all communication with the command post, Leims personally advanced and laid telephone lines across the isolating expanse of open fireswept terrain. Ordered to withdraw his command after he had joined his forward platoons, he immediately complied, adroitly effecting the withdrawal of his troops without incident. Upon arriving at the rear, he was informed that several casualties had been left at the abandoned ridge position beyond the front lines. Although suffering acutely from strain and exhaustion of battle, he instantly went forward despite darkness and the slashing fury of hostile machine gun fire, located and carried to safety one seriously wounded Marine and then, running the gauntlet of enemy fire for the third time that night, again made his tortuous way into the bullet-riddled death trap and rescued another of his wounded men. . . ."

LEJEUNE, John Archer. Lieutenant General. 13th Commandant of the Marine Corps – July 1, 1920 to Mar. 4, 1929: b. Pointe Coupee, La., Jan. 10, 1867; d. Baltimore, Md., Nov. 20, 1942. John Lejeune attended Louisiana State University, Baton Rouge, from which he was graduated with a Bachelor of Arts degree. Subsequently he secured an appointment as a midshipman at the U.S. Naval Academy, from which he was graduated in 1888. At the expiration of a two-year cruise as a cadet midshipman he was commissioned a second lieutenant in the Marine Corps on July 1, 1890, and during the succeeding years saw action in the Spanish-American War aboard the USS *Cincinnati*. In the fall of 1903 Le-

Lejeune

jeune, now a major, was dispatched to Panama with a battalion of Marines when conditions became critical in the revolution in Colombia. He returned to Panama three years later following a brief tour of duty at the MB in Washington, D.C. During the following years he was transferred to duty in the Philippines, arriving in May 1907. While there he commanded the MB, Navy Yard, Cavite, and later the 1st Brig. of Marines. He was detached to the States in June 1909. His next tour of foreign shore duty was served in Cuba with the 2nd Prov. Brig. Marines from May 1912 to Dec. of the same year. After a short period in the States, he was again detached to expeditionary service in Cuba in Feb. 1913, this time with the 2nd Brig. at Guantanamo Bay. In Nov. 1913, he sailed from

New York with the 2nd Advanced Base Regt., his ultimate destination Vera Cruz, Mex. where he landed with his unit in Apr. of 1914. He returned home in Dec. 1914, this time reporting to HQMC in Washington, D.C. to become assistant to the Major General Commandant of the Marine Corps. With the outbreak of WWI, Lejeune assumed command of the newly constructed MB at Quantico, Va. Overseas service was, however, inevitable and in June 1918 he arrived at Brest, France. Upon reporting to the commander of the AEF, he was assigned to command a brigade of the 32nd Div., and assumed command of the 4th Brig. of Marines of the 2nd Div. immediately following the attack of that division in the Soissons offensive. On July 28, 1918, Gen. Lejeune assumed command of the 2nd Div. and remained in that capacity until Aug. 1919 when the unit was demobilized. He was the first Marine officer to hold an Army divisional command, and following the Armistice he led his division in the march into Germany. During WWI he was recognized by the French government as a strategist and leader, receiving the Legion of Honor and the Croix de Guerre from that country. In Oct. 1919, he again was appointed CG, MB, Quantico, prior to his appointment as Major General Commandant of the Marine Corps on June 30, 1920. Upon the expiration of his second term as Commandant, Gen. Lejeune indicated his reluctance to retire from the Marine Corps, but was still relieved as Commandant in Mar. 1929. The following Nov. of that year, he retired in order to accept the position of superintendant of the Virginia Military Institute, serving there until poor health necessitated his resignation in Oct. 1937. In Feb. 1942, he was advanced to the rank of lieutenant general on the Marine Corps retired list. Gen.

Lejeune died on Nov. 20, 1942, at the Union Memorial Hospital, Baltimore, Md., and was interred in the Arlington National Cemetery with full military honors. Today Camp Lejeune, N.C., bears the name of one of the ablest officers of the American military forces, and one of the most distinguished soldiers of WWI.

LEONARD, Joseph. Sergeant. Medal of Honor: b. Cohoes, N.Y., Aug. 28, 1876. Joseph Leonard enlisted in the Marine Corps at Brooklyn, N.Y. on June 7, 1897. He was awarded the nation's highest military honor for bravery during the Philippine Insurrection. His citation reads, in part: "... for distinguished conduct in the presence of the enemy, while with the 8th Army Corps on Mar. 25, 27, and 29, and on Apr. 4, 1899...." He was discharged from the Corps, but reenlisted to serve during WWI. On July 3, 1918, at Quantico, he was discharged as a sergeant.

LITTLETON, Herbert A. Private First Class. Medal of Honor: b. Blackhawk, S.D., July 1, 1930; d. KIA, Korea, Apr. 22, 1951. P.F.C. Littleton's citation reads, in part: "... while serving as a radio operator with an artillery forward observation team of Co. C, 1st Bn., 7th Marines, 1st Mar. Div. (Reinf.), in action against enemy aggressor forces in Korea on Apr. 22, 1951. Standing watch when a well-concealed and numerically superior enemy force launched a violent night attack from nearby positions against his company, P.F.C. Littleton quickly alerted the forward observation team and immediately moved into an advantageous position to assist in calling down artillery fire on the hostile force. When an enemy hand grenade was thrown into his vantage point shortly after the arrival of the remainder of the team, he un-hesitatingly hurled himself on the deadly missile, absorbing its full, shattering impact in his own body. By his prompt action and heroic spirit of self-sacrifice, he saved the other members of his team from serious injury or death. . . ."

Liversedge

LIVERSEDGE, Harry Bluett. "Harry the Horse." Brigadier General: b. Volcanoe, Calif., Sept. 21, 1894; d. Navy Medical Center, Bethesda, Md., Nov. 25, 1951. After attending the University of California, Harry Liversedge began his career in the Marine Corps in May 1917, when he enlisted as a private. He was commissioned a second lieutenant in Sept. 1918. He was promoted to first lieutenant in July 1919, while serving with the 5th

Brig. in France. Following his return to the States in Aug. 1919, he was ordered to the MB, Quantico, but shortly thereafter was assigned to the 2nd Prov. Mar. Brig. at Santo Domingo, arriving in Oct. of that year. In Apr. of the following year he was returned to the States. Upon return from the Olympic Games in 1920 and after a tour at the Naval Academy at Annapolis, he was ordered to MB, Quantico in Mar. 1922. As aide to Brig. Gen. John H. Russell, he later sailed to Port au Prince, Haiti, but was ordered back to Quantico in Aug. of the same year. He returned to Haiti in Dec. 1922 for duty as aide to the American High Commissioner. In July 1923, he reported for duty again at Quantico, and in the early part of the following year was transferred to the Naval Academy for participation in the 1924 Olympics. He returned to Quantico in Aug. of that year, this time to attend the Company Officers' Course at the MCS. Upon completion of this course he was transferred to Mare Is., Calif. He served at Quantico from Sept. 1926 to Feb. 1927, when he was detached for duty in China. Following his arrival in the Orient he was temporarily detached to the 3rd Brig. at Tientsin to act as boxing coach, and while in Shanghai participated in the International Track and Field Meets. In Aug. 1929, he was transferred to Quantico and in Nov. of the same year was ordered to the MCB at San Diego, Calif. Following his promotion to captain in Jan. 1930, he was ordered to HQ, Department of the Pacific, San Francisco, in May 1932. There he served as Aide-de-Camp to the CG. He served aboard the USS *California* from June 1933 to June 1935, when he returned to Quantico. He completed the Senior Course at the MCS and in June 1936, was transferred to serve on the Staff of the Basic School, MB, Navy Yard,

Philadelphia. He was appointed a major in July of that year. Early in 1938 he was again ordered to Quantico, this time to serve with the 1st Mar. Brig. In May 1940, another transfer took him to the west coast. There he was assigned duty as the Inspector-Instructor, 14th Bn., MCR at Spokane, Wash. Following his promotion to the rank of lieutenant colonel in Aug. 1940, he was ordered to the MCB, San Diego, and was subsequently assigned to the 8th Marines, 2nd Mar. Div. In Jan. 1942, Lt. Col. Liversedge departed from the States for American Samoa, in command of the 2nd Bn., 8th Marines. He was promoted to colonel in May of that same year and in Aug. he assumed command of the 3rd Mar. Raider Bn. He led this unit ashore at Pavuvu in the unopposed occupation of the Russell Is. He commanded the battalion until Mar. 1943 when he was given command of the newly organized 1st Mar. Raider Regt. In Jan. 1944, he was transferred to the 5th Mar. Div. and assumed command of the 28th Marines. He gallantly led the "28th" ashore in the Iwo Jima campaign, for which he was awarded a Gold Star in lieu of his Second Navy Cross. Following a brief tour of duty with the occupation forces in Japan, he was ordered to the MCB in San Diego in Mar. 1946. In July 1946 he was assigned duties as Director of the 12th Mar. Reserve District and District Marine Officer, 12th Naval District, San Francisco. He served in that capacity until he was named assistant commander of the 1st Mar. Div., Camp Pendleton, Calif., in Feb. 1948. In May of that year, he was promoted to brigadier general, and the following May he took command of Fleet Marine Force, Guam, where he remained until Apr. 1950. He then served briefly as Deputy Commander, MB, Camp Pendleton, before becoming Director of the Marine Corps Reserve in June 1950. He died at the Navy Medical Center, Bethesda, Md. on Nov. 25, 1951.

LOPEZ, Baldomero. First Lieutenant. Medal of Honor: b. Tampa, Fla., Aug. 23, 1925; d. KIA, Inchon, Korea, Sept. 15, 1950. Lt. Lopez' citation reads, in part: "... as a rifle platoon commander of Co. A, 1st Bn., 5th Marines, 1st Mar. Div. (Reinf.), in action against enemy aggressor forces during the Inchon invasion in Korea on Sept. 15, 1950. With his platoon, 1st Lt. Lopez was engaged in the reduction of immediate enemy beach defenses after landing with the assault waves. Exposing himself to hostile fire, he moved forward alongside a bunker and prepared to throw a hand grenade into the next pillbox whose fire was pinning down that sector of the beach. Taken under fire by an enemy automatic weapon and hit in the right shoulder and chest as he lifted his arm to throw, he fell backward and dropped the deadly missile. After a moment, he turned and dragged his body forward in an effort to retrieve the grenade and throw it. In critical condition from pain and loss of blood, and unable to grasp the hand grenade firmly enough to hurl it, he chose to sacrifice himself rather than endanger the lives of his men and, with a sweeping motion of his wounded right arm, cradled the grenade under him and absorbed the full impact of the explosion. ...."

LUCAS, Jacklyn Harrell. Private First Class. Medal of Honor: b. Plymouth, N.C., Feb. 14, 1928. On D-Day plus one on Iwo Jima, P.F.C. Lucas was creeping through a twisting ravine in company with three other men of his rifle team when the Japanese opened a hand grenade attack on them. The men jumped into two shallow foxholes. A grenade landed in Lucas' foxhole and he threw his body over it. Another one came hurtling in, and he reached out and pulled it beneath himself shortly before the explosion which lifted him off the ground and blew parts of his clothing into the air. Severely wounded in the right arm and wrist, right leg and thigh, and chest, P.F.C. Lucas had undoubtedly saved his companions from serious injury and possible death. He was evacuated and treated at various field hospitals prior to his arrival at San Francisco, Calif., Mar. 28, 1945. He was discharged from the MCR because of disability resulting from his wounds on Sept. 18, 1945.

Luckey

LUCKEY, Robert Burneston. Lieutenant General. CG, Fleet Marine Force, At-

lantic, Norfolk, Va.: b. Hyattsville, Md., July 9, 1905. After graduation from high school, Robert Luckey entered the University of Maryland, from which he was graduated in 1927. He accepted a commission as a Marine second lieutenant, Aug. 10, 1927. After completing the Basic School for Marine Corps Officers at the Philadelphia Navy Yard in Feb. 1928, Lt. Luckey sailed for Nicaragua the following month to serve on expeditionary duty with the 2nd Mar. Brig. He returned from Nicaragua in July 1929, and was assigned to the MB, U.S. Naval Academy, prior to completing the Sea School at the Navy Yard, Portsmouth, Va. In June 1930, he began a tour of sea duty with the Marine Detachment aboard the USS *Rochester*. From Sept. to Nov. 1930, he was temporarily detached from that ship to serve again in Nicaragua as commander of the Electoral Guard Detachment in the Department of Carazo. Leaving the *Rochester* in Feb. 1932, he served with Marine Detachments aboard the USS *Memphis* and *Fulton* until July of that year. In Sept. 1933, after a year's duty at the Norfolk Navy Yard, Lt. Luckey entered the Battery Officers' Course at the Army Field Artillery School, Fort Sill, Okla. Completing the course in June 1934, he was ordered to San Diego, Calif., where he served as a battery officer with the 6th and 10th Marines. He was promoted to first lieutenant in Jan. 1935. He sailed for China in Jan. 1936, and was assigned to the Marine Detachment at the American Embassy in Peiping. While there, he was promoted to captain in Nov. 1936. Luckey joined the 2nd Mar. Brig. at Shanghai in Jan. 1938, and returned with it to the States in Apr. That June he reported to the MB, Quantico, where in Sept. 1938 he was named Aide-de-Camp to the CG. He served in that capacity until July 1939, then served briefly as Post Adjutant. In Oct. 1939, he became a battery commander with the 1st Bn., 10th Marines, at Quantico. From Oct. 1940 to Apr. 1941, Capt. Luckey served with the 1st Mar. Brig., FMF, on temporary duty at Guantanamo Bay, Cuba. On his return, he served as a battalion operations and executive officer with the 11th Marines, 1st Mar. Div., at Parris Is., S.C., and later at Camp Lejeune, N.C. He was promoted to major in Jan. 1942. He was named Division Antitank Officer and commander of the 1st Special Weapons Bn., 1st Mar. Div., at Camp Lejeune in Feb. 1942, and embarked for the Pacific area with his battalion that June. Arriving on Guadalcanal in Aug., he took part in the fighting there. While on Guadalcanal, he was promoted to lieutenant colonel in Sept. 1942. Lt. Col. Luckey became Regimental Executive Officer of the 11th Marines in Oct. 1942. He held that post during the later stages of the Guadalcanal operation and in the Cape Gloucester campaign. In addition, he served as Artillery Officer on the staff of the Assistant CG, 1st Mar. Div., Cape Gloucester, and earned the Bronze Star Medal with Combat "V." He returned to the States in Feb. 1944. From Mar. to Oct. 1944, he was Director of the Artillery School, MCS, Quantico. He was ordered overseas again in Nov. 1944, and in Dec. 1944 was promoted to colonel. He served as Division Artillery Officer and Regimental Commander of the 15th Marines, 6th Mar. Div., on Okinawa and Guam, and in Tsingtao, China. In this capacity he earned the Legion of Merit with Combat "V" at Okinawa, and another Bronze Star Medal (Army) in Tsingtao during the surrender and repatriation of Japanese forces in that area. He returned from China in Apr. 1946 to enter the Naval War College, Newport, R.I. Upon grad-

uation in June 1947, Col. Luckey joined the 2nd Mar. Div., Camp Lejeune, as Division Artillery Officer and Regimental CO of the 4th and 10th Marines. He took command of the MB, Washington, D.C., in June 1949, and after two years there, returned to Camp Lejeune in July 1951. He served at Camp Lejeune as Assistant Chief of Staff, G-3, and later Chief of Staff, 2nd Mar. Div., until June 1953, when he became Chief of Staff, MCS, Quantico. In Aug. 1954, he was promoted to brigadier general. Gen. Luckey returned to Camp Lejeune in Sept. 1954, and served as CG, Force Troops, FMF, Atlantic, until June 1955. He then reported to HQMC, Washington, D.C., as Deputy Assistant Chief of Staff, G-3 (Plans), and in June 1956 began a year's assignment as Deputy Chief of Staff (Research and Development). While serving in this capacity, he was promoted to the rank of major general in Nov. 1956. In July 1957, Gen. Luckey became CG of the MCRD, Parris Is. Following this assignment, he reported in June 1959 as CG, 3rd Mar. Div. on Okinawa. On his return to the States in Oct. 1960, he served for one year as CG, MCB, Camp Lejeune. On Nov. 1, 1961, he assumed his current duties as CG, FMF, Atlantic, and was promoted to lieutenant general.

LUMMUS, Jack. First Lieutenant. Medal of Honor: b. Ennis, Tex., Oct. 22, 1915; d. Iwo Jima, Mar. 8, 1945. Lt. Lummus' citation reads, in part: ". . . as leader of a rifle platoon, attached to Co. E, 2nd Bn., 27th Marines, 5th Mar. Div., in action against enemy Japanese forces on Iwo Jima Mar. 8, 1945. Resuming his assault tactics with bold decision after fighting without respite for two days and nights, 1st Lt. Lummus slowly advanced his platoon against an enemy deeply entrenched in a network of mutually supporting positions. Suddenly halted by a terrific concentration of hostile fire, he unhesitatingly moved forward of his front lines in an effort to neutralize the Japanese position. Although knocked to the ground when an enemy grenade exploded close by, he immediately recovered himself and, again moving forward despite the intensified barrage, quickly located, attacked, and destroyed the occupied emplacement. Instantly taken under fire by the garrison of a supporting pillbox and further assailed by the slashing fury of hostile rifle fire, he fell under the impact of a second enemy grenade but, courageously disregarding painful shoulder wounds, staunchly continued his heroic one-man

assault and charged the second pillbox, annihilating all the occupants. Subsequently returning to his platoon position, he fearlessly traversed his lines under fire, encouraging his men to advance and directing the fire of supporting tanks against other holding Japanese emplacements. Held up again by a devastating barrage, he again moved into the open, rushed a third heavily fortified installation and killed the defending enemy. Determined to crush all resistance, he led his men indomitably, personally attacking foxholes and spider-traps with his carbine and systematically reducing the fanatic opposition until, stepping on a land mine, he sustained fatal wounds. . . ."

M

McCARD, Robert Howard. Gunnery Sergeant. Medal of Honor: b. Syracuse, N.Y., Nov. 25, 1918; d. KIA, Saipan, June 16, 1944. Sgt. McCard left the States on Jan. 13, 1944, and on Jan. 31, landed at Kwajelein in the Marshalls. From then until Feb. 26, he fought in the battles for Ennugaret, Ennumennett, and Namur Is. Leaving the Marshalls, he went to the Hawaiian Is. for two months, then sailed for Saipan. D-Day was June 15, 1944. On the 16th, Gy. Sgt. McCard participated in an advance when his tank was put out of action by a battery of Japanese 77-mm. guns. Cut off from the rest of his platoon, McCard brought all his tank's weapons to bear on the enemy, but the intensity of the Japanese fire caused him to order his crew out of the escape hatch. While they made their escape, McCard exposed himself and hurled hand gre-

nades at the enemy until his supply was exhausted. Severely wounded, he nevertheless dismantled one of the tank's machine guns, then faced the enemy again and delivered such effective fire that he killed 16 of the enemy before he himself was killed.

McCARTHY, Joseph Jeremiah. Captain, USMCR. Medal of Honor: b. Chicago, Ill., Aug. 10, 1911. Joseph McCarthy enlisted in the Marine Corps on Feb. 20, 1937 at Chicago, Ill., and served for four years. He was discharged and, after a year of civilian life, he reenlisted in Feb. 1942. He was again discharged in June of that year to accept a commission in the MCR. He joined the 4th Mar. Div. shortly thereafter and went overseas in Jan. 1944. He earned the Medal of Honor for gallantry on Iwo Jima. His citation reads, in part: "... as CO of Co. G, 2nd Bn., 24th Marines, 4th Mar. Div., in action against enemy Japanese forces during the seizure of Iwo Jima, Volcano Is., on Feb. 21, 1945. Determined to break through the enemy's cross-island defenses, Capt. McCarthy acted on his own initiative when his company advance was held up by uninterrupted Japanese rifle, machine gun and high velocity 47-mm. fire during the approach to Motoyama Airfield Number 2. Quickly organizing a demolitions and flame thrower team to accompany his picked rifle squad, he fearlessly led the way across 75 yards of fire-swept ground, charged a heavily fortified pillbox on the ridge to the front and, personally hurling hand grenades into the emplacement as he directed the combined operations of his small assault group, completely destroyed the hostile installation. Spotting two Japanese soldiers attempting an escape from the shattered pillbox, he boldly stood upright in full view of the enemy and dispatched both soldiers before advancing to a second emplacement under greatly intensified fire and blasted the strong fortifications with a well-planned demolitions attack. Subsequently entering the ruins, he found a Japanese taking aim at one of his men and with alert presence of mind jumped the enemy, disarmed and shot him with his own weapon. Then, intent on smashing through the narrow breach, he rallied the remainder of his company and pressed a full attack with furious aggressiveness until he had neutralized all resistance and captured the ridge."

McCAWLEY, Charles G. Colonel. 8th Commandant of the Marine Corps — Nov. 1, 1876 to Jan. 29, 1891: b. Philadelphia, Pa., Jan. 29, 1827; d. Rosemont, Pa., Oct. 13, 1891. Charles McCawley was appointed a second lieutenant in the Marine Corps on Mar. 3, 1847 and served during the war with Mexico. He participated in the storming of the Castle of Chapultepec and taking of the City of Mexico, being brevetted first lieutenant for gallant and meritorious conduct in these actions. He served throughout the Civil War. In May 1862, he was ordered with a detachment of Marines to reoccupy the Norfolk Navy Yard and aided in the destruction of large stores of ammunition, which would otherwise have fallen into the hands of the Confederate forces. He also aided in the capture of Port Royal, S.C., and served with a battalion of Marines on Morris Is. during the bombardment and destruction of Fort Sumter and the capture of Forts Wagner and Gregg. He commanded a detachment of 100 officers and men in the boat attack on Fort Sumter, Sept. 8, 1863, and received a brevet as major for gallant and meritorious conduct during this engagement. In 1876 he was appointed to the highest post in the Marine Corps, Colonel Commandant. One of Col. McCawley's first duties as Commandant was to dispatch Marines to eastern cities where labor riots had gone beyond control of local and state authorities. In each instance, the disorders were dispersed shortly after the arrival of the Marines. Among other accomplishments attributed to his tenure was a plan that resulted in the assignment of several members of each graduating class of the U.S. Naval Academy to the Marine Corps as second lieutenants. The Quartermaster Department, under Commandant McCawley, became more self-sustaining by manufacturing a considerable portion of its own clothing and equipment at its supply depot in Philadelphia. In 1880, he assigned one of the Corps' most famous officers — John Philip Sousa — to serve as leader of the Marine Corps

Band. During McCawley's 15-year term as Commandant, U.S. Marines staged successful landings in Panama, Chile, Egypt, Korea, Haiti, Samoa, Argentina, Japan, and the Hawaiian Is. to protect American lives and property. Marines also served in Alaska where they patrolled the Bering shores to eliminate seal poaching. Col. McCawley retired from active service at the age of 64 on Jan. 29, 1891.

McCUTCHEON, Keith Barr. Brigadier General. Assistant Chief of Staff J-3, Staff of the Commander in Chief, Pacific, Hawaii (1963): b. East Liverpool, Ohio, Aug. 10, 1915. After graduation from high school in 1933, Keith McCutcheon obtained his Bachelor of Science degree in management engineering from Carnegie Institute of Technology at Pittsburgh, Pa., in 1937. An honor graduate of the ROTC unit at Carnegie Tech, he resigned his Army Reserve commission to accept appointment as a Marine second lieutenant, Aug. 13, 1937. The following June, after completing the Basic School for Marine Corps officers at the Philadelphia Navy Yard, he began a tour of sea duty with the Marine Detachment aboard the USS *Yorktown*, remaining on that ship until May 1939. A month later he entered flight training at Pensacola, Fla. In July 1940, he completed flight school and was designated a naval aviator. He was promoted to first lieutenant the following month. Lt. McCutcheon's first duty station in aviation was with Marine Observation Squadron 1 (which later became Observation Squadron 151). With that squadron he served aboard the carriers *Ranger, Wasp,* and *Yorktown,* and at Guantanamo Bay, Cuba, and San Juan, Puerto Rico, during extensive Caribbean maneuvers. He was detached from the squadron in Sept.

1941 to enter the Postgraduate School, U.S. Naval Academy, where he completed the course in aeronautical engineering. While there he was promoted to captain in Feb. 1942, and to major in Aug. 1942. From Annapolis, Maj. McCutcheon was ordered to the Massachusetts Institute of Technology at Cambridge in Oct. 1943 for graduate work in aeronautical engineering. He was promoted to lieutenant colonel in May 1944, and that June received his Master of Science degree. In Sept. 1944, after a short tour as Executive Officer, MAG 41, at El Toro, Calif., he departed for the Pacific area. He served as Operations Officer of MAG 24 on Bougainville; and later on Luzon and Mindanao, Philippine Is. He saw additional duty, subsequently, as Operations Officer of MAGs, Dagupan, on Luzon, and later Operations Officer of MAGs, Zamboanga, on Mindanao. The Silver Star Medal was awarded Lt. Col. McCutcheon for gallantry in action from April 12 to 17, 1945, at Malabang, Mindanao, where he flew into a guerrilla-held airstrip four days before the American invasion to obtain vital information from guerrilla leaders on Japanese strength in the area. On the last day before the landings, he and the Australian Army officer who led the guerrillas joined the invasion convoy by small boat to turn over their information to the task force commander. Prior to the Luzon invasion, he directed a program of intensive close air support training for MAGs 24 and 32. Both these groups earned Navy Unit Commendations for their support of the U.S. 6th Army at Luzon and, afterward, as part of MAGs, Zamboanga, went on to share another Navy Unit Commendation with MAG 12 for their support of the 8th Army on Mindanao and in the Sulu Archipelago. He also earned the Distinguished Flying

Cross and six Air Medals during WWII. Detached from MAG 24 in Aug. 1945, he remained in the Philippines for a short time after the war as Operations Officer of MAG 32, and Executive Officer of MAG 61, respectively. He returned to the States in Nov. 1945, and shortly after was assigned as an instructor in the Aviation Section, MCS, Quantico. Following this, he served from Oct. 1946 until Dec. 1949 in the Bureau of Aeronautics, Navy Department, Washington, D.C. He served in the Guided Missiles (then Pilotless Aircraft) Division of the Design and Engineering Group, and was Branch Chief at various times of the Liaison, Experimental Projects, and Target Drone branches. He also performed additional duty in 1947 as Senior Marine Corps Aide to the White House. Lt. Col. McCutcheon was transferred to Norfolk, Va. in Jan. 1950, completing the course at the Armed Forces Staff College in June 1950. He was then ordered to Quantico for duty as CO of Marine Helicopter Squadron 1 (HMX-1), the Corps' only helicopter squadron at that time. After undergoing transitional helicopter training with the Navy's Helicopter Squadron 2, at Lakehurst, N.J. he was designated a helicopter pilot in Aug. 1950. During the next 18 months, HMX-1 served as the focal point for the expansion of the Marine Corps helicopter program. In addition, he served as a member of the Marine Corps Schools Advanced Base Problem Team during a demonstration in England in 1951. He was promoted to colonel in June 1951. In Nov. 1951, he left Quantico and the following month took command of Marine Helicopter Transport Squadron 161 in Korea. He earned his second Legion of Merit with Combat "V" and his seventh through tenth Air Medal in this capacity, prior to his return from Korea in Aug. 1952.

That Oct., after a short time at HQMC, Washington, he reported to HQ, United States European Command in Frankfurt, Germany, where he served successively as Operations Officer, Assistant Chief, and later Chief, Operations Branch, J-3 Division, until May 1954. Upon his return to the States, Col. McCutcheon assumed duties in June 1954 as Chief, Air Section, Marine Corps Equipment Board, Quantico. In Aug. 1957, he reported to MAG 26 at New River, Camp Lejeune, N.C., as CO. He commanded the helicopter group until June 1959, when he was detached to Washington, D.C., to attend the National War College. Following graduation, Col. McCutcheon was assigned to HQMC in July 1960 as Assistant Director of Aviation, and in Sept. 1961 was named Director of Aviation. He departed Washington in Feb. 1962, and that Mar. was promoted to his present rank of brigadier general and assumed command of the Hawaii-based 1st Mar. Brig. Gen. McCutcheon commanded the brigade until Jan. 1963, when he joined the staff of Commander in Chief Pacific as Assistant Chief of Staff, J-3.

McLAUGHLIN, Alford Lee. Technical Sergeant. Medal of Honor: b. Leeds, Ala., Mar. 18, 1928. Sgt. McLaughlin's citation reads, in part: " . . . while serving as a machine gunner of Co. I, 3rd Bn., 5th Marines, 1st Mar. Div. (Reinf.), in action against enemy aggressor forces in Korea on the night of Sept. 4-5, 1952. Volunteering for his second continuous tour of duty on a strategic combat outpost far in advance of the main line of resistance, (then) P.F.C. McLaughlin, although operating under a barrage of enemy artillery and mortar fire, set up plans for the defense of his position which proved decisive in the successful defense of the outpost. When hostile forces attacked in battalion strength during the night, he maintained a constant flow of devastating fire upon the enemy, alternately employing two machine guns, a carbine, and hand grenades. Although painfully wounded, he bravely fired the machine guns from the hip until his hands became blistered by the extreme heat from the weapons and, placing the guns on the ground to allow them to cool, continued to defend the position with his carbine and grenades. Standing up in full view, he shouted words of encouragement to his comrades above the din of battle and, throughout a series of fanatical enemy attacks, sprayed the surrounding area with deadly fire, accounting for an estimated 150 enemy dead and 50 wounded. . . ."

McNALLY, Michael Joseph. Sergeant Major. Medal of Honor: b. New York, N.Y., June 29, 1860; d. Washington *Star* obituary records death of a Michael Joseph McNally at the Naval Medical Center, Bethesda, Md., on May 24, 1957. Michael McNally enlisted in the Marine Corps on Dec. 1, 1897, and was awarded the Medal of Honor for "distinguished conduct in the presence of the enemy at Samoa on Apr. 1, 1899." He retired from the Corps on Dec. 1, 1914.

McNAMARA, Michael. Private. Medal of Honor: b. Clure, Ireland, 1841. Michael McNamara enlisted in the Marine Corps at Brooklyn, N.Y. on Nov. 19, 1868. His citation reads, in part: ". . . while serving on board the USS *Benicia* . . . for gallantry in advancing to the parapet, wrenching the match-lock from the hands of an enemy and killing him, at the capture of the Korean Forts, June 11, 1871. . . ."

McTUREOUS, Robert Miller, Jr. Private.

Medal of Honor: b. Altoona, Fla., Mar. 26, 1924; d. KIA, aboard hospital ship USS *Relief,* June 11, 1945. Pvt. McTureous' citation reads, in part ". . . while serving with Co. H, 3rd Bn., 29th Marines, 6th Mar. Div., in action against enemy Japanese forces on Okinawa, June 7, 1945 . . . following his company's seizure of an important hill-objective, Pvt. McTureous was quick to observe the plight of company stretcher-bearers who were suddenly assailed by slashing machine gun fire as they attempted to evacuate wounded at the rear of the newly won position. Determined to prevent further casualties, he quickly filled his shirt with hand grenades and charged the enemy-occupied caves from which the concentrated barrage was emanating . . . as he waged his furious one-man assault, he smashed grenades into the cave entrances, thereby diverting the heaviest fire from the stretcher-bearers to his own person and, resolutely returning to his own lines under a blanketing hail of rifle and machine gun fire to replenish his supply of grenades, dauntlessly he continued his systematic reduction of Japanese strength until he himself sustained serious wounds after silencing a large number of the hostile guns. Aware of his own critical condition and unwilling to further endanger the lives of his comrades, he stoically crawled a distance of 200 yards to a sheltered position within friendly lines before calling for aid. By his fearless initiative and bold tactics, Pvt. McTureous had succeeded in neutralizing the enemy fire, killing six of the Japanese and effectively disorganizing the remainder of the savagely defending garrison. . . ."

MacNEAL, Harry Lewis. Private. Medal of Honor: b. Philadelphia, Pa., Mar. 22, 1875. Harry MacNeal enlisted in the

Marine Corps on Nov. 16, 1896. He was awarded the Medal of Honor on Aug. 9, 1899 for his gallantry while serving on board the USS *Brooklyn* during the battle of Santiago, Cuba, on July 3, 1898.

Mackie

MACKIE, John Freeman. Corporal. First Marine to win the Medal of Honor: b. New York, N.Y., 1836; d. Philadelphia, Pa., 1910. John Mackie enlisted in the Marine Corps at Brooklyn, N.Y. on Aug. 23, 1861. He was awarded the Medal of Honor on July 10, 1863, for bravery ". . . while serving on board the USS *Galena* in the attack on Fort Darling at Drurys Bluff, James River, May 15, 1862 . . . particularly mentioned for his gallant conduct and services and signal acts of devotion to duty. . . ." Mackie was discharged from the Corps on July 10, 1863.

MANGRUM, Richard Charles. Major General. CG, 2nd Marine Aircraft Wing, MCAS, Cherry Point, N.C.: b. Seattle, Wash., Oct. 27, 1906. After attending Franklin High School and the University of Washington in Seattle, Richard Mangrum enlisted in the MCR on Sept. 28, 1928, and entered primary flight training at the Naval Reserve Aviation Base, Seattle. He completed advanced flight training at Pensacola, Fla., in Feb. 1929, and was commissioned a Marine Reserve second lieutenant on Apr. 27, 1929. Lt. Mangrum was next assigned to NAS, San Diego, Calif., where he was designated a naval aviator, Aug. 20, 1929, then served as a squadron officer until Mar. 1931. During the next ten years, he was active in Marine aviation on the west coast, serving as commander of the Marine Corps Reserve Aviation Unit in Seattle, and in Oakland, Calif., respectively, and also as a squadron inspector-instructor. During this period, he was promoted to first lieutenant in June 1931, and then to captain in Jan. 1937. He was integrated in the regular Marine Corps in Feb. 1941. The following month he joined Bombing Squadron 2, 2nd MAG, on Ewa, Oahu, Hawaii. In July 1941, the group was integrated with the newly formed 2nd MAW, and the squadron and group were redesignated Marine Scout Bombing Squadron 232 (VMSB-232), MAG 21. When the Japanese struck Pearl Harbor on Dec. 7, 1941, Capt. Mangrum took part in the defense of Ewa Field, Oahu. He was promoted to major in Jan. 1942. That month he was named commander of VMSB-232 and moved with the squadron to Guadalcanal, where his unit became the first dive-bomber squadron to operate in the Solomons. He was awarded the Distinguished Flying Cross and the Navy Cross for his action in the Solomons campaign. During this

Mangrum

campaign, he was promoted to lieutenant colonel in Sept. 1942. In Jan. 1943, following his return to the States, Lt. Col. Mangrum assumed command of the Aviation Cadet Regiment at NAS, Corpus Christi, Tex. He was promoted to colonel in Dec. 1943. In May 1944, Col. Mangrum was transferred to Cherry Point, N.C., and became CO of MAG 93, 9th MAW, Marine Corps Auxiliary Air Facility, Bogue Field. He returned to the Pacific area in Nov. 1944 as Chief of Staff, 3rd MAW and, later, as CO, MAG 45, 4th MAW. He served at Ulithi in the

western Caroline Is. as Air Defense Commander from Jan. to Oct. 1945. Following WWII, he reported to HQMC, Washington, D.C., as Head of the Reserve Section, Division of Aviation, to reactivate the Aviation Reserve Program. In July 1948, he was enrolled at the Naval War College, Newport, R.I. Completing the Strategy and Tactics Course in June 1949, he served on the faculty until July 1951. The following month he flew to Korea for duty with the 1st MAW. His service as CO, MAG 12, and later as Wing Liaison Officer with HQ, 5th Air Force, Seoul, earned him a second Legion of Merit with Combat "V," and the Navy Commendation Ribbon with Combat "V." Col. Mangrum returned to this country in June 1952, and was ordered to Quantico, where he served as Chief of Staff of the Marine Corps Educational Center. In Aug. 1954, he was transferred to MCAS, Miami, Fla., for duty as CO. While at Miami he rejoined the FMF as CO, MAG 31 (Reinf.) for a brief period, and also commanded an air-ground task group for the TRAEX 2-56 maneuvers in the Caribbean area. He became Deputy Assistant Chief of Staff, G-3 (Plans), at HQMC, Washington, D.C., in June 1956. He was promoted to brigadier general in July 1957. Departing Washington early in 1959, Gen. Mangrum became Assistant Wing Commander, 1st MAW, at Iwakuni, Japan, in Feb. 1959. He was promoted to his present rank of major general in Nov. 1959, and assumed duties as CG of the 1st MAW. He served in this capacity until Apr. 1960 when he returned to the States. In May 1960, Gen. Mangrum was assigned to Norfolk, Va., as CG, Aircraft, FMF, Atlantic, and Deputy Commander, FMF, Atlantic. Upon consolidation of the two activities, July 1, 1960, he continued as Deputy Commander, FMF, Atlantic, until Sept. 1961. The following month, he assumed his current assignment as CG, 2nd MAW.

MARGULIES, Samuel. Private. Served under the name of GROSS, Samuel (*q.v.*).

MARTIN, Harry Linn. First Lieutenant. Medal of Honor: b. Bucyrus, Ohio, Jan. 4, 1911; d. KIA, Iwo Jima, Mar. 26, 1945. Lt. Martin landed on Iwo Jima on Feb. 19, 1945 – D-Day. Less than a month later, on Mar. 16, the day the Iwo campaign officially closed, the Japanese launched a concentrated attack and penetrated the Marine lines in the area where Lt. Martin's platoon was bivouacked. "He immediately organized a firing line among the men in the foxholes closest to his own and temporarily stopped the headlong rush of the enemy. Several of his men lay wounded in positions overrun by the Japanese and, in a determined effort to rescue them, he was severely wounded twice as he defied intense hostile fire and made his way through the Japanese to his men, guiding them back to their own lines. Four of the enemy had entrenched themselves in an abandoned machine gun pit and were subjecting the area to a barrage of hand grenades. Lt. Martin, alone and armed only with a pistol, charged the pit and killed all four of its occupants. Realizing that his few remaining men could not repulse another organized attack, he called to them to follow him and then charged into the midst of the strong enemy force, firing his weapon and scattering them until he fell mortally wounded by a grenade. He died 10 days later. . . ."

MARTIN, James. Sergeant. Medal of Honor: b. Derry, Ireland, 1826. James Martin enlisted in the Marine Corps at Philadelphia, Pa. on July 9, 1847. He earned the nation's highest military award ". . . while serving on board the USS *Richmond,* Mobile Bay . . . was commended for coolness and good conduct as a captain of a gun in the action of Mobile Bay on the morning and forenoon of Aug. 5, 1864 . . . was in actions with Forts Jackson and St. Philip, the Chalmettes, the rebel ironclads and gunboats below New Orleans, Vicksburg, Port Hudson, and was present at the surrender of New Orleans, on board the *Richmond.* . . ." He was awarded the Medal of Honor on Dec. 31, 1864. He retired from the Corps after seven reenlistments, having served 33 years.

MASON, Leonard Foster. Private First Class. Medal of Honor: b. Middleborough, Ky., Feb. 2, 1920; d. KIA, Guam, July 23, 1944. P.F.C. Mason was awarded the Medal of Honor for conspicuous gallantry in singlehandedly charging and wiping out a Japanese machine gun position on Guam, July 22, 1944, despite serious wounds. Mason, an automatic rifleman, made the initial landing on July 21. The next day he was proceeding with his comrades through a gully when Japanese machine guns opened fire on them. Resolving to clear out the enemy position, Mason left the gully to blast the enemy from the rear. Wounded numerous times in the arm and shoulder, he nevertheless wiped out the enemy position and rejoined his platoon to report, before consenting to be evacuated. The following day he died aboard a hospital ship offshore.

MASTERS, James Marvin, Sr. Major General. CG, Marine Corps Base, Camp Pendleton, Calif.: b. Atlanta, Ga., June 16, 1911. James Masters attended The Citadel before entering the U.S. Naval Academy at Annapolis in 1929. Upon graduation from the Academy, he was commissioned a Marine second lieutenant, June 1, 1933. He completed the Basic Course at the Philadelphia Navy Yard in May 1934, and the following month began a year's tour of sea duty, serving with the Marine Detachment aboard the USS *New Mexico*. In July 1935, he joined the 1st Mar. Brig. at Quantico, Va. He was promoted to first lieutenant in July 1936. Lt. Masters remained at Quantico until Jan. 1937, and the following month embarked for Shanghai, China, where he served with the 4th Marines until Nov. 1939. While in China, he was promoted to captain in Sept. 1939. On his return to the States, he was ordered to the MB, Washington, D.C. in Dec. 1939, and later served briefly at Quantico. In Sept. 1940, he was assigned to the MCB, Parris Is., S.C., as a battery CO with the 4th Defense Bn. He was transferred with the battalion to Guantanamo Bay, Cuba, in Feb. 1941, and in Nov. 1941 embarked with the battalion for Pearl Harbor. On Dec. 7, 1941, Capt. Masters participated in the defense of that base against the Japanese aerial attack. On Dec. 25, he departed Pearl Harbor en route to and in command of the first reinforcements for Johnston Is., where he remained until Nov. 1942. He was promoted to major in May 1942. Maj. Masters then joined the 10th Defense Bn. at Pearl Harbor in Nov. 1942. Later, as Executive Officer of the battalion, attached to the 1st Mar. Amphibious Corps, he served in the Solomon and Russell Is. He was promoted to lieutenant colonel in Apr. 1943. In Aug. 1943, he joined the 2nd Bn., 1st Marines, 1st Mar. Div., and served briefly in Australia prior to going into combat again in Dec. 1943 and Jan. 1944 as a battalion CO at Cape Gloucester. Following this, he returned to the States and, in Mar. 1944, assumed duty at HQMC with the Division of Plans and Policies, G-3. In

Sept. he was assigned detached duty at Pearl Harbor, and on Guam, Saipan, and Tinian, Marianas Is. In Nov. 1944, he was transferred to the 7th Marines, 1st Mar. Div. The following month, he began serving as Regimental Executive Officer at Pavuvu, Russell Is. In this capacity he took part in combat on Okinawa, in Apr., May, and June of 1945, during which action he earned the Navy Cross. Ordered to Tientsin, China, in Oct. 1945, Lt. Col. Masters served with the 1st Mar. Div. as Assistant Chief of Staff, G-2, until Mar. 1946, then returned to the States. Upon his return, he was again assigned to HQMC where in May 1946 he began a two-year assignment in the Inspection Division. In May 1948, he was ordered to the MCS, Quantico, serving as Executive Officer and, later, CO of the Basic School. He was promoted to colonel in Aug. 1949. He was then transferred to Camp Lejeune, N.C., and assumed command of the 8th Mar. Regt., 2nd Mar. Div. in Sept. 1950. He commanded the regiment for 18 months, then returned to Washington where he was enrolled as a student at the National War College from Aug. 1952 to June 1953. The following month he became a Member of the Joint Strategic Plans Group, Joint Staff, Office of the Joint Chiefs of Staff, serving in this capacity for two years. In Aug. 1955, Col. Masters assumed duty as Regimental Commander of the 4th Marines (Reinf.), 3rd Mar. Div., at MCAS, Kaneohe Bay, Hawaii. He commanded this regiment until he was named FMF Pacific Liaison Officer to the Commander in Chief, Pacific Fleet in Hawaii in June 1956. While serving in this capacity, he was promoted to brigadier general in July 1957. Gen. Masters reported to HQMC as Assistant Chief of Staff, G-2, in Sept. 1957. He was assigned additional duty as Inspector

General of the Marine Corps in June 1960, and was promoted to major general the following month. He continued in the post of Inspector General of the Marine Corps from Aug. 1960 until July 1961. Transferred to the west coast, Gen. Masters assumed command of the 1st Mar. Div. (Reinf.), FMF, at Camp Pendleton, Calif., July 31, 1961. He served in this capacity until June 1962, when he became CG, MCB, Camp Pendleton.

MASTERS, John Hillary. Brigadier General. Assistant Division Commander, 3rd Mar. Div., Okinawa: b. Atlanta, Ga., May 23, 1913. John Masters attended The Citadel, Charleston, S.C., for a year and a half, before entering the U.S. Naval Academy in 1932. On graduating from the Academy he was appointed a Marine second lieutenant, June 4, 1936. Lt. Masters served as a company officer at the Portsmouth, N.H. Navy Yard, then completed the Basic School at the Philadelphia Navy Yard in June 1937. Assigned to the 5th Marines, 1st Mar. Brig., FMF, Quantico, he served as a platoon leader in a machine gun company and Officer in Charge of the Special Weapons and Antitank Platoons, and took part in maneuvers in the Caribbean. He was promoted to first lieutenant in June 1939. That month he became Aide-de-Camp to the CG, MB, Quantico. In May 1940, he departed Quantico to assume duty aboard the USS *Tuscaloosa* as CO of the Marine Detachment. While serving in this capacity, he was promoted to captain in Jan. 1942, and to major in Sept. 1942. On completing his tour of sea duty in Sept. 1942, Maj. Masters embarked for China where he served for 21 months as Commander, U.S. Naval Unit 1, U.S. Naval Group, China, and trained Chinese guerrilla troops. During this assignment, he was promoted to lieutenant colonel

in Jan. 1944, and remained in China until June 1944. The following month, Lt. Col. Masters assumed duty at HQMC, Washington, D.C., as Aide-de-Camp to the CMC, Gen. A. A. Vandegrift. He returned to China in Sept. 1945, and participated in the occupation of northern China until May 1947. During this time, he commanded the 1st Bn., 5th Marines, then served as Regimental Executive Officer from Oct. 1946 to May 1947. In July 1947, he resumed his former duties in the States as Aide-de-Camp to the CMC, and continued in the same capacity with Gen. Vandegrift's successor, Gen. Clifton B. Cates, from Jan. 1948 through May 1949. Ordered next to MCS, Quantico, he completed the Senior Course, Sept. 1949 to June 1950. He then served as Chief, General Subjects Group, Combined Arms Section, until Mar. 1951; and Assistant Director, Junior School, until Mar. 1952. He was promoted to colonel in Feb. 1951. He was transferred to Camp Lejeune, N.C., in Mar. 1952, as Regimental Commander, 8th Marines, 2nd Mar. Div. In Feb. 1954, he became Assistant Chief of Staff, MCB, Camp Pendleton, then served as Assistant Chief of Staff, G-3, from July 1954 through Aug. 1955. Remaining at Camp Pendleton, he was named CO, 2nd Inf. Training Regt., in Sept. 1955, and held this post until June 1957. Col. Masters assumed duties in Aug. 1957 as Force Inspector, FMF, Pacific, Honolulu, Hawaii. In May 1958, he was named CO, 4th Marines (Reinf.), 1st Mar. Brig., on Kaneohe Bay, Oahu, Hawaii. He served there until July 1959 and, on his return to Washington, D.C., assumed duties in Aug. 1959 as Assistant Director of Personnel, HQMC. Following this assignment, Col. Masters was named Legislative Assistant to the CMC in Feb. 1960. While serving in that capacity, he was promoted to his present rank of brigadier general in July 1960. Gen. Masters departed from HQMC in Sept. 1962, and assumed duty as Assistant Division Commander, 3rd Mar. Div., on Okinawa.

MATHIAS, Clarence Edward. Sergeant Major. Medal of Honor: b. Royalton, Pa., Dec. 12, 1876; d. U.S. Naval Hospital, Washington, D.C., Dec. 9, 1935. Clarence Mathias enlisted in the Marine Corps at Harrisburg, Pa. on Sept. 20, 1899. His citation reads, in part: ". . . for distinguished conduct in the presence of the enemy in the advance on Tientsin, China, June 21, 1900. . . ." Mathias was retired from the Corps on June 15, 1923 as a sergeant major.

MATTHEWS, Daniel Paul. Sergeant. Medal of Honor: b. Van Nuys, Calif., Dec. 31, 1931; d. KIA, Vegas Hill, Korea, Mar. 28, 1953. Sgt. Matthews' citation reads, in part: ". . . while serving as a Squad Leader of Co. F, 2nd Bn., 7th Marines, 1st Mar. Div. (Reinf.), in action against enemy aggressor forces in Korea on Mar. 28, 1953. Participating in a counterattack against a firmly entrenched and well concealed hostile force which had repelled six previous assaults on a vital enemy-held outpost far forward of the main line of resistance, Sgt. Matthews fearlessly advanced in the attack until his squad was pinned down by a murderous sweep of fire from an enemy machine gun located on the peak of the outpost. Observing that the deadly fire prevented a corpsman from removing a wounded man lying in an open area fully exposed to the brunt of the devastating gunfire, he worked his way to the base of the hostile machine gun emplacement, leaped onto the rock fortification surrounding the gun and, taking the enemy by complete surprise, singlehandedly

charged the hostile emplacement with his rifle. Although severely wounded when the enemy brought a withering hail of fire to bear upon him, he gallantly continued his valiant one-man assault and, firing his rifle with deadly effectiveness, succeeded in killing two of the enemy, routing a third, and completely silencing the enemy weapon, thereby enabling his comrades to evacuate the stricken Marine to a safe position. Succumbing to his wounds before aid could reach him, Sgt. Matthews, by his indomitable fighting spirit, courageous initiative, and resolute determination in the face of almost certain death, served to inspire all who observed him and was directly instrumental in saving the life of his wounded comrade. . . ."

MAUSERT, Frederick William, III. Sergeant. Medal of Honor: b. Cambridge, N.Y., May 2, 1930; d. KIA, Songnap-yong, Korea, Sept. 12, 1951. Sgt. Mausert's citation reads, in part: ". . . while serving as a squad leader in Co. B, 1st Bn., 7th Marines, 1st Mar. Div. (Reinf.), in action against enemy aggressor forces in Korea on Sept. 12, 1951. With his company pinned down and suffering heavy casualties under murderous machine gun, rifle, artillery, and mortar fire laid down from heavily fortified, deeply entrenched hostile strongholds on Hill 673, Sgt. Mausert unhesitatingly left his covered position and ran through a heavily mined and fire-swept area to bring back two critically wounded men to the comparative safety of the lines. Staunchly refusing evacuation despite a painful head wound sustained during his voluntary act, he insisted on remaining with his squad and, with his platoon ordered into the assault moments later, took the point position and led his men in a furious bayonet charge against the first of a series of literally impregnable bunkers. Stunned and knocked to the ground when another bullet struck his helmet, he regained his feet and resumed his drive, personally silencing the machine gun and leading his men in eliminating several other emplacements in the area. Promptly reorganizing his unit for a renewed fight to the final objective on top of the ridge, Sgt. Mausert boldly left his position when the enemy's fire gained momentum and, making a target of himself, boldly advanced alone into the face of the machine gun, drawing the fire away from his men and enabling them to move into position to assault. Again severely wounded when the enemy's fire found its mark, he still refused aid and continued spearheading the assault to the topmost machine gun nest and bunkers, the last bulwark of the fanatic aggressors. Leaping into the wall of fire, he destroyed another machine gun with grenades before he was mortally wounded by bursting grenades and machine gun fire. . . ."

Megee

MEGEE, Vernon E. Lieutenant General (Retired). Veteran of Korean fighting, three WWII campaigns, and prewar expeditionary duty in Haiti, China, and Nicaragua: b. Tulsa, Okla., June 5, 1900. Vernon Megee enlisted in the Marine Corps on Mar. 8, 1919, and was commissioned a second lieutenant May 4, 1922. After completing the Officers' Basic Course, he served his first tour of expeditionary duty with the 1st Mar. Brig. in Haiti from Oct. 1923 to Nov. 1925. He was then stationed with the 10th Marines at Quantico. He was promoted to first lieutenant in Mar. 1926. In Apr. of the following year, Lt. Megee was ordered to China for his second tour of expeditionary duty. Returning from China in Mar. 1928, he was assigned to preliminary aviation training at the NAS,

San Diego, Calif. until Jan. 1929. He then began another tour of expeditionary service as Squadrons Quartermaster, Aircraft Squadrons, 2nd Mar. Brig., in Nicaragua. After earning the Navy and Marine Corps Medal there, he returned to the States to enter flight training at Pensacola, Fla. in Jan. 1931. Awarded his wings in Feb. 1932, Lt. Megee was next assigned to Aircraft Squadrons, West Coast Expeditionary Forces at San Diego, where he remained until May 1933. The following month he began a three-year tour of duty at Quantico as a student and instructor in the MCS, then as Executive Officer of Marine Fighter Squadron 9. He was promoted to captain in Nov. 1934. Capt. Megee entered the Air Corps Tactical Training School at Maxwell Field, Ala., in Aug. 1936. After graduating in June 1937, he returned to Quantico for another two years as an instructor in aviation tactics. He was promoted to major in Aug. 1938. In July 1939, Megee took command of Marine Fighter Squadron 2, 2nd MAG, with which he participated in fleet exercises the following year. In Oct. 1940, Maj. Megee was assigned to the U.S. Naval Aviation Mission to Peru as special advisor to that government's Minister of Aviation. He was promoted to lieutenant colonel in Jan. 1942, and to colonel in Dec. 1942. He returned to the States in Oct. 1943. The following month Col. Megee reported to Cherry Point, N.C. as Chief of Staff of the 3rd MAW. He went overseas with that unit in May 1944. Assigned to Aircraft, FMF, Pacific in Oct. 1944, he was named commander of the Prov. Air Support Command. After leading Control Unit 1 at Iwo Jima, he became Chief of Staff, Air Support Control Units, Pacific Fleet, with additional duty as Commander, Marine Air Support Control Units. He served in that capacity until he returned to the States in Sept. 1945. Reporting to HQMC that Oct., Col. Megee became a member of the Joint Amphibious Operations and Doctrines Committee until Aug. 1946. He then served briefly as an instructor at the National War College, Washington, D.C. He was promoted to brigadier general in Dec. 1946. Ordered to Norfolk, Va., the general became Chief of Staff, FMF, Atlantic the following month. Gen. Megee returned to Washington in Aug. 1949 to serve as Assistant Director of Marine Corps Aviation until Jan. 1950. That month he joined the Joint Staff, Department of Defense. In Aug. 1951, he was promoted to major general and named commander of MCAS and Marine Corps Air Bases, Cherry Point, N.C. The gen-

eral remained there until Feb. 1952, then served for almost a year as CG, Aircraft, FMF, Pacific at El Toro, Calif. He took command of the 1st MAW in Korea in Jan. 1953. The following Jan. he reported to Pearl Harbor, where he served as Deputy Commander, FMF, Pacific, until June 1955. A month later he was appointed CG, Aircraft, FMF, Atlantic, serving in that capacity at Norfolk until Dec. 1955. Gen. Megee was promoted to lieutenant general Jan. 1, 1956. On the same date, he was appointed Assistant Commandant of the Marine Corps and Chief of Staff, HQMC. He was the first Marine aviator to serve in that capacity. Following two years in this assignment, he moved to Honolulu, T.H., where he served as CG, FMF, Pacific, from Dec. 1957 until his retirement Nov. 1, 1959.

MEREDITH, James. Private. Medal of Honor. See FORD, Patrick F., Jr.

MILLER, Andrew. Sergeant. Medal of Honor: b. Germany, 1836. Andrew Miller enlisted in the Marine Corps at Washington, D.C. on Aug. 21, 1854. His citation reads, in part ". . . while serving on board the USS *Richmond*, Mobile Bay . . . commended for coolness and good conduct as captain of a gun in the action of Mobile Bay, on the morning and forenoon of Aug. 5, 1864 . . . was on board the USS *Brooklyn* in the actions with Forts Jackson and St. Philip, the Chalmettes; the rebel ironclads and gunboats below New Orleans; batteries below Vicksburg; and present at the surrender of New Orleans. . . ." Miller was discharged from the Corps on Aug. 21, 1858, but served three additional enlistments.

MILLER, John Carroll. Brigadier General. CG, Landing Force Training Unit,

Atlantic, Norfolk, Va.: b. Lake Andres, S.D., Dec. 25, 1912. John Miller graduated from high school at Lake Andres and, in 1931, he entered the University of South Dakota, where he was a member of the ROTC. Graduating in June 1935, he was commissioned a second lieutenant in the Army Infantry Reserve. Shortly after, he resigned that commission to accept appointment as a Marine second lieutenant on Sept. 10, 1935. He completed Basic School for Marine officers at the Philadelphia Navy Yard in May 1936, and the following month began a year of sea duty with the Marine Detachment aboard the USS *New Mexico*. Ordered to China in Aug. 1937, he served with the 6th Marines, 2nd Brig., at the International Settlement in Shanghai during hostilities between China and Japan. He returned to San Diego with the 6th Marines in Apr. 1938. He was promoted to first lieutenant in Oct. 1938. In May 1939, he was transferred to the MB at the Navy Yard, Mare Island, Calif., becoming Commander of the Barracks Detachment in Oct. 1940. He also saw temporary duty in connection with the Western Division Rifle and Pistol Matches, and served briefly with the Marine Detachment at the Receiving Ship, San Francisco, Calif. In Aug. 1940, he joined the 1st Def. Bn. at San Diego, and in Feb. 1941 sailed with the battalion for Pearl Harbor. He was promoted to captain in Nov. 1941, and to major in May 1942. Miller continued to serve at Pearl Harbor and on Palmyra Island until Dec. 1942. In Feb. 1943, he joined the 16th Def. Bn. on Johnston Is. as Executive Officer. He was promoted to lieutenant colonel in July 1943. He returned to San Diego in Aug. 1943 to become Area Ordnance Officer. In Feb. 1944, Miller departed again for Hawaii to command the 3rd Bn., 8th Marines,

2nd Mar. Div., and that May embarked with the battalion for Saipan. Although severely wounded during the approach to the beach on D-Day, June 15, 1944, he disembarked and directed the operation of his battalion, earning a Bronze Star Medal with Combat "V" for his heroism. After being hospitalized at San Diego, Lt. Col. Miller went overseas again in Jan. 1945, joining the 5th Marines, 1st Mar. Div., as Regimental Operations Officer. He also served temporarily as liaison officer with the Army's 7th Infantry Division in the Philippines and on Okinawa. Rejoining the 5th Marines in Apr., he commanded the 3rd Bn. during the Okinawa campaign, and was awarded a second Bronze Star Medal for meritorious achievement from Apr. 4 to May 18, 1945. He returned to the States in June 1945 and that Sept. entered the Command and Staff Course at the MCS, Quantico. Completing the course in Feb. 1946, he served as an instructor in the Senior Course, Amphibious Warfare School, until June 1948. The following month, he began a two-year tour of duty as Assistant Chief of Staff, G-3 (Operations and Training), 1st Mar. Div., Camp Pendleton, Calif. In July 1950, he sailed for the Panama Canal Zone, where he was Executive Officer of the MB, 15th Naval District. On his return to the States in Feb. 1951, he was promoted to colonel. That Mar., Col. Miller reported to the Troop Training Unit, Amphibious Training Command, Pacific Fleet at Coronado, Calif. Besides his chief assignment there as Director of Training, he also saw temporary duty in Japan in 1952 as Chief of Staff, Troop Training Team, Amphibious Force, Far East. He left Coronado in July 1953 to join the 3rd Mar. Div. at Camp Pendleton. Embarking for Japan the following month, he served as Chief of Staff of the 3rd Mar. Div.'s Advance Echelon, before taking command of the 4th Marines in Oct. 1953. He served in the latter capacity until Apr. 1954 when he became the division's Assistant Chief of Staff, G-4 (Logistics). In Sept. 1954, Col. Miller moved to Pearl Harbor as Assistant Chief of Staff, G-3 (Operations and Training), FMF, Pacific. On his return to the States, he joined MCS, Quantico, in July 1956 as a member of the Advanced Research Group. The following July he reported to London, England, as Force Marine Officer, Staff of the Commander in Chief, U.S. Naval Forces, Eastern Atlantic and Mediterranean. During the Lebanon crisis in the summer of 1958, he served as Senior Marine Officer on the Staff of the Commander in Chief, U.S. Specified Command, Middle East. Assigned to Quantico on his return to the States in July 1959, he served as Deputy Director, Marine Corps Educational Center, until Nov. 1959, when he became Director of the Educational Center. While serving in this capacity he was promoted to his present rank of brigadier general, Jan. 1, 1960. In Sept. 1961, Gen. Miller became Director of the Marine Corps Landing Force Development Center at Quantico. He served in this capacity until June 1962, when he reported to Norfolk as CG, Landing Force Training Unit, Atlantic.

MITCHELL, Frank Nicias. First Lieutenant. Medal of Honor: b. Indian Gap, Tex., Aug. 18, 1921; d. KIA, Hansan-ni, Korea, Nov. 26, 1950. Lt. Mitchell's citation reads, in part: "... as leader of a rifle platoon of Co. A, 1st Bn., 7th Marines, 1st Mar. Div. (Reinf.) in action against enemy aggressor forces in Korea on Nov. 26, 1950. Leading his platoon in point position during a patrol by his company through a thickly wooded and snow

covered area in the vicinity of Hansan-ni, Lt. Mitchell acted immediately when the enemy suddenly opened fire at point-blank range, pinning down his forward elements and inflicting numerous casualties in his ranks. Boldly dashing to the front under blistering fire from automatic weapons and small arms, he seized an automatic rifle from one of the wounded men and effectively trained it against the attackers and, when his ammunition was expended, picked up and hurled grenades with deadly accuracy, at the same time directing and encouraging his men in driving the outnumbering enemy from his position. Maneuvering to set up a defense when the enemy furiously counterattacked to the front and left flank, Lt. Mitchell, despite wounds sustained early in the action, reorganized his platoon under the devastating fire and spearheaded a fierce hand-to-hand struggle to repulse the onslaught. Asking for volunteers to assist in searching for and evacuating the wounded, he personally led a party of litter bearers through the hostile lines in growing darkness and, although suffering intense pain from multiple wounds, stormed ahead and waged a singlehanded battle against the enemy, successfully covering the withdrawal of his men before he was fatally struck down by a burst of small arms fire...."

MONEGAN, Walter Carleton, Jr. Private First Class. Medal of Honor: b. Melrose, Mass., Dec. 25, 1930; d. KIA, Sosa-ri, Korea, Sept. 20, 1950. P.F.C. Monegan's citation reads, in part: "... while serving as a rocket gunner attached to Co. F, 2nd Bn., 1st Marines, 1st Mar. Div. (Reinf.) in action against enemy aggressor forces near Sosa-ri, Korea, and on Sept. 17 and 20, 1950. Dug in on a hill overlooking the main Seoul highway when six enemy tanks threatened to break through the battalion position during a pre-dawn attack on Sept. 17, P.F.C. Monegan promptly moved forward with his bazooka under heavy hostile automatic weapons fire and engaged the lead tank at a range of less than 50 yards. After scoring a direct hit and killing the sole surviving tankman with his carbine as he came through the escape hatch, he boldly fired two more rounds of ammunition at the oncoming tanks, disorganizing the attack and enabling our tank crews to continue blasting with their 90-mm guns. With his own and an adjacent company's position threatened with annihilation when an overwhelming enemy tank-infantry force by-passed the area and proceeded toward the battalion CP during the early morning of Sept. 20, Monegan seized his rocket launcher and, in total darkness, charged down the slope of the hill where the tanks had broken through. Quick to act when an illuminating shell lit the area, he scored a direct hit on one of the tanks as hostile rifle and automatic weapons fire raked the area at close range. Again exposing himself, he fired another round to destroy a second tank and, as the rear tank turned to retreat, stood upright to fire and was fatally struck down by hostile machine gun fire when another illuminating shell silhouetted him against the sky. . . ."

MOORE, Albert. Private. Medal of Honor: b. Merced, Calif., Dec. 25, 1862. Albert Moore enlisted in the Marine Corps at Mare Is., Calif. on Jan. 18, 1898. He was awarded the nation's highest military honor ". . . for distinguished conduct in the presence of the enemy at Peking, China, July 21 to Aug. 17, 1900. Moore assisted to erect barricades under heavy fire. . . ." He was discharged from the Corps at San Francisco, Calif. on Jan. 17, 1903.

MORELAND, Whitt Lloyd. Private First Class. Medal of Honor: b. Austin, Tex., Mar. 7, 1930; d. KIA, Kwagch'i-dong, Korea, May 29, 1951. P.F.C. Moreland's citation reads, in part: ". . . while serving as an Intelligence Scout attached to Co. C, 1st Bn., 5th Marines, 1st Mar. Div. (Reinf.), in action against enemy aggressor forces in Korea. Voluntarily accompanying a rifle company in a daring assault against a strongly defended enemy hill position, P.F.C. Moreland delivered accurate rifle fire on the hostile emplacement and thereby aided materially in seizing the objective. After the position had been secured, he unhesitatingly led a party forward to neutralize an enemy bunker which he had observed some 400 meters beyond and, moving boldly through a fire-swept area, almost reached the hostile emplacement when the enemy launched a volley of hand grenades on his group. Quick to act despite the personal danger involved, he kicked several of the grenades off the ridgeline where they exploded harmlessly and, while attempting to kick away another, slipped and fell near the deadly missile. Aware that the sputtering grenade would explode before he could gain his feet and dispose of it, he shouted a warning to his comrades, covered the missile with his body and absorbed the full blast of the explosion, but in saving his companions from possible injury or death, was mortally wounded. . . ."

MORRIS, John. Corporal. Medal of Honor: b. Dublin, Ireland, Feb. 12, 1862. John Morris enlisted in the Marine Corps at Brooklyn, N.Y. He was awarded the Medal of Honor ". . . for leaping overboard from the flagship USS *Lancaster* at Villefranche, France, Dec. 25, 1881, and rescuing from drowning Robert Blizzard, ordinary seaman, a prisoner who had jumped overboard. . . ." Morris was discharged from the Corps at Brooklyn on Apr. 20, 1895.

Munn

MUNN, John Calvin. Lieutenant General. CG, Marine Corps Base, Camp Pendleton, California: b. Prescott, Ark., Oct. 17, 1906. After completing high school in 1923, John Munn entered the U.S. Naval Academy the same year. Upon graduation he was commissioned a Marine second lieutenant on June 2, 1927. In Jan. 1928, after further instruction at Annapolis and completion of the Marine Officers' basic course at the Philadelphia Navy Yard, he joined the 2nd Mar. Brig. in Nicaragua. Returning from Nicaragua in Sept. 1929, he reported to Quantico, and during Oct. and Nov. served with the Ma-

rine Detachment at former President Herbert Hoover's summer camp near Criglersville, Va. That Dec., he was designated a student naval aviator and ordered to Hampton Roads, Va. for preliminary training. From there, he was assigned to Pensacola, Fla., in May 1930. Following his designation as a naval aviator in Jan. 1931, he remained at Pensacola for two months of advanced training, then served for six months at the NAS, San Diego, Calif. In Oct. 1931, Lt. Munn joined Scouting Squadron 14-M, which went aboard the USS *Saratoga* the following month, as one of the first two Marine squadrons to serve aboard Navy carriers. He was promoted to first lieutenant in Jan. 1934. He remained on the *Saratoga* until June 1934, then returned to San Diego. There, he joined Bombing Squadron 4-M for two years' duty aboard the *Lexington* and *Langley*. Leaving the west coast in June 1936, he was assigned aviation duty at Quantico. He was promoted to captain in Aug. 1936. In May 1938, he sailed for Colombia to serve as Naval Attaché and Naval Attaché for Air, at the American embassies in Colombia, Panama, Venezuela, Ecuador, and Peru. He returned to the States in Mar. 1941, and was stationed briefly in Washington. In June, he was assigned to Marine Observation Squadron 151 of MAG 11, 1st MAW, at Quantico and later saw duty aboard the *Ranger*. He was promoted to major in July 1941. Munn was ordered to San Diego with Squadron 151 in Dec. 1941 when the U.S. entered WWII. In Aug. 1942, upon his promotion to lieutenant colonel, he departed for the Pacific area. On Sept. 3, 1942, he arrived on Guadalcanal in the first transport plane to land there. While on Guadalcanal, he served as Assistant Chief of Staff, G-2, 1st MAW, and Assistant Chief of Staff, G-3, 2nd MAW, respectively. Lt. Col.

Munn was awarded the Navy Commendation Ribbon with Combat "V" for service on Guadalcanal. In Mar. 1943, he assumed command of MAG 11 in the New Hebrides. He returned to the States in July 1943. From Sept. 1943 until Feb. 1945, he served in Washington as Assistant Head of the Aviation Planning Section, HQ, Commander in Chief, U.S. Fleet. While serving in this capacity, he was promoted to colonel in Nov. 1943. In Mar. 1945, he returned to the Pacific area to take command of MAG 31. The group, under his command, destroyed 180 Japanese planes in the Okinawa campaign. For service in this capacity, he was awarded both the Silver Star Medal and his first Legion of Merit with Combat "V." After the war, he commanded the group in Japan. He returned briefly to the States in Apr. 1946 for temporary duty in Washington. Col. Munn reported to Pearl Harbor in June 1946 as Aviation Plans Officer on the staff of the Commander in Chief, Pacific Fleet, and as Fleet Marine Officer. He returned from Hawaii in June 1948. During the next two years, he served at Cherry Point, N.C., as Commander of Marine Wing Service Group 2 (Prov.), and Chief of Staff of Air, FMF, Atlantic, and the 2nd MAW, respectively. He entered the National War College, Washington, in Aug. 1950, and graduated the following summer. In June 1951, Col. Munn was named a member of the Joint Strategic Plans Group, Joint Staff. He served in that capacity until Feb. 1952, when he was assigned to the Division of Aviation at HQMC, as Executive Officer and, later, as Assistant Director. Col. Munn embarked for Korea in Apr. 1953 to become Chief of Staff of the 1st MAW. For outstanding service in that capacity, he was awarded his second Legion of Merit with Combat "V." On his return from Korea

in Apr. 1954, he assumed command of MCAS, El Toro, Calif. While there, he was promoted to brigadier general in Aug. 1954. In Oct. 1954, Gen. Munn was transferred to Norfolk, Va., as Assistant CG, Aircraft, FMF, Atlantic. Ordered to Washington in Feb. 1955, he was assigned to the Office of the Vice Chief of Naval Operations, as Marine Corps Liaison Officer, until Oct. of the same year. He then served as Inspector General of the Marine Corps until Jan. 1956, when he returned to Cherry Point to assume command of the 2nd MAW. He was promoted to major general in Aug. 1956. Upon his detachment from Cherry Point in Feb. 1958, Gen. Munn was named Director of Aviation at HQMC. On Jan. 1, 1960, he was promoted to his present rank, lieutenant general, on assuming his assignment as Assistant Commandant of the Marine Corp.

MURPHY, John Alphonsus. Drummer. Medal of Honor: b. New York, N.Y., Feb. 26, 1881; d. Nov. 29, 1935. John Murphy enlisted in the Marine Corps at Washington, D.C. on Jan. 5, 1897. His citation reads, in part: ". . . for distinguished conduct in the presence of the enemy at Peking, China, July 21 to Aug. 17, 1900. . . ." He received the Medal of Honor on Dec. 11, 1901.

MURPHY, Raymond Gerald. Captain. Medal of Honor: b. Pueblo, Col., Jan. 14, 1930. Capt. Murphy's citation reads, in part: ". . . as a platoon commander of Co. A, 1st Bn., 5th Marines, 1st Mar. Div. (Reinf.), in action against enemy aggressor forces in Korea on Feb. 3, 1953. Although painfully wounded by fragments from an enemy mortar shell while leading his evacuation platoon in support of assault units attacking a cleverly concealed and well-entrenched hostile force occupying commanding ground, (then) 2nd Lt. Murphy steadfastly refused medical aid and continued to lead his men up a hill through a withering barrage of hostile mortar and small arms fire, skillfully maneuvering his force from one position to the next and shouting words of encouragement. Undeterred by the increasingly intense enemy fire, he immediately located casualties as they fell and made several trips up and down the fire-swept hill to direct evacuation teams to the wounded, personally carrying many of the stricken Marines to safety. When reinforcements were needed by the assaulting elements, 2nd Lt. Murphy employed part of his unit as support and, during the ensuing battle personally killed two of the enemy with his pistol. With all the wounded evacuated and the assaulting units beginning to disengage, he remained behind with a carbine to cover the movement of friendly forces off the hill and, though suffering intense pain from his previous wounds, seized an automatic rifle to provide more firepower when the enemy reappeared in the trenches. After reaching the base of the hill, he organized a search party and again ascended the slope for a final check on missing Marines, locating and carrying the bodies of a machine gun crew back down the hill. Wounded a second time while conducting the entire force to the line of departure through a continuing barrage of enemy small arms, artillery and mortar fire, he again refused medical assistance until assured that every one of his men, including all casualties, had preceded him to the main lines. . . ."

MURRAY, Raymond Leroy. Brigadier General. Selected for promotion to major general in July 1962. Now serving as CG, Marine Corps Recruit Depot, Parris Is., S.C.: b. Los Angeles, Calif., Jan. 30, 1913.

Raymond Murray attended schools in Alhambra, Calif., and Harlingen, Tex., graduating from high school in 1930. On July 9, 1935, following graduation from Texas A&M College, he accepted his commission as a Marine second lieutenant. After completing Basic School at the Philadelphia Navy Yard in Mar. 1936, he joined the 2nd Mar. Brig. in San Diego, Calif. Embarking with the brigade for China in Sept. 1937, he served for a short time with the 2nd Bn. in Shanghai. In Jan. 1938, he joined the Marine Detachment at the American Embassy in Peiping. He was promoted to first lieutenant in Aug. 1938. Upon his return to San Diego in Sept. 1940, he again saw duty with the 2nd Brig. While there, he was promoted to captain in Mar. 1941. That May, he sailed for duty in Iceland with the 6th Marines (Reinf.), 1st Prov. Mar. Brig., and later graduated from the British Force Tactical School. After the brigade was disbanded, he returned to San Diego in Apr. 1942, and the following month was promoted to major. In Oct. 1942, Murray embarked with the 6th Marines for the Pacific area. For conspicuous gallantry on Guadalcanal in Jan. 1943, as commander of the 2nd Bn., 6th Marines, he was awarded his first Silver Star Medal. He was promoted to lieutenant colonel in June 1943. Lt. Col. Murray was awarded a second Silver Star Medal for conspicuous gallantry while commanding the same unit on Tarawa in Nov. 1943. Serving in this same capacity on Saipan, his heroism in remaining at his post although seriously wounded and continuing to direct his battalion during the initial assault earned him his first Navy Cross on June 15, 1944. Returning to the States in Aug. 1944, he entered the Command and Staff School at Quantico the following month. After brief duty as an instructor, he was named Assistant Chief of Staff, G-3, 1st Special Mar. Brig., moving with the brigade to Camp Lejeune, N.C., in Feb. 1946. In Oct. 1946, he departed for duty in the Pacific area as Deputy Chief of Staff, HQ, Marine Garrison Forces, Pacific, and the following Apr. was named Inspector of Marine Garrison Forces. He returned to Quantico in July 1948 for temporary duty on the Marine Corps Board at Marine Corps Schools. Transferred to Camp Pendleton, Calif., in Jan. 1949, he served consecutively as Assistant Chief of Staff, G-4; as CO, 3rd Marines; and as Executive Officer, 5th Marines, 1st Mar. Div. In July 1950, when the 1st Prov. Mar. Brig. was formed for duty in Korea, he was ordered overseas with the 5th Mar. Regt. which was to be the nucleus for the brigade. As CO, 5th Marines, he was awarded his third and fourth Silver Star Medal (Army) and the Legion of Merit during action in Aug. and Sept. 1950. With his unit, he participated in the battles of the Naktong River perimeter, Wolmi-Inchon, Seoul, and Wonsan; and in the Marine advance north toward the Yalu River. He was subsequently awarded the Army Distinguished Service Cross for extaordinary heroism in the 1st Division's historic breakout from the Chosin Reservoir area to the sea at Hamhung, and two days later took part in the action which earned him his second Navy Cross. Shortly afterward, with his regiment committed to fighting on the central Korean front, he was advanced to the rank of colonel in Jan. 1951. Following his return from Korea, he served from May until Aug. 1951 at HQMC, Washington, D.C., then entered the National War College. On completing the course in June 1952, he saw two years' duty as CO, Basic School, MCS, Quantico. In July 1954, he was ordered to the MCB, Camp Pendleton.

Col. Murray remained at Camp Pendleton four years, serving first as CO, 1st Inf. Training Regt. until Feb. 1955; then as Chief of Staff of the MCB until July 1957. During his final year there, he was assigned to the 1st Mar. Div., serving as Division Inspector, Chief of Staff, and Assistant Chief of Staff, respectively. In July 1958, he assumed duties as Chief of Staff, MCB, Camp Lejeune. He was promoted to his present rank of brigadier general in June 1959. Gen. Murray departed for Okinawa the following month and assumed duties as Assistant Division Commander, 3rd Mar. Div., in Aug. 1959. In July 1960, he reported to Camp Pendleton, as Deputy Base Commander and subsequently, in Mar. 1961, became CG of the MCB, Camp Pendleton. He served in the latter capacity until June 1962. On July 1, 1962, he assumed command of the MCRD, Parris Is.

MURRAY, William H. Private. Medal of Honor: b. Brooklyn, N.Y., June 3, 1876. (Served under the name of Henry W. Davis.) William Murray enlisted in the Marine Corps at Brooklyn, N.Y., on Apr. 8, 1898. His citation reads, in part: ". . . for meritorious conduct in the presence of the enemy at Peking, China, July 21 to Aug. 17, 1900. . . ." He was discharged from the Corps on Apr. 8, 1903.

MYERS, John Twiggs. Lieutenant General: b. Weisbaden, Germany, Jan. 29, 1871; d. Coconut Grove, Fla., Apr. 17, 1952. John Myers entered the U.S. Naval Academy in Sept. 1887. Graduating in 1892, he continued to hold the rank of naval cadet. He was transferred from the Navy to the Marine Corps on Mar. 6, 1895, and accepted appointment as a second lieutenant the following day. In May 1896, after completing the course at the School of Application in Washington,

J. T. Myers

D.C., he was ordered to the Naval War College at Newport, R.I. He then served briefly at the MB, Boston, Mass. before joining the barracks detachment at Mare Is., Calif. in Nov. of the same year. He left Mare Is. May 7, 1898, to join the Marine Detachment aboard the USS *Charleston*, which sailed a few days later to convoy six troop ships to the Philippines. En route, the *Charleston* stopped at Guam, and on June 21, Lt. Myers accompanied the captain of the *Charleston* ashore as head of a landing party of 16 sailors and 30 Marines. They disarmed and made prisoners of the Spanish garrison on the island. After that, the convoy moved on to the Philippines, where Myers was transferred to the USS *Baltimore* in July 1899. While attached to that ship during the Philippine Insurrection,

he commanded a landing expedition which went ashore under fire to capture and destroy an Insurrecto gun at Port Olongapo on Sept. 23 and made another landing under fire at Bacoor on Oct. 2. He also commanded a 100-man landing force which took over the naval station at Subic Bay on Dec. 10, 1899, the day after it was captured by the Army. On Apr. 18, 1900, he was transferred from the *Baltimore* to the USS *Oregon*, and on May 24 of the same year he was detached to the USS *Newark*. Meanwhile, a wave of violence, led by an athletic society known as the Boxers, was erupting in China, during which a number of foreigners were killed or subjected to gross indignities. The Imperial Government, sympathizing with the movement, did little to stop it, and the foreigners in Peking were soon forced to take refuge in the legations there. On May 28, E. H. Conger, the American Minister at Peking, telegraphed the Commander in Chief of the U.S. Asiatic Squadron at Taku to send an armed force for the protection of the legation. The following day Myers set out for that city as commander of a force of 48 Marines and three sailors from the *Oregon* and *Brooklyn*. Together with detachments of British, Russian, French, Italian and Japanese Marines, they reached Peking at 11 o'clock on the night of May 31, just before the city was encircled. On June 24 serious fighting broke out on the walls of the legation as hordes of Boxers, armed with swords, spears, clubs, stones, noise-makers, and several 3-inch field pieces, attempted to overwhelm the handful of foreign troops. A German detachment repulsed the first attack and the U.S. Marines hurled back a second, causing heavy losses among the Boxers. After that the Chinese changed their tactics and began building a tower on the ancient wall above the American Lega-tion, only about 25 feet from the Marines' position. Since this would have allowed the Boxers to fire at will on the troops and civilians below, Minister Conger re-ported this danger to the British Minister, Sir Claude M. MacDonald, who had been picked by common consent as command-er of the international defense. He agreed to the American's suggestion that an at-tack should be made on the tower and the Chinese barricade behind it. Myers was picked to head the attacking force, composed of himself and 14 other Ameri-can Marines, 16 Russian and 25 British Marines. His plan was to have the Rus-sians hit the barricade from the north, while the American and British Marines were to assault the tower, then fight their way to the barricade, along a trench which ran from it to the tower. At a sig-nal from Myers, the attack began about 3 o'clock on the morning of July 3. The Anglo-American force, with Myers in the lead, found the tower empty when they reached it, then proceeded along the trench, where they ran into bitter, hand-to-hand fighting. Myers was badly wounded by a spear during the action in the trench, but the attack continued until the barricade was in friendly hands. In addition to the wounded Myers, the allied losses included two U.S. Marines and one Russian killed and two Russian and three British Marines severely wounded. Estimates of enemy losses ran as high as 50 dead. The disheartened Boxers agreed to an uneasy truce on July 16. Myers was brevetted a major and ad-vanced four numbers in rank for his brav-ery. A relief column finally reached Peking on Aug. 14 and the following month Myers, convalescing from typhoid fever and the spear wound in his leg, was ordered to the U.S. Naval Hospital at Yokohama, Japan. From there he was transferred to the Naval Hospital at Mare Is. He remained there until Dec. 1902, when he took command of the MB at Bremerton, Wash. Myers left Bremerton in May 1903, arriving on the east coast the following month to take command of the Marine Detachment aboard the USS *Brooklyn*. He held that command until Apr. 1905, then served at the Naval War College in Newport, afterward taking command of the School for Noncommis-sioned Officers at the MB, Washington, D.C. in Oct. of the same year. In May 1906, he took command of the barracks detachment there, serving in that assign-ment until he left Washington that July. The following month he returned to the Philippines, commanding the 1st Mar. Regt. there until Jan. 1907, when he was assigned to the USS *West Virginia* as commander of its Marine Detachment and Fleet Marine Officer of the Asiatic Fleet. In May 1909, Maj. Myers was transferred from the *West Virginia* to the USS *Tennessee* for duty as Fleet Marine Officer, Pacific Fleet, but the following month, because of a serious intestinal infection, he was ordered once more to the Naval Hospital at Mare Is. Myers was hospitalized or on sick leave until Jan. 1911, when he entered the Army Field Officers' Course at Fort Leavenworth, Kans. Completing that course in Mar. 1911, he was stationed briefly at the MB, Philadelphia, Pa. and on recruiting duty in Boston before he entered the Army War College in Washington that Aug. Graduating in July 1912, he took com-mand of the MB at the Washington Navy Yard the following month. His service there was interrupted by expeditionary duty as a battalion commander with the 2nd Prov. Mar. Regt. off Santo Domingo in 1912 and with the 2nd Regiment, 2nd Prov. Mar. Brig. at Guantanamo Bay, Cuba the following year. He left Washington in Apr. 1913, to serve for the next year as commander of the MB, Honolulu, T.H. In Apr. 1914, he returned from that assignment to take command of the 1st Bn., 4th Mar. Regt. at Mare Is., sailing with that unit for the west coast of Mexico later the same month. The regiment remained aboard the battleship *South Dakota* in Mexican waters during a period of strained relations between the United States and that country, but did not land. The regiment returned to the States in July and Myers, still commanding its 1st Bn., was stationed with it at San Diego, Calif. until Feb. 1915, when that unit was assigned duty at the Panama Pacific International Exposition in San Francisco, Calif. The battalion was ordered to sea duty with the Pacific Fleet in Nov. 1915 and in Feb. of the following year, after service on the USS *San Diego* and USS *Buffalo*, it returned to San Diego. Myers, now a lieutenant colonel, was detached from the 1st Bn., 4th Marines in June 1916, and assigned to the Atlantic Fleet as Fleet Marine Officer and Counterintelligence Officer on the staff of its commander. Serving in those capacities for most of WWI, he was stationed aboard the USS *Wyoming* until Oct. 1916, and on the USS *Pennsylvania* from then until Aug. 1918, when he took command of the MB at Parris Is., S.C. He remained there until the war ended that Nov. In Jan. 1919, after a short time at Quantico, Myers assumed command of the MB at Pearl Harbor, where he was stationed until Aug. 1921. He was then named Adjutant and Inspector of the Department of the Pacific, with headquarters at San Francisco, Calif., serving in that assignment until May 1924. After that, he commanded the MCB at San Diego from June of that year to Nov. 1925. Myers then sailed for Haiti to take command of

the 1st Mar. Brig. He returned from that tour of expeditionary duty in Jan. 1928 and the following month reported to HQMC in Washington. There, after serving on various boards, he was named Assistant to the Major General Commandant in Apr. 1930, serving in that capacity until Feb. 1933. A month later he returned to San Francisco where he was CG, Department of the Pacific and Western Recruiting Area, until he was placed on the retired list, Feb. 1, 1935 at the statutory retirement age of 64. A major general when he retired, Gen. Myers was promoted to lieutenant general on the retired list in 1942, when the law was passed authorizing such promotions for officers who had been specially commended in combat.

MYERS, Reginald Rodney. Colonel. Medal of Honor: b. Boise, Idaho, Nov. 26, 1919. Reginald Myers graduated from high school in Salt Lake City, Utah, and then from the University of Idaho, Moscow, Idaho, in June 1941 with a Bachelor of Science degree in mechanical engineering. He attained the rank of cadet colonel in the ROTC at the university. On Sept. 1, 1941, he resigned his Army Reserve commission to accept appointment as a second lieutenant in the Marine Corps. He completed Marine Officers' Basic School at the Philadelphia Navy Yard, then served as a company commander at the MCB, San Diego, Calif. In June 1942, he joined the Marine Detachment on board the USS *New Orleans* for a year's duty at sea. He was promoted to first lieutenant in Oct. 1942, and to captain in Apr. 1943. In July 1943, Capt. Myers became CO of the Marine Detachment on board the USS *Minneapolis.* While serving on the *New Orleans,* he fought the Japanese at Guadalcanal, Tulagi, the Eastern Solomons, and Tassafaronga. Later, aboard the *Minneapolis,* he participated in the Gilbert, Marshall, Marianas, and western Caroline Is. campaigns. Returning briefly to the States in Oct. 1944, he was promoted to major in Jan. 1945. Maj. Myers again returned to the Pacific area in June 1945, and served with the 5th Marines, 1st Mar. Div., during the assault on Okinawa, and in the landing on and occupation of northern China. He returned to the States in May 1946, and served at Mare Island, Calif., Norfolk, Va., and Cherry Point, N.C. At Cherry Point, he served as Assistant G-4, Aircraft, FMF, Atlantic, and 2nd MAW, from Aug. 1948 until May 1950. Ordered to Korea in July 1950, Maj. Myers served as Executive Officer, 3rd Bn., 1st Marines, 1st Mar. Div. For his part in the Inchon landing, Sept. 15, 1950, he was awarded the Bronze Star Medal with Combat "V"; and for his heroism in helping rescue two wounded Marines four days later, he was awarded a Gold Star in lieu of a second Bronze Star Medal. He earned the Medal of Honor in Korea for fearlessly leading 250 United Nations troops to victory over 4000 of the enemy. The battle occurred Nov. 29, 1950, as the Chinese Communists threatened to envelop United States 10th Army Corps forces at the Chosin Reservoir. His citation reads, in part: "... as executive officer of the 3rd Bn., 1st Marines, 1st Mar. Div. (Reinf.), in action against enemy aggressor forces in Korea on Nov. 29, 1950. Assuming command· of a composite unit of Army and Marine service and headquarters elements totaling approximately 250 men, during a critical stage in the vital defense of the strategically important military base at Hagaru-ri, Maj. Myers immediately initiated a determined and aggressive counterattack against a well-entrenched and cleverly concealed enemy force numbering an estimated 4000. Severely handicapped by a lack of trained personnel and experienced leaders in his valiant efforts to regain maximum ground prior to daylight, he persisted in constantly exposing himself to intense, accurate and sustained hostile fire in order to direct and supervise the employment of his men and to encourage and spur them on in pressing the attack. Inexorably moving forward up the steep, snow-covered slope with his depleted group in the face of apparently insurmountable odds, he concurrently directed artillery and mortar fire with superb skill and, although losing 170 of his men during 14 hours of raging combat in sub-zero temperatures, continued to reorganize his unit and spearhead the attack which resulted in 600 enemy killed and 500 wounded."

Maj. Myers returned to the States in June 1951. That Aug. he reported to the Basic School, MCS, Quantico, as a battalion commander. While stationed at Quantico, he was promoted to lieutenant colonel in Dec. 1951. Assigned next to Washington, D.C., Lt. Col. Myers served as Inspector-Instructor of the 5th Special Inf. Bn., USMCR, from Sept. 1952 through Aug. 1953, and Inspector-Instructor, 13th Inf. Bn., USMCR, from Sept. 1953 through July 1955. Following this assignment, he entered the Senior School at MCS, Quantico, and completed the course in June 1956. He remained at Quantico until Apr. 1958, serving as CO, H&S Bn., and as Executive Officer, Basic School, respectively. Following temporary duty at the Foreign Service Institute, Washington, D.C., he was assigned as Assistant Naval Attaché at the U.S. Embassy in London, England. He left London July 31, 1961, to become Head, International Planning Section, Office of the Chief of Naval Operations, Pentagon, Washington, D.C.

N

NEVILLE, Wendell Cushing. Major General. 14th Commandant of the Marine Corps — Mar. 5, 1929, to July 8, 1930. Medal of Honor: b. Portsmouth, Va., May 12, 1870; d. July 8, 1930. Wendell Neville entered the Naval Academy at Annapolis, Md. in 1886, after learning that an appointment to the Academy had not been filled in his district. He received his diploma in 1890 and following a two-year cruise aboard a warship was commissioned a second lieutenant in the Marine Corps. At the outbreak of the Spanish-American War, Lt. Neville was assigned to the 1st Mar. Bn., hurriedly organized under Lt. Col. W. R. Huntington for service in Cuba. The battalion staged an attack under heavy gunfire at Guantanamo Bay, established a beachhead and routed enemy forces in that area. For outstanding valor and leadership in that action, Lt. Neville was awarded the Brevet Medal, highest Marine Corps decoration at that time, and was promoted to the brevet rank of captain. Promoted to the permanent rank of captain a few months after the war, he was assigned to a battalion of Marines ordered to China to relieve the hard-pressed garrison at Peking during the Boxer Rebellion. He took part in four battles in that area and was again commended for his gallantry. In the Philippine Is. not long afterward, he was appointed military governor of Basilan Province. Following that assignment he served in Cuba, Nicaragua, Panama, and Hawaii. While in command of Marines landing at Vera Cruz on Apr. 21, 1914, he displayed conspicuous gallantry. In that operation, Lt. Col. Neville was awarded the Medal of Honor for his distinguished conduct. His citation reads, in part "... his duties required him to be at points of great danger in directing his officers and men, and he exhibited conspicuous courage, coolness, and skill in his conduct of the fighting. Upon his courage and skill depended, in great measure, success or failure...." Prior to his embarkation for France in 1917, Col. Neville returned to China where he was chosen to command the combined Allied guard at Peking. On Jan. 1, 1918, he was placed in command of the 5th Mar. Regt. in France, and in May moved his regiment into action at Belleau Wood where Germany's big drive was decisively halted. In July Gen. Neville's command was enlarged to include the 4th Mar. Brig. which he directed during the remaining days of the war and during its occupation service in Germany. After service with the Army of Occupation in Germany, Gen. Neville and his brigade returned to the States in July 1919. Promoted to major general in Mar. 1920, he served as assistant to the CMC and later became CG, Department of the Pacific, with headquarters in San Francisco. Prior to becoming Commandant on Mar. 5, 1929, he was in command of the MB, Quantico, Va. Gen. Neville's sudden death on July 8, 1930, while in office as Major General Commandant, closed one of the most brilliant military careers of his day — a career of service that extended through many important chapters of Marine Corps history: Guantanamo Bay, the Siege of Peking, Tientsin, the Philippine Insurrection, Panama, Vera Cruz, Belleau Wood, Soissons, St.-Mihiel, Meuse-Argonne, the Rhine, and Coblenz.

NEW, John Dury. Private First Class. Medal of Honor: b. Aug. 12, 1924; d. KIA, Peleliu Is., Sept. 25, 1944. P.F.C. New's citation reads, in part: " . . . while serving with the 2nd Bn., 7th Marines, 1st Mar. Div., in action against enemy Japanese forces on Peleliu Is., Sept. 25, 1944. When a Japanese soldier emerged from a cave in a cliff directly below an observation post and suddenly hurled a hand grenade into the position from which two of our men were directing mortar fire against enemy emplacements, P.F.C. New instantly perceived the dire peril to the other Marines and, with utter disregard for his own safety, unhesitatingly flung himself upon the grenade and absorbed the full impact of the explosion, thus saving the lives of the two observers."

NICHOLAS, Samuel. 1st Commandant of the Marine Corps — Nov. 28, 1775 to Aug. 1783: b. 1744, Philadelphia, Pa.; d. Aug. 27, 1790, Philadelphia, Pa. First officer commissioned in the Marine Corps by the Second Continental Congress on Nov. 5, 1775, five days before the recognized birth of the Corps itself. His commission, however, was confirmed on Nov. 28th when the President of Congress signed an order making him a captain at the wage of $32 a month. Nicholas immediately set up a recruiting station in the old Tun Tavern to enlist Marines for duty aboard the *Black Prince* (later named the *Alfred*). The *Black Prince* and several other vessels were outfitted and received Marine Detachments; then, in the spring of 1776, they sailed to the Bahamas and, at New Providence, they surprised the British garrison. Capt. Nicholas and a landing force of 200 Marines and 50 bluejackets captured the town and the forts which defended it, taking away with them valuable stores

Nicholas

and ammunition. This was the first amphibious operation the Marine Corps had ever attempted. Following this successful action, the fleet returned north. On June 25, 1776, in Philadelphia, Nicholas was promoted to Major of Marines and ordered to "discipline four companies of Marines for guards on frigates. . . ." In Dec. of the same year, Maj. Nicholas received orders to march with three companies of his Marines "to be under the command of his excellency, The Commander in Chief, in operations against the British in New Jersey." The battles of Trenton and Princeton followed. Nicholas and his Marines remained with Gen. Washington's army until the end of winter. In the spring of 1777, Nicholas returned to Philadelphia and served as Commanding Officer of Marines. His duties, since he exercised general supervision over the Continental Marines, closely coincided with those of the Commandant today. Throughout the remainder of the war he continued to serve in this capacity in the vicinity of Philadelphia. When the Revolutionary War ended the Marines, along with the Navy, were temporarily disbanded in 1783 and Nicholas returned to civilian life. He remained in Philadelphia until his death in 1790. On May 12, 1919, he was honored by the Navy when a new destroyer was christened the USS *Nicholas*.

Nickerson

NICKERSON, Herman, Jr. Major General. CG, 1st Mar. Div. (Reinf.), Fleet Marine Force, Camp Pendleton, Calif.: b. Boston, Mass., July 30, 1913. Following graduation from high school at Arlington, Mass., Herman Nickerson entered Boston University where he was a member of the ROTC unit for four years. Upon graduation he resigned an Army Reserve commission to accept appointment as a Marine second lieutenant on July 10, 1935. After completing Basic School at the Philadelphia Navy Yard in Feb. 1936, he embarked for Shanghai, China, where he served for two and a half years with the 4th Marines. While in China, he was promoted to first lieutenant in Aug. 1938. On his return to the States in Nov. 1938, he served as CO of the Marine Detachment at NAS, Seattle, Wash. Joining the 2nd Defense Bn. in Sept. 1940, he served with them in San Diego, Calif., and Parris Is., S.C. In May 1941, he was promoted to captain while on temporary duty under instruction at the Coast Artillery School, Fort Monroe, Va. In Dec. 1941, following the attack on Pearl Harbor, Nickerson departed Parris Is. for San Diego with the 2nd Defense Bn. to join the 2nd Mar. Brig. overseas. Arriving on American Samoa in Jan. 1942, he served consecutively as Battery Commander, Group Executive Officer, and finally Group Commander, 3-Inch Antiaircraft Artillery Group. While overseas, he was promoted to major in May 1942, and to lieutenant colonel in June 1943. He returned to the States in July 1943. That Oct., Lt. Col. Nickerson was assigned to MCS, Quantico, as CO of the Ordnance School, and subsequently completed the Command and Staff School. In Feb. 1945, he joined the 4th Inf. Training Regt. at Camp Pendleton, Calif., and again embarked for duty in the Pacific area, serving as Ordnance Officer, 4th Mar. Div., and Executive Officer, 25th Marines. He later saw duty as Ordnance Officer with the III Amphibious Corps in Tientsin, China, and following dissolving of the 3rd Amphibious Corps, served as Division Ordnance Officer and Division Legal Officer, respectively, of the 1st Mar. Div. In Jan. 1947, on his return to the States, he began a three-year assignment at the MCRD, Parris Is., serving consecutively as Assistant G-3, Recruit Training Battalion Commander, Weapons Training Battalion Commander, and Assistant Chief of Staff, G-3. He also saw temporary duty from Jan. through Aug. 1949 as a U.S. Military Observer with the United Nations Mission in Palestine and seven Arab States. Following this, he completed the Armed Forces Staff College, Norfolk, Va., and was promoted to colonel in July 1950. That same month, upon the outbreak of hostilities in Korea, he departed for the Far East. From Aug. 1950 to Apr. 1951, he served as Advisor on Marine Corps Matters, GHQ, Far East Command, and also performed temporary additional duty in Korea. For conspicuous gallantry in Sept. 1950 as Liaison Officer, 1st Marines, 1st Mar. Div., during the advance along the Inchon-Seoul highway and the Han River crossing, he was awarded the Silver Star Medal. In Apr. 1951, he became CO of the 7th Marines in Korea, serving in this capacity through Sept. 1951. During the early part of this period, he earned both the Legion of Merit with Combat "V" and, subsequently, the Army Distinguished Service Cross. Col. Nickerson was named Inspector of FMF, Pacific, in Oct. 1951. In Mar. 1952, he returned to MCS, Quantico, where he served as Director, Advance Base Problem Section until June 1954, and Director, Senior School, until July 1956. He served next

as Assistant Chief of Staff, G-3, FMF, Pacific, at Pearl Harbor, from Aug. 1956 to Dec. 1957. In Jan. 1958, he joined FMF, Atlantic, at Norfolk as Assistant Chief of Staff, G-3. Transferred to HQMC in Sept. 1958, Col. Nickerson served as Special Assistant to the Fiscal Director until Apr. 1959, when he was named Fiscal Director of the Marine Corps. He was promoted to brigadier general on Jan. 1, 1959. While at HQMC, Gen. Nickerson was elected President of the American Society of Military Comptrollers in 1959 and again in 1960. He completed his tour of duty as Fiscal Director of the Marine Corps in May 1962. That June he assumed command of the 1st Mar. Div. at Camp Pendleton. He was promoted to his present rank of major general, July 1, 1962, having been authorized the title and uniform of a major general while en route and prior to reporting to his current command.

NUGENT, Christopher. Orderly Sergeant. Medal of Honor: b. County Caven, Ireland, 1840; d. New York, 1898. Christopher Nugent enlisted in the Marine Corps on Feb. 8, 1858 at Boston, Mass. During a seven-year career in the Corps he served aboard various ships and, while an orderly sergeant on the USS *Fort Henry*, he was awarded the Medal of Honor for "displaying extraordinary zeal, skill, and discretion in driving a guard of rebel soldiers into a swamp, capturing their arms, and destroying their camp equipage while in charge of a reconnoitering party sent into Crystal River, Fla., on June 15, 1863." Nugent was discharged from the Corps on Oct. 9, 1865.

O

O'Bannon

O'BANNON, Presley Neville. First Lieutenant: b. Fauquier County, Va., 1776; d. Logan County, Ky., Sept. 12, 1850. Presley O'Bannon was appointed a second lieutenant in the Marine Corps on Jan. 18, 1801. He was promoted to first lieutenant on Oct. 15, 1802. When the Barbary States were levying unfair tribute from nations who sent merchant ships through the Mediterranean, O'Bannon, in charge of seven Marines, was sent to Egypt where he and his small force joined "General" William Eaton who had organized a motley horde of Greek mercenaries, Arab cavalrymen, and French soldiers of fortune for the purpose of overthrowing the ruling Tripolitan pasha and replacing him with the rightful owner of the throne. After unbelievable mutinies and disappointments, suffered in a 600-mile trek across the desert, Eaton's "Army" reached Derne, Tripoli, on Apr. 26, 1805. The following day, led by Lt. O'Bannon and his few Marines, they stormed the old fortress and raised the American flag, for the first time, over foreign soil. O'Bannon's heroism and leadership throughout the desert journey and the final battle contributed heavily to the success of the expedition. In recognition for his gallantry, the pasha presented O'Bannon with a jeweled sword with a Mameluke hilt. On his return to the States, Virginia awarded him another sword, a true scimitar. The blade of this sword has more curve than the similar sword worn by Marine officers today. O'Bannon retired from the Corps on Mar. 6, 1807. He spent the remainder of his life in Kentucky and, after his death, a monument was erected in Frankfort to commemorate his heroic service to his country.

OBREGON, Eugene Arnold. Private First Class. Medal of Honor: b. Los Angeles, Calif., Nov. 12, 1930; d. KIA, Seoul, Korea, Sept. 26, 1950. P.F.C. Obregon's citation reads, in part: ". . . while serving with Co. G, 3rd Bn., 5th Marines, 1st Mar. Div. (Reinf.), in action against enemy aggressor forces at Seoul, Korea on Sept. 26, 1950. While serving as an ammunition carrier of a machine gun squad in a Marine rifle company which was temporarily pinned down by hostile fire, P.F.C. Obregon observed a fellow

Marine fall wounded in the line of fire. Armed only with a pistol, he unhesitatingly dashed from his covered position to the side of the casualty. Firing his pistol with one hand as he ran, he grasped his comrade by the arm with his other hand and, despite the great peril to himself, dragged him to the side of the road. Still under enemy fire, he was bandaging the man's wounds when hostile troops of approximately platoon strength began advancing toward his position. Quickly seizing the wounded Marine's carbine, he placed his own body as a shield in front of him and lay there firing accurately and effectively into the hostile group until he himself was fatally wounded by enemy machine gun fire. . . ."

O'BRIEN, George Herman, Jr. Captain. Medal of Honor: b. Fort Worth, Tex., Sept. 10, 1926. Capt. O'Brien's citation reads, in part: ". . . as a rifle platoon commander of Co. H, 3rd Bn., 7th Marines, 1st Mar. Div. (Reinf.), in action against enemy aggressor forces in Korea on Oct. 27, 1952. With his platoon subjected to an intense mortar and artillery bombardment while preparing to assault a vitally important hill position on the main line of resistance which had been overrun by a numerically superior enemy force on the preceding night, (then) 2nd Lt. O'Brien leaped from his trench when the attack signal was given and, shouting for his men to follow, raced across an exposed saddle and up the enemy-held hill through a virtual hail of deadly small arms, artillery, and mortar fire. Although shot through the arm and thrown to the ground by hostile automatic weapons fire as he neared the well-entrenched enemy position, he bravely regained his feet, waved his men onward, and continued to spearhead the assault, pausing

only long enough to go to the aid of a wounded Marine. Encountering the enemy at close range, he proceeded to hurl hand grenades into the bunkers and, utilizing his carbine to best advantage in savage hand-to-hand combat, succeeded in killing at least three of the enemy. Struck down by the concussion of grenades on three occasions during the subsequent action, he steadfastly refused to be evacuated for medical treatment and continued to lead his platoon in the assault for a period of nearly four hours, repeatedly encouraging his men and maintaining superb direction of the unit. With the attack halted, he set up a defense with his remaining forces to prepare for a counterattack, personally checking each position, attending to the wounded, and expediting their evacuation. When a relief of the position was effected by another unit, he remained to cover the withdrawal and to assure that no wounded were left behind. . . ."

ORNDOFF, Harry Westley. Private. Medal of Honor: b. Sandusky, Ohio, Nov. 9, 1872; d. July 14, 1938. Harry Orndoff enlisted in the Marine Corps at Mare Is., Calif. on Oct. 17, 1896. He was awarded the Medal of Honor on Dec. 10, 1901 ". . . for distinguished conduct in the presence of the enemy in battles on June 13, 20, 21 and 22, 1900, while with the relief expedition of the Allied Forces in China. . . ." He was discharged from the Corps with a medical survey on Jan. 21, 1902.

OSTERMANN, Edward Albert. Major General (Retired). Medal of Honor: b. Columbus, Ohio, Nov. 23, 1882. Edward Ostermann accepted a commission as a second lieutenant in the Marine Corps on Mar. 20, 1907. His long career took him to Cuba, Panama, China, Nicaragua,

Mexico, Haiti, Hawaii, and the Philippines. He was awarded the Medal of Honor in 1917 for his conspicuous gallantry in action, incident to the capture of Fort Dipitie, Haiti, on Oct. 24, 1915. The citation accompanying the medal states that a Marine detachment was crossing a river in a deep ravine at night when it was suddenly fired upon from three sides by about 400 Cacos concealed in the bushes about 100 yards from the objective, Fort Dipitie. The Marines fought their way forward to a good position and maintained it throughout the night despite the continuous fire of the Cacos. At daybreak, the Marines in three squads commanded by Lt. Ostermann, Capt. William P. Upshur, and Gy. Sgt. Daniel Daly, advanced in three different directions, surprising and scattering the Cacos in all directions. Capt. Upshur's and Lt. Ostermann's squads then went on to capture the fort with a total of 13 Marines. The fort was demolished and burned and the garrison was put to flight. "These men were in pitch darkness surrounded by ten times their number and fighting for their lives...." the citation states; "... Had one squad failed, not one man of the party would have lived to tell the story...." Gen. Ostermann, Capt. Upshur (who also became a general), Gy. Sgt. Dan Daly, and Maj. Smedley D. Butler all received the Medal of Honor for this battle. Gen. Ostermann was retired because of physical disability on Jan. 1, 1943 and, because of having been "specially commended for his performance of duty in actual combat," he was promoted to the rank of major general on the retired list.

OVIATT, Miles M. Corporal. Medal of Honor: b. Cattaraugus County, N.Y., 1841. Miles Oviatt enlisted in the Marine Corps at Brooklyn, N.Y. on Aug. 19,

1862. His citation reads, in part: ". . . while serving on board the USS *Brooklyn* in the engagement in Mobile Bay, Aug. 5, 1864: conspicuous for good conduct at his gun. . . ."

OWENS, Michael. Private. Medal of Honor: b. New York, N.Y. Michael Owens enlisted in the Marine Corps at New York, N.Y. on Aug. 17, 1865. His citation reads, in part: ". . . while serving on board the USS *Colorado* during the capture of Korean forts, June 11, 1871 . . . fighting hand-to-hand with the enemy . . . and badly wounded. . . ." After four reenlistments, Owens was discharged from the Corps with a medical survey on Aug. 17, 1888.

OWENS, Robert Allen. Sergeant. Medal of Honor: b. Greenville, S.C., Sept. 13, 1920; d. KIA, Bougainville, Nov. 1, 1943. The landing on the beach at Cape Torokina, Bougainville, was strongly resisted by a well-camouflaged 75-mm. regimental gun. Strategically placed, the gun had already scored direct hits on several of the landing craft and it was seriously threatening the success of the operation. No boats could approach the beach without passing within 150 yards or less from the muzzle. The emplacement was so situated that it could only be attacked from the front and also in a position whereby rifle fire and grenades could not reach the gun crew. Sizing up the situation, Sgt. Owens decided that the only way to neutralize the gun was to charge it directly from the front. Calling on four volunteers to cover him, he placed them where they could keep adjacent bunkers under fire. At the moment when he judged he had a fair chance of reaching his objective, he charged right into the emplacement through the fire port, and chased the Japanese out the back where they were cut down by his riflemen. Pursuing them, he in turn was instantly killed. It was discovered that a round had been placed in the chamber and the breech was almost closed at the moment that Sgt. Owens came through the fire port. More than 150 rounds of high-explosive shells were stacked and ready for firing. The enemy had counted heavily on this weapon to stop the Marine landing. On July 22, 1946, the destroyer, USS *Robert A. Owens* was christened at Bath, Maine, in his honor.

OZBOURN, Joseph William. Private. Medal of Honor: b. Herrin, Ill., Oct. 24, 1919; d. KIA, Tinian Is., July 30, 1944. Pvt. Ozbourn's citation reads, in part: ". . . as a BAR man serving with the 1st

Bn., 23rd Marines, 4th Mar. Div., during the battle for enemy Japanese-held Tinian Is., Marianas Is. on July 30, 1944. As a member of a platoon assigned the mission of clearing the remaining Japanese troops from dugouts and pillboxes along a tree line, Pvt. Ozbourn, flanked by two men on either side, was moving forward to throw an armed hand grenade into a dugout when a terrific blast from the entrance severely wounded the four men and himself. Unable to throw the grenade into the dugout and with no place to hurl it without endangering the other men, Pvt. Ozbourn unhesitatingly grasped it close to his body and fell upon it, sacrificing his own life to absorb the full impact of the explosion but saving his comrades. . . ."

P

PAIGE, Mitchell. Colonel (Retired). Medal of Honor: b. Charleroi, Pa., Aug. 31, 1918. Mitchell Paige enlisted in the Marine Corps on Sept. 1, 1936 at Baltimore, Md. Completing his boot camp training at Parris Is., S.C. in Nov. 1936, he was transferred to Quantico. Later he served aboard the USS *Wyoming* as a gunner. In Feb. 1937, he was transferred to Mare Is. Navy Yard for guard duty, and two months later was ordered to Cavite in the Philippine Is. While in Cavite he became a member of the All-Navy-Marine baseball team which gained prominence throughout the island and the Orient. He served in China from Oct. 1938 to Sept. 1939. He left north China and returned to the States in Apr. 1940 for guard duty at the Brooklyn and Philadelphia Navy Yards. In Sept. 1940, he rejoined the 5th

Marines, at Quantico, and the following month participated in maneuvers at Guantanamo Bay, Cuba and Culebra, Puerto Rico. In Mar. 1941, he was transferred back to the States and ordered to New River, N.C. to help construct and prepare a new training base for Marines which later became Camp Lejeune. After the Japanese attack on Pearl Harbor, Paige was once more sent overseas with the 7th Marines and landed at Apia, British Samoa. From Samoa the 7th Marines went to Guadalcanal, landing in Sept. of 1942. There he won the nation's highest decoration in Oct. 1942 when he made a desperate lone stand against enemy Japanese after they had broken through the lines and killed or wounded all of the Marines in his machine gun section. His citation reads, in part:

Paige

"...while serving with a company of Marines in combat against enemy Japanese forces in the Solomon Is. on Oct. 26, 1942. When the enemy broke through the line directly in front of his position, (then) Plat. Sgt. Paige, commanding a machine gun section with fearless determination, continued to direct the fire of his gunners until all his men were either killed or wounded. Alone, against the deadly hail of Japanese shells, he fought his gun and, when it was destroyed, took over another, moving from gun to gun, never ceasing his withering fire against the advancing hordes until reinforcements finally arrived. Then, forming a new line, he dauntlessly and aggressively led a bayonet charge, driving the enemy back and preventing a breakthrough in

our lines...." He remained there until Jan. 1943 when he went to Melbourne, Australia with the 1st Mar. Div. While on Guadalcanal he was commissioned a second lieutenant in the field on Dec. 19, 1942, with date of rank from Oct. 2, 1942, following his heroic one-man stand. In June 1943, he was promoted to first lieutenant. In Sept. 1943, he left with the 1st Mar. Div. for New Guinea where his unit joined the 6th Army for the attack on Cape Gloucester, New Britain, on Dec. 26, 1943. In May 1944, the division left Cape Gloucester for a rest area in the Russell Is., Pavuvu. In July 1944, Paige was sent back to the States and assigned duty at Camp Lejeune, N.C. In June 1945, he became Tactical Training Officer at Camp Matthews, Calif., and the following Sept., was sent to the MCRD as a recruit training officer. He was promoted to captain in Feb. 1945. Capt. Paige was placed on inactive duty in May 1946, returning to active duty again in July 1950, and was assigned duty at Camp Pendleton, Oceanside, Calif. He was later transferred to the MCRD at San Diego, Calif., as Plans and Operations Officer of the 2nd Recruit Training Bn. At this time he also went on a special assignment as Plans and Training Officer in charge of setting up a PLC training program for the Special Training Co. He was promoted to the rank of major on Jan. 1, 1951. In Oct. 1951, Maj. Paige became Executive Officer of the 2nd Recruit Training Bn., MCRD, San Diego, Calif. until Oct. 1952, when he was transferred to the 4th Special Junior Course, Marine Corps Educational Center, B Co., HQ Bn., MCS, Quantico. He attended school there until May 1953, then served as Division Recruiting Officer, 2nd Mar. Div., Camp Lejeune, N.C. until Feb. 1954. Maj. Paige was next assigned to Sub-Unit 2, HQ Co., HQ Bn., 3rd Mar.

Div., San Francisco, Calif., serving as Officer in Charge, Division Noncommissioned Officers' School, 3rd Mar. Div. until Apr. 1955. During this period he also served briefly as Assistant Officer in Charge of Sub-Unit 1. From there he served as Battalion Executive Officer and later CO of the 3rd Bn., 7th Marines, 1st Mar. Div. at Camp Pendleton from Apr. 1955 until Aug. 1955. That month he reported to the 12th MCR and Recruitment District to serve as Officer in Charge of Marine Corps Recruiting Station in San Francisco; he was promoted to lieutenant colonel in May 1957. In Aug. 1957, he was assigned duty as Inspector-Instructor, 7th Infantry Bn., USMCR, at San Bruno, Calif. until Aug. 1958, when he was detached to HQMC, Washington, D.C. In May 1959, he entered the U.S. Army Language School in Monterey, Calif., and remained there for 9 months until he was ordered to the MB, U.S. Naval Station, San Diego, Calif. to serve as Executive Officer until Oct. 1959. He was placed on the Disability Retired List on Nov. 1, 1959. For being specially commended for performance of duty in actual combat he was promoted to colonel upon retirement.

PARKER, Pomeroy. Private. Medal of Honor: b. Gates County, N.C., Mar. 17, 1874. Pomeroy Parker enlisted in the Marine Corps at Norfolk, Va. on Sept. 13, 1892. His citation reads, in part: ". . . while serving on board the USS *Nashville*, for extraordinary bravery and coolness while cutting the cables leading from Cienfuegos, Cuba, May 11, 1898, under heavy fire of the enemy. . . ."

PATE, Randolph McCall. General. 21st Commandant of the Marine Corps: b. Port Royal, S.C., Feb. 11, 1898; d. U.S. Naval Hospital, Bethesda, Md., July 31, 1961. Randolph Pate served a brief tour of enlisted service with the U.S. Army in 1918. Following WWI, he graduated from the Virginia Military Institute in June 1921 with a Bachelor of Arts degree. He was commissioned a second lieutenant in the MCR in Sept., and accepted a commission in the regular Marine Corps the following May. In addition to expeditionary duty in Santo Domingo during 1923 and 1924, Pate served in China from 1927 to 1929, and at various posts throughout the States during his 38-year Marine Corps career. During WWII Pate, then a colonel serving as Deputy Chief of Staff, FMF, Pacific, was awarded the Legion of Merit for outstanding service during operations on Palau, Iwo Jima, and Okinawa. In 1947 he was awarded a Gold Star in lieu of a second Legion of Merit for exceptionally meritorious service at Guadalcanal during the first U.S. offensive against Japan. Following WWII, he served as Director of the Division of Reserve at HQMC, Washington, D.C. and as Director of the Marine Corps Educational Center at the MCS, Quantico. He was promoted to brigadier general in 1948. Ordered to Korea in June 1953, Gen. Pate commanded the 1st Mar. Div. until May 1954, earning the Distinguished Service Medal and the Republic of Korea's Order of Military Merit Taiguk. Promoted to the rank of general on Jan. 1, 1956, he became the 21st Commandant of the Marine Corps, succeeding Gen. Lemuel C. Shepherd, Jr. Serving in that capacity for four years, Gen. Pate was retired with the rank of general on Dec. 31, 1959.

PENDLETON, Joseph Henry. "Uncle Joe." Major General: b. Rochester, Pa., June 2, 1860; d. San Diego, Calif., Feb. 4, 1942. Joseph Pendleton was appointed to

Pendleton

the U.S. Naval Academy from Pennsylvania in 1878. After graduating from the Academy he was appointed a second lieutenant in the Marine Corps on July 1, 1884, following two years at sea as a cadet engineer. His first duty was performed at the MB, Navy Yard, N.Y., where he served from Aug. 31, 1884 to Feb. 7, 1885. From here the new lieutenant joined the USS *Pensacola* on Mar. 20, 1885. In Mar. 1888, he reported to the MB, N.Y. His next station was the MB, Mare Is., Calif. where he served from May 24, 1889 to May 12, 1892; but between June 21 and Oct. 14, 1891 he was on temporary duty on board the *Al-Ki*, cruising the Bering Sea. Lt. Pendleton again served in Alaska at the MB, Sitka, from June 1892 to June 1894, and from Nov. 1899 to Mar. 1904. He was advanced

to first lieutenant on June 28, 1891. During the period intervening between these two tours of duty in Alaska, Lt. Pendleton served at the MB, Washington, D.C., New York, Annapolis, and on board the USS *Yankee*. He was promoted to captain on Mar. 3, 1899, and to major Mar. 3, 1903. After being detached from the MB, Sitka, Alaska on Mar. 21, 1904, Maj. Pendleton reported to the MB, Mare Is., Calif., Apr. 2, 1904. On May 28, 1904, he joined the 1st Brig. of Marines in the Philippine Is., and on Apr. 7, 1905 he reported to Olongapo where he served until Jan. 1906. From Feb. to July 1906, Maj. Pendleton commanded the MB, Guam. From Sept. 1906 to Sept. 1909, he commanded the MB, Puget Sound, Bremerton, Wash. On Jan. 1, 1908, he was advanced to the rank of lieutenant colonel. Pendleton joined the 1st Brig. of Marines in the Philippine Is. for his second tour of duty there on Nov. 4, 1909. He performed duty as CO, 1st Brig. and as Post Quartermaster, and CO of the 1st Regt., Olongapo, Philippine Is. On May 23, 1911, he was promoted to colonel. He was detached from the Philippine Is. in May 1912, and returned to the States via the Suez Canal and Europe, reporting at the MB, Portsmouth, N.H. in Aug. 1912. Col. Pendleton, while attached to Portsmouth, was absent on temporary foreign shore service from Aug. 1912 to Dec. of that year. This duty covered the period of the 1912 operations in Nicaragua. He was in command of the Marines during the campaign. The skirmishes at Masaya and Chichigalpa, and the capture of Coyotepe and Leon, occupy high places in Marine Corps history. From Feb. to June 1913, Col. Pendleton was with an expeditionary force at Guantanamo Bay, Cuba. In Aug. 1913, he was detached from the MB, Portsmouth, N.H. From Sept. 1913 to Dec. 1914, Col. Pendleton was in command of the MB, at Puget Sound, Wash., and was on expeditionary duty for a good part of this period. He was in command of the 4th Regt. from Apr. to Dec. 1914 on board the USS *South Dakota*, and at San Diego, Calif. From Dec. 1914 to Feb. 1916, Col. Pendleton was in command of the 4th Regt. at San Diego, California; part of the time, however, he was on expeditionary duty and temporary sea duty with the Pacific Fleet. From Feb. 3 to Dec. 31, 1916, Col. Pendleton was in command of the MB, San Diego, Calif.; but, from June 6 to Dec. 31, 1916, he was absent on expeditionary duty in command of the 4th Regt. He was placed in command of all naval forces ashore in Santo Domingo on June 19, 1916. He participated in engagements with the enemy at Las Trencheras, at Dona Antonia, at Guayacanes, and was in command of the forces that occupied Santiago. During this period (on Aug. 29, 1916) he was promoted to brigadier general. On Nov. 22, 1916, Brig. Gen. Pendleton was detailed to command the 2nd Prov. Brig. in Santo Domingo, and on Dec. 31, 1916 was detached from the MB, San Diego, and assigned to permanent duty in Santo Domingo. Gen. Pendleton was acting Military Governor of Santo Domingo from Oct. 29 to Nov. 29, 1917, and on Mar. 18, 1918, was designated Military Governor temporarily, in the absence of the Military Governor. He was detached from Santo Domingo Oct. 21, 1918 and reported to HQMC in Washington, D.C., Oct. 28, 1918. From Nov. 11, 1918 to Sept. 25, 1919, Gen. Pendleton commanded the MB, Parris Is., S.C., and on Oct. 1, 1919, joined the 2nd Advanced Base Force at San Diego, Calif. as its CG. From Oct. 1, 1921 to Nov. 7, 1921, he was in command of the Department of Pacific at San Francisco. Upon the establishment

of the 5th Brig. of Marines in Oct. 1921, Gen. Pendleton was assigned to that organization as the CO. In addition to these duties he was assigned as CG of the Department of the Pacific in the absence of Gen. Barnett, from May 1922 to Sept. 1922. He was advanced to major general Dec. 10, 1923. From Feb. 1924 to Mar. 1924, he was on duty inspecting Marine Corps stations and organizations in Central America and the West Indies. After this inspection trip he was on a short tour of duty at HQMC and in May 1924, he resumed duties at San Diego as CO of the 5th Brig. of Marines. On June 2, 1924, Gen. Pendleton was retired, having reached the age of 64. He died in San Diego, Calif., on Feb. 4, 1942 at the age of 81.

PFEIFER, Louis Fred. Private. Medal of Honor. Served under the name of THIES, Louis Fred (*q.v.*).

PHELPS, Wesley. Private First Class. Medal of Honor: b. Neafus, Ky., June 12, 1923; d. KIA, Peleliu Is., Oct. 4, 1944. P.F.C. Phelps' citation reads, in part: " . . . while serving with the 3rd Bn., 7th Marines, 1st Mar. Div., in action against enemy Japanese forces on Peleliu Is., during a savage hostile counterattack on the night of Oct. 4, 1944. Stationed with another Marine in an advanced position when a Japanese hand grenade landed in his foxhole, P.F.C. Phelps instantly shouted a warning to his comrade and rolled over on the deadly bomb, absorbing with his own body the full, shattering impact of the exploding charge. Courageous and indomitable, P.F.C. Phelps fearlessly gave his life that another might be spared serious injury. . . ."

PHILLIPS, George. Private. Medal of Honor: b. Rich Hill, Mo., July 14, 1926;

d. KIA, Iwo Jima, Mar. 14, 1945. Pvt. Phillips' citation reads, in part: "...while serving with the 2nd Bn., 28th Marines, 5th Mar. Div., in action against enemy Japanese forces during the seizure of Iwo Jima in the Volcano Is., on Mar. 14, 1945. Standing the foxhole watch while other members of his squad rested after a night of bitter hand-grenade fighting against infiltrating Japanese troops, Pvt. Phillips was the only member of his unit alerted when an enemy hand grenade was tossed into their midst. Instantly shouting a warning, he unhesitatingly threw himself on the deadly missile, absorbing the shattering violence of the exploding charge in his own body and protecting his comrades from serious injury...."

PHILLIPS, Lee Hugh. Corporal. Medal of Honor: b. Stockbridge, Ga., Feb. 3, 1930. Cpl. Phillips' citation reads, in part: "...while serving as a squad leader of Co. E, 2nd Bn., 7th Marines, 1st Mar. Div. (Reinf.), in action against enemy aggressor forces in Korea on Nov. 4, 1950. Assuming the point position in the attack against a strongly defended and well-entrenched numerically superior enemy force occupying a vital hill position which had been unsuccessfully assaulted on five separate occasions by units of the Marine Corps and other friendly forces, Cpl. Phillips fearlessly led his men in a bayonet charge up the precipitous slope under a deadly hail of hostile mortar, small arms, and machine gun fire. Quickly rallying his squad when it was pinned down by a heavy and accurate mortar barrage, he continued to lead his men through the bombarded area and, although only five members were left in the casualty ridden unit, gained the military crest of the hill where he was immediately subjected to an enemy counterattack. Although greatly outnumbered by

an estimated enemy squad, Cpl. Phillips boldly engaged the hostile force with hand grenades and rifle fire and, exhorting his gallant group of Marines to follow him, stormed forward to completely overwhelm the enemy. With only three men now left in his squad, he proceeded to spearhead an assault on the last remaining strong point which was defended by four of the enemy on a rocky and almost inaccessible portion of the hill position. Using one hand to climb up the extremely hazardous precipice, he hurled grenades with the other and, with two remaining comrades, succeeded in annihilating the pocket of resistance and in consolidating the position. Immediately subjected to a sharp counterattack by an estimated enemy squad, he skillfully directed the fire of his men and employed his own weapon with deadly effectiveness to repulse the numerically superior hostile force...."

PHILLIPS, Reuben Jasper. Corporal. Medal of Honor: b. Cambria, Calif., July 28, 1874. Reuben Phillips enlisted in the Marine Corps at Mare Is., Calif. on July 16, 1898. He was awarded the Medal of Honor "... for distinguished conduct in the presence of the enemy in the battles on June 13, 20, 21 and 22, 1900, while with the relief expedition of the Allied Forces in China...." He was discharged from the Corps on July 21, 1903.

PIERCE, Philip Nason. Lieutenant Colonel (Retired). Marine Corps writer: b. Gardiner, Me., Sept. 20, 1917. Philip Pierce enlisted in the Marine Corps as a private on Mar. 12, 1942. He was assigned to Officer's School at MCS, Quantico on June 15, and was commissioned a second lieutenant on Aug. 22, 1942. Spending two years with various combat units in the Pacific Theater during WWII, he took part in campaigns in the Marshall Is., and at Saipan, Tinian, and Iwo Jima. He was promoted to captain on Nov. 30, 1944. Following WWII, Capt. Pierce served at various posts in the States, including HQMC; Camp Pendleton, Calif.; and Fort Sill, Okla. He returned to combat duty with the advent of the Korean War. As a battalion operations officer he was with the famed Mar. Prov. Brig. which President Syngman Rhee called "the saviors of Korea" as a result of their battle successes along the Pusan Perimeter during the summer of 1950. Joining the 1st Mar. Div. in Sept., Pierce took part in the Inchon landing and the liberation of Seoul. Throughout the following year his division fought in central, eastern and northern Korea, including the epic Chosin Reservoir Campaign. He was promoted to major on Jan. 1, 1951, and to his present rank on July 1, 1955. Since the Korean War, Lt. Col. Pierce has served at many posts and stations throughout the States; in the Pacific; and the Orient. A qualified Russian interpreter, he has served with Naval Intelligence and is a graduate of Strategic Intelligence School. From 1951 to 1953 he was assigned as CO, Artillery Demonstration Unit, at MCS, Quantico. This duty was followed by an assignment as Chief Instructor at the Navy's Amphibious Training School in Coronado, Calif. Following a third tour of duty in the Orient, where he served as a special staff officer on the staffs of the CG, 1st Mar. Div. and the 3rd Mar. Div., he became successively executive officer and then CO of the MB, U.S. Naval Base, Brooklyn, N.Y. He also served as District Marine Officer on the staff of the Commander, 3rd Naval District. From 1958 until his retirement, Lt. Col. Pierce was Director of Media Branch, Division of Information, at HQMC, Washington, D.C. Lt. Col. Pierce's articles and feature stories have been published in national magazines and newspapers throughout the country. His work has appeared in such publications as *Bluebook, Argosy, Navy, Marine Corps Gazette, Leatherneck,* and the *Encyclopaedia Britannica.* He is the author of *The Compact History of the U.S. Marine Corps,* and co-author (with Karl Schuon) of *John H. Glenn: Astronaut.*

POPE, Everett Parker. Major. Medal of Honor: b. Milton, Mass., July 16, 1919. Maj. Pope's citation reads, in part: ". . . while serving as CO of Co. C, 1st Marines, 1st Mar. Div., during action against enemy Japanese forces on Peleliu Is. on Sept. 19 and 20, 1944. Subjected to point-blank cannon fire which caused heavy casualties and badly disorganized his company while assaulting a steep coral hill, (then) Capt. Pope rallied his men and gallantly led them to the summit in the face of machine gun, mortar, and sniper fire. Forced by widespread hostile attack to deploy the remnants of his company thinly in order to hold the ground won, and with his machine guns out of order and insufficient water and ammunition, he remained on the exposed hill with 12 men and 1 wounded officer, determined to hold through the night. Attacked continuously with grenades, machine guns, and rifles from three sides, he and his valiant men fiercely beat back or destroyed the enemy, resorting to hand-to-hand combat as the supply of ammunition dwindled, and still maintaining his lines with his eight remaining riflemen when daylight brought more deadly fire and he was ordered to withdraw. . . ."

PORTER, David Dixon. Colonel. Medal

of Honor: b. Washington, D.C., Apr. 29, 1877; d. Feb. 25, 1944, Naval Hospital, Philadelphia, Pa. Col. Porter's citation reads, in part: ". . . in battle at the junction of the Cadacan and Sohoton Rivers, Samar, P.I., Nov. 17, 1901. Capt. Porter, in command of the columns upon their uniting ashore in the Sohoton region, made a surprise attack of the fortified cliffs and completely routed the enemy, killing 30 and capturing and destroying the powder magazine, 40 lantacas (guns), rice, food, and cuartels. Due to his courage, intelligence, discrimination, and zeal, he successfully led his men up the cliffs by means of bamboo ladders to a height of 200 feet. The cliffs were of soft stone of volcanic origin, in the nature of pumice, and were honeycombed with caves. Tons of rocks were suspended in platforms held in position by vine cables in readiness to be precipitated upon people below. After driving the insurgents from their position which was almost impregnable — being covered with numerous trails lined with poisoned spears, pits, etc. — Capt. Porter led his men across the river, scaled the cliffs on the opposite side, and destroyed the camps there. He and the men under his command overcame incredible difficulties and dangers in destroying positions which, according to reports from old prisoners, had taken three years to perfect, were held as a final rallying point, and were never before penetrated by white troops. Capt. Porter also rendered distinguished public service in the presence of the enemy at Quinapundan River, Samar, P.I. on Oct. 26, 1901."

POWER, John Vincent. First Lieutenant. Medal of Honor: b. Worcester, Mass., Nov. 20, 1918; d. KIA, Roi-Namur, Kwajalein, Feb. 1, 1944. In mid-January 1944, Lt. Power sailed from San Diego harbor in a combat-loaded transport — the first group to sail directly from the States to an enemy beach. Its destination: Roi-Namur Is. in the Kwajalein Atoll. Roi was conquered in short order and the surviving Japanese fled to nearby Namur. Advancing about 75 yards inland, Lt. Power's platoon made contact with a large enemy pillbox. The platoon leader and one of his men advanced upon the position and placed a charge upon it. In the process, both were wounded. Taken back to a shell hole by his comrades, the lieutenant's stomach wound was dressed and he turned over command of his platoon to his sergeant, after promising that he would help as much as possible. The sergeant and some of his men urged the lieutenant to return to the beach where he could be properly cared for, but Lt. Power refused. The platoon sergeant and his men continued to demolish the pillbox which contained about 30 Japanese and then moved on to another. While the Marines were preparing to blow up that one, Lt. Power rejoined them. The charge was placed and set off. Even before the smoke cleared away, Lt. Power charged into the opening firing his carbine with his right hand and holding his wounded stomach with his left. Emptying his clip, Lt. Power attempted to reload his weapon to continue the attack. It was then that the fatal shots struck him in the stomach again and in the head. By the time his men reached him, he was dead.

POYNTER, James Irsley. Sergeant. Medal of Honor: b. Bloomingdale, Ind., Dec. 1, 1916; d. KIA, south of Sudong, Korea, Nov. 4, 1950. Sergeant Poynter's citation reads, in part: ". . . while serving as a squad leader in a rifle platoon of Co. A, 1st Bn., 7th Marines, 1st Mar. Div. (Reinf.), in action against enemy aggressor forces during the defense of Hill 532, south of Sudong, Korea, on Nov. 4, 1950. When a vastly outnumbering, well-concealed hostile force launched a sudden, vicious counterattack against his platoon's hasty defensive position, Sgt. Poynter displayed superb skill and courage in leading his squad and directing its fire against the onrushing enemy. With his ranks critically depleted by casualties and he himself critically wounded as the onslaught gained momentum and the hostile force surrounded his position, he seized his bayonet and engaged in bitter hand-to-hand combat as the breakthrough continued. Observing three machine guns closing in at a distance of 25 yards, he dashed from his position and, grasping hand grenades from fallen Marines as he ran, charged the emplacements in rapid succession, killing the crews of two and putting the other out of action before he fell, mortally wounded. . . ."

PRENDERGAST, Thomas Francis. Corporal. Medal of Honor: b. Waterford, Ireland, Apr. 2, 1871. Thomas Prendergast enlisted in the Marine Corps on May 16, 1893. He was awarded the Medal of Honor on July 19, 1901 ". . . for distinguished conduct in the presence of the enemy in battles while with the 8th Army Corps (during the Philippine Insurrection) on Mar. 25, 27, and 29, and April 4, 1899. . . ."

PRESTON, Herbert Irving. Private. Medal of Honor: b. Berkeley, N.J., Aug. 6, 1876. Herbert Preston enlisted in the Marine Corps at Philadelphia, Pa. on June 29, 1899. His citation reads, in part: ". . . for distinguished conduct in the presence of the enemy at Peking, China, July 21 to Aug. 17, 1900. Preston assisted to erect barricades under heavy fire. . . ."

PRUITT, John Henry. Corporal. Medal of Honor: b. Faderville, Ark., Oct. 4, 1896; d. KIA, France, Oct. 1918. Cpl. Pruitt's citation reads, in part: ". . . in action with the enemy at Mont Blanc Ridge, France, Oct. 3, 1918. Cpl. Pruitt, singlehanded, attacked two machine guns, capturing them and killing two of the enemy. He then captured 40 prisoners in a dugout nearby. This gallant soldier was killed soon afterwards by shell fire while he was sniping at the enemy. . . ."

Puller

PULLER, Lewis Burwell. "Chesty." Lieutenant General (Retired). Colorful veteran of the Korean fighting, four World War campaigns, and expeditionary service in China, Nicaragua, and Haiti: b. West Point, Va., June 26, 1898. Lewis Puller attended Virginia Military Institute until enlisting in the Marine Corps in Aug. 1918. He was appointed a Marine Reserve second lieutenant on June 16, 1919, but due to the reduction of the Corps after WWI, was placed on inactive duty ten days later. He rejoined the Marines as an enlisted man on the 30th of that same month, then served later as an officer in the Gendarmerie d'Haiti, a military force set up in that country under a treaty with the States. Most of its officers were U.S. Marines, while its enlisted personnel were Haitians. After nearly five years in Haiti, where he saw frequent action against the Caco rebels, Puller returned to the States in Mar. 1924. He was commissioned a Marine second lieutenant that same month, and during the next two years served at the MB, Norfolk, Va.; completed the Basic School at Philadelphia, Pa.; and served with the 10th Mar. Regt. at Quantico, Va. He was then detailed to duty as a student naval aviator at Pensacola, Fla. in Feb. 1926. In July of that year, he embarked for a two-year tour of duty at the MB, Pearl Harbor. Returning in June 1928, he served at San Diego, Calif., until he joined the Nicaraguan National Guard Detachment that Dec. After winning his first Navy Cross in Nicaragua he returned to the States in July 1931, to enter the Company Officers' Course at the Army Infantry School, Fort Benning, Ga. He completed the course in June 1932, and returned to Nicaragua the following month to begin the tour of duty which brought him his second Navy Cross. In Jan. 1933, Puller left Nicaragua for the west coast of the United States. A month later he was called from San Francisco to join the Marine Detachment of the American Legation at Peiping, China. There, in addition to other duties, he commanded the famed "Horse Marines." Without coming back to the States, he began a tour of sea duty in Sept. 1934, as CO of the Ma-

rine Detachment aboard the USS *Augusta* of the Asiatic Fleet. In June 1936, he returned to the States to become an instructor in the Basic School at Philadelphia. He left there in May 1939, to serve another year as commander of the *Augusta*'s Marine Detachment. From that ship, he joined the 4th Mar. Regt. at Shanghai, China, in May 1940. After serving as a battalion executive and CO with the 4th Marines, Puller sailed for the States in Aug. 1941, just four months before the attack on Pearl Harbor. In Sept. he took command of the 1st Bn., 7th Marines, 1st Mar. Div. at Camp Lejeune. That regiment was detached from the 1st Div. in Mar. 1942 and, the following month, as part of the 3rd Mar. Brig., it sailed for the Pacific theater. The 7th Regt. rejoined the 1st Mar. Div. in Sept. 1942, and Puller, still commanding its 1st Bn., went on to win his third Navy Cross at Guadalcanal. The action which brought him that medal occurred on the night of Oct. 24-25, 1942. For a desperate three hours his battalion, stretched over a mile-long front, was the only defense between vital Henderson Airfield and a regiment of seasoned Japanese troops. In pouring jungle rain, the Japanese smashed repeatedly at his thin line, as Puller moved up and down its length to encourage his men and direct the defense. After reinforcements arrived he commanded the augmented force until late the next afternoon. The defending Marines suffered fewer than 70 casualties in the engagement, while 1400 of the enemy were killed and 17 truckloads of Japanese equipment were recovered by the Americans. After Guadalcanal, Puller became executive officer of the 7th Marines. He was fighting in that capacity when he won his fourth Navy Cross at Cape Gloucester in Jan. 1944. There, when the commanders of two battalions were wounded, he took over their units and moved through heavy machine gun and mortar fire to reorganize them for attack, then led them in taking a strongly fortified enemy position. In Feb. 1944, Col. Puller took command of the 1st Marines at Cape Gloucester. After leading that regiment for the remainder of the campaign, he sailed with it for the Russell Is. in Apr. 1944, and went on from there to command it at Peleliu in Sept. and Oct. 1944. He returned to the States in Nov. 1944, was named executive officer of the Inf. Training Regt. at Camp Lejeune in Jan. 1945 and took command of that regiment the following month. In Aug. 1946, he became Director of the 8th Marine Corps Reserve District, with headquarters at New Orleans, La. After that assignment, he commanded the MB at Pearl Harbor until Aug. 1950, when he arrived at Camp Pendleton, Calif. to re-establish and take command of the 1st Marines, the same regiment he had led at Cape Gloucester and Peleliu. Landing with the 1st Marines at Inchon, Korea, in Sept. 1950, he continued to head that regiment until Jan. 1951, when he was promoted to brigadier general and named Assistant Commander of the 1st Mar. Div. That May he returned to Camp Pendleton to command the newly reactivated 3rd Mar. Brig., which was redesignated the 3rd Mar. Div. in Jan. 1952. After that, he was assistant division commander until he took over the Troop Training Unit, Pacific, at Coronado, Calif. that June. He was promoted to major general in Sept. 1953, and in July 1954 assumed command of the 2nd Mar. Div. at Camp Lejeune. Despite his illness he retained that command until Feb. 1955, when he was appointed Deputy Camp Commander. He served in that capacity until Aug., when he entered the U.S. Naval Hospital at Camp Lejeune. On Nov. 1, 1955 he was promoted to lieutenant general and placed on the temporary disability retired list.

PURVIS, Hugh. Private. Medal of Honor: b. Philadelphia, Pa., Mar. 5, 1846. Hugh Purvis enlisted in the Marine Corps on Oct. 27, 1869 at Philadelphia, Pa. He won the Medal of Honor while serving aboard the USS *Alaska* in the conflict against hostile Korean forces who had been attacking and destroying American ships and cargoes and killing American crews. During a final battle for a fiercely defended Korean fort, Purvis distinguished himself by tearing down the fort's 12-foot yellow cotton flag thereby greatly demoralizing the hostile forces. His citation reads, in part: "...On board the USS *Alaska* during the attack on and capture of the Korean forts, June 11, 1871, braving the enemy fire, Purvis was the first to scale the walls of the fort and capture the flag of the Korean forces...."

Q

QUICK, John Henry. Sergeant Major. Medal of Honor: b. Charlestown, W. Va., June 20, 1870; d. St. Louis, Mo., Sept. 10, 1922. John Quick enlisted in the Marine Corps on Aug. 10, 1892 at Philadelphia, Pa. He served continuously in the Corps on board naval vessels and ashore in all parts of the world until Nov. 20,

Quick

1918, when he was placed on the retired list. It was in Cuba during the war with Spain that Quick's gallantry was the subject of official dispatches and a number of commendations, which resulted in his being awarded the Medal of Honor. The USS *Panther* arrived in Guantanamo Bay at about 1:00 P.M., June 10, 1898, and soon began landing Lt. Col. Robert W. Huntington's battalion of Marines. A camp site was selected on the top of McCalla hill where the old Spanish blockhouses had been located. After repulsing a number of Spanish attacks during the first few days, it was decided to capture Cuzco Well (located about six miles southeast of Camp McCalla and near the coast), the only water supply for the Spanish forces in the vicinity. During the morning of June 14, 1898,

Companies C and D and approximately 50 Cubans moved through the hills to seize Cuzco Well. The USS *Dolphin* moved east along the shore ready to furnish naval gunfire support upon call. The Spanish soon discovered the movement and their main body near the Well was alerted. The Marines and Cubans occupied the hill which overlooked the enemy's position, but were immediately subjected to heavy long-range rifle fire. Capt. George F. Elliott, in command of the Marine Detachment, signaled the *Dolphin* to shell the Spanish position; but due to the fact that the sender was not clearly visible, the message was misinterpreted, and the vessel began dropping shells on a small detachment of Marines who were enroute to join the fight. The problem of directing the fire of the USS *Dolphin* was solved by Sgt. Quick who heroically placed himself in plain sight of the vessel — but in danger of falling shells — and signaled for the fire to be stopped, using a blue flag belonging to the Cubans. Due to the poor visibility, Sgt. Quick scrambled to the top of the hill where he was plainly silhouetted against the horizon. As he calmly turned his back to the enemy and began waving his flag, he was immediately subjected to a furious enemy rifle fire. While enemy bullets cut through the bushes and screamed overhead, Quick continued to signal the *Dolphin* as coolly as though he were on a parade ground. Letter by letter the message to the ship was spelled out in the dot-dash code. When Sgt. Quick finished his message, the ship answered. Quick then picked up his rifle and resumed his place on the firing line. The *Dolphin* shifted her fire and by 2:00 P.M. the Spaniards had begun to retreat. For this deed, Quick was awarded the Medal of Honor and this citation: "John Quick, sergeant, United States Marine

Corps, for distinguished and gallant conduct in the Battle of Cuzco, Cuba, on June 14, 1898, signaling to the USS *Dolphin* on three different occasions while exposed to heavy fire from the enemy." During the Philippine Insurrection, Quick served in the Samoan campaign from Oct. 26, 1901 to Mar. 26, 1902, participating in the heroic march across Samar. Shortly after the personnel of Co. C, 9th U.S. Infantry, had been massacred at Balangiga by the insurrectionists, a vigorous campaign against the rebellious elements of the island of Samar began. A battalion of Marines (14 officers and approximately 300 enlisted men) under Maj. L. W. T. Waller was organized at Cavite on Luzon Island and sent to take part in the campaign. John Quick was a member of the force commanded by Maj. Waller which left Basey on Dec. 8, 1901, to hack its way through jungles and swamps across the island. Later it was the fortitude and leadership of Capt. D. D. Porter and Sgt. Quick which gave the other members of the party the courage and strength to carry on while suffering great hardships and privations. After that expedition, John Quick settled down to a more peaceful routine. He performed various duties in many places until the trouble of 1906 in Cuba where he served with the Marines in the Army of Cuban Pacification. After serving in the various enlisted grades, Quick was appointed to the rank of sergeant major on Nov. 12, 1905, and continued in that rank throughout the remainder of his service. During another period of quiet, Sgt. Maj. Quick served as first sergeant at St. Juliens Creek, MB, Washington, D.C., and other stations in the States. Then came the Battle of Vera Cruz, Mex., in Apr. 1914 when Marines advanced into the city. The Secretary of the Navy commended John Quick for his gallantry during the occupation: "He was continually exposed to fire during the first two days of the operation and showed coolness, bravery, and judgment in the prompt manner in which he performed his duties." Vera Cruz was the end of the lull before the storm. There was trouble in Haiti, in Santo Domingo, and the approaching world war in Europe was looming more portentous every day. When it came, John Quick was ready, sailing for France as sergeant major of a battalion of the 6th Regt., U.S. Marines. Belleau Wood was only the opening battle of WWI for Quick; he participated in every battle that was fought by the Marines in France until Oct. 16, 1918: the Toulon sector at Verdun; the battle of Belleau Wood; the Aisne-Marne offensive (popularly known as the Battle of Soissons); the Marbache sector near Pont-a-Mousson; the St.-Mihiel offensive; the Battle of Mont Blanc Ridge; and the Meuse-Argonne sector. His gallantry at Belleau Wood won for him the Distinguished Service Cross and the Navy Cross. He won these decorations on June 6, 1918, when "he volunteered and assisted in taking a truckload of ammunition and materiel into Bouresches, France, over a road swept by artillery and machine gun fire, thereby relieving a critical situation." He was further awarded the 2nd Div. Citation and the French fourragère. Sgt. Maj. Quick participated in all the campaigns in which the Marine Corps took part during his service. They were the West Indian Campaign, Spanish Campaign, Philippine Campaign, Cuban Campaign, Mexican Campaign and WWI. Sgt. Maj. John H. Quick died in St. Louis, Mo., on Sept. 10, 1922.

R

RAMER, George Henry. Second Lieutenant. Medal of Honor: b. Myersdale, Pa., Mar. 27, 1927; d. KIA, Korea, Sept. 12, 1951. Lt. Ramer's citation reads, in part: ". . . as leader of the 3rd Platoon in Co. I, 3rd Bn., 7th Marines, 1st Mar. Div. (Reinf.), in action against enemy aggressor forces in Korea on Sept. 12, 1951. Ordered to attack and seize hostile positions atop a hill vigorously defended by well-entrenched enemy forces . . . 2nd Lt. Ramer fearlessly led his men up the steep slopes and, although he and the majority of his unit were wounded during the ascent, bolding continued to spearhead the assault. With the terrain becoming more precipitous near the summit and the climb more perilous as the hostile forces added grenades to the devastating hail of fire, he staunchly carried the attack to the top, personally annihilated one enemy bunker with grenade and carbine fire and captured the objective with his remaining eight men. Unable to hold the position against an immediate, overwhelming hostile counterattack, Ramer ordered his group to withdraw and singlehandedly fought the enemy to furnish cover for his men and for the evacuation of three fatally wounded Marines. Severely wounded a second time, Lt. Ramer refused aid when his men returned to help him and, after ordering them to seek shelter, courageously manned his post until the hostile troops overran his position and he fell mortally wounded. . . ."

RANNAHAN, John. Corporal. Medal of Honor: b. County of Monahan, Ireland, 1836. John Rannahan enlisted in the Marine Corps at Philadelphia, Pa. on June 21, 1861. His citation reads, in part: ". . . while serving on board the USS *Minnesota*; especially commended for bravery in the assault on Fort Fisher, Jan. 15, 1865, remaining at the front near the fort when the panic carried the mass away. . . ." Rannahan was discharged from the Corps at Boston, Mass. on Jan. 24, 1865.

REEM, Robert Dale. Second Lieutenant. Medal of Honor: b. Lancaster, Pa., Oct. 20, 1925; d. Chinhungni, Korea, Nov. 6, 1950. 2nd Lt. Reem's citation reads, in part: ". . . as a Platoon Commander in Co. H, 3rd Bn., 7th Marines, 1st Mar. Div. (Reinf.), in action against enemy aggressor forces. . . . Grimly determined to dislodge a group of heavy enemy infantry units occupying well-concealed and strongly fortified positions on commanding ground overlooking unprotected terrain, 2nd Lt. Reem moved slowly forward up the side of the ridge with his platoon in the face of a veritable hail of shattering hostile machine gun, grenade, and rifle fire. Three times repulsed by a resolute enemy force in achieving his objective, and pinned down by the continuing fury of hostile fire, he rallied and regrouped the heroic men in his depleted and disorganized platoon in preparation for a fourth attack. Issuing last-minute orders to his noncommissioned officers when an enemy grenade landed in a depression of the rocky ground in which the group was standing, 2nd Lt. Reem unhesitatingly chose to sacrifice himself and, springing upon the deadly missile, absorbed the full impact of the explosion in his own body, thus protecting others from serious injury and possible death. . . ."

REID, George Croghan. Brigadier General. Medal of Honor: b. Lorain, Ohio, Dec. 9, 1876; d. U.S. Air Force Hospital, Harlingen Air Force Base, Texas, Feb. 19, 1961. George Reid was appointed a second lieutenant in the Marine Corps during the War with Spain, May 20, 1898. He served on the Asiatic Station from May 1899 to May 1902. This duty included service with the China Relief Expedition during the Boxer Rebellion from June 1900 to Oct. 1900. Returning from the Orient, he was stationed at various posts in the States for the next few years, this service being interrupted by expeditionary duty on the Isthmus of Panama during the early part of 1904. In 1906 he returned to the Philippine Is., remaining there until Sept. 1908. He was on duty at posts in the States until 1912 when he again went on expeditionary duty, this time to Nicaragua with the forces dispatched there to protect American interests, during the insurrectionary troubles in that country. During this service he took part in the assault and capture of Coyotepe and Barranca on Nov. 19, 1912, for which he received a letter of commendation for gallantry and conspicuous service in action. In Jan. 1914, he went to sea as Division Marine Officer of the Atlantic Fleet, remaining on this duty until May 1916. While serving in this capacity he landed with the Marines of the Fleet in Vera Cruz, Mex., April 21, 1914, and took part in the engagements incident to the occupation of that city. For distinguished conduct in the face of the enemy he was awarded the Medal of Honor.

REYNAUD, Joseph Sinclair. Brigadier General. CG, Marine Corps Supply Activity, Philadelphia, Pa.: b. New Orleans, La., Apr. 9, 1915. Joseph Reynaud graduated from Jesuit High School in Phila-

delphia in 1932. He entered Tulane University and upon graduation, received an engineering degree in June 1936. While in college, he enlisted in the MCR, July 5, 1935, and the following summer entered the Platoon Leaders' Class at Quantico, Va. Upon completing the course, he was commissioned a Marine Reserve second lieutenant, Sept. 19, 1936, with rank from July 1, 1936. He was assigned to extended active duty in Aug. 1940 and has served continuously since that time. He was integrated in the regular Marine Corps following WWII. In Nov. 1940, he completed the Reserve Officers' Course at MCS, Quantico, then served variously as a staff instructor, supply officer, and company commander. While at Quantico, he was promoted to first lieutenant in Feb. 1941, and to captain in Feb. 1942. Ordered overseas in Jan. 1943, he was promoted to major that Mar., and subsequently joined the 18th Marines, 2nd Mar. Div., in New Zealand. From there he participated in combat on Tarawa in the Gilbert Is., and on Saipan and Tinian in the Marianas. For heroic action in the assault on Saipan, he was awarded the Bronze Star Medal with Combat "V." Following the Marianas campaign, he was assigned as Executive Officer of the 2nd Engineer Bn. in Aug. 1944, and that same month was promoted to lieutenant colonel. Reynaud became commander of the 2nd Engineer Bn. in Nov. 1944, and in this capacity participated in the Okinawa campaign in Apr. 1945. He returned to the States in June 1945, and following a brief assignment at Camp Lejeune, N.C., was ordered to HQMC, Washington, D.C., in Oct. 1945. He served there for almost four years as Executive Officer and, later, Head, Engineer Supply Division, Supply Department. In July 1949, he was assigned to the Marine Corps Supply Depot, Barstow, Calif., as Supply Officer, and a year later was named CO of the Fifth Base Depot, Barstow. In Dec. 1951, he was transferred to the Marine Corps Supply Depot, Philadelphia, Pa., where he served as Chief of the Industrial Branch (Clothing and Equipment Factory) for almost three years. During this assignment he was promoted to colonel in June 1952. In Sept. 1954, Col. Reynaud joined the FMF, Atlantic, at Norfolk, Va., as Force Supply Officer. He remained there until Mar. 1956, when he was ordered to the Far East. He served as Wing Supply Officer of the 1st MAW in Japan until Apr. 1957. The following month he returned to HQMC where he served consecutively as Director of the Services Division, Supply Department through Mar. 1959, and Plans and Programs Officer, Supply Department until Aug. 1959. He then entered the Industrial College of the Armed Forces, Washington, D.C., and on completion of the course in June 1960, was assigned to the Marine Corps Supply Activity, Philadelphia, as Chief of Staff. In Jan. 1962, he was assigned to a general officer's billet as CO of the Supply Activity. While serving in this capacity, he was promoted to brigadier general in Aug. 1962.

RILEY, Thomas Felton. Brigadier General. Inspector General of the Marine Corps at HQMC, Washington, D.C.: b. Harrisonburg, Va., July 6, 1912. After graduation from high school in 1931, Thomas Riley attended Virginia Military Institute. Here he obtained his Bachelor of Science degree in 1935. A member of the National Guard and the ROTC while in college, he resigned an Army Reserve commission to accept appointment as a Marine second lieutenant on July 10, 1935. On completing Basic School at the Philadelphia Navy Yard in Mar. 1936,

he was ordered to the Norfolk, Va. Navy Yard where he remained until Jan. 1937. He then joined the Marine Detachment aboard the USS *Vincennes*. Returning from sea duty in June 1938, he was assigned to the 29th U.S. Army Engineers at Portland, Ore. for instruction in aerial photo mapping. He was promoted to first lieutenant the following month. Lt. Riley joined the 1st Mar. Brig. at Quantico, in Dec. 1938, serving with and later commanding the 1st Engineer Co. until Sept. 1939, when the unit was expanded into the 1st Engineer Bn. Embarking for Guantanamo Bay, Cuba, in Sept. 1940, he continued as a company commander with the battalion until the following spring. In May 1941, he was promoted to captain and assigned command of the Marine Detachment aboard the USS *New York*. He was serving in this capacity when the United States entered WWII. In May 1942, he was promoted to major, and the same month reported to Camp Lejeune, N.C., as commander of the 1st Aviation Engineer Bn., FMF. Maj. Riley sailed with the battalion for the Pacific area in Aug. 1942. That Nov., after taking part in the construction of a landing field on New Caledonia, he arrived with his unit on Guadalcanal. There he subsequently earned the Bronze Star Medal with Combat "V" for his service from Nov. 1942 through Feb. 1943 in the rehabilitation of Henderson Field and the construction of Sailor Field. He was promoted to lieutenant colonel in Aug. 1943. In Oct. 1943, he joined the staff of the 3rd Amphibious Corps, serving as Assistant Engineer and Executive Officer of the Engineering Section at Bougainville, Emirau, Saipan, and Guam. After organizing and training the 3rd Amphibious Corps' Service Shore Party, he commanded it under fire during the Guam operation. For outstanding service in this campaign, from July 21 to Aug. 10, 1944, he was awarded the Legion of Merit with Combat "V." He returned to the States in Sept. 1944. Shortly after his return, he was named Officer in Charge of the Engineer Supply Division, Quartermaster General's Department, HQMC. He left Washington in Oct. 1946 to become Inspector-Instructor of the 11th Engineer Bn., MCR, in Baltimore, Md. In July 1948, Lt. Col. Riley embarked for Guam to become Executive Officer of the 5th Service Depot. He served in this capacity until July 1949 when he assumed command of the Depot. He returned to the States in Feb. 1950, following the Depot's transfer to the Marine Corps Supply Annex at Barstow, Calif. That Aug. he entered the Armed Forces Staff College at Norfolk. He completed the course in Jan. 1951, and that same month was promoted to colonel. He remained in Norfolk until May 1952, serving consecutively as Assistant Engineer Officer, and Engineer Officer, FMF, Atlantic. He was next assigned to HQMC in June 1952, and served for two years as Head, Planning Branch, G-4 Division. In June 1954, he became a member of the Advanced Research Group at Quantico. Following this assignment, Col. Riley was ordered to MCB, Camp Lejeune, in July 1955 for a two-year tour of duty as Chief of Staff, 2nd Mar. Div. In June 1957, he reported at Camp Pendleton as Chief of Staff of the MCB. Upon his detachment from this post in Jan. 1959, he reported to the CG, 1st Mar. Div. for duty as Assistant Division Commander. While serving in this capacity, he was promoted to his present rank of brigadier general in July 1959. Gen. Riley departed Camp Pendleton in July 1960, and the following month became Assistant Division Commander, 3rd Mar. Div., on Okinawa. He departed

Okinawa late in May 1961, and in July assumed his current post as Inspector General of the Marine Corps.

ROAN, Charles Howard. Private First Class. Medal of Honor: b. Claude, Tex., Aug. 16, 1923; d. KIA, Peleliu, Sept. 18, 1944. P.F.C. Roan's citation reads, in part: ". . . while serving with the 2nd Bn., 7th Marines, 1st Mar. Div., in action against enemy Japanese forces on Peleliu, Palau Islands, Sept. 18, 1944. . . . P.F.C. Roan and his companions were suddenly engaged in a furious exchange of hand grenades with Japanese forces emplaced in a cave on higher ground and to the rear of the squad. Seeking protection with four other Marines in a depression in the rocky, broken terrain, P.F.C. Roan was wounded by an enemy grenade which fell close to their position and, immediately realizing the imminent peril to his comrades when another grenade landed in the midst of the group, unhesitatingly flung himself upon it, covering it with his body and absorbing the full impact of the explosion. . . ."

ROANTREE, James S. Sergeant. Medal of Honor: b. Dublin, Ireland, 1835. James Roantree enlisted in the Marine Corps at Brooklyn, N.Y. on Jan. 15, 1858. His citation reads, in part: ". . . while serving on board the USS *Oneida* in the engagement in Mobile Bay, Aug. 5, 1864 . . . conducted himself with distinguished gallantry and is mentioned as particularly deserving of notice. . . ." Roantree was discharged from the Corps at Brooklyn, N.Y. on Dec. 17, 1870.

ROBERTS, Carson Abel. Lieutenant General. CG, Fleet Marine Force, Pacific, Oahu, Hawaii: b. Lancaster, Wis., Sept. 4, 1905. Carson Roberts graduated from University High School, Madison, Wis.,

Roberts

in 1925, and from the University of Wisconsin in 1929 with a Bachelor of Philosophy degree. He was appointed a Marine second lieutenant July 30, 1929. The following July he completed the Basic School for Marine Corps officers at the Philadelphia Navy Yard. In Mar. 1932, after service at the MB, Pensacola, Fla., Lt. Roberts sailed for Haiti where he served with the 1st Mar. Brig. He returned to this country in Jan. 1934 to enter flight training at Pensacola and was designated an aviator on Nov. 12 of that year. He was promoted to first lieutenant in Nov. 1934. In Jan. 1935, he was ordered to Quantico, where he saw service with Observation and Fighter Squadrons 7 and 9-M and Aircraft 1, FMF. He was promoted to captain in July 1937. Leaving

Quantico in May 1938, he completed a course at the Army Chemical Warfare School, Edgewood Arsenal, Md. the following month. He then served with Scouting Squadron 2 and MAG 2 at San Diego, Calif., from July 1938 until June 1940, when he returned to Quantico. There he served successively with Base Air Detachment 1, Bombing Squadron 1, and MAG 11. In addition, he was stationed with Bombing Squadron 1 at Guantanamo Bay, Cuba, from Nov. 1940 to Apr. 1941. Capt. Roberts was serving as Adjutant of MAG 11 when the United States entered WWII, and with that unit was ordered from Quantico to San Diego a few days after the attack on Pearl Harbor. He was promoted to major in Jan. 1942. That May, Maj. Roberts was named Group Operations Officer. He was promoted to lieutenant colonel in Aug. 1942, and the following month was detached from the group. After instruction at the Army Air Force School of Fighter Command in Orlando, Fla., Lt. Col. Roberts left for the Pacific area. As Operations Officer, 4th MAW, he saw duty in Hawaii, Samoa, and the Ellice and Gilbert Is. He was promoted to colonel in Jan. 1944. Col. Roberts became Assistant Operations Officer on the Staff of the Commander, Shore Based Aircraft, Forward Area, Central Pacific, in Apr. 1944. For meritorious service in this capacity during operations against the Japanese in the Marshall, Caroline, and Mariana Is., he was awarded his first Bronze Star Medal with Combat "V." He returned to the States in Nov. 1944 to serve as Assistant Chief of Staff, Marine Fleet Air, West Coast, San Diego. In Mar. 1945, he was assigned to Hawaii, heading the Future Plans Section, Aircraft, FMF, Pacific, until the end of the war. While serving in this capacity, he was awarded a second Bronze Star Medal for meritorious achievement in planning the employment of Marine air units in the Okinawa campaign and the occupation of Japan. He was named Assistant Chief of Staff, G-3 (Operations and Training), 1st MAW, in Sept. 1945, and in that assignment his duties took him to the Philippines, Okinawa, and China. Returning to the States in Nov. 1945, Col. Roberts commanded the MCAS at Eagle Mountain Lake, Texas, until Apr. 1946. He then served briefly with the 2nd MAW at Cherry Point, N.C., and entered the Army Command and General Staff College, Fort Leavenworth, Kans., that Aug. He completed the course in July 1947 and for the next two years was Chief of the Aviation Section, MCS, Quantico. From July 1949 to Apr. 1951, he was Assistant Chief of Staff, G-3, MARTC, Glenview, Ill. Ordered to Korea in May 1951, he saw action there until Mar. 1952, serving successively as Deputy Chief of Staff, 1st MAW; Commander, MAG 33; and Chief of Staff, 1st Wing. He was awarded the Legion of Merit with Combat "V" for outstanding service as group commander, and the Distinguished Flying Cross for heroism in that capacity on Nov. 10, 1951 while leading a close air support strike near Sohui-ri. In May 1952, he became Chief of Staff, Aircraft, FMF, Atlantic, at Norfolk, Va. He was ordered to Quantico in July 1953, serving there consecutively as a member of the Advanced Research Group, MCS, and as Assistant Commander, MCAS. In Aug. 1954, he became Director of the Marine Corps Development Center. He was promoted to brigadier general in July 1955. Gen. Roberts was transferred from Quantico in Jan. 1956. Assigned to Washington, D.C., he served as Inspector General of the Marine Corps until Oct. 1956, at which time he joined the staff of the Secretary of

Defense as Director of Armed Forces Information and Education. He resumed temporarily his former duties as Inspector General of the Marine Corps in Oct. 1957. He was promoted to major general in Nov. 1957. In Dec. 1957, Gen. Roberts became Deputy Chief of Staff (Plans) at HQMC. He served in this capacity until Mar. 1959, and the following month assumed duties in Japan as CG, 1st MAW. On his return to the States in Dec. 1959, he served for more than a year and a half as CG, 3rd MAW, El Toro. Following this assignment, he remained at El Toro where he subsequently assumed duties as CG, Aircraft, FMF, Pacific, in June 1961. In June 1962, he was promoted to lieutenant general and moved to CG, FMF Pac, Oahu, Hawaii.

ROBERTSHAW, Louis Bentham. Brigadier General. Commander, Marine Air Reserve Training, Glenview, Ill.: b. Philadelphia, Pa., Aug. 1, 1912. Louis Robertshaw graduated from Haverford Township High School, Havertown, Pa., in 1930, and attended Friends Central School, and Swavely School in Manassas, Va. He entered the U.S. Naval Academy in 1932. While there, he captained the 1935 football team, and received the Naval Academy Sword for personal excellence in athletics. He was commissioned a Marine second lieutenant upon graduation, June 4, 1936. He then served at the Philadelphia Navy Yard, the San Diego MCB, and the MB, Washington, D.C., prior to completing the Basic School for Marine Corps Officers at the Philadelphia Navy Yard in June 1937. That month he embarked for duty in China with the 6th Marines, 2nd Mar. Brig., and participated in the defense of the International Settlement in Shanghai from Oct. 1937 to Feb. 1938. In May 1938, he returned with the brigade to

San Diego, and remained until Feb. 1939 when he again sailed for China. While serving with the 2nd Bn., 4th Marines, in Shanghai, he was promoted to first lieutenant in July 1939. Following his return to the States in Aug. 1940, Robertshaw was assigned to the Naval Academy as Executive Officer of the Marine Detachment, and as a coach in football and basketball. In Apr. 1941, he was assigned to the Philadelphia Navy Yard as an instructor. He was promoted to captain in Oct. 1941. He entered flight school at the NAS, Pensacola, Fla. in Feb. 1942. Upon graduation in Aug. 1942, he was designated a naval aviator and promoted to major. He embarked from San Diego for Noumea, New Caledonia, in Oct. 1942. After serving as Executive Officer, Marine Scout Bombing Squadron 132, MAG 11, he assumed command of the squadron in Dec. 1942 when the CO became a casualty. Maj. Robertshaw was awarded the Distinguished Flying Cross for his air attack on a group of Japanese transports in which he scored a direct hit on one transport and severely damaged land installations in the Solomons' area in Nov. and Dec. 1942. A second Distinguished Flying Cross and six Air Medals were also awarded him for bombing operations in the Solomons. In Apr. 1943, he became Group Operations Officer. He was promoted to lieutenant colonel in Dec. 1943. On his arrival in the States in January 1944, he was named Executive Officer and, later, CO of Marine Base Defense Aircraft Group 41, MCAS, El Toro, Calif. He was again ordered overseas in June 1945, serving as Assistant G-3, Aircraft, FMF, Pacific, Ewa, Hawaii, and, later, as Marine Aviation Officer on the Staff of Commander, Naval Activities, Japan. He returned to the States in July 1946, and was assigned to Marine Air West

Coast, Miramar, San Diego. Shortly after, Lt. Col. Robertshaw was transferred to MCAS, El Toro, where he served as Executive Officer and CO, respectively, of Marine Transport Squadron 152. In July 1948, he began a two-year tour of duty as CO, Marine Air Detachment, Marine Air Reserve Training Command, NAS, Willow Grove, Pa. After leaving Willow Grove, he saw two years' duty in the Division of Aviation, HQMC. While there, he was promoted to colonel in Feb. 1951. Ordered to Korea in Aug. 1952, Col. Robertshaw served briefly as Assistant Chief of Staff, 1st MAW, prior to becoming CO of MAG 33. For outstanding service in Korea from Sept. 1952 to May 1953, during which time he flew 77 missions, he was awarded the Legion of Merit with Combat "V," a third Distinguished Flying Cross, and his seventh through eleventh Air Medals. In June 1953, following his return to the States, he was stationed at Quantico, where he later entered and completed the Senior Course, MCS. He went overseas again in July 1954 for two years' duty on the Staff of the Commander in Chief, Pacific, at Pearl Harbor. In Aug. 1956, he returned to Quantico as a member of the Advanced Research Group, Marine Corps Educational Center. After a year at Quantico, Col. Robertshaw was transferred to Cherry Point, N.C., serving as Assistant Chief of Staff, G-3 and later, Chief of Staff, 2nd MAW, Aircraft, FMF, Atlantic. He also served on temporary duty in 1957 as Marine Corps Liaison Officer during Operation Deep-Water in Turkey. On his detachment from Cherry Point, he departed for the Far East in Oct. 1959 and, the following month, assumed duties as Assistant Wing Commander, 1st MAW, in Iwakuni, Japan.

ROBINSON, Robert Guy. Gunnery Sergeant. Medal of Honor: b. New York, N.Y., Apr. 30, 1896. Gy. Sgt. Robinson's citation reads in part: ". . . as observer in the 1st Marine Aviation Force at the front in France. He not only participated successfully in numerous raids into the enemy territory, but on Oct. 8, 1918, while conducting an air raid in company with planes from Squadron 218, R.A.F., he was attacked by nine enemy scouts and in the fight which followed he shot down one of the enemy planes. Also, on Oct. 14, 1918, while on an air raid over Pittham, Belgium, his plane and one other became separated from their formation on account of motor trouble and were attacked by 12 enemy scouts. In the fight which ensued, he behaved with conspicuous gallantry and intrepidity. After shooting down one of the enemy planes he was struck by a bullet which carried away most of his elbow, and his gun jammed at the same time. He cleared the jam with one hand while his pilot maneuvered for position. With the gun cleared, he returned to the fight though his left arm was useless, and fought off the enemy scouts until he collapsed after receiving two more bullet wounds, one in the stomach and one in the thigh."

ROCKEY, Keller E. Lieutenant General (Retired). CG of the 5th Mar. Div. in the battle for Iwo Jima: b. Columbia City, Ind., Sept. 22, 1888. Keller Rockey was commissioned as a second lieutenant in the Marine Corps on Nov. 18, 1913. Upon reporting for duty he was assigned as a student to the Marine Officers' School, MB, Norfolk, Va. where, upon graduation in May 1915, he went to sea. First, he was a member of the Marine Detachment aboard the USS *Nebraska*, then a member of the Marine Detachment aboard the USS *Nevada*. Following

Rockey

sea duty he sailed for France in June 1917, and one year later, as a member of the 5th Mar. Regt., participated in the Aisne-Marne defensive (Chateau-Thierry). He was awarded a Navy Cross for his actions at Chateau-Thierry where, on July 6, 1918, "he performed distinguished service by bringing up supports and placing them in the front lines at great personal exposure, showing exceptional ability and extraordinary heroism." Shortly after returning to the States in 1919, Rockey went to foreign shore duty in Haiti as a member of the Haitian Constabulary. He remained there until 1921, then returned to the States and joined the MB, Washington, D.C. Following duty at HQMC, Washington, D.C., he became a student at the Field Officers'

Course, MCS, Quantico. After graduation in July, 1925, he was again assigned to school, this time as a student at the Command and General Staff School, Fort Leavenworth, Kans. Upon graduation in June 1926, he became an instructor in the Department of Tactics, MCS. From Jan. 1928 to Nov. 1928, he was CO of the 1st Bn., 11th Regt., 2nd Mar. Brig., stationed in Nicaragua. He then became Base Intelligence, Operations, and Training Officer of the MCB, San Diego, Calif., and later Chief of Staff of the Base. In June 1934, he was assigned to duty in the Major General Commandant's Department, HQMC, following which he became Force Marine Officer, Battle Force aboard the USS *California*. He returned to Washington in July 1939 to assume duties with Operations, Navy Department (War Plans) and in Aug. 1941 became Chief of Staff of the 2nd Mar. Div., the position he held when the United States entered WWII. He was assigned duties as Director, Division of Plans and Policies at HQMC in Aug. 1942 and, one year later, assumed duties as Assistant to the Commandant. In Feb. 1944, he went to the Pacific where he was successively CG of the 5th Mar. Div. and the 3rd Amphibious Corps. Following the deactivation of the 3rd Corps, he assumed command of the 1st Mar. Div. (Reinf.), with headquarters at Tientsin, China. He returned to the States and became CG of the Department of the Pacific in Sept. 1946, which position he held until ordered to duty on Jan. 2, 1947 as CG of the newly activated FMF, Atlantic. Gen. Rockey was retired from the Corps on Sept. 1, 1950.

ROTTET, Ralph Kaspar. Major General. Director of the Marine Corps Educational Center, Quantico, Va.: b. Jasper, Ind., Feb. 25, 1911. Ralph Rottet graduated from high school in Shelbyville, Ind., where he was a member of the Indiana National Guard. A year later he was appointed to the U.S. Naval Academy. Upon graduation from the Academy, he was awarded a Bachelor of Science degree and commissioned a Marine second lieutenant, May 31, 1934. He then completed Basic School at the Philadelphia Navy Yard in Apr. 1935, and that June joined the Marine Detachment aboard the USS *Salt Lake City*. In June 1936, he entered flight training at the NAS, Pensacola, Fla. In July 1937, he was promoted to first lieutenant and designated a naval aviator. During the next three years, Rottet served at NAS, San Diego, Calif. He was promoted to captain in July 1940. He returned to Pensacola as an instructor in Nov. 1940. Upon being transferred to Washington, D.C. in Oct. 1941, he saw a year's duty at the Bureau of Aeronautics, Navy Department. He was promoted to major in May 1942. In Nov. 1942, he joined the 3rd MAW, MCAS, Cherry Point, N.C. There he served as CO, Marine Fighting Squadron 311, and later as CO of MAG 31. He was promoted to lieutenant colonel in June 1943. Deployed with the group to the Marshall Is. area in Sept. 1943, Lt. Col. Rottet served as Executive Officer, Operations Officer, and finally CO of MAG 31, then a part of the 4th MAW in the Pacific. Flying F4U Corsairs with his group, he operated from Wallis Is., American Samoa, Funafuti in the Ellice Islands, Makin in the Gilbert Islands, and Roi-Namur in the Marshalls. Twenty-one combat missions in this area earned him the Distinguished Flying Cross and the Air Medal with two Gold Stars. Under his command, MAG 31 developed an effective napalm bombing method, and conducted the first napalm bombing strikes, inflicting extensive damage on the enemy. For meritorious service in this capacity, he was awarded the Bronze Star Medal with Combat "V." He returned to the States in Dec. 1944. From Jan. to June 1945, Lt. Col. Rottet attended the Army-Navy Staff College, Washington, D.C. Upon completing the course, he was transferred to MCAS, Cherry Point, where he commanded Aircraft Engineering Squadron 46, then served as Assistant Chief of Staff (G-3), Operations and Training. Following his detachment from Cherry Point in Aug. 1946, he served on the faculty of the Armed Forces Staff College, Norfolk, Va. until July 1948. That Sept. he reported to NAS, San Diego, as Marine Aviation Planning Officer, on the Staff of Commander, Air Force, Pacific Fleet. While there, he was promoted to colonel in July 1949. Col. Rottet joined NAS, Minneapolis, Minn., in June 1950, as CO, Marine Air Detachment, Marine Air Reserve Training Command. In July 1951, he was assigned to HQMC, Washington, D.C., where he served briefly as Executive Officer, Operations and Training Branch, Division of Aviation, prior to becoming Head of the branch. He was transferred to MCAS, El Toro, Calif., in July 1953, completing the Jet Indoctrination Course that Aug. before leaving for Korea. In Korea, he saw duty from Aug. 1953 to July 1954, earning the Legion of Merit for outstanding service as Commander of MAG 12, and later MAG 11, 1st MAW. On his return to the States, he was stationed at MCS, Quantico, serving as Member of the Advanced Research Group, Marine Corps Educational Center, from Aug. 1954 to June 1955. The following month, he reported to HQ, Aircraft, FMF, Atlantic, in Norfolk as Assistant Chief of Staff, G-3. In July 1956, he became Chief of Staff, FMF, Atlantic, the first aviator appointed to

that position. In July 1957, he was promoted to brigadier general. That same month, Gen. Rottet was named CG, 4th Prov. Marine Air-Ground Task Force. Six months later he was ordered to the Far East, arriving in Japan in Dec. 1957 to assume duty as Assistant Commander, 1st MAW, Aircraft, FMF, Pacific. He returned to the States in Mar. 1959 as Commander, Marine Corps Air Bases, Eastern Area, and CG, MCAS, Cherry Point, N.C. While serving in this capacity, he was promoted to his present rank of major general in July 1960. In Sept. 1960, Gen. Rottet began a year's assignment as CG, 2nd MAW. He remained at Cherry Point until Oct. 1961, when he assumed his current duties as Director of the Marine Corps Educational Center at Quantico.

ROUH, Carlton Robert. Captain. Medal of Honor: b. Lindenwold, N.J., May 11, 1919. Capt. Rouh's citation reads, in part: ". . . while attached to the 1st Bn., 5th Marines, 1st Mar. Div., during action against enemy Japanese forces on Peleliu Is., Sept. 15, 1944. Before permitting his men to use an enemy dugout as a position for an 81-mm. mortar observation post, (then) 1st Lt. Rouh made a personal reconnaissance of the pillbox and, upon entering, was severely wounded by Japanese rifle fire from within. Emerging from the dugout, he was immediately assisted by two Marines to a less exposed area but, while receiving first aid, was further endangered by an enemy grenade which was thrown into their midst. Quick to act in spite of his weakened condition, he lurched to a crouching position and thrust both men aside, placing his own body between them and the grenade and taking the full blast of the explosion himself. . . ."

RUHL, Donald Jack. Private First Class. Medal of Honor: b. Columbus, Mont., July 2, 1923; d. KIA, Iwo Jima, Feb. 21, 1945. On Feb. 19, 1945 — D-Day at Iwo Jima — Pvt. Ruhl singlehandedly attacked a group of eight Japanese who had been driven from a blockhouse. Killing one with his bayonet, he killed another with rifle fire before the rest fled. Early the next morning he left the safety of his tank trap and moved out under a tremendous volume of mortar and machine gun fire to rescue a wounded Marine lying in an exposed position about 40 yards forward of the front lines. Half carrying and half pulling the wounded man, Ruhl removed him to a position out of reach of enemy rifles. Calling for an assistant and a stretcher, the young man again braved the heavy fire to carry the casualty 300 yards back to an aid station on the beach. Returning to his outfit, he volunteered to investigate an apparently abandoned Japanese gun emplacement 75 yards forward of the right flank. Subsequently he occupied the position through the night, thus preventing the enemy from again taking possession of the valuable weapon. The next morning, D plus two, E Co. of the 28th Marines pushed forward in the assault against the vast network of fortifications surrounding the base of Mt. Suribachi. During the advance, P.F.C. Ruhl, with his platoon guide, crawled to the top of a Japanese bunker to bring fire to bear on enemy troops located on the far side of the bunker. Suddenly a hostile grenade landed between the two Marines. Calling a warning to his senior NCO, he instantly dove upon the deadly missile and absorbed the full charge of the exploding grenade into his own body.

RUSSELL, John Henry, Jr. Major General. 16th Commandant of the Marine Corps: b. Mare Is., Calif., Nov. 14, 1872; d. Coronado, Calif., Mar. 6, 1947. John Russell entered the Naval Academy at Annapolis in May 1888. He graduated with the class of 1892 and, after two years as a naval cadet, he was commissioned a second lieutenant in the Marine Corps on July 1, 1894. He served at shore stations until June 1, 1896, then went aboard the USS *Massachusetts*. During the Spanish-American War he served on that ship in the blockading operations around the West Indies and in the bombardment of the forts of Santiago, Cuba. In Nov. 1898, he was promoted to first lieutenant and was assigned, in turn, to Philadelphia, Norfolk and Washington, D.C. He was promoted to captain on Mar. 28, 1899 while serving aboard the USS *Yosemite*. Duty followed on Guam, in the States at east coast stations and at Mare Is., Calif., and aboard the USS *Oregon*. He was promoted to major in July 1906, and transferred to the command of the Marine Barracks, Honolulu, Hawaii. From Hawaii his duty assignments took him to the Canal Zone, back to the States on the staff of the Navy War College, to the legation guard at Peking, China, then to Washington, D.C. and the Office of Naval Intelligence. Early in 1914, he was given command of the 2nd Bn. 3rd Marines and landed with that unit at Vera Cruz, Mex. on Apr. 30, 1914. The battalion remained in Mexico until Dec. when it was withdrawn, and Maj. Russell returned to his regular assignment with the Navy Department. He was promoted to lieutenant colonel and took command of the 3rd Mar. Regt. in Santo Domingo, then was placed in command of the 1st Prov. Brig. of Marines occupying Haiti. During his tour of duty in Haiti he became thoroughly familiar with its political and economic difficulties and, on Feb. 11,

1922 after promotion to brigadier general, he was appointed as High Commissioner of Haiti with the rank of Ambassador Extraordinary. He remained in this important assignment for nearly nine years before being transferred to the MCB at San Diego where he took command in Nov. 1930. A year later he was assigned to Quantico, and from there he returned to HQMC as Assistant to the Commandant. He was promoted to major general and continued as Assistant to the CMC until he was appointed Commandant on Apr. 5, 1934. Gen. Russell's administration lasted only two years and eight months, but it brought significant changes and progress within the Corps. The old system of seniority promotions of officers was changed to that of advancement by selection. The 1st Mar. Brig. was withdrawn from Haiti, while the 4th Marines continued to occupy Shanghai, but carried out no military operations. Organization, education, and training of the Corps progressed rapidly. The FMF assumed a new importance. The Reserves were given more attention, including summer training camps for selected college students. And the number of ships carrying Marine Detachments continued to increase throughout the period. Gen. Russell reached the statutory age limit in Nov. 1936, and was retired from active duty on Dec. 1, 1936.

S

SANTELMANN, William Frederick. Lieutenant Colonel (Retired). Leader of the Marine Band — 1940 to 1955: b. Washington, D.C., 1902. After completion of his studies at the New England Conservatory of Music at Boston, William Santelmann enlisted in the Marine Corps on Sept. 5, 1923. Immediately upon enlistment he was assigned to the orchestral group which performed regularly at all White House affairs. During this time he served under the direction of his father who had already been leader of the band four years before William's birth. Although the son had begun conducting small groups soon after entering the band, it was not until 1935, with his appointment as Assistant Leader, that he had to devote full time to conducting. On Apr. 1, 1940, the Commandant of the Marine Corps appointed him the Leader and with that responsibility went the rank of captain. Promotion to major followed in 1947 and in 1951, Santelmann attained the highest rank ever held by a musician in the Marine Corps, lieutenant colonel. In his 32 years of service with the Marine Band, Santelmann made concert tours into every state in the country and into every large city from coast to coast. He appeared as Director on 12 of these tours and established a firm reputation as a conductor. Perhaps the most important duties assigned to Col. Santelmann were those connected with the White House, the Presidents, and their guests. Planning and providing the music for all official functions during the administrations of Presidents Coolidge, Hoover, Roosevelt, Truman, and the first term of President Eisenhower was a very exacting yet stimulating responsibility. In addition to his duties as Leader of the Marine Band, Col. Santelmann was also

Supervisor of all Marine Bands throughout the world, Music Director of the famous Gridiron Club of Washington, and
Music Director of the Military Order of
the Carabao.

SCANNELL, David John. Private. Medal of Honor: b. Boston, Mass., Mar. 30,
1875. David Scannell enlisted in the
Marine Corps at Boston, Mass. on Feb.
1, 1898. He was awarded the nation's
highest military honor ". . . for distinguished conduct in the presence of the
enemy at Peking, China, July 21 to Aug.
17, 1900. Scannell assisted in erecting
barricades under heavy fire. . . ." He was
discharged from the Corps on Mar. 6,
1903.

SCHILT, Christian Frank. General (Retired). Medal of Honor. Pioneer of Marine Corps aviation: b. Richland County,
Ill., Mar. 1, 1895. Christian Schilt enlisted
in the Marine Corps June 23, 1917. As an
enlisted man he served at Ponta Delgada
in the Azores with the 1st Mar. Aeronautical Co., a seaplane squadron assigned to antisubmarine patrol. This was
the first organized American air unit of
any service to go overseas during WWI.
Returning to the States as a corporal,
Schilt entered flight training at the Marine Flying Field, Miami, Fla. He was
designated an aviator June 5, 1919, and
commissioned a second lieutenant 5 days
later. That Oct. he began his first tour of
expeditionary duty as a member of
Squadron D, Marine Air Forces, 2nd
Prov. Brig. in Santo Domingo. He returned to the States in Feb. 1920 to enter
the Marine Officers' Training School,
Quantico, Va. Completing the course in
Aug. 1920, he went overseas again the
following month, joining Squadron E of
Marine Aviation Forces, 1st Prov. Brig.
at Port-au-Prince, Haiti. He was trans-

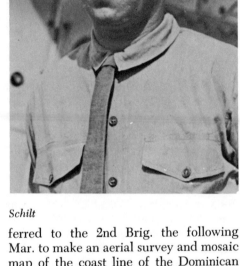

Schilt

ferred to the 2nd Brig. the following
Mar. to make an aerial survey and mosaic
map of the coast line of the Dominican
Republic. After completing this assignment he returned to Quantico in Oct.
1922. Except for service at NAS, Pensacola, Fla. from Jan. to July 1923, and
completing a three-month photographic
course at the Air Service Technical
School, Chanute Field, Ill. in 1925, he
remained at Quantico for the next five
years. While attached to that post he won
second place in the Schneider International Seaplane Race at Norfolk, Va. in
Nov. 1926, flying a special Curtiss racer
at a speed of 231.3 miles per hour over
seven laps of a triangular 50-kilometer
course. In Nov. 1927, Schilt was ordered
to Managua, Nicaragua where he joined
Observation Squadron 7-M. It was during

this tour of duty that he won the Medal of Honor. He was awarded the Medal for heroism from Jan. 6 to 8, 1928, at Quilali, Nicaragua, where two Marine patrols were ambushed and cut off by rebel bandits. Lt. Schilt voluntarily risked his life to make 10 flights into the besieged town, evacuating 18 casualties and carrying in a replacement commander and badly needed medical supplies. To make a landing strip on the village's rough, rolling main street, the Marines on the ground had to burn and level part of the town and, since the plane had no brakes, they had to stop it by dragging from its wings as soon as it touched down. Hostile fire on landings and take-offs, plus low-hanging clouds, mountains, and tricky air currents, added to the difficulty of the flights, which the citation describes as feats of "almost superhuman skill combined with personal courage of the highest order." Schilt returned to the States in Aug. 1929 and, after commanding Fighter Squadron 5-N at Quantico, was named Chief Test Pilot and Flight and Aerological Officer at the Naval Aircraft Factory, Philadelphia, Pa. He served in that capacity for two years before returning to Quantico in June 1932 to enter the Company Officers' Course at the MCS. He completed that course in July 1933, and a month later entered the Air Corps Tactical School at Montgomery, Ala. Graduating in June 1934, he began another four years at Quantico, where he was Air Officer on the Staff of the CG, FMF, and later a squadron commander with Aircraft 1, FMF. He then served from May 1938 to June 1940, as Executive Officer of MCAS at St. Thomas, Virgin Is. After that assignment he returned to Quantico to complete the Senior Course in the MCS and serve with Base Air Detachment 1, FMF. He left Quantico in May 1941, when he was as-

signed to the American Embassy in London, England, as an Assistant Naval Attaché for Air. In that capacity he traveled through England and Scotland and served as a naval observer in north Africa and the middle east. He returned to the States in Aug. 1941, and was assigned to Quantico as Engineer and Supply Officer of the 1st MAW. In Sept. 1942, he arrived on Guadalcanal as Assistant Chief of Staff, 1st MAW. After that he was commander of MAG 11, Chief of Staff of the 1st Wing and CO of the Strike and Search Patrol Commands, Solomon Is. He returned to the States in Sept. 1943 and took command of the MCAS at Cherry Point, N.C. until Mar. of the following year. From Apr. to June 1944, Schilt headed the 9th MAW during the organization of that unit. He then served for six months as Chief of Staff of the wing and for another month as its commander before returning to the Pacific theater in Feb. 1945. This time he was Island Commander at Peleliu from Mar. to Aug. 1945, and CG, Air Defense Command, 2nd MAW, on Okinawa until Oct. 1945, when he took command of the 2nd Wing. Returning from Okinawa in Mar. 1946, he reported to NAS, Glenview, Ill. the following month. There he headed the MARTC until July 1949, when he was ordered to Norfolk as Chief of Staff, FMF, Atlantic. He served in that capacity until he took command of the 1st MAW in Korea in July 1951. In Apr. 1952, he returned from Korea to serve in Hawaii as Deputy Commander, FMF, Pacific until Feb. 1953, when he became CG, Aircraft, FMF, Pacific, at MCAS, El Toro, Calif. He left El Toro in July 1955. Ordered to HQMC, he was promoted to lieutenant general Aug. 1, 1955 and, on that same date, assumed duties as Director of Aviation, Assistant Commandant of the Marine Corps for Air, and Assistant Chief of Naval Operations for Marine Aviation. He served in this capacity until his retirement from the Marine Corps on Apr. 1, 1957. He was promoted to his present rank by reason of having been specially commended for heroism in combat.

SCHWAB, Albert Ernest. Private First Class. Medal of Honor: b. Washington, D.C., July 17, 1920; d. KIA, Okinawa, May 7, 1945. P.F.C. Schwab's citation reads, in part: ". . . as a flame thrower operator serving with HQ Co., 1st Bn., 5th Marines, 1st Mar. Div., in action against enemy Japanese forces on Okinawa May 7, 1945. Quick to take action when his company was pinned down in a valley and suffering resultant heavy casualties under blanketing machine gun fire emanating from a high ridge to the front, P.F.C. Schwab, unable to flank the enemy emplacement because of steep cliffs on either side, advanced up the face of the ridge in bold defiance of the intense barrage and, skillfully directing the fire of his flame thrower, quickly demolished the hostile gun position, thereby enabling his company to occupy the ridge. Suddenly a second Japanese machine gun opened fire, killing or wounding several Marines with its initial bursts. Estimating with split-second decision the tactical difficulties confronting his comrades, P.F.C. Schwab elected to continue his one-man assault despite a diminished supply of fuel for his flame thrower. Cool and indomitable, he moved forward in the face of the direct concentration of hostile fire, relentlessly closed in on the enemy position and attacked. Although severely wounded by a final vicious blast from the enemy weapon, P.F.C. Schwab had succeeded in destroying two highly strategic Jap-

anese gun positions during a critical stage of the operation. . . ."

SCOTT, Joseph Francis. Corporal. Medal of Honor: b. Boston, Mass., June 4, 1864. Joseph Scott enlisted in the Marine Corps at Boston, Mass. on Aug. 11, 1888. His citation reads, in part: ". . . while serving on board the USS *Nashville,* for extraordinary bravery and coolness while cutting the cables leading from Cienfuegos, Cuba, May 11, 1898, under a heavy fire of the enemy. . . ." He was discharged from the Corps on May 7, 1901.

Shapley

SHAPLEY, Alan. Lieutenant General (Retired). Former CG, Fleet Marine Force, Pacific, in Honolulu, Hawaii: b. New York, N.Y., Feb. 9, 1903. Alan Shapley received his early schooling at Vallejo, Calif., and was graduated from the Peddie School at Hightstown, N.J. in

1922. He then entered the U.S. Naval Academy, graduating on June 2, 1927 as a Marine second lieutenant. After further training at the Academy, duty at Quantico, Va., and completion of the Marine officers' Basic School at the Philadelphia Navy Yard, he sailed for Hawaii in Jan. 1929 to begin almost three years of duty at the MB, Pearl Harbor. He returned to the States in Oct. 1931, and served in various capacities at San Diego, Calif., before taking command of the Marine Detachment aboard the USS *San Francisco* in Jan. 1934. He was promoted to first lieutenant that same month. Detached from the USS *San Francisco* in June 1936, he returned to Quantico where he served as Aide-de-Camp to the CG of the MB. He was promoted to captain in July 1936. In June 1937, Shapley entered the Junior Course of the MCS at Quantico. He completed the course in May 1938, and was ordered to San Francisco, Calif. as Aide-de-Camp to the CG, Department of the Pacific. After serving in that capacity until July 1939, he served as Operations, Training and Intelligence Officer of the Department of the Pacific until May 1940. A month later he departed for Hawaii, where he took command of the Marine Detachment on the USS *Arizona*. He was promoted to major in Aug. 1941. He was awarded the Silver Star Medal for heroism on Dec. 7, 1941, when the USS *Arizona* was sunk at Pearl Harbor. There, in the water after the ship had been bombed and set afire by the Japanese, he disregarded his own exhaustion and the enemy's bombing and strafing to rescue one of his men from drowning. Two days after the attack on Pearl Harbor, he sailed for San Diego to become personnel officer of the Amphibious Corps, Pacific Fleet. He was promoted to lieutenant colonel in Aug. 1942. Lt.

Col. Shapley assumed a similar post with the 1st Amphibious Corps in Oct. 1942, and that same month he sailed with the 1st Corps for the Pacific area. There he commanded the 2nd Raider Bn., 1st Mar. Raider Regt. from Mar. to Sept. 1943. Later, he led the crack 2nd Mar. Raider Regt. in the fighting at Bougainville, earning the Legion of Merit with Combat "V" for outstanding service at Bougainville in Nov. 1943. After the Bougainville campaign, Lt. Col. Shapley was given command of the 1st and 2nd Mar. Raider Regts., from which he organized the 4th Marines, which he commanded at Emirau, Guam, and Okinawa. In addition to the Navy Cross for heroism on Guam, he was also awarded a second Legion of Merit with Combat "V" for outstanding service at Okinawa from Apr. to June 1945. He was promoted to colonel in Nov. 1944. Following the Okinawa campaign, Col. Shapley returned to the States in July 1945 to become Assistant Inspector in the Inspection Division at HQMC, Washington, D.C. In Sept. he entered the National War College in Washington. After graduation in June 1947, he served for two years at Norfolk, Va., as Assistant Chief of Staff, G-3 (Operations and Training), of FMF, Atlantic. Subsequently, he was ordered to the Marine Corps Recruit Depot at San Diego in June 1949, and after serving as personnel officer, became that unit's chief of staff in Sept. 1949. In Jan. 1951, Col. Shapley was ordered again to Washington where he served on the International Planning Staff of the Standing Group, North Atlantic Treaty Organization, until June 1953. Ordered to Korea, he served as Chief of Staff, 1st Mar. Div., earning the Bronze Star Medal with Combat "V" for meritorious achievement during this period. For subsequent service as Senior Advisor to the Korean Marine Corps, he was awarded the Republic of Korea's Ulchi Medal with Silver Star. From Korea, Col. Shapley was ordered to Japan in May 1954. He served there as CO, and subsequently as CG, Troop Training Team, Amphibious Group, Western Pacific. He was promoted to brigadier general in July 1954. In July 1955, on his return to the States, Gen. Shapley became Assistant Commander of the 1st Mar. Div., Camp Pendleton, Calif. Following his detachment from the 1st Div. in May 1956, he commanded the Recruit Training Command at the Marine Corps Recruit Depot, San Diego, for a brief time prior to being ordered to the Far East. Upon his promotion to major general in Sept. 1956, he assumed duties on Okinawa as CG, 3rd Mar. Div., FMF. Gen. Shapley returned to the States in July 1957, reporting to HQMC, Washington, as Director of the MCR. After holding this post for over two years, he returned to the west coast in Nov. 1959, and served as CG, MCB, Camp Pendleton, until Mar. 1961. In Apr. 1961, upon assuming his assignment as CG, FMF, Pacific, he was promoted to his present rank of lieutenant general. He was placed on the retired list July 1, 1962.

SHAW, Samuel Robert. Brigadier General (Retired). Recalled to active duty, Sept. 30, 1962, as Director of Programs on the Staff of the Preparedness Sub-Committee, Senate Armed Services Committee, Washington, D.C.: b. Cleveland, Ohio, June 6, 1911. After graduating from high school at Dayton, Ohio, Samuel Shaw enlisted in the Marine Corps in Sept. 1928, and was appointed to the U.S. Naval Academy from the ranks in July 1930. Upon graduation he was commissioned a Marine second lieutenant May 31, 1934. After completing the Marine Officers' Basic School at the

Philadelphia Navy Yard and a year of sea duty with the Marine Detachment aboard the USS *Tuscaloosa*, he joined the 5th Marines at Quantico, Va. in June 1936. He was promoted to first lieutenant in July 1937. Shortly afterward, Shaw was temporarily detached from the regiment to complete the Army Ordnance Field Service School at Raritan Arsenal, Metuchen, N.J. He was also a member of the Marine Corps Rifle and Pistol Teams of 1937 and 1938, and commanded the Marine Detachment at the Rifle Range, Cape May, N.J., from Mar. to Aug. 1939. Upon his return from Cape May, he entered the Junior Course at the MCS, Quantico. He completed the course in June 1940, and later fired on the 1940 Rifle and Pistol Team. He was promoted to captain in July 1940. Shaw sailed in Oct. 1940 for Pearl Harbor. As a company commander at the MB, Pearl Harbor Navy Yard, he took part in the defense of Pearl Harbor when the Japanese struck on December 7, 1941. He was promoted to major in May 1942 and to lieutenant colonel in Apr. 1943. In July 1943, after his return to the States, Lt. Col. Shaw was appointed Assistant Chief of Staff, A-3 (Operations and Training), FMF, San Diego area. He served in that capacity until he entered the Army Command and General Staff School, Fort Leavenworth, Kans., and completed the course in Oct. 1944. Departing for the Pacific area the following month, he assumed command of the 6th Pioneer Bn., 6th Mar. Div. In this capacity, he saw action in the Okinawa campaign and earned the Legion of Merit with Combat "V." He held that command until Oct. 1945, when he landed with the battalion at Tsingtao, China. There, as Assistant Chief of Staff, G-4, 6th Mar. Div., he was awarded the Bronze Star Medal. He returned from China in Sept. 1946. From

Oct. 1946 to Jan. 1949, Lt. Col. Shaw was stationed at Quantico as a member of a special Marine Corps Board convened to conduct research and prepare material relative to postwar legislation concerning the role of the Marine Corps in national defense. Transferred to Washington, D.C., in Jan. 1949, he served as Research Officer in the Organizational Research and Policy Division, Office of the Assistant Chief of Naval Operations, until Nov. 1949; and, subsequently, as Shore Party Officer in the Engineer Section, Division of Plans and Policies, at HQMC; as a member of the Navy Department Management Survey Board; and as Chief of the Joint Action Panel in the Marine Corps' Division of Plans and Policies. He was promoted to colonel in Aug. 1949. He left Washington in Feb. 1952 to become Senior Marine Corps Representative on the Joint Amphibious Board at Little Creek, Va., where he remained until July 1953. He returned to Quantico that Aug. as a member of the Advanced Research Group, Marine Corps Educational Center. Ordered overseas in June 1954, Col. Shaw joined the 1st Mar. Div. in Korea the following month as Assistant Chief of Staff, G-4. He returned to HQMC, Washington, in July 1955, serving as Director, Policy Analysis Branch, until June 1957, when he was named Deputy Chief of Staff, Research and Development. He was promoted to brigadier general in Nov. 1957. Gen. Shaw departed Washington for Quantico in July 1958 to become Director of the Marine Corps Development Center. Following this assignment, he was named CO, Landing Force Training Unit, Pacific Fleet, in Nov. 1959, serving in this capacity until his retirement, Mar. 1, 1962.

SHEPHERD, Lemuel Cornick, Jr. General. 20th Commandant of the Marine

Shepherd

Corps – Jan. 1, 1952 to Dec. 31, 1955. Retired but recalled to active duty and appointed Chairman of the Inter-American Defense Board: b. Norfolk, Va., Feb. 10, 1896. Lemuel Shepherd, a graduate of Virginia Military Institute, was commissioned a second lieutenant in the Marine Corps on Apr. 11, 1917. On May 19, he reported for active duty at the MB, Port Royal, S.C. Less than a month later, he sailed for France as a member of the 5th Mar. Regt., with the first elements of the AEF. He served in defensive sectors in the vicinity of Verdun and participated in the Aisne-Marne offensive (Chateau-Thierry) where he was twice wounded in action at Belleau Wood during the fighting there in June 1918. Upon returning to the front in Aug., he rejoined the 5th Marines and saw action in the St.-

Mihiel and Meuse-Argonne (Champagne) offensive where he was wounded for the third time. For his gallantry in action at Belleau Wood, Lt. Shepherd was awarded the Army Distinguished Service Cross, the Navy Cross, the French Croix de Guerre, and was cited in the general orders of the 2nd Inf. Div., AEF. After duty with the Army of Occupation in Germany, Shepherd sailed for home in July 1919. In Sept., he returned to France for duty in connection with the preparation of relief maps of the battlefields over which the 4th Brig. of Marines had fought. Upon Shepherd's return to the States in Dec. 1920, he was assigned as Aide-de-Camp to the Commandant and Aide at the White House. In July 1922, he was assigned duty in command of a selected company of Marines at the Brazilian Exposition at Rio de Janeiro. In June of 1923, he was ordered to sea duty as CO of the Marine Detachment aboard the USS *Idaho*. This tour was followed by duty at the MB, Norfolk, Va., where he commanded the Sea School. In Apr. 1927, he sailed for expeditionary duty in China, where he served in the 3rd Mar. Brig. in Tientsin and Shanghai. Upon returning to the States in 1929, he attended the Field Officers' Course, MCS. After graduation, Capt. Shepherd was assigned to overseas duty again, this time on detached duty with the Garde d'Haiti where he served for four years as a District and Department Commander. Following the withdrawal of Marines from Haiti in 1934, Shepherd, now a major, was detailed to the MB, Washington, D.C., as Executive Officer and as Registrar of the Marine Corps Institute. Promoted to lieutenant colonel in 1936, he was assigned to the Naval War College at Newport, R.I. Following graduation in May 1937, he commanded the 2nd Bn., 5th Mar. Regt., part of the

newly formed FMF, Atlantic, which was being extensively employed in the development of amphibious tactics and techniques. In June 1939, he was ordered to the Staff of the MCS, Quantico, Va., where he served during the next three years as Director, Correspondence School; Chief of the Tactical Section; Officer in Charge of the Candidates Class; and Assistant Commandant. In Mar. 1942, four months after the United States' entry into WWII, Col. Shepherd was ordered to command the 9th Mar. Regt. He organized, trained, and took this unit overseas as part of the 3rd Mar. Div. Upon appointment to flag rank in July 1943, while serving on Guadalcanal, Brig. Gen. Shepherd was assigned as Assistant Division Commander of the 1st Mar. Div. In this capacity, he participated in the Cape Gloucester operation on New Britain from Dec. 1943 through Mar. 1944, where he was awarded a Legion of Merit for distinguished service in command of the operations in the Borgan Bay area. In May 1944, Gen. Shepherd assumed command of the 1st Prov. Mar. Brig. and led this organization in the invasion and subsequent recapture of Guam during July and Aug. of 1944. For distinguished leadership in this operation, Gen. Shepherd received his first Distinguished Service Medal, and was promoted to major general. After organizing the 6th Mar. Div. from the Brigade, Maj. Gen. Shepherd commanded it throughout the Okinawa Operation and subsequently took that unit to Tsingtao, China. There, on Oct. 25, 1945, he received the surrender of the Japanese forces in this area. For exceptionally meritorious service as CG of the 6th Mar. Div. in the assault and occupation of Okinawa (Apr. 1 to June 21, 1945) he was awarded a Gold Star in lieu of a second Distinguished Service Medal. The citation for this decoration reads in part: "Schooled by grim experience in the art of countering Japanese strategies, Maj. Gen. Shepherd organized a major Marine Corps fighting unit for the second time within a year, planned its commitment into battle with brilliant military acumen... and demonstrated a superior ability to use the men and weapons at his command. His indomitable courage and astute judgment were important factors in the success of his division's operations." Several months later, the general returned to the States and in Mar. 1946, organized the Troop Training Command, Amphibious Forces, Atlantic Fleet, at Little Creek, Va. On Nov. 1 of the same year, he was ordered to duty as Assistant to the Commandant and Chief of Staff of HQMC. He remained at this post until Apr. 1948, when he was assigned to Quantico, where he served as Commandant of the MCS until June 1950. When the Korean War erupted, Gen. Shepherd was in command of the FMF, Pacific, with HQ at Pearl Harbor. In this capacity, he participated in the landing at Inchon and the evacuation of our forces from Hungnam following the withdrawal from the Chosin Reservoir in north Korea in Dec. 1950. On Jan. 1, 1952, he was appointed Commandant of the Marine Corps by the President of the United States. During Gen. Shepherd's four-year appointment as the 20th CMC, he initiated a number of important policies which resulted in an increased military proficiency of the Corps. He was the first Commandant to become a member of the Joint Chiefs of Staff, and upon his retirement on Jan. 1, 1956 he was awarded a third Distinguished Service Medal. Two months after his retirement, Gen. Shepherd was recalled to active duty and appointed Chairman of the Inter-American Defense Board.

SHIVERS, John. Private. Medal of Honor: b. Canada, 1830. John Shivers enlisted in the Marine Corps at Philadelphia, Pa. on Sept. 17, 1864. His citation reads, in part: "... while serving on board the USS *Minnesota*, especially commended for bravery in the assault on Fort Fisher, Jan. 15, 1865, remaining at the front near the fort when the panic carried the mass away...."

Shoup

SHOUP, David Monroe. General. 22nd Commandant of the U.S. Marine Corps. A Marine officer since 1926, he assumed his present duties and was promoted to his present rank on Jan. 1, 1960: b. Battle Ground, Ind., Dec. 30, 1904. As a colonel in WWII, Gen. Shoup earned the nation's highest award, the Medal of Honor, while commanding the 2nd Marines, 2nd

Mar. Div., at Betio, a bitterly contested island of Tarawa Atoll. The British Distinguished Service Order was also awarded him for this action. The following citation accompanied his award of the Medal of Honor: "For conspicuous gallantry and intrepidity at the risk of his own life above and beyond the call of duty as CO of all Marine Corps troops in action against enemy Japanese forces on Betio Island, Tarawa Atoll, Gilbert Is., from Nov. 20 to 22, 1943. Although severely shocked by an exploding shell soon after landing at the pier, and suffering from a serious painful leg wound which had become infected, Shoup (then a colonel) fearlessly exposed himself to the terrific relentless artillery, machine gun, and rifle fire from hostile shore emplacements and, rallying his hesitant troops by his own inspiring heroism, gallantly led them across the fringing reefs to charge the heavily fortified island and reinforced our hard-pressed thinly held lines. Upon arrival at the shore, he assumed command of all landed troops and, working without rest under constant withering enemy fire during the next two days, conducted smashing attacks against unbelievably strong and fanatically defended Japanese positions despite innumerable obstacles and heavy casualties. By his brilliant leadership, daring tactics, and selfless devotion to duty, Col. Shoup was largely responsible for the final, decisive defeat of the enemy and his indomitable fighting spirit reflects great credit upon the United States Naval Service." David Shoup was the 25th Marine to receive the Medal of Honor in WWII. It was presented to him on Jan. 22, 1945, by the late James V. Forrestal, Secretary of the Navy. The general was a 1926 graduate of DePauw University, Greencastle, Ind., where he was a member of the ROTC. He served

for a month as a second lieutenant in the Army Infantry Reserve before he was commissioned a Marine second lieutenant on July 20, 1926. Ordered to Marine Officers' Basic School at the Philadelphia Navy Yard, Lt. Shoup's instruction was interrupted twice by temporary duty elsewhere in the States, and by expeditionary duty with the 6th Marines in Tientsin, China. After serving in China during most of 1927, he completed Basic School in 1928. He then served at Quantico, Va.; Pensacola, Fla.; and San Diego, Calif. From June 1929 to Sept. 1931, Lt. Shoup was assigned to the Marine Detachment aboard the USS *Maryland*. By coincidence, the USS *Maryland* was the flagship for the assault on Tarawa 12 years later — providing emergency naval gunfire support with her 16-inch guns early on D-Day. On his return from sea duty, Shoup served as a company officer at the MCB (later Marine Corps Recruit Depot), San Diego, until May 1932, when he was ordered to the Puget Sound Navy Yard, Bremerton, Wash. He was promoted to first lieutenant in June 1932. Lt. Shoup later served on temporary duty with the Civilian Conservation Corps in Idaho and New Jersey from June 1933 to May 1934. Following duty in Seattle, Wash., he was again ordered to China in Nov. 1934, serving briefly with the 4th Marines in Shanghai and, subsequently, at the American Legation in Peiping. He returned to the States, via Japan, early in June 1936 and was again stationed at the Puget Sound Navy Yard. He was promoted to captain in Oct. 1936. Capt. Shoup entered the Junior Course, Marine Corps Schools, Quantico, in July 1937. On completing the course in May 1938, he served as an instructor for two years. In June 1940, he joined the 6th Marines in San Diego. He was promoted to major in Apr. 1941. One month later, Maj.

Shoup was ordered to Iceland with the 6th Marines and, after serving as Regimental Operations Officer, became Operations Officer of the 1st Mar. Brig. in Iceland in Oct. 1941. For his service in Iceland during the first three months after the United States entered WWII, he was awarded the Letter of Commendation with Commendation Ribbon. He assumed command of the 2nd Bn., 6th Marines, in Feb. 1942. On returning to the States in Mar., the 1st Mar. Brig. was disbanded and he returned with his battalion to San Diego. In July 1942, he became Assistant Operations and Training Officer of the 2d Mar. Div. He was promoted to lieutenant colonel in Aug. 1942. Sailing from San Diego aboard the USS *Matsonia* in Sept. 1942, Lt. Col. Shoup arrived at Wellington, New Zealand, later that month. From then until Nov. 1943, he served as G-3, Operations and Training Officer of the 2nd Mar. Div. during its training period in New Zealand. His service in this capacity during the planning of the assault on Tarawa earned him his first Legion of Merit with Combat "V." During this period he also served briefly as an observer with the 1st Mar. Div. on Guadalcanal in Oct. 1942, and with the 43rd Army Division on Rendova, New Georgia, in the summer of 1943, earning a Purple Heart in the latter operation. Promoted to colonel, Nov. 9, 1943, Col. Shoup was placed in command of the 2nd Marines (Reinf.), the spearhead of the assault on Tarawa. During this action he earned the Medal of Honor as well as a second Purple Heart. In Dec. 1943, he became Chief of Staff of the 2nd Mar. Div. For outstanding service in this capacity from June to Aug. 1944, during the battles for Saipan and Tinian, he was again awarded the Legion of Merit with Combat "V." He returned to the States in Oct.

1944. On his return Col. Shoup served as Logistics Officer, Division of Plans and Policies, HQMC. He was again ordered overseas in June 1947. Two months later he became CO, Service Command, FMF, Pacific. In June 1949, he joined the 1st Mar. Div. at Camp Pendleton as Division Chief of Staff. A year later he was transferred to Quantico where he served as CO of the Basic School from July 1950 until Apr. 1952. He was then assigned to the Office of the Fiscal Director, HQMC, serving as Assistant Fiscal Director. He was promoted to brigadier general in Apr. 1953. In July 1953, Gen. Shoup was named Fiscal Director of the Marine Corps. While serving in this capacity, he was promoted to major general in Sept. 1955. Subsequently, in May 1956, he began a brief assignment as Inspector General of the Marine Corps from Sept. 1956 until May 1957. He returned to Camp Pendleton in June 1957 to become CG of the 1st Mar. Div. Gen. Shoup joined the 3rd Mar. Div. on Okinawa in Mar. 1958 as CG. Following his return to the States, he served as CG of the MCRD, Parris Is., from May to Oct. 1959. On Nov. 2, 1959, he was promoted to lieutenant general and assigned duties as Chief of Staff, HQMC. He served in this capacity until he assumed his current assignment. Gen. Shoup was nominated by President Dwight D. Eisenhower on Aug. 14, 1959, to be the 22nd Commandant of the Marine Corps. Subsequently, his nomination for a four-year term, beginning Jan. 1, 1960, was confirmed by the Senate.

SHUCK, William Edward, Jr. Staff Sergeant. Medal of Honor: b. Ridgely, W.Va., Aug. 16, 1926; d. KIA, Korea, July 3, 1952. S. Sgt. Shuck's citation reads, in part: ". . . while serving as a squad leader of Co. G, 3rd Bn., 7th Marines,

1st Mar. Div. (Reinf.), in action against enemy aggressor forces in Korea on July 3, 1952. When his platoon was subjected to a devastating barrage of enemy small arms, grenade, artillery, and mortar fire during an assault against strongly fortified hill positions well forward of the main line of resistance, S. Sgt. Shuck, although painfully wounded, refused medical attention and continued to lead his machine gun squad in the attack. Unhesitatingly assuming command of a rifle squad when the leader became a casualty, he skillfully organized the two squads into an attacking force and led two more daring assaults upon the hostile positions. Wounded a second time, he steadfastly refused evacuation and remained in the foremost position under heavy fire until assured that all dead and wounded were evacuated. Mortally wounded by an enemy sniper bullet while voluntarily assisting in the removal of the last casualty, S. Sgt. Shuck, by his fortitude and great personal valor in the face of overwhelming odds, served to inspire all who observed him. . . ."

SIGLER, Franklin Earl. Private First Class. Medal of Honor: b. Montclair, N.J., Nov. 6, 1924. On Iwo Jima, Franklin Sigler, then a private, took command of his squad when his squad leader became a casualty and unhesitatingly led them in a bold rush against an enemy gun position which had been holding up the advance of his company for several days. Reaching the gun position first, he personally annihilated the gun crew with grenades. When more enemy troops began firing from tunnels and caves leading to the gun position, he successfully scaled the rocks leading up to the position and alone assaulted the Japanese completely surprising them. Although painfully wounded in this one-man assault, he re-fused to be evacuated and, crawling back to his squad, directed machine gun fire and rocket fire on the cave entrances. In the ensuing fight three of his men were wounded and Pvt. Sigler, disregarding the pain from his wound and the heavy enemy fire, carried them to safety behind the lines. Returning to his squad he remained with his men, directing their fire until ordered to retire and seek medical aid. Hospitalized in the U.S. Naval Hospital, Bethesda, Md., he was discharged with the rank of private first class in June 1946 because of disability resulting from his wounds.

SILVA, France. Private. Medal of Honor: b. Hayward, Calif., May 8, 1876. France Silva enlisted in the Marine Corps at San Francisco, Calif. on Sept. 12, 1899. His citation reads, in part: " . . . for distinguished conduct in the presence of enemy at Peking, China, June 28 to Aug. 17, 1900. . . ." He was discharged from the Corps on Jan. 6, 1901.

SILVERTHORN, Merwin Hancock. Lieutenant General (Retired): b. Minneapolis, Minn., Sept. 22, 1896. Merwin Silverthorn attended the University of Minnesota before enlisting in the Marine Corps on Apr. 27, 1917. In Aug. of that year, he sailed for France with the 5th Mar. Regt. He was commissioned a second lieutenant on June 9, 1918 while in France, and fought in the Aisne-Marne defensive (Chateau-Thierry), Aisne-Marne offensive (Soissons), Marbache Sector (Pont-a-Mousson), and the Meuse-Argonne offensive (Champagne). After WWI he remained in Europe with the Army of Occupation of Germany until ordered to the States in Sept. 1919. In May 1923, following tours of duty at Washington, D.C., Mare Is., Calif., and Quantico, he went to Haiti with the 1st

Brig. Marines. In Mar. 1924, he was transferred to the Gendarmerie d' Haiti, serving with that organization as District Commander, Aux Cayes, and Chief of Police, Port-au-Prince. Returning to the MB at Quantico in July 1926, he served there for almost four years before he was assigned to the MB on Guam in Apr. 1930 as an assistant quartermaster. He was detached to the States in Jan. 1932, and for the next several years he served at various posts and stations in this country. During those years he completed a course at the Army Quartermaster Subsistence School in Chicago and the Senior Course in the MCS, Quantico. After two years as an instructor at Quantico he entered the Naval War College at Newport, R.I. in July 1938. Completing the course at Newport in May 1939, Silverthorn began a tour of sea duty which included service in various capacities aboard the USS *Indianapolis*, USS *Enterprise*, USS *Houston*, and the USS *Chester*, returning to Washington in Aug. 1941. He was a lieutenant colonel, attached to the War Plans Section of the Operations Division, Navy Department, when the States entered WWII. Silverthorn was then assigned to HQ, Commander-in-Chief, U.S. Fleet, where he served as a naval member of the Joint U.S. Strategic Committee, Joint Chiefs of Staff, from Jan. 1942 until June 1943. He remained in Washington for the next six months as Chief of the Amphibious Warfare Section at the Army and Navy Staff College, winning the Letter of Commendation Ribbon from the Army for his service in that capacity. In Jan. 1944, he joined the 1st Mar. Amphibious Corps in the Pacific theater, serving as Chief of Staff of that unit until it was redesignated the 3rd Amphibious Corps. He then served in the same capacity with the 3rd Corps until June 1945. The

following month he became Chief of Staff, FMF, Pacific. A brigadier general when the war ended, he remained with FMF, Pacific until Sept. 1946. The following month he took command of the Troop Training Unit, Training Command, Amphibious Forces, Atlantic Fleet, at Little Creek, Va. Gen. Silverthorn returned once more to Washington in Sept. 1947, serving as Marine Corps Liaison Officer with the Office of the Chief of Naval Operations until May 1949, then as Director of the MCR at HQMC. He was named Assistant Commandant of the Marine Corps in July 1950, and was temporarily promoted to the rank of lieutenant general the following Feb., when the office of Assistant Commandant was elevated to that rank. He took command of the Marine Corps Recruit Depot at Parris Is. in Feb. 1952, reverting to the rank of major general for that assignment, and was again promoted to lieutenant general upon retirement on June 30, 1954.

SIMANEK, Robert Ernest. Private First Class. Medal of Honor: b. Detroit, Mich., Apr. 26, 1930. P.F.C. Simanek's citation reads, in part: "... while serving with Co. F, 2nd Bn., 5th Marines, 1st Mar. Div. (Reinf.), in action against enemy aggressor forces in Korea on Aug. 17, 1952. While accompanying a patrol en route to occupy a combat outpost forward of friendly lines, P.F.C. Simanek exhibited a high degree of courage and a resolute spirit of self-sacrifice in protecting the lives of his fellow Marines. With his unit ambushed by an intense concentration of enemy mortar and small arms fire, and suffering heavy casualties, he was forced to seek cover with the remaining members of the patrol in a nearby trench line. Determined to save his comrades when a hostile grenade was hurled into their midst, he unhesitatingly threw himself on the deadly missile, absorbing the shattering violence of the exploding charge in his own body and shielding his fellow Marines from serious injury or death. . . ."

SIMPSON, Ormond Ralph. Brigadier General. Assistant Chief of Staff, G-1, HQMC, Washington, D.C. (1963): b. Corpus Christi, Tex., Mar. 16, 1915. Ormond Simpson was a member of the ROTC unit at Texas A&M College where he was designated Military Honor Graduate and awarded a Bachelor of Science degree in mechanical engineering upon graduation in June 1936. He held an Army Reserve commission until July 11, 1936 when he was commissioned a Marine second lieutenant. After serving variously for 15 months at San Diego, Calif., Philadelphia, Pa., and Quantico, he resigned his commission to accept a position at Texas A&M in Oct. 1937. The following month he was granted a commission in the MCR, and two years later was promoted to first lieutenant in the Reserve. In Nov. 1940, Lt. Simpson requested assignment to extended active duty and was ordered to the MCB, San Diego, where he served as a company commander with the 8th Marines until the outbreak of WWII. Shortly after his promotion to captain in Dec. 1941, he sailed with the 8th Marines, 2nd Mar. Brig. for the Pacific area. Stationed on Samoa, Capt. Simpson served as Regimental Adjutant of the 8th Marines until Aug. 1942, when he was promoted to major and named Assistant Operations Officer of the Samoan Group Defense Force. In Mar. 1944, he joined the Emirau Landing Force, 3rd Mar. Div. He was promoted to lieutenant colonel in Apr. 1944, and returned to the States the following month. After completing the In-

fantry Course, Command and General Staff School at Fort Leavenworth, Kans., Lt. Col. Simpson returned to the Pacific area in Nov. 1944. He served at Leyte and Manila, Philippine Is., as Assistant G-4, GHQ, Southwest Pacific Area; and later, in occupied Japan, joined the Staff of Supreme Commander, Allied Powers (SCAP), as Assistant G-4. The Army Legion of Merit was awarded Lt. Col. Simpson for exceptionally meritorious conduct from Dec. 1944 to Jan. 1946 during the planning for the invasion of Japan and its subsequent occupation. Following his return to the States, he was assigned to MCS, Quantico, in Mar. 1946, and served as an instructor in the Logistics Section for over three years. While at Quantico, he was integrated into the regular Marine Corps. In June 1949, he was transferred to HQMC, Washington, D.C. as Special Assistant to the Director of the Division of Plans and Policies. He was promoted to colonel in Nov. 1951, and the following month was detached from Headquarters. In Jan. 1952, Col. Simpson joined the 2nd Mar. Div., Camp Lejeune, N.C., serving as Regimental Commander of the 6th Marines until Apr. 1953 when he became Division Assistant Chief of Staff, G-4. In Sept. 1953, he departed for Korea where he subsequently earned the Bronze Star Medal for meritorious service as CO, 1st Marines, 1st Mar. Div. The following Feb. he became Division Assistant Chief of Staff, G-3. On his return from Korea in July 1954, Col. Simpson was assigned as a student to the Army War College, Carlisle Barracks, Pa., graduating in June 1955. Ordered to HQMC that July, he served briefly in the Policy Analysis Division, then was named Secretary of the General Staff in Oct. In Jan. 1956, he became Military Secretary to the CMC, serving in this capacity for two and a half years. From July 1958 until June 1960, Col. Simpson served as Chief of Staff, MCS, Quantico. Following this assignment, he joined the staff at Duke University in July 1960, serving for one year as CO, Naval Reserve Officers' Training Corps unit and Professor of Naval Science. Departing for Okinawa in Aug. 1961, he assumed duty as Assistant Division Commander, 3rd Mar. Div., and was promoted to brigadier general. In May 1962, when American troops were requested by the Government of Thailand during the Laotian crisis, Gen. Simpson was ordered to Thailand as CG of the 3rd Mar. Expeditionary Brig. and Naval Component Commander, Joint Task Force 116. He remained in Thailand until Aug. 7, 1962, then resumed his duties on Okinawa. In Nov. 1962, following his return to the States, he assumed duty at HQMC as Assistant Director of Personnel. He served in this capacity through Mar. 1963, then assumed his assignment as Assistant Chief of Staff, G-1, HQMC.

SITTER, Carl Leonard. Lieutenant Colonel. Medal of Honor: b. Syracuse, Mo., Dec. 2, 1921. Carl Sitter enlisted in the Marine Corps on June 22, 1940. After eight months' duty in Iceland, he was ordered to the Pacific. He was serving as a corporal in the Wallis Is. when, on Dec. 12, 1942, he was given a field commission as a second lieutenant in the MCR. He later received a regular commission. Sitter saw combat at Eniwetok in the Marshall Is., and Guam in the Marianas. He was first wounded Feb. 20, 1944 at Eniwetok, but went back into action almost immediately. He was wounded again the following July on Guam. Removed to the States, he served at San Diego, Quantico, Brooklyn Naval Shipyard, Panama Canal Zone, Key West,

Fla., Camp Lejeune, N.C., and Camp Pendleton, Calif. before going overseas again to Korea in Aug. 1950. His citation reads, in part: ". . . as commanding officer of Co. G, 3rd Bn., 1st Marines, 1st Mar. Div. (Reinf), in action against enemy aggressor forces at Hagaru-ri, Korea, on Nov. 29 and 30, 1950. Ordered to break through enemy-infested territory to reinforce his battalion on the early morning of Nov. 29, Capt. Sitter continuously exposed himself to enemy fire as he led his company forward and, despite 25 per cent casualties suffered in the furious action, succeeded in driving through to his objective. Assuming the responsibility of attempting to seize and occupy a strategic area occupied by a hostile force of regiment strength deeply entrenched on a snow-covered hill commanding the entire valley southeast of the town, as well as the line of march of friendly troops withdrawing to the south, he reorganized his depleted units the following morning and boldly led them up the steep, frozen hillside under blistering fire, encouraging and redeploying his troops as casualties occurred and directing forward platoons as they continued the drive to the top of the ridge. During the night a vastly outnumbering enemy launched a sudden, vicious counterattack, setting the hill ablaze with mortar, machine gun, and automatic weapons fire. . . . With the enemy penetrating his lines in repeated counterattacks which often required hand-to-hand combat and, on one occasion infiltrating to the command post with hand grenades, he fought gallantly with his men in repulsing and killing the fanatic attackers in each encounter. Painfully wounded in the face, arms, and chest by bursting grenades, he staunchly refused to be evacuated and continued to fight on until a successful defense of the area was assured with a loss to the enemy of more than 50 per cent dead, wounded, and captured. . . ."

SKAGGS, Luther, Jr. Private First Class. Medal of Honor: b. Henderson, Ky., Mar. 3, 1923. P.F.C. Skaggs' citation reads, in part: ". . . . while serving as squad leader with a mortar section of a rifle company in the 3rd Bn., 3rd Marines, 3rd Mar. Div., during action against enemy Japanese forces on Guam, July 21-22, 1944. When the section leader became a casualty under a heavy mortar barrage shortly after landing, P.F.C. Skaggs promptly assumed command and led the section through intense fire for a distance of 200 yards to a position where it could deliver effective coverage of the assault on a strategic cliff. Valiantly defending this vital position against strong enemy counterattacks during the night, P.F.C. Skaggs was critically wounded when a Japanese grenade lodged in his foxhole and exploded, shattering the lower part of one leg. Quick to act, he applied an improvised tourniquet and, while propped up in his foxhole, gallantly returned the enemy's fire with his rifle and hand grenades for a period of eight hours, later crawling unassisted to the rear to continue the fight until the Japanese had been annihilated. . . ."

SKINNER, Sherrod Emerson, Jr. Second Lieutenant. Medal of Honor: b. Hartford, Conn., Oct. 29, 1929; d. KIA, Korea, Oct. 6, 1952. Lt. Skinner's citation reads, in part: ". . . as an artillery forward observer of Battery F, 2nd Bn., 11th Marines, 1st Mar. Div. (Reinf.), in action against enemy aggressor forces in Korea on the night of Oct. 26, 1952. When his observation post in an extremely critical and vital sector of the main line of resistance was subjected to a sudden and fanatical attack by hostile forces, sup-

ported by a devastating barrage of artillery and mortar fire which completely severed communication lines connecting the outpost with friendly firing batteries, 2nd Lt. Skinner, in a determined effort to hold his position, immediately organized and directed the surviving personnel in the defense of the outpost, continuing to call down fire on the enemy by means of radio alone until this equipment became damaged beyond repair. Undaunted by the intense hostile barrage and the rapidly closing attackers, he twice left the protection of his bunker in order to direct accurate machine gun fire and to replenish the depleted supply of ammunition and grenades. Although painfully wounded on each occasion, he steadfastly refused medical aid until the rest of the men received treatment. As the ground attack reached its climax, he gallantly directed the final defense until the meager supply of ammunition was exhausted and the position overrun. During the three hours that the outpost was occupied by the enemy, several grenades were thrown into the bunker serving as protection for 2nd Lt. Skinner and his remaining comrades. Realizing that there was no chance for other than passive resistance, he directed his men to feign death even though the hostile troops entered the bunker and searched their persons. Later, when an enemy grenade was thrown between him and two other survivors, he immediately threw himself on the deadly missile in an effort to protect the others, absorbing the full force of the explosion and sacrificing his life for his comrades. . . ."

SMITH, Albert Joseph. Sergeant. Medal of Honor: b. Calumet, Mich., July 31, 1898. Albert Smith's rescue of a Navy pilot from a burning airplane which had crashed at the NAS, Pensacola, Fla. in

Feb. 1921, won for him the Medal of Honor. Then a private, Smith was on duty as a sentry the morning of Feb. 11, 1921, when suddenly a seaplane piloted by Machinist's Mate 2nd Cl. Plen M. Phelps went into an erratic spin and crashed to the flying field, imprisoning the pilot. Almost at the same instant, a gravity gasoline tank exploded and the plane burst into flame. The citation accompanying Smith's award credits him with having "pushed himself to a position where he could reach Phelps," despite the explosion of the gas tank and "with total disregard for his own personal safety." He later freed Phelps but sustained painful burns about the head, neck, and both hands. Having enlisted in the Marine Corps in Oct. 1919, he served three years, including a tour of duty in Santo Domingo.

SMITH, Holland McTyeire. General (Retired). One of the United States' top commanders in the Pacific during WWII, he led the 5th Amphibious Corps in the assaults on the Gilberts, the Marshalls, and Saipan and Tinian in the Marianas. In the latter operation, he commanded all Expeditionary Troops in the Marianas, including those which recaptured Guam. Later, he served as the first CG of the Fleet Marine Force, Pacific, and headed Task Force 56 (Expeditionary Troops) at Iwo Jima: b. Seale, Ala., Apr. 20, 1882. Holland Smith received a Bachelor of Science degree from Alabama Polytechnic Institute in 1901, obtained his Bachelor of Laws degree from the University of Alabama in 1903, and practiced law in Montgomery, Ala., for a year before he was appointed a Marine second lieutenant Mar. 20, 1905. In Apr. 1906, after completing the School of Application at Annapolis, Md., he sailed for the Philippines, where he served on ex-

H. M. Smith

peditionary duty with the 1st Mar. Brig. until Sept. 1908. He returned to the States the following month and was stationed at the MB, Annapolis, until Dec. 1909, when he embarked for expeditionary duty in Panama. Returning from there in Apr. 1910, he served variously at Annapolis; Puget Sound, Wash.; San Diego, Calif., and the Recruiting Station, Seattle, Wash., before sailing in Sept. 1912, to rejoin the 1st Mar. Brig. in the Philippines. This time he remained with the 1st Brig. until Apr. 1914, when he took command of the Marine Detachment aboard the USS *Galveston*. He served in that capacity in Asiatic waters until July 1915, then returned to the States the following month for duty at the Navy Yard, New Orleans, La. From there he was ordered to the Dominican Republic in June 1916, as a member of the 4th Mar. Regt. During that unit's operations against rebel bandits he saw action in the march to Santiago and engagements at La Pena and Kilometer 29. Returning to the States May 30, 1917, he sailed for France just two weeks later as commander of the 8th Machine Gun Company, 5th Marines. In France, Gen. Smith was detached from the 5th Marines and sent to the Army General Staff College at Langres, from which he was graduated in Feb. 1918. He was then named Adjutant of the 4th Mar. Brig., in which capacity he fought in the Verdun Sector and Aisne-Marne defensive, including the epic battle of Belleau Wood. Transferred to the 1st Corps, 1st Army, in July 1918 he served as assistant operations officer in charge of liaison during the Aisne-Marne, Oisne-Aisne, St.-Mihiel and Meuse-Argonne offensives. After the Armistice he participated in the march to the Rhine through Belgium and Luxembourg as an assistant operations officer with the 3rd Army, and served with the General Staff, U.S. Army, during the occupation of Germany. For his service at Belleau Wood he was awarded the Croix de Guerre with palm by the French government. Returning to the States in Apr. 1919, Smith's assignments in the next four years included duty at Norfolk, Va., study at the Naval War College, Newport, R.I., and service in Washington, D.C. with the War Plans Section of the Office of Naval Operations. There he was the first Marine officer to serve on the Joint Army-Navy Planning Committee. Leaving Washington in May 1923, he served aboard the battleships *Wyoming* and *Arkansas* as Fleet Marine Officer, U.S. Scouting Fleet, until Sept. of that year. In Feb. 1924, after serving at HQMC and in connection with joint Army-Navy maneuvers, Smith joined the

Mar. Brig. on expeditionary duty in Haiti, serving as that unit's Chief of Staff and Officer in Charge of Operations and Training. He returned from that country in Aug. 1925, to serve as Chief of Staff of the 1st Mar. Brig. at Quantico, until Sept. 1926; as a student in the MCS, Quantico, from then until June 1927; and as Post Quartermaster of the MB, Philadelphia Navy Yard, from July 1927 to Mar. 1931. In Apr. 1931, he began another tour of sea duty, this time aboard the USS *California* as Aide to the Commander and Force Marine Officer of the Battle Force, U.S. Fleet. He served in those capacities until June 1933, then commanded the MB at the Washington Navy Yard until Jan. 1935. The next two years he served at San Francisco, Calif., as Chief of Staff, Department of the Pacific. From there he was ordered to HQMC in Mar. 1937 to serve two years as Director of the Division of Operations and Training, after which he was Assistant Commandant of the Marine Corps under Maj. Gen. Thomas Holcomb from Apr. to Sept. 1939. After the latter assignment Gen. Smith assumed command of the 1st Mar. Brig. at Quantico, taking that unit to Guantanamo Bay, Cuba, for extended amphibious training in Oct. 1940. In Feb. 1941, when the brigade was redesignated the 1st Mar. Div., he became that organization's first commander. He returned with the division to Quantico in Apr. 1941, and in June of that year he was detached from it to take command of the organization which eventually became the Amphibious Force, Atlantic Fleet. Under this command, the 1st Mar. Div. and the 1st and 9th Army Divisions received their initial training in amphibious warfare. Moving to San Diego in Aug. 1942, the general took command of the Amphibious Corps, Pacific Fleet, under which he completed the amphibious indoctrination of the 2nd and 3rd Mar. Divs. before they went overseas and the 7th Army Division and other units involved in the Aleutians operation. The Amphibious Corps, Pacific Fleet, was later redesignated the 5th Amphibious Corps, and in Sept. 1943, as commander of that unit, Gen. Smith arrived at Pearl Harbor to begin planning for the Gilbert Is. campaign. He continued to head the 5th Amphibious Corps until Aug. 1944, when he was named CG, FMF, Pacific, at Pearl Harbor. In addition to that post, he commanded Task Force 56 at Iwo Jima before returning to the States in July 1945, to head the Marine Training and Replacement Command at Camp Pendleton, Calif. A lieutenant general when he was retired on May 15, 1946 at the age of 64, he was promoted to general on the retired list for having been especially commended in combat.

SMITH, John Lucian. Colonel. Marine Corps ace. Medal of Honor: b. Lexington, Okla., Dec. 26, 1914. During the crucial battle for the Solomons, Col. Smith led Marine Fighter Squadron 223 on sorties against the enemy, during which the squadron accounted for 83 enemy aircraft destroyed. His citation reads, in part: "...as CO of Marine Fighting Squadron 223, during operations against enemy Japanese forces in the Solomon Is. Area, Aug.-Sept. 1942. Repeatedly risking his life in aggressive and daring attacks, Smith (then a major) led his squadron against a determined force, greatly superior in numbers, personally shooting down 16 Japanese planes between Aug. 21 and Sept. 15, 1942. In spite of the limited combat experience of many of the pilots of this squadron, they achieved the notable record of a total of 83 enemy aircraft destroyed in

this period, mainly attributable to the thorough training under Maj. Smith and to his intrepid and inspiring leadership. . . ." Col. Smith retired from active duty in the Marine Corps on Sept. 1, 1960.

J. C. Smith

SMITH, Julian C. Lieutenant General (Retired): b. Elkton, Md., Sept. 11, 1885. Julian Smith, one of the Marine Corps' outstanding leaders in the field of amphibious warfare, was graduated from the University of Delaware with a Bachelor of Arts degree prior to receiving his appointment as a second lieutenant in the Marine Corps in Jan. 1909. Smith received his basic training as a Marine officer at the MB, Port Royal, S.C. Following his promotion to first lieutenant in Sept. 1912, Smith was ordered to the MB, Navy Yard, Philadelphia, Pa. In

Dec. of the following year he was transferred to Panama, at which station he remained until Jan. 1914. As a member of an expeditionary force, Lt. Smith departed from Panama and took part in the occupation at Vera Cruz, Mex., from Apr. to Dec. 1914. Upon return to the States, he again was ordered to Philadelphia, this time as a member of the 1st Brig. of Marines. In Aug. of the following year he departed for and arrived in Haiti for duty, and in Apr. of 1916 he was transferred to Santo Domingo with the 2nd Bn., 1st Regt., 1st Brig. In Dec. of the same year, he was again ordered to return to the Philadelphia Navy Yard, this time with the Advance Base Force there. Following his promotion to captain in Mar. 1917, he was ordered to attend a course of instruction at the Naval War College in Newport, R.I. Several months later he was ordered to Quantico to instruct in the Marine Officers' Training Camp. In the early part of 1919, Smith, now a captain in command of a machine gun battalion, sailed for Cuba. Following his appointment to major, he was returned to the Navy Yard at Philadelphia, and a short time later was transferred to HQMC, Washington, D.C. In Aug. 1920, he again assumed duties at Quantico. In July of the following year he was detached to serve at sea on the staff of the Commander, Scouting Fleet. After two years' service as a sea soldier, he was again returned to HQMC, this time to serve in the office of the Chief Coordinator, Bureau of the Budget, Washington, D.C. Immediately following graduation from the Army Command and General Staff School, Fort Leavenworth, Kans. in 1928, he was again ordered to duty at HQMC. Smith captained the Marine Corps Rifle and Pistol Team Squad for the year 1928, while detached to temporary duty at Quantico. He also

captained the 1930 squad. His next assignment found him with the Marines in Corinto, Nicaragua in Aug. 1930. Upon return from Nicaragua after a three-year tour of duty, he returned to Quantico. Shortly afterward he was appointed to the rank of lieutenant colonel. After another short tour of duty in Philadelphia, he returned to HQMC for duty with the Division of Operations and Training. With his promotion to colonel, he assumed the duties of Director of Personnel. In June 1938, he became CO, 5th Marines, with the 1st Mar. Brig., Quantico. After his promotion to brigadier general, Gen. Smith was sent to London, England, where he served with the Naval Attaché, American Embassy, as a naval observer. He returned to the States in Aug. 1941, and again reported to Quantico. Upon appointment to major general in Oct. 1942, he assumed command of the FMF Training Schools, New River, N.C. Following his command of the 2nd Mar. Div., which he assumed in the spring of 1943, Gen. Smith was appointed CG, Expeditionary Troops, 3rd Fleet which captured the southern Palau Islands and occupied Ulithi Atoll. For his services in that capacity he was awarded a Gold Star in lieu of a second Distinguished Service Medal. In Dec. 1944, Gen. Smith took command of the Department of the Pacific with headquarters in San Francisco, Calif. In Feb. 1946, he was sent to Parris Is., S.C., to assume command of that post. On Dec. 1, 1946, he was retired and advanced to his present rank of lieutenant general for having been specially commended for performance of duty in actual combat.

SMITH, Oliver P. General (Retired). CG of the 1st Mar. Div. during its historic breakthrough to the sea in Korea in 1950: b. Menard, Tex., Oct. 26, 1893.

Oliver Smith attended the University of California, Berkeley, Calif., and graduated in 1916. He reported for active duty as a second lieutenant in the Marine Corps on May 14, 1917. The following month he was assigned his first overseas tour at Guam, Marianas Is., where he served with the MB, Naval Station. In May 1919, he returned to the States for duty with the MB at Mare Is., Calif. Ordered to sea duty in Oct. 1921, he served as CO of the Marine Detachment aboard the USS *Texas* until May 1924. At that time he was ordered to HQMC, Washington, D.C., for duty with the personnel section. Returning overseas in June 1928, he joined the Gendarmerie d' Haiti, Port-au-Prince, as Assistant Chief of Staff. Following his return from foreign shore duty in June 1931, he became a student at the Field Officers' Course, Army Infantry School, Fort Benning, Ga. Graduating in June 1932, he was ordered to duty at the MCS, Quantico, Va., as an instructor in the Company Officers' Course. In Sept. 1933, he was named Assistant Operations Officer of the 7th Mar. Regt. at Quantico. He sailed for France in Jan. 1934, where he joined the staff of the American Embassy at Paris for duty with the Office of the U.S. Naval Attaché. From Nov. 1934 to July 1936, while in Paris, he studied at the Ecole Superieure de Guerre. He returned to the States in Aug. 1936, and joined the staff of the MCS at Quantico as an instructor in the Three Section (Operations and Training), then was transferred to the west coast in July 1939, where he joined the FMF as Operations Officer at the MCB, San Diego, Calif. In June of the following year he became CO of the 1st Bn., 6th Marines, and in May 1941, sailed with the regiment for Iceland where he remained until returning to the States in March 1942. In May of

the same year Smith was ordered to HQMC, Washington, D.C., where he became Executive Officer of the Division of Plans and Policies. He remained in this capacity until Jan. 1944, when he joined the 1st Mar. Div. on New Britain. There he took command of the 5th Marines and subsequently led the regiment in the Talasea phase of the Cape Gloucester operation. In Apr. 1944, he was named Assistant Division Commander of the 1st Mar. Div. and participated in operations against the Japanese in the Peleliu operation during Sept. and Oct. 1944. Gen. Smith became Marine Deputy Chief of Staff of the 10th Army in Nov. 1944, and participated in the Okinawa operation from Apr. through June 1945. In July 1945, the general returned to the States and became Commandant of the MCS, Quantico, and in Jan. 1948, was named CG, MB, Quantico, in addition to his duties at the school. Three months later he became Assistant Commandant of the Marine Corps, Chief of Staff, HQMC, Washington, D.C. Named CG of the 1st Mar. Div. in June 1950, Gen. Smith led his division through the bitter campaigns of the Korean War. After leading the 1st Mar. Div. in the assault of Inchon and subsequent capture of Seoul, Gen. Smith moved his division to Wonsan for the Corps' 280th and least opposed landing. After driving toward the Yalu, the division reached the Chosin reservoir where the Chinese Communist forces entered the war. With the flanking forces collapsing, Gen. Smith rallied the 1st Mar. Div. and began the historic 70-mile, 13-day fight to the sea. In the face of sub-zero temperatures and the onslaught of eight Chinese Communist divisions, Gen. Smith brought his forces to Hungnam for the amphibious operation in reverse. Gen. Smith returned to the States in May 1951 and was assigned duties as CG, MCB, Camp Pendleton, Calif. In July 1953 he became CG, FMF, Atlantic. He served in this capacity until his retirement on Sept. 1, 1955.

SMITH, Willard M. Corporal. Medal of Honor: b. Allegheny, N.Y., 1840. Willard Smith enlisted in the Marine Corps on Aug. 19, 1862. His citation reads, in part: " . . . while serving on board the USS *Brooklyn*, in the engagement in Mobile Bay, Aug. 5, 1864; conspicuous for good conduct at his gun. . . ." He was discharged from the Corps on Aug. 19, 1866.

SNEDEKER, Edward Walter. Lieutenant General. Commandant, Marine Corps Schools, Quantico, Va.: b. Peoria, Ill., Feb. 19, 1903. After attending schools in Peoria and at Dallas, S.D., he was graduated from high school at Benkelman, Neb., in 1922. He was appointed to the U.S. Naval Academy the same year and commissioned a Marine second lieutenant upon graduation, June 3, 1926. His first tour of expeditionary duty was with the 11th Marines in Nicaragua from May to Aug. 1927. He was then transferred from Nicaragua to the MB at Cape Haitien, Haiti, where he remained until Aug. 1929. He returned to Haiti in Jan. 1931 and that Oct. was promoted to first lieutenant. He remained in Haiti until May 1933. In addition to expeditionary duty, he served at various posts and stations in the States before the war, chiefly in communications. He also completed the Marine Officers' Basic School at the Philadelphia Navy Yard; the Communication Officers' Course at the Army Signal School, Fort Monmouth, N.J.; the post-graduate course in applied communications at the Naval Academy; and the Senior Course in the MCS at Quantico. He was promoted to captain in July 1936, and to major in Sept. 1940. On completing the Senior Course, he served as transport quartermaster aboard the USS *Barnett* for six months before he was named signal officer of the 1st Mar. Div. in June 1941. That Sept., after participating in landing exercises with the division, he moved with it to New River, N.C. He sailed with its advance echelon for New Zealand, via the Panama Canal, in May 1942. In Aug. 1942, he landed with the 1st Div. at Guadalcanal. He was promoted to lieutenant colonel in Sept. 1942. While taking part in the capture and defense of Guadalcanal, Lt. Col. Snedeker was awarded both the Silver Star Medal and the Bronze Star Medal. After serving several months in Australia, he was detached from the division in July 1943, to become signal officer of the 1st Marine Amphibious Corps. Then, following service as an observer at Vella Lavella, he was named Assistant Chief of Staff, G-3 (Operations), of the 1st Corps in Sept. 1943. He also served in that capacity in the Treasury-Bougainville campaign. Returning to the States in Jan. 1944, he served at HQMC as Chief, G-3 Section, Division of Plans and Policies. He was promoted to colonel in June 1944. In Nov. 1944, he rejoined the 1st Mar. Div. in the Russell Is. As CO, 7th Marines, he led his regiment in the assault and capture of Okinawa, during which action he earned the Navy Cross. He returned to HQMC in Oct. 1945, to serve again as Chief of the G-3 Section. He continued in that capacity until May 1946, then served briefly as Chief, Instructors Section, Quantico, before taking command of the Basic School there in Aug. 1946. He left Quantico for Guam in June 1949 to become Assistant Chief of Staff for Plans and Area Marine Officer, Naval Forces, Marianas. Col. Snedeker returned from Guam in July 1950, and departed for Korea later the same month as Chief of Staff, 1st Prov. Mar. Brig. After the Pusan Perimeter fighting, the brigade was absorbed by the 1st Mar. Div. and he became the division's Deputy Chief of Staff, serving in that capacity in the Inchon-Seoul campaign and the Oct. landing at Wonsan. During Nov. 1950, he served on temporary duty with the Pacific Fleet Evaluation Group, returning to the 1st Div. on Dec. 3 to establish a control and regulating post at Chinghung-ni, along the division's withdrawal route from the Chosin Reservoir. Following that campaign he became the division's Chief of Staff in Feb. 1951. He served in that capacity until late May 1951 during operations in Central Korea. For meritorious service in Korea, he received three separate awards of the Legion of Merit with Combat "V." Col. Snedeker returned to the States in July 1951, to serve as Chief of Staff of the 3rd Mar. Brig. at Camp Pendleton. He was promoted to brigadier general in Dec. 1951. In May 1952 he became Deputy Director of the Marine Corps Educational Center at Quantico, where he remained until June 1954. The following month he was appointed Assistant Commander, 2nd Mar. Div., Camp Lejeune, and in Feb. 1955, was given command of the division. He was promoted to major general in Apr. 1955. The general began serving as Assistant Chief of Staff, G-3, at HQMC in Aug. 1955. He served in this capacity for two and a half years, and in Feb. 1958 assumed command of the 1st Mar. Div. at Camp Pendleton. On assuming his current assignment as Commandant of the Marine Corps Schools, he was promoted to lieutenant general in Nov. 1959.

SORENSON, Richard Keith. First Lieutenant. Medal of Honor: b. Anoka, Minn., Aug. 28, 1924. Lt. Sorenson's citation

reads, in part: "... while serving with an assault battalion attached to the 4th Mar. Div. during the battle of Namur Island, Kwajalein Atoll, Marshall Is., on Feb. 1-2, 1944. Putting up a brave defense against a particularly violent counter-attack by the enemy during invasion operations, Sorenson (then a private) and five other Marines occupying a shellhole were endangered by a Japanese grenade thrown into their midst. Unhesitatingly, and with complete disregard for his own safety, Pvt. Sorenson hurled himself upon the deadly weapon, heroically taking the full impact of the explosion... he was severely wounded but the lives of his comrades were saved."

Sousa

SOUSA, John Philip. "The March King." American composer, bandmaster, and

Leader of the Marine Band: b. Washington, D.C., Nov. 6, 1854; d. Reading, Pa., Mar. 6, 1932. As a boy of mixed Portuguese and German ancestry, John Sousa spent a great deal of his time playing on the lawn of the Marine Commandant's house at 8th and Eye Streets in Washington, D.C. His father, Antonio Sousa, not only played in the Marine Band, but also worked as a carpenter on the CMC's house. When, shortly after his 13th birthday, John decided to run away, his father consulted Commandant Jacob Zeilin. In the opinion of the father, the boy needed the discipline and training traditionally offered by the Marines. The Commandant agreed. In those years it was not at all uncommon for the Marine Corps to enlist an apprentice. So John Philip Sousa, who had begun his musical education at the age of six, became a "boy bound to learn music." His enlistment, as such, lasted seven years and five months. Already a promising student of the violin, young Sousa also was given military training and was taught "to read, write and cipher as far as the single rule of three." To defray the expense of this schooling, one dollar was deducted from his pay each month. Young Sousa reenlisted after his first "hitch" and he and his father served together in the Marine Band until 1875, when they both received special discharges. John Sousa then became a civilian bandmaster, traveling through the New England States and as far west as St. Louis. Antonio remained in Washington and continued to work for the Commandant as a civilian cabinet maker. Five years later, in 1880, when the Marine Corps needed a new leader for the Band, Sousa's father again appealed to the Commandant in behalf of his son. The appeal was successful. John Philip Sousa, one-time apprentice, was asked to return to Washington to become 14th Leader of the Marine Band. He took his new position on Oct. 1, 1880. Under his direction, the band continued its White House engagements, played weekly concerts at the Marine Barracks as well as on the Capitol Plaza, took part in parades and celebrations, and began making annual concert tours of the United States. Requests had been coming in from every part of the country for the band to play at historical celebrations. Sousa finally asked President Benjamin Harrison for permission to take the band on tours. Presidential approval of the idea was prompt. Thus, in 1891, the first tour began; since then, the band has regularly made an annual fall tour. Sousa's showmanship, together with his musical and executive ability, were all instrumental in making the Marine Band popular from coast to coast. Meanwhile, Sousa himself had become interested in composing new marches. He wrote *Semper Fidelis*, which later was adopted as the official march of the Marine Corps. As it turned out, this march sparked the genius of the young composer. In the years that followed, march after march flowed from his prolific pen. Among the best known are *Stars and Stripes Forever, Washington Post, Liberty Bell, High School Cadets, Invincible Eagle, El Capitan, The Thunderer, Manhattan Beach, Yorktown Centennial, Hands Across the Sea, Man Behind the Gun, King Cotton, Bullets and Bayonets, Boy Scouts of America, Liberty Loan March, Naval Reserve March, Sabre and Spurs March,* and *On the Campus March.* On July 30, 1892, Sousa had resigned from the Marine Band to organize a band of his own. Later, during the Spanish-American War, Sousa tried to join the Marine Corps again, but there was no vacancy for a bandmaster. Undaunted, he joined the

Army. Illness, however, prevented him from serving a single day. When WWI came along, the same situation prevailed; this time Sousa joined the Navy. He was assigned to the Naval Training Station at Great Lakes, Ill., in the capacity of musical director. His rank: Lieutenant Commander, USNR. During that time he gave countless concerts in behalf of Liberty Loan Drives and served with the Navy until 1919. Years later, at the request of Marine Corps officers who had served in north China during the Boxer Rebellion, Sousa composed a march called *The Royal Welsh Fusiliers* to commemorate the Marines' association with that British regiment. In June, 1930, he was at Tidworth, England, when a "beautifully bound score of the march" was formally presented to the Royal Welsh Fusiliers (the oldest regiment in Wales) to perpetuate the regiment's friendship with the United States Marines. Sousa's last appearance before the Marine Band was on the occasion of the Carabao Wallow of 1932 at Washington. The band furnished the music for the big event. Sousa, as a distinguished guest, arose from the speakers' table, took the baton from Capt. Taylor Branson, then Leader of the Band, and led the musicians through the stirring strains of *Stars and Stripes Forever*. John Philip Sousa died on Mar. 6, 1932, at Reading, Pa., where he was scheduled to conduct the Ringgold Band the following day. His body was brought to his native Washington to lie in state in the band hall of the Marine Barracks, 8th and Eye Streets, S.E. Four days later, two companies of Marines and bluejackets, the Marine Band, and honorary pallbearers from the Army, Navy and Marine Corps headed the funeral cortege from the Marine Barracks to Congressional Cemetery.

SPROWLE, David. Orderly Sergeant. Medal of Honor: b. Lisbon, N.Y., 1811. David Sprowle enlisted in the Marine Corps on June 16, 1848 at Boston, Mass. His citation reads, in part: " . . . while serving on board the USS *Richmond*, Mobile Bay . . . commended for coolness and setting a good example to the Marine guard working a division of great guns in the action of Mobile Bay on the morning and forenoon of Aug. 5, 1864. . . ." He was discharged from the Corps on Dec. 1, 1866 at Washington, D.C.

STEIN, Tony. Corporal. Medal of Honor: b. Dayton, Ohio, Sept. 30, 1921; d. KIA, Iwo Jima, Mar. 1, 1945. Cpl. Stein's citation reads, in part: " . . . while serving with Co. A, 1st Bn., 28th Marines, 5th Mar. Div., in action against enemy Japanese forces on Iwo Jima, Feb. 19, 1945. The first man of his unit to be on station after hitting the beach in the initial assault, Cpl. Stein, armed with a personally improvised aircraft-type weapon, provided rapid covering fire as the remainder of his platoon attempted to move into position and, when his comrades were stalled by a concentrated machine gun and mortar barrage, gallantly stood upright and exposed himself to the enemy's view, thereby drawing the hostile fire to his own person and enabling him to observe the location of the furiously blazing hostile guns. Determined to neutralize the strategically placed weapons, he boldly charged the enemy pillboxes one by one and succeeded in killing 20 of the enemy during the furious singlehanded assault. Cool and courageous under the merciless hail of exploding shells and bullets which fell on all sides, he continued to deliver the fire of his skillfully improvised weapon at a tremendous rate of speed which rapidly exhausted his ammunition. Undaunted, he removed his helmet and shoes to expedite his movements and ran back to the beach for additional ammunition, making a total of eight trips under intense fire and carrying or assisting a wounded man back each time. He rendered prompt assistance to his platoon whenever the unit was in position, directing the fire of a half-track against a stubborn pillbox until he had effected the ultimate destruction of the Japanese fortification. Later in the day, although his weapon was twice shot from his hands, he personally covered the withdrawal of his platoon to the company position."

STEWART, James A. Sergeant. Medal of Honor: b. Philadelphia, Pa., 1839. James Stewart enlisted in the Marine Corps on Apr. 13, 1868. His citation reads, in part: "... while serving on board the USS *Plymouth,* jumped overboard in the harbor of Villefranche, France, Feb. 1, 1872, and saved Midshipman Osterhaus from drowning...." Stewart was discharged from the Corps on July 11, 1873.

STEWART, Joseph Lester. Brigadier General. CG, Force Troops, Fleet Marine Force, Pacific, and CG, Marine Corps Base, Twentynine Palms, Calif.: b. Newton, Ala., May 31, 1915. Joseph Stewart graduated from Butler County High School in Greenville, Ala., in 1933. He was awarded a Bachelor of Science degree on May 31, 1937, upon graduation from Alabama Polytechnic Institute and was an honor graduate of the ROTC course there. While in college he was a a three-letter athlete. He was commissioned a Marine second lieutenant on July 28, 1937. He completed Basic School at the Philadelphia Navy Yard in May 1938, then served for one year with the Marine Detachment aboard the USS

California. This was followed by assignments with the 1st Bn., 6th Marines, and the 2nd Bn., 10th Marines. In Sept. 1940, he was promoted to first lieutenant. He graduated from the Battery Officers' Course at Fort Sill, Okla., in May 1941, then returned to the 10th Marines. When WWII broke out, Lt. Stewart was deployed with the 2nd Mar. Brig. for Samoa as CO of B Battery, 1st Bn., 10th Marines, in Jan. 1942. He was promoted to captain in Feb. 1942, and remained overseas until Aug. In Oct. 1942, while attending the Field Officers' Course at Fort Sill, he was promoted to major. Later, he completed the Command and General Staff School at Fort Leavenworth, Kans. Ordered to Kiska, Alaska, in July 1943, he served on the Staff of the Amphibious Corps, Pacific Fleet, during the Aleutian campaign. From Sept. 1943 through Oct. 1945, he served in the Pacific area as Executive Officer, G-3 Section, 5th Amphibious Corps. He participated in combat at Kwajalein and Eniwetok in Jan. and Feb. 1944. Later, following his promotion to lieutenant colonel, he took part in the Saipan-Tinian and Iwo Jima campaigns, earning the Legion of Merit and the Bronze Star Medal, both with Combat "V." He also participated in the occupation of Japan, then returned to the States in Dec. 1945. Lt. Col. Stewart served as an instructor in the Senior Course, MCS, from Jan. 1946 through June 1949. In July 1949, he joined the 1st Mar. Div. at Camp Pendleton, Calif., serving as Assistant G-3, Commander of the 1st Bn., 5th Marines, and Division G-3, respectively, until June 1950. Upon the outbreak of the Korean War, he was ordered to Korea where he served with both the 1st Prov. Mar. Brig. and the 1st Mar. Div., as Brigade G-3 and later Division G-3. He participated in action at the Pusan Perimeter and in the assault and seizure of Inchon. Subsequently, as Executive Officer of the 5th Marines, he took part in the bitter Chosin Reservoir campaign in Nov. and Dec. 1950; and commanded the 3rd Bn., 5th Marines in the first United Nations counteroffensive early in 1951. The Silver Star Medal was awarded Lt. Col. Stewart for conspicuous gallantry as Executive Officer, 5th Marines, in Korea, Dec. 3, 1950, during his regiment's attack from Yudam-ni toward Hagaru-ri against elements of three enemy divisions. He was also awarded his second Legion of Merit and his second Bronze Star Medal, as well as an Air Medal for his service in Korea. Following his return from Korea in June 1951, he was assigned to HQ, FMF, Pacific, as Assistant G-3 and later G-3. He was promoted to colonel in Nov. 1951. In Aug. 1953, Col. Stewart began a three-year assignment at HQMC where he served consecutively as Assistant G-4 and Head of the G-4 Planning Branch. In Aug. 1956, he entered the National War College, Washington, D.C. Following graduation in June 1957, he assumed duty as Deputy Plans Director on the Staff of the Supreme Allied Commander, Atlantic (SACLANT), at Norfolk, Va. In Sept. 1958, he was named Assistant Chief of Staff, G-3, FMF, Atlantic. Col. Stewart departed from Norfolk for MCS, Quantico, in Aug. 1959. There he served as Director of the Senior School until May 1961, when he became Deputy Director of the Marine Corps Educational Center. He was promoted to his present grade of brigadier general in Aug. 1962. In Sept. 1962, Gen. Stewart became CG, Force Troops, FMF, Pacific, and CG, MCB, Twentynine Palms, Calif.

STEWART, Peter. First Sergeant. Medal of Honor: b. Airdrie, Scotland, Feb. 17, 1858; d. June 17, 1914. Peter Stewart enlisted in the Marine Corps at New York, N.Y. on Jan. 5, 1894. His citation reads, in part: " . . . for distinguished conduct in the presence of the enemy in battles on June 13, 20, 21 and 22, 1900, while with the relief expedition of the Allied Forces in China. . . ."

STOCKHAM, Fred William. Gunnery Sergeant. Medal of Honor (Army): b. Detroit, Mich., Mar. 16, 1881; d. Belleau Wood, France, June 22, 1918. Sgt. Stockham's citation reads, in part: " . . . with the 96th Co., 2nd Bn., 6th Regt. . . . in action with the enemy in Bois-de-Belleau, France, on the night of June 13-14, 1918. During an intense enemy bombardment with high explosive and gas shells which wounded or killed many members of the company, Sgt. Stockham, noticing that the gas mask of a wounded comrade was shot away, without hesitation, removed his own gas mask and insisted upon giving it to the wounded man, well knowing that the effects of the gas would be fatal to himself. Despite the fact that he was without protection of a gas mask, he continued with undaunted courage and valor to direct and assist in the evacuation of the wounded in an area saturated with gas and swept by heavy artillery fire, until he himself collapsed from the effects of gas, dying as a result thereof a few days later."

STREETER, Ruth Cheney. Colonel. First Director of the U.S. Marine Corps Women's Reserve: b. Brookline, Mass., Oct. 2, 1895. Ruth Streeter attended schools abroad and graduated from Bryn Mawr College at Bryn Mawr, Pa. in 1918. During the depression years following 1930, she worked in public health and welfare, unemployment relief, and old-age assistance in her home state of New Jersey. Long interested in aviation, she completed a course in aeronautics at New York University and served as adjutant of Group 221, Civil Air Patrol. She learned to fly in 1940 and in 1941 became the only woman member of the Committee on Aviation of the New Jersey Defense Council. The same year she also acted as chairman of the Citizens' Committee for Army and Navy, Inc. for Fort Dix, N.J. She received her commercial pilot's license in Apr. 1942. Col. Streeter was the first woman to hold the rank of major in the Marine Corps. She was appointed to that rank on Jan. 29, 1943. She was promoted to lieutenant colonel on Nov. 22, 1943, and then to the rank of colonel on Feb. 1, 1944. She left the Corps in Dec. 1945.

SULLIVAN, Edward. Private. Medal of Honor: b. Cork, Ireland, May 16, 1870; d. Boston, Mass., Mar. 14, 1955. Edward Sullivan enlisted in the Marine Corps at Boston, Mass., on July 23, 1896. He was awarded the Medal of Honor on Aug. 15, 1899 for extraordinary bravery and coolness while serving aboard the USS *Marblehead,* cutting cables leading from Cienfuegos, Cuba, May 11, 1898, under heavy fire of the enemy. He was discharged from the Corps at Newport, R.I., on July 30, 1901.

SUTTON, Clarence Edwin. Sergeant. Medal of Honor: b. Middlesex Co., Va., Feb. 18, 1871; d. Oct. 9, 1916. Clarence Sutton enlisted in the Marine Corps on

July 5, 1899. He was awarded the Medal of Honor "... for distinguished conduct in the presence of the enemy at the battle of Tientsin, China, July 13, 1900. Sutton carried a wounded officer from the field under a heavy fire. . . ." He was discharged from the Corps on Sept. 3, 1903.

SWETT, James Elms. Lieutenant Colonel. Medal of Honor: b. Seattle, Wash., June 15, 1920. Lt. Col. Swett's citation reads, in part: ". . . as a division leader in a Marine fighting squadron in action against enemy Japanese aerial forces in the Solomon Is. area, Apr. 7, 1943. In a daring flight to intercept a wave of 150 Japanese planes, 1st Lt. Swett unhesitatingly hurled his four-plane division into action against a formation of 15 enemy bombers and during his dive personally exploded 3 hostile planes in mid-air with accurate and deadly fire. Although separated from his division while clearing the heavy concentration of antiaircraft fire, he boldly attacked 6 enemy bombers, engaged the first 4 in turn, and unaided shot them down in flames. Exhausting his ammunition as he closed with the fifth Japanese bomber, he relentlessly drove his attack against terrific opposition which partially disabled his engine, shattered the windscreen and slashed his face. In spite of this, he brought his battered plane down with skillful precision in the water off Tulagi without further injury. . . ."

T

TALBOT, Ralph. Second Lieutenant. Medal of Honor: b. South Weymouth, Mass., Jan. 6, 1897; d. near the Belgian front, Oct. 25, 1918. Ralph Talbot enrolled on May 26, 1918, as a second lieutenant (provisional) in Class 5A, Marine Corps Reserve Flying Corps. On June 4, 1918, he was appointed a second lieutenant (provisional) in Class 5, by the Major General Commandant, with rank from Apr. 3, 1918. Upon enrollment he was assigned to active service with the First Marine Aviation Force, Miami, Fla. He was detached on July 12, 1918, to foreign shore expeditionary service in France. He sailed from the States July 17, 1918, aboard the USS *DeKalb,* arrived and disembarked at Brest, France, Aug. 1, 1918, and was assigned to duty with the Northern Bombing Group. He participated in numerous air raids into enemy territory while attached to Squadron C, and on Oct. 8, 1918, while on such a raid, he was attacked by nine enemy scouts. In the fight that followed, he shot down an enemy plane. On Oct. 14, 1918, while on a raid over Pittham, Belgium, Lt. Talbot and one other plane became detached from the formation on account of engine trouble, and were attacked by 12 enemy scouts. During the severe fight that followed, his plane shot down one of the enemy scouts. His observer was shot through the elbow and his gun jammed. He cleared the jam with one hand while Lt. Talbot maneuvered to gain time; then they returned to the fight. The observer fought until shot twice in the stomach and once in the hip. When he collapsed, Lt. Talbot attacked the nearest enemy scout with his front guns and shot him down. With his observer unconscious and his motor failing he dived to escape the rest of the enemy and crossed the German trenches at an altitude of 50 feet, landing at the nearest hospital and left his observer and returned to his aerodrome. For this feat Lt. Talbot was awarded the Navy Medal of Honor. On Oct. 25, 1918, while attached to the 9th Squadron, Day Wing, Northern Bombing Group, and while flying a DH-4 bombing plane, Talbot struck a hump. The plane capsized, caught fire, and Lt. Talbot was killed.

THARIN, Frank Cunningham. Major General. One of the defenders of Wake Is. at the outbreak of WWII. CG, 3rd Marine Aircraft Wing, Fleet Marine Force, Pacific, MCAS, El Toro (Santa Ana) Calif. (1963): b. Washington, D.C., Oct. 23, 1910. After graduation from Central High School in the nation's capital, Frank Tharin entered the U.S. Naval Academy in 1930. Upon graduation, May 31, 1934, he was appointed a Marine second lieutenant. After completing Basic School at the Philadelphia Navy Yard in June 1935, he saw a year of sea duty with the Marine Detachment aboard the USS *Northampton,* then entered flight school at the NAS, Pensacola, Fla. He was promoted to first lieutenant in July 1937, and that same month was designated a naval aviator. That Sept. Tharin reported for duty at the North Is. NAS, near San Diego, Calif., with Marine Fighter Squadron 2. In Nov. 1938, he was assigned duty under instruction at the Air Corps Technical School, Lowry Field, Denver, Colo. Returning to North Is. in Aug. 1939, he joined MAG 21. He was promoted to captain in July 1940.

Tharin

Early in 1941, he was transferred with his group to Ewa, Hawaii. There he was assigned to Marine Fighter Squadron 211 in Oct. 1941, and the following month moved with the squadron to Wake Is. He was one of the senior pilots on Wake in Dec. 1941 when the Japanese attacked the small Pacific island. During the initial attack, he was wounded by shrapnel, and in the bitter fighting that followed, he was credited with destroying and damaging several enemy aircraft, and assisting in the destruction of a large destroyer. His action during the defense of Wake earned him the Silver Star Medal, the Distinguished Flying Cross, two Air Medals, and the Purple Heart. Taken prisoner Dec. 23, 1941, he was interned for almost four years by the Japanese

in prison camps at Woosung, Kiangwan, Fengtai (China), Fusan (Korea), and Hokkaido (Japan). Liberated on Sept. 14, 1945, Capt. Tharin was flown to the States for hospitalization. He was promoted to major in Nov. 1945 with rank from May 1942, and to lieutenant colonel in January 1946 with rank from Oct. 1942. He then completed Instrument Flight Instructors' Course, Atlanta, Ga., and the Command and Staff Course, Quantico, Va. Leaving Quantico in Aug. 1946, he served at the MCAS, Cherry Point, N.C. for 18 months as Assistant G-3, 2nd MAW. Following this assignment, he assumed duty in the Division of Plans and Policies, HQMC, Washington, D.C., in Jan. 1948. He was promoted to colonel in Aug. 1949. Col. Tharin remained at HQMC until June 1950. Two months later, he assumed duty in Hawaii on the Staff of Commander in Chief, Pacific. On his return to the continental U.S. in Aug. 1952, he became CO of MAG 32, 3rd MAW, Miami, Fla. In July 1953, he entered the National War College and completed the course the following June. From June 1954 until June 1956, he served in the Office of the Joint Chiefs of Staff as a member of the Joint Strategic Plans Group. Ordered to the Far East, he saw duty as CO, MAG 11, 1st MAW, in Japan from July 1956 until June 1957, then served briefly as Chief of Staff, 1st MAW. In Sept. 1957, he became Chief of Staff, Aircraft, FMF, Atlantic, Norfolk, Va. Transferred to Cherry Point in July 1958, he was promoted to brigadier general and appointed Assistant Wing Commander, 2nd MAW. Gen. Tharin remained at Cherry Point four years, serving consecutively as: Assistant Wing Commander until Dec. 1959; CG of the 2nd Wing until Oct. 1960; and, finally, Commander, Marine Corps Air Bases, Eastern Area and CG, MCAS, until Sept. 1962. While there, he was promoted to major general in Aug. 1962. Assigned next to El Toro, Gen. Tharin assumed command of the 3rd MAW there in Oct. 1962.

THIES, Louis Fred. Private. Medal of Honor: b. Philadelphia, Pa., June 19, 1876. (Served first tour under assumed name of Thies, then reenlisted under real name of Pfeifer, Louis Fred.) Louis Thies enlisted in the Marine Corps at Brooklyn, N.Y. on Jan. 5, 1898. His citation reads, in part: ". . . while serving on board the USS *Petrel*, for heroism and gallantry, fearlessly exposing his own life to danger for the saving of the others on the occasion of the fire on board said vessel, Mar. 31, 1901. . . ." He was discharged from the Corps on Aug. 27, 1917.

THOMAS, Herbert Joseph. Sergeant. Medal of Honor: b. Columbus, Ohio, Feb. 8, 1918; d. KIA, Bougainville, Nov. 7, 1943. Sgt. Thomas' citation reads, in part: ". . . in action against enemy Japanese forces during the battle of Koromokina River, Bougainville Is., on Nov. 7, 1943. Although several of his men were struck by enemy bullets as he led his squad through dense jungle undergrowth in the face of severe hostile machine gun fire, Sgt. Thomas and his group fearlessly pressed forward into the center of the Japanese position and destroyed the crews of two machine guns by accurate rifle fire and grenades. Discovering a third gun more difficult to approach, he carefully placed his men closely around him in strategic positions from which they were to charge after he had thrown a grenade into the emplacement. When the grenade struck vines and fell back into the midst of the group, Sgt. Thomas deliberately flung himself upon it to

smother the explosion, valiantly sacrificing his life for his comrades. . . ."

THOMASON, Clyde. Sergeant. Medal of Honor: b. Atlanta, Ga., May 23, 1914; d. KIA, Makin Is., Aug. 18, 1942. Sgt. Thomason's citation reads, in part: ". . . during the Marine Raider Expedition against the Japanese-held island of Makin on Aug. 17-18, 1942. Leading the advance element of the assault echelon, Sgt. Thomason disposed his men with keen judgment and discrimination. On one occasion, he dauntlessly walked up to a house which concealed an enemy Japanese sniper, forced in the door, and shot the man before he could resist. Later in the action, while leading an assault on an enemy position, he gallantly gave up his life in the service of his country."

THOMPSON, Henry. Private. Medal of Honor: b. Philadelphia, Pa., 1833. Pvt. Thompson's citation reads, in part: ". . . while serving on board the USS *Minnesota*; especially commended for bravery in the assault on Fort Fisher, Jan. 15, 1865, remaining at the front near the fort when the panic carried the mass away. . . ."

TIMMERMAN, Grant Frederick. Sergeant. Medal of Honor: b. Americus, Kan., Feb. 19, 1919; d. KIA, Saipan, July 8, 1944. Sgt. Timmerman's citation reads, in part: ". . . as Tank Commander serving with the 2nd Bn., 6th Marines, 2nd Mar. Div., during action against enemy Japanese forces on Saipan, on July 8, 1944. Advancing with his tank a few yards ahead of the infantry in support of a vigorous attack on hostile positions, Sgt. Timmerman maintained steady fire from his antiaircraft sky mount machine gun until progress was impeded by a series of enemy trenches and pillboxes. Observing a target of opportunity, he immediately ordered the tank stopped and, mindful of the danger from the muzzle blast as he prepared to open fire with the 75mm., fearlessly stood up in the exposed turret and ordered the infantry to hit the deck. Quick to act as a grenade, hurled by the Japanese, was about to drop into the open turret hatch, Sgt. Timmerman unhesitatingly blocked the opening with his body, holding the grenade against his chest and taking the brunt of the explosion . . . saving his men at the cost of his own life. . . ."

TOMLIN, Andrew J. Corporal. Medal of Honor: b. Goshen, N.J., 1844. Andrew Tomlin enlisted in the Marine Corps at Philadelphia, Pa. on July 10, 1862. His citation reads, in part: " . . . while serving aboard the USS *Wabash*. During the assault on Fort Fisher, Jan. 15, 1865, he advanced under a heavy fire from the enemy's sharpshooters into an open space to the fort and assisted a wounded comrade to a place of safety. . . ."

TOMPKINS, Rathvon McClure. Brigadier General. Assistant Division Commander, 2nd Mar. Div., Fleet Marine Force, Camp Lejeune, N.C. (1963): b. Boulder, Colo., Aug. 23, 1912. Following completion of high school in South Kent, Conn., Rathvon Tompkins entered the University of Colorado from which he was graduated in 1935 with a Bachelor of Arts degree. At the university he boxed and played hockey and polo. He enlisted in the MCR, June 5, 1935, and was a member of the Western Platoon Leaders' Class, 1935 (Reserve), at the MCB, San Diego, Calif. July to Aug. 1935. He accepted appointment as a Marine Reserve second lieutenant Mar. 25, 1936. In Oct. 1939, he was assigned active duty and entered the Reserve Officers' Class, MCS, Quantico, Va. Upon completion of the

course that Nov., he joined the 2nd Bn., 6th Marines, 2nd Mar. Brig. He was promoted to first lieutenant in Feb. 1940. In May 1941, he sailed for Iceland with the 1st Prov. Mar. Brig. He was serving there when the U.S. entered WWII. He was promoted to captain in Jan. 1942. On his return to the States in Mar. 1942, Tompkins was assigned to the 6th Marines, 2nd Mar. Div., in San Diego. He was promoted to major in Aug. 1942. Maj. Tompkins was ordered overseas in Oct. 1942, and subsequently participated in combat in the capture and defense of Guadalcanal, the consolidation of the southern Solomons, the Gilbert Is. operation, and the Marianas operation. For heroic achievement on Guadalcanal as Regimental Operations Officer, 6th Marines (Reinf.), 2nd Mar. Div., from Jan. to Feb. 1943, he was awarded the Bronze Star Medal with Combat "V." Subsequently, during landing operations on Tarawa, he earned the Silver Star Medal for conspicuous gallantry in rescuing seven wounded Marines under continuous enemy fire, Nov. 20, 1943. He was promoted to lieutenant colonel in Dec. 1943. During the next six months he served as Operations Officer, Infantry, Assistant Division Commander Section, 2nd Mar. Div. Arriving on Saipan in June 1944, he took part in the action which earned him the Navy Cross as commander of the 1st Bn., 29th Marines, 2nd Mar. Div. On July 3 he was wounded by shrapnel on Saipan, and later evacuated to the States for hospitalization. Lt. Col. Tompkins served at HQMC, Division of Plans and Policies, from Mar. 1945 until Dec. 1946. In Jan. 1947, he reported to Naval Forces, Eastern Atlantic and Mediterranean, London, England, for duty under instruction as a student in the Joint Services Staff College. Following graduation, he was designated a Naval Observer in the Office of the U.S. Naval Attaché, London, and assigned duty as an instructor on the staff of the School of Combined Operations, in Aug. 1947. In Apr. 1948, he returned to the States, and assumed duty at MCS, Quantico, as Chief, Infantry Section, Amphibious Warfare School, Junior Course; and, later, Instructor, Tactical Operations Group, Combined Arms Section. He was promoted to colonel in Feb. 1951. In Aug. 1951, Col. Tompkins began a two-year tour of duty as a member of the War Plans Section, Joint Strategic Plans Group, Joint Staff, Office of the Joint Chiefs of Staff. Ordered to Korea in June 1953, he served with the 1st Mar. Div. as commander of the 5th Marines (Reinf.), and later as Assistant Chief of Staff, G-2. A Gold Star in lieu of a second Bronze Star Medal with Combat "V" was awarded him for meritorious achievement during the period July 24, 1953 to Apr. 18, 1954. He returned to the States in July 1954. He entered the Naval War College, Newport, R.I., in Aug. 1954. Upon completing the Senior Resident Course in Naval Warfare, he was assigned in June 1955 to the Staff of the Naval War College, and served subsequently as Assistant Head and Head, Strategy and Tactics Department, and Senior Marine, Staff, Naval War College. In July 1957, he was transferred to Camp Pendleton, where he commanded the 1st Service Bn. (Reinf.), 1st Mar. Div., until Dec. 1957, then served as the Division's Assistant Chief of Staff, G-3, until Mar. 1958. In Apr. 1958, Col. Tompkins arrived in the Far East for duty as Chief of Staff, 3rd Mar. Div., (Reinf.), in Okinawa. The following Apr. he became Assistant Division Commander, serving in this capacity until his detachment in June 1959. He joined the Personnel Department, HQMC,

in Aug. 1959, and remained there for three years. He served first as Head of the Military Personnel Procurement Branch until June 1960, when he became Assistant Director of Personnel. Shortly after assuming this post, he was promoted to brigadier general in July 1960. In Aug. 1962, Gen. Tompkins was detached from HQMC, and the following month assumed duty as Assistant Division Commander, 2nd Mar. Div., at Camp Lejeune.

TOWLE, Katherine A. Colonel. Director of Women Marines — Nov. 4, 1948 to May 1, 1953: b. Towle, Calif., Apr. 30, 1898. Katherine Towle was graduated from the University of California at Berkeley in May 1920. In addition she also studied at Columbia University in New York City. When called to active duty simultaneously with the receipt of her commission as captain in the U.S. Marine Corps Women's Reserve on Feb. 25, 1943, she was employed as Assistant to the Manager at the University of California. In early Mar. 1943, she was ordered directly from civil life to HQMC in Washington, D.C. Later that month she was ordered to the Marine Detachment, Naval Training School (Women Reserve), Hunter College, New York City as the senior woman officer of the detachment. In May of the same year she was detached from Hunter College, ordered to temporary duty in Washington, and in early June was assigned to the special staff of the CG, Camp Lejeune, New River, N.C. as Assistant for Women's Reserve, with the opening of the Women's Reserve Training Center there. While serving in that capacity in Feb. 1944, she was advanced to the rank of major. Her next duty assignment, beginning in Sept. 1944, was at HQMC as Assistant Director of the Marine Corps Women's Reserve. In Mar. 1945, she was promoted to lieutenant colonel, and with the resignation of the Director of the Women's Reserve, she became the second Director on Dec. 7, 1945. Her advancement to the rank of colonel came simultaneously with her appointment by Gen. A. A. Vandegrift, then CMC. On June 12, 1946, Col. Towle relinquished her position as Director of the Women's Reserve and returned to the University of California at Berkeley following her release from active service on Aug. 18, 1946. From that time until she reported to the CG, Department of Pacific, San Francisco for active duty on Sept. 23, 1948, she was assistant dean of women at that university. Col. Towle reported for duty at HQMC Oct. 18, 1948, and served as Director of Women Marines until her retirement on May 1, 1953.

TRUESDELL, Donald Leroy. Commissioned Warrant Officer. Medal of Honor: b. Lugoff, S.C., Aug. 26, 1906. Donald Truesdell enlisted in the Marine Corps in Nov. 1924. He earned the nation's highest award when, as a corporal in the Marines and a lieutenant in the Nicaraguan native army, he was second in command of a patrol pushing through that country's trackless forests on the trail of bandits. A rifle grenade fell from the pack of one member of the patrol, hitting a rock and the impact ignited the detonator of the grenade, threatening the safety of the entire patrol. Without hesitation, Cpl. Truesdell grabbed the missile and attempted to hurl it away. He was seconds late, and the grenade exploded while still in his grasp, blowing off his hand and inflicting multiple wounds in his body. For his heroism he was awarded the Medal of Honor and also the Nicaraguan Cross of Valor by that government. The citation accompanying Cpl. Truesdell's award stated

that he "could easily have sought cover and safety for himself," being several yards away but he chose to try and save the patrol at the risk of his own life. Although he had lost an arm, officer Truesdell continued to serve with the Marine Corps until his retirement as a Commissioned Warrant Officer in May 1946.

TWINING, Merrill Barber. General (Retired): b. Monroe, Wis., Nov. 28, 1902. Merrill Twining was commissioned a Marine second lieutenant upon graduation from the U.S. Naval Academy, June 7, 1923. During the next two years, he completed the Marine Officers' Basic School; served at Quantico; participated in Caribbean maneuvers with the 10th Marines; and was stationed at the MB, Pensacola, Fla. Lt. Twining was ordered to the MB at Pearl Harbor in Nov. 1925, and after six months in Hawaii he sailed for China via the Philippine Is. In China he served with the 4th and 12th Mar. Regts. at Shanghai, Taku, Hsin Ho, Tientsin, and Peking. He returned to the States in Aug. 1928. Twining was promoted to first lieutenant in Dec. 1928 while serving as Commander of the MB at the Pacific Coast Torpedo Station, Keyport, Wash. He then served briefly as Editor and Publisher of *Leatherneck* Magazine in Washington, D.C. In Sept. 1929, Lt. Twining was assigned to the Office of the Judge Advocate General of the Navy. While stationed there, he obtained his Bachelor of Laws degree from George Washington University in 1932. He reported again to the MB at Pearl Harbor in Nov. 1932, remaining there until Jan. 1935. In Mar. 1935, while attached to the MB at the NAS, Sunnyvale, Calif., he earned the Distinguished Pistol Shot's Gold Badge in the Western Division Rifle and and Pistol Matches at San

Diego, Calif. He was promoted to captain in May 1935. From July 1935 to Aug. 1936, Capt. Twining was a student in the Army Infantry School, Fort Benning, Ga. During the next year he served at Philadelphia as an instructor in the Marine Officers' Basic School. Moving to Quantico in June 1937, he served as a company commander with the 5th Marines, and two years later became an instructor in the Marine Corps Schools. He also participated in Caribbean maneuvers in 1938 and 1939. He was promoted to major in July 1939. In Nov. 1941, Maj. Twining joined the 1st Mar. Div. at Camp Lejeune, N.C. He was promoted to lieutenant colonel in Jan. 1942 and moved with his division to the Pacific area in May 1942. He earned his first Legion of Merit with Combat "V" for meritorious service from June 25 to Dec. 10, 1942 as the Division's Assistant Operations Officer and, later, Assistant Chief of Staff, G-3. In that capacity, he helped prepare and execute plans for the Guadalcanal campaign. During the planning phase, Lt. Col. Twining and Maj. William B. McKean were flown over the then-Japanese-held island on July 17, 1942 for the first sighting of Guadalcanal by U.S. Marines in WWII. Following the Guadalcanal campaign, he served as Assistant Chief of Staff, G-3, of the 1st Mar. Amphibious Corps, then commanded by Gen. Alexander A. Vandegrift. Returning to the States in Nov. 1943, Lt. Col. Twining remained until 1947 at the MCS, Quantico. While there, he served successively as Chief of Operations and Training, Executive Officer, and as a member of the Schools' Administrative Staff. He was promoted to colonel in Feb. 1945. In Aug. 1947, Col. Twining reported to Pearl Harbor as Chief of Staff, FMF, Pacific. The following June, he was named Fleet Marine

Officer on the Staff of the Commander-in-Chief, Pacific Fleet. He served in that capacity until July 1949, when he returned to the MCS as Senior Resident Member of the Marine Corps Board. In Aug. 1950, he reported to Camp Pendleton and the following month was promoted to brigadier general. He served there as CG, Marine Corps Training and Replacement Command until Nov. 1951, and later as Commander of FMF Troops and CG, 3rd Mar. Div. Upon leaving Camp Pendleton, Gen. Twining joined the 1st Mar. Div. in Korea in Mar. 1952. He returned to the States that June, and subsequently served in the Office of the CMC. He was promoted to major general in Sept. 1952. In Jan. 1954, he was named Deputy Chief of Staff at HQMC. Gen. Twining returned to Korea in Jan. 1955 as Commander of the 1st Mar. Div. In Mar. of that year, he accompanied the division to Camp Pendleton, where he served until Aug. 1956. In Sept. 1956, he was promoted to lieutenant general and assumed duties as Commandant, MCS, Quantico, the 25th Marine officer to head the Schools. He served in that capacity until his retirement on Oct. 31, 1959.

TYLER, Paul Robert. Brigadier General. Serving with the Defense Supply Agency, Department of Defense, Washington, D.C.: b. Rochester, N.Y., Aug. 13, 1913. After graduation from high school at Kenmore, N.Y., in 1930, he attended Canisius College at Buffalo prior to his appointment to the Naval Academy in 1932. Upon graduation, he was commissioned a Marine second lieutenant, June 4, 1936. During the next year, he served at the MB, Parris Is., S.C., then attended Basic School at the Philadelphia Navy Yard. Following this, he served with the Marine Detachment at the U.S. Naval Prison,

Portsmouth, N.H. until June 1938, when he joined the 5th Marines, 1st Mar. Brig., FMF, at Quantico. In June 1939, he was promoted to first lieutenant. That Sept., Tyler entered the Signal Corps School, Fort Monmouth, N.J., completing the course in Feb. 1940. He then returned to Quantico as Regimental Communications Officer of the 5th Marines, and subsequently took part in fleet exercises in the Caribbean area. In Sept. 1941, he was transferred to New River (later Camp Lejeune), N.C., as Assistant Communications Officer with the 1st Mar. Div. He was promoted to captain in Oct. 1941, and was serving in this capacity when the U.S. entered WWII. In Apr. 1942, he joined the 3rd Mar. Brig., FMF, as Brigade Communications Officer, and in May arrived with his unit for duty in western Samoa. While stationed there, he was promoted to major in Aug. 1942. On his return to the States in July 1943, he served in the Signal Supply Division, Quartermaster Department, HQMC, Washington, D.C., with temporary duty at the supply depots in Philadelphia and San Francisco. He was promoted to lieutenant colonel in Dec. 1943. In Mar. 1944, Lt. Col. Tyler was transferred to the San Francisco Depot of Supplies as Officer in Charge of the Signal Supply Division. In Apr. 1945, while assigned to FMF, Pacific, he began two years' duty overseas, serving consecutively as Signal Officer, U.S. Marine Corps Section, Army Forces, Western Pacific; and as Regimental Executive Officer and Regimental Supply Officer, 7th Service Regt., Signal Corps, at Manila in the Philippines, and Tientsin, China. Ordered to Washington, D.C., in Apr. 1947, he served briefly in the Office of the Chief of Naval Operations until Sept. 1947, when he became Officer in Charge of the Electronics Supply Division, Marine Corps Supply Depot, Camp Lejeune. He returned to Washington in Aug. 1949 for duty with the Electronics Divisions, Bureau of Ships, Navy Department; and in Nov. 1950, became Marine Corps Liaison Officer, Planning and Coordination Division, Office of Naval Materiel, Navy Department. During this assignment, he was promoted to colonel in Feb. 1951. In Aug. 1952, Col. Tyler entered the Armed Forces Industrial College, completing the course the following June. Ordered overseas, he arrived in Korea in Aug. 1953 as Division Supply Officer, 1st Mar. Div. (Reinf.), subsequently becoming CO of the 1st Service Bn. in Apr. 1954. Following his return from Korea in June 1954, he was assigned to the MCSC, Barstow, Calif., where he served as Head of the Supply Branch and Chief of Staff. In Oct. 1955, he was named Executive Officer of the Marine Corps Supply Forwarding Annex in San Francisco, and in Feb. 1956 became CO of the Annex. He returned to HQMC in July 1957 to serve as Head of the Supply Management Branch, Materiel Division. In Aug. 1958, he was promoted to brigadier general and assumed duties as Director of the Materiel Division. In Apr. 1959, Gen. Tyler became Assistant Quartermaster General of the Marine Corps, and in Aug. 1959 was named CG, Marine Corps Supply Activity, Philadelphia, Pa. He served in the latter capacity until Jan. 1962 when he assumed his current assignment with the Defense Supply Agency.

U

UPHAM, Oscar J. Private. Medal of Honor: b. Toledo, Ohio, Jan. 14, 1871; d. Guthrie, Okla., Feb. 19, 1949. Oscar Upham enlisted in the Marine Corps at the age of 25, shortly before the war with Spain. After a year of duty at Mare Is., Calif., he was ordered to sea duty aboard the USS *Oregon.* He was a powder monkey for a six-inch gun on the *Oregon*'s bridge during the Spanish-American War, when the Spanish fleet tried to escape from the harbor at Santiago, Cuba, on July 3, 1898. During the Boxer Rebellion in 1900, Pvt. Upham and his fellow Marines were erecting barricades in Peking, China, when the Chinese rebels surrounded the group and settled down for a three-month siege. A quotation from his diary, kept during the siege, reads: "We are holding out no hope for rescue and many do not give rescue a second thought." He was awarded the Medal of Honor for this action — one of 33 Marines to win that award during the rebellion.

UPSHUR, William Peterkin. Major General. Medal of Honor: b. Richmond, Va., Oct. 28, 1881; d. Sitka, Alaska, Aug. 18, 1943. William Upshur was graduated from the Virginia Military Institute in 1902. He was appointed a second lieutenant in the Marine Corps on Feb. 1, 1904, and subsequently served on the high seas aboard naval vessels at foreign stations throughout the world, and at various posts and stations in the States. His foreign shore duty included service with an expeditionary force to Havana, Cuba, in Oct. 1906, and duty at Camp Evans, Deer Point, Guantanamo, Cuba from Jan. 9 to Feb. 8, 1907. He again was detailed to

Upshur

expeditionary duty with a force of Marines on the Isthmus of Panama from June 19 to Aug. 8, 1908. Arriving at Olongapo, Philippine Is. in Jan. 1912, he joined the 1st Brig. Marines and was again detached in Feb. 1914, this time to the Marine Detachment, American Legation, Peking, China, where he served until Oct. 16, 1914. On Aug. 4, 1915, he assumed command of the 15th Co., 2nd Regt., Port au Prince, Haiti, where he participated in engagements against hostile Cacos bandits. It was during this action that he was awarded the Medal of

Honor. Other decorations for service in Haiti include the Haitian Campaign Medal and Marine Corps Expeditionary Medal. Upon the United States' entry into WWI, Gen. Upshur was again detailed for foreign shore duty, this time with the 13th Regt. Marines in France from Sept. 1918 to Aug. 1919, during which time he was in command of the American Military Prison, Casino des Lilas, Bordeaux, and the American Guard Camp, also Guards of American and French docks, Bassens from Feb. 1919 to May of the same year. He was on temporary duty at the Naval Station, St. Thomas, Virgin Is. in July and Aug. 1921. He also served in Haiti for a period of two years with the 1st Brig. Marines, from 1922-24. In Jan. and Mar., 1929 he was on temporary duty as Chief Umpire, Fleet Training Exercise No. 5, Culebra, Puerto Rico, and again in Jan., Feb., and Mar. 1940. In Sept. 1939 he was assigned to the MCB, San Diego, Calif. In addition to his foreign shore stations he served aboard the USS *Maine*, USS *Kearsarge*, USS *Rainbow*, USS *Buffalo*, and the USS *California*. During his career he also served as Commandant of the MCS at MB, Quantico, Va.; Director of the Marine Corps Reserve; with the War Plans Division, Office of the Chief of Naval Operations, Navy Department; and as CG of the MCB at San Diego. He was a graduate of the Marine Corps School of Application, the Army Command and General Staff School, Fort Leavenworth, Kans. and of the Army and Navy War Colleges. The general's last station of duty was with the Department of the Pacific, where he served as CG with headquarters in San Francisco, Calif. from Jan. 1, 1942 until the time of his death. The general died in an airplane crash near Sitka, Alaska, on Aug. 18, 1943, while on an inspection tour of his command which included Alaska and the Hawaiian Islands.

V

VANDEGRIFT, Alexander Archer. General (Retired). 18th Commandant of the Marine Corps — Jan. 1, 1944 to Jan. 1, 1948. Commanded the 1st Marine Amphibious Corps in the landing at Empress Augusta Bay, Bougainville, and the 1st Mar. Div. (Reinf.), in the battle for Guadalcanal during WWII. For outstanding services as CG of the 1st Mar. Div., (Reinf.), during the attack on Guadalcanal, Tulagi, and Gavutu in the Solomon Is. on Aug. 7, 1942, was awarded the Navy Cross; and for the subsequent occupation and defense from Aug. 7 to Dec. 9, 1942, awarded the Medal of Honor: b. Charlottesville, Va., Mar. 13, 1887. Alexander Vandegrift attended the University of Virginia and was commissioned in the Marine Corps as a second lieutenant on Jan. 22, 1909. Following instruction at the Marine Officers' School, Port Royal, S.C., and a tour of duty at the MB, Portsmouth, N.H., he went to foreign shore duty in the Caribbean area where he participated in the bombardment, assault, and capture of Coyotepe in Nicaragua. He further participated in the engagement and occupation of Vera Cruz, Mexico. In Dec. 1914, Vandegrift attended the Advance Base Course at

Vandegrift

where he became Assistant Chief Co-ordinator, Bureau of the Budget. Following duty in Washington, he joined the MB, Quantico, where he became Assistant Chief of Staff, G-1 Section, FMF, in which post he remained until ordered to China in June 1935. Here he was successively Executive Officer and CO of the Marine Detachment at the American Embassy in Peiping. He reported to HQMC, Washington, D.C., in June 1937, where he became Military Secretary to the Major General Commandant. In Mar. 1940, he was appointed Assistant to the Major General Commandant, in which position he remained until Nov. 1941, when he was detached to the 1st Mar. Div. Gen. Vandegrift sailed with the division as CG in May 1942 for the south Pacific, where on Aug. 7, 1942, in the Solomon Is., he led ashore the 1st Mar. Div. (Reinf.), in the first large scale offensive action against the Japanese. In July 1943, he assumed command of the 1st Mar. Amphibious Corps and commanded this organization in the landing at Empress Augusta Bay, Bougainville, northern Solomon Is., on Nov. 1, 1943. Upon establishing the initial beachhead, he relinquished command and returned to HQMC, where on Jan. 1, 1944 he became Commandant of the Marine Corps. His first gigantic task was the chore of building the Marine Corps to meet the demands of the two years to follow. Under "Archie" Vandegrift's cool, tenacious direction the Corps was increased by another 125,000 men. At war's end Gen. Vandegrift was faced with the twin tasks of demobilization and the establishment of the Marine Corps on a permanent, post-war basis commensurate with the needs and demands which might arise in the future. Gen. Vandegrift left active service on Dec. 31, 1947. He was placed on the retired list Apr. 1, 1949.

the MB, Philadelphia. Upon completion of schooling, he sailed for Haiti with the 1st Brig. and participated in action against hostile Cacos bandits at Le Trou and Fort Capois. In Aug. 1916, he became a member of the Haitian Constabulary, Port au Prince, where he remained until detached to the States in Dec. 1918. He returned to Haiti again in July 1919 to serve with the Gendarmerie d' Haiti as an Inspector of Constabulary. He returned to the States in Apr. 1923, and was assigned to the MB at Quantico. He completed the Field Officers' Course, MCS, in May 1926, after which he went to the MCB, San Diego, Calif. as Assistant Chief of Staff. In Feb. 1927, he sailed for China where he served as Operations and Training Officer of the 3rd Mar. Brig. with HQ at Tientsin. He was ordered to Washington, D.C., in Sept. 1928,

VAN RYZIN, William John. Brigadier General. Chief of Staff for the Commander in Chief, U.S. Naval Forces, Eastern Atlantic and Mediterranean (CINCNELM), London, England: b. Appleton, Wis., Apr. 20, 1914. After graduation from high school in 1931, William Van Ryzin entered the University of Wisconsin. There he completed four years of service in the ROTC unit and was commissioned a Marine second lieutenant on July 8, 1935. After attending Basic School at the Philadelphia Navy Yard, he embarked for China in May 1936 for duty with the Marine Detachment at the American Embassy, Peiping. While in China, he was promoted to first lieutenant in Aug. 1938. In Feb. 1939, he was ordered to the MCB, San Diego, Calif., and from Nov. 1939 to Aug. 1940 served with the 1st Defense Bn. there. Assigned temporary duty at the Coast Artillery School, Fort Monroe, Va., Van Ryzin completed the Antiaircraft Artillery Course in Dec. 1940. He rejoined the 1st Defense Bn. in Jan. 1941 for duty at Pearl Harbor, Hawaii. He was promoted to captain in May 1941. That Oct. he was named CO of the Marine Detachment, 1st Defense Bn., Palmyra Is. He was serving in this capacity when the Japanese attacked Pearl Harbor on Dec. 7. For meritorious achievement in this assignment and, later, as Commander of the 3-inch Antiaircraft Artillery Group on Palmyra, from Dec. 7, 1941 to July 1942, he was awarded the Bronze Star Medal with Combat "V." He was promoted to major in May 1942. On his return to Pearl Harbor in July 1942, Maj. Van Ryzin was assigned to Marine Forces, 14th Naval District. In May 1943, he was ordered to the MCB, Camp Lejeune, N.C. The following month he was promoted to lieutenant colonel. In July 1943, as Commander of the 18th Antiaircraft Bn., Lt.

Col. Van Ryzin again embarked for the Pacific area. While serving in that capacity, he participated in the occupation and defense of Tinian. In Apr. 1945, he joined the 3rd Mar. Div., 12th Marines, and served consecutively as a battalion commander, as Regimental Executive Officer, and as the division's Assistant Chief of Staff, G-1. From Feb. to Aug. 1946, he was attached to the 1st Mar. Div., 11th Marines, as a battalion commander, and took part in the occupation of northern China. Ordered to HQMC in Sept. 1946, he served almost three years as Executive Officer, Division of Plans and Policies, G-1 Section (Personnel). In June 1949, he was assigned to MCS, Quantico, as a student in the Senior Course. After graduating the following June, he joined the Staff of Commander Amphibious Force, U.S. Atlantic Fleet, as Assistant Chief of Staff, Military Operations. He was promoted to colonel in Jan. 1951. He returned to MCS, Quantico, in Aug. 1952, and remained there three years, serving successsively as Chief, Supporting Arms Section, Tactics and Techniques Board; as a member of the Advanced Research Group; and as Chief, Advanced Base Problem Section, Marine Corps Educational Center. In Aug. 1955, he reported overseas as Chief of Staff of the 3rd Mar. Div. (Reinf.), FMF, on Okinawa. Departing Okinawa the following summer, Col. Van Ryzin assumed duty at HQ, United Nations and Far East Command, Japan, in late June 1956, serving as Chief, Operations Branch, J-3 Division until Aug. 1957. On his return to the States, he reported to HQMC, Washington, D.C. in Sept., as Director of the Policy Analysis Division. In Dec. 1957, he became Secretary of the General Staff. While serving in this capacity, he was promoted to brigadier general in Feb. 1959. In Mar. 1959, Gen.

Van Ryzin was named Deputy Assistant Chief of Staff, G-3, at HQMC. He departed Washington in July 1960 and late that month, on his arrival in London, assumed his current duties as Chief of Staff, CINCNELM.

VAN STOCKUM, Ronald Reginald. Brigadier General. Director of the Marine Corps Reserve, HQMC, Washington, D.C.: b. in England, July 8, 1916. Ronald Van Stockum grew up in the state of Washington. He graduated from high school in Yakima, Wash. and, in June 1937, he was awarded a Bachelor of Arts degree in economics upon graduation from the University of Washington, where he had been a member of the Army ROTC unit for four years. He was commissioned a Marine second lieutenant on Aug. 4, 1937, and entered the Marine Officers' Basic School at the Philadelphia Navy Yard. After completing the course, he was assigned his first tour of sea duty with the Marine Detachment aboard the USS *Tennessee* from June 1938 until May 1939. He then served with the 1st and 3rd Bns., 6th Marines, at the MCB, San Diego, until Dec. 1940. During this tour of duty, he was promoted to first lieutenant. In Jan. 1941, he joined the Marine Detachment aboard the USS *Wasp*, where he was serving when WWII broke out. Upon his promotion to captain in Feb. 1942, he was named CO of the *Wasp*'s Marine Detachment. During this period the *Wasp* made two trips into the Mediterranean area with British Spitfires for the relief of Malta. In July 1942, Van Stockum was transferred to the 1st Bn., 21st Marines (later part of the 3rd Mar. Div.). He was promoted to major in Aug. 1942, and in Feb. 1943 embarked for the Pacific area. Maj. Van Stockum was awarded the Bronze Star Medal with Combat "V" for his service as Infantry

Weapons CO with the 1st Bn., 21st Marines, during the occupation and defense of Cape Torokina, Bougainville. He was promoted to lieutenant colonel in May 1944, and during the succeeding months served as Battalion Executive Officer in the Guam campaign. In Sept. 1944, he assumed command of the 1st Bn., 3rd Marines, which was in floating reserve off Iwo Jima during that operation. On his return to the States in Apr. 1945, he served briefly at Camp Pendleton, Calif., then was an instructor with the Troop Training Unit, Amphibious Force, Pacific, in San Diego, for 18 months. From Jan. 1947 until June 1948, he was Inspector-Instructor, 4th Infantry Bn., MCR, Minneapolis, Minn. From July 1948 until Aug. 1949, he held that same post with the 1st Infantry Bn., MCR, New York City. Next he completed the Senior Course at MCS, Quantico, in June 1950. He was then assigned to the Staff of the Commander, Amphibious Group 2, on board the USS *Mt. Olympus*, where he served in the Operations and Training Section. It was during this period, while the flagship was in the Navy Yard, that he attended the Army Arctic Indoctrination School in Alaska. Also during this period, Commander, Amphibious Group 2 and the staff participated in Operation Blue Jay above the Arctic Circle, at Thule, Greenland. He was promoted to colonel in Jan. 1952, and was detached from the *Mt. Olympus* in July 1952. Col. Van Stockum then completed a two-year tour of duty as CO of the MB and District Marine Officer at the Naval Training Center, Great Lakes, Ill. In Aug. 1954, he became Assistant Chief of Staff, G-2, 3rd Mar. Div. and Prov. Corps, then in Japan. From June 1955 until July 1957, he served as HQ Commandant for the Commander in Chief, Far East and United Nations Commands in Tokyo. On his return from the Far East in Aug. 1957, Col. Van Stockum entered the Canadian National Defence College at Fort Frontenac, Kingston, Ont., the first U.S. Marine to receive this assignment. Upon graduation in July 1958, he reported to the 2nd Mar. Div., Camp Lejeune, N.C., where he served consecutively as Deputy Chief of Staff, Regimental Commander of the 8th Marines, Division Inspector, and Chief of Staff, until June 1961. In July 1961, he became Director of the 4th Marine Corps Reserve and Recruitment District with headquarters in Philadelphia. He served in this capacity until June 1962, when he assumed his present assignment as Director of the Marine Corps Reserve at HQMC, and on July 1, 1962 was promoted to the grade of brigadier general.

VAN WINKLE, Archie. Second Lieutenant. Medal of Honor: b. Juneau, Alaska, Mar. 17, 1925. Archie Van Winkle entered the University of Washington to study physical education, but left after a few months to enlist in the MCR on Dec. 14, 1942. During almost three years of active duty, he served as an aviation radioman-gunner and mechanic, participating in the Solomons, Philippines, and Emirau operations. On Oct. 22, 1945, he was discharged. He continued his studies in physical education for two years at Everett Junior College and for another year at the University of Washington. In Mar. 1948, he rejoined the Reserve and became a member of A Co., 11th Infantry Bn. at Seattle. On Aug. 7, 1950 the battalion was mobilized and ordered to Camp Pendleton, Calif. for training. Van Winkle, then a staff sergeant, arrived in Korea late that month and participated in the Inchon landing. He was cited for gallantry in action near Sudong, Korea on Nov. 2, 1950. His citation reads, in

part: "... immediately rallying the men in his area after a fanatical and numerically superior enemy force penetrated the center of the line under cover of darkness and pinned down the platoon with a devastating barrage of deadly automatic weapons and grenade fire, S. Sgt. Van Winkle boldly spearheaded a determined attack through withering fire against hostile frontal positions and, though he and all the others who charged with him were wounded, succeeded in enabling his platoon to gain the fire superiority and the opportunity to reorganize. Realizing that the left-flank squad was isolated from the rest of the unit, he rushed through 40 yards of fierce enemy fire to reunite his troops despite an elbow wound which rendered one of his arms totally useless. Severely wounded a second time when a direct hit in the chest from a hostile hand grenade caused serious and painful wounds, he staunchly refused evacuation and continued to shout orders and words of encouragement to his depleted and battered platoon. Finally carried from his position unconscious from shock and loss of blood, S. Sgt. Van Winkle served to inspire all who observed him to heroic efforts in successfully repulsing the enemy attack...." Evacuated to Japan and later to the States, he served for several months with the Marine guards at the Bremerton (Wash.) Naval Base before his release from active duty on July 16, 1951.

VAUGHN, Pinkerton R. Sergeant. Medal of Honor: b. Downington, Pa., 1839. Pinkerton Vaughn enlisted in the Marine Corps at Philadelphia, Pa. on Oct. 31, 1860. His citation reads, in part: "... while serving aboard the USS *Mississippi*, in the attack on the Port Hudson batteries, night of Mar. 14, 1863; commended for zeal and courage displayed in the performance of unusual and trying service while the vessel was aground and exposed to a heavy fire. . . ." Vaughn was discharged from the Corps at Philadelphia, Pa. on Nov. 7, 1864.

VITTORI, Joseph. Corporal. Medal of Honor: b. Beverly, Mass., Aug. 1, 1929; d. KIA, near Songnae-dong, Korea, Sept. 16, 1951. Cpl. Vittori was cited for action which occurred on Hill 749 where his company was engaged in an assault on well-entrenched Chinese Communist positions. A vicious enemy counterattack drove back a forward platoon with heavy casualties, and Cpl. Vittori, with two other volunteers from his reserve platoon, plunged into hand-to-hand combat in the midst of the swarming enemy soldiers to give the Marine company time to con-

solidate its positions. Later, when a call went up for an automatic rifleman to defend an isolated heavy machine gun position on the flank of his company's sector, Cpl. Vittori again volunteered. With heavy casualties leaving a 100-yard gap in the Marine lines at the position, he fought a singlehanded battle to prevent an enemy breakthrough. Leaping from one side of the position to the other, he kept up a withering fire of over 1000 rounds in three hours. He made repeated trips through heavy shellfire to replenish his ammunition, manned a machine gun after its gunner fell, and despite enemy penetration to within feet of his position, kept the enemy out of the breach in his company's lines until he was mortally wounded.

W

WADE, Sidney Scott. Major General. CG, Marine Corps Recruit Depot, San Diego, Calif.: b. Bloomington, Ill., Sept. 30, 1909. Sidney Wade graduated from high school in Bloomington and, following enlisted service in the Marine Corps from May 1928 to July 1929, he was appointed to the U.S. Naval Academy. Upon graduation, he was commissioned a Marine second lieutenant, June 1, 1933. After completing Basic School at the Philadelphia Navy Yard in June 1934, he saw duty at sea aboard the USS *Pennsylvania* and the USS *Salt Lake City* until June 1935, prior to embarking for duty in China with the 4th Marines. In China he was promoted to first lieutenant in June 1936. Shortly after his return to the States in Oct. 1937, he was ordered to the NAS,

Pensacola, Fla., serving at the MB until June 1939, when he reported to MCS, Quantico. He was promoted to captain in Aug. 1939. Capt. Wade completed the Junior Course at MCS in May 1940, then served two years on board the USS *Louisville* as CO of the Marine Detachment. With the outbreak of WWII, he saw action during the latter assignment in the raid on the Gilbert-Marshall Is., and in the New Guinea, Bismarck, and Solomon Is. area. He was promoted to major in May 1942. That month Maj. Wade joined the Amphibious Corps, Pacific Fleet, at the MCB, San Diego, Calif. While attached to that organization, he completed a course of instruction at the Command and General Staff School, Fort Leavenworth, Kans. in Nov.

1942. In Dec. 1942, he reported for duty with the 1st Mar. Amphibious Corps and embarked for the Pacific area, where the 1st Corps was subsequently redesignated the 3rd Amphibious Corps. He was promoted to lieutenant colonel in Apr. 1943. For outstanding service as Assistant Chief of Staff, G-2 and Assistant G-2 on the Staff of the 3rd Amphibious Corps, FMF, during the planning and execution of the Bougainville, Emirau, Guam, Palau, and Okinawa operations, from Dec. 1942 through May 1945, he was awarded his first Legion of Merit with Combat "V." On his return to the States in June 1945, Lt. Col. Wade served briefly at the Marine Training and Replacement Command, San Diego. That Oct. he was assigned to MCS, Quantico, serving there until Aug. 1947, when he was ordered to Washington, D.C., as one of the original members of the Joint Logistics Plans Group, Joint Chiefs of Staff. He was promoted to colonel in Aug. 1949. In Aug. of the following year, he was again ordered overseas and on his arrival at Pearl Harbor, Hawaii, assumed duty as Assistant Chief of Staff, G-2, FMF, Pacific. From Hawaii he was ordered to Korea in Oct. 1951. In Korea he earned a second Legion of Merit with Combat "V" and an Air Medal for outstanding service as CO, 1st Marines, 1st Mar. Div. He returned to the States in May 1952. Col. Wade entered the National War College, Washington, D.C., in Aug. 1952. In Aug. 1953, after completing the course, he reported to HQMC as Head, Plans Branch, G-3 Division. Transferred from Washington to MCS, Quantico, in July 1955, he served as Senior Member, Advanced Research Group, until June 1956. At that time, he was assigned a year's duty in the Office of the Chief of Naval Operations, Washington, D.C. He was promoted to brigadier general in May 1957. Subsequently

ordered to Camp Lejeune, N.C., Gen. Wade assumed duty as CG, Force Troops, FMF, Atlantic, in June 1957. On Jan. 10, 1958, he assumed command of the 2nd Prov. Mar. Force, FMF, Atlantic, and on May 14 departed for the Mediterranean area. At the request of the government of Lebanon, the first units of the 2nd Prov. Mar. Force under his command went ashore at Beirut on July 15. He remained in command of all Marine Forces in Lebanon during the entire operation. Gen. Wade departed from Lebanon Oct. 4 with the 2nd Prov. Mar. Force headquarters staff and returned to Camp Lejeune. There he assumed his duties as Assistant Commander of the 2nd Mar. Div., having been named to this assignment July 15, 1958, while still in the Middle East. On May 22, 1959, he was awarded the Distinguished Service Medal for exceptionally meritorious service as CG, 2nd Prov. Mar. Force, American Land Forces, Middle East, during the Lebanon operation. In July 1959, Gen. Wade assumed duties as CG, MCB, Camp Lejeune. While serving in this capacity, he was promoted to his present rank of major general in July 1960. Following a 15-month tour of duty, Gen. Wade relinquished command of the MCB, Camp Lejeune, in Oct. 1960, and reported as Assistant Chief of Staff, G-3, HQMC. In Sept. 1961, he was assigned to the Pentagon as Marine Corps Liaison Officer to the Vice Chief of Naval Operations. He served in this capacity until Feb. 1962, when he assumed his current assignment as CG, Marine Corps Recruit Depot, San Diego.

WALKER, Edward Alexander. Sergeant. Medal of Honor: b. Huntley, Scotland, Oct. 2, 1864; d. July 1948. Edward Walker enlisted in the Marine Corps at Brooklyn, N.Y. on Oct. 30, 1896. His citation reads, in part: "... for distinguished conduct in the presence of the enemy at the battle of Peking, China, June 20 to July 16, 1900. ..." Walker was discharged from the Corps at Bremerton, Wash., on Oct. 29, 1901.

WALSH, Kenneth Ambrose. Lieutenant Colonel (Retired). Medal of Honor: b. Brooklyn, N.Y., Nov. 24, 1916. Kenneth Walsh enlisted in the Marine Corps on Dec. 15, 1933, and underwent recruit training at Parris Is., S.C. Upon graduation, he spent two years as an aviation mechanic and radioman at MCB, Quantico, Va. In Mar. 1936, Walsh was selected for flight training and was transferred to Pensacola, Fla. He won his wings there as a private in Apr. 1937, and spent four years in scout and observation flying. During this time he served aboard the aircraft carriers *Yorktown, Wasp,* and *Ranger.* Meanwhile, Walsh was promoted through the enlisted ranks to master technical sergeant and then to marine gunner, equivalent to the present rank of warrant officer. The latter promotion took place on May 11, 1942, while he was serving with MAG 12, 1st MAW, FMF, San Francisco, Calif. In Oct. 1942, he was commissioned a second lieutenant, and, in June 1943, was promoted to first lieutenant. He was promoted to captain (temporary) in Feb. 1944 (this appointment became permanent Nov. 13, 1948); to major in Apr. 1955; and to lieutenant colonel in Oct. 1958. When the Japanese attacked Pearl Harbor, he was serving on the west coast with Marine Fighting Squadron 122. He transferred to Marine Fighting Squadron 124 in Sept. 1942, to be shipped overseas in Jan. 1943 for duty in the Solomon Is. area. He was particularly active in aerial combat in the Vella LaVella vicinity in Aug. 1943 while he was division

leader of his squadron. He scored all his 21 victories in the Vought Corsair F4U fighter. The citation accompanying his Medal of Honor, awarded for this action, states, in part: "... as a pilot in Marine Fighting Squadron 124 in aerial combat against enemy Japanese forces in the Solomon Islands Area. Determined to thwart the enemy's attempt to bomb Allied ground forces and shipping at Vella LaVella on Aug. 15, 1943, Walsh (then a first lieutenant) repeatedly dove his plane into an enemy formation outnumbering his own division six-to-one and, although his plane was hit numerous times, shot down two Japanese dive bombers and one fighter. After developing engine trouble on Aug. 30 during a vital escort mission, 1st Lt. Walsh landed his mechanically disabled plane at Munda, quickly replaced it with another and proceeded to rejoin his flight over Kahili. Separated from his escort group when he encountered approximately 50 Japanese Zeros, he unhesitatingly attacked, striking with relentless fury in his lone battle against a powerful force. He destroyed four hostile fighters before cannon shellfire forced him to make a dead-stick landing off Vella LaVella where he was later picked up." Ordered to return to the States in Nov. 1943, Walsh was assigned special temporary aviation duty with the Division of Aviation, HQMC. During the same month, he received the Medal of Honor. In Jan. 1944, he joined Aviation Casual Co., MB, NAS, Jacksonville, Fla., to serve as flight instructor. In Apr. 1945, he was transferred to the Philippine Islands and served in that area and in the Okinawa campaign as Operations Officer for Marine Fighter Squadron 222 and, later, as Assistant Operations Officer of MAG 14. He returned to HQMC in March 1946, to be reassigned with the Bureau of Aeronautics, Navy Department. After more than three years with the Bureau, he joined the 1st MAW, FMF, in Jan. 1949, at El Toro, Santa Ana, Calif., as Assistant Group Engineering Officer. He transferred from there in July 1949, to MCAS, Quantico, as an aircraft engineering and maintenance student. Upon completion, he returned to El Toro and MAG 25 as Assistant Engineering Officer. With this group he went overseas on July 15, 1950, shortly after the outbreak of the Korean Conflict. He served in Korea until July 27, 1951. He returned to El Toro in late July 1951, remaining there until Apr. 1, 1952, when he was transferred to Staff, Commander Air Force, Atlantic Fleet, Norfolk, Va., as Marine Liaison Officer for Aircraft Materiel and Maintenance. He remained there until Sept. 28, 1955, when he was assigned to the 3rd MAW, Aircraft, FMF, Pacific, El Toro, as Aircraft Maintenance and Repair Officer and transport commander. In Jan. 1959, Col. Walsh was assigned to the 1st MAW, Aircraft, FMF, Pacific, as Wing Aircraft Maintenance Officer. He held this assignment until Apr. 1960, and the following month returned to the 3rd MAW at El Toro, serving consecutively as Executive Officer and Operations Officer of Marine Transport Squadron 352 until Oct. 1961. That month he was assigned to HQ and HQ Squadron, Marine Wing Service Group 37, 3rd MAW. He retired from active service in Jan. 1962.

WALSH, William Gary. Gunnery Sergeant. Medal of Honor: b. Roxbury, Mass., Apr. 7, 1922; d. KIA, Iwo Jima, Feb. 27, 1945. William Walsh attended public schools in Boston before enlisting in the Marine Corps in Apr. 1942. He received his basic training at Parris Is., S.C. and advanced training at Camp Lejeune, N.C. From there, he went to Samoa and was assigned to a unit of Marine Scouts. His next assignment was with the famed Carlson's Raiders. During WWII, Walsh saw action at Guadalcanal, Bougainville, Tarawa and the Russell Is. Following two years in the Pacific theatre, he returned to the States. He was sent overseas later with the 5th Div. in time for the Iwo Jima invasion. It was at Iwo, while leading his men against a fortified hill on Feb. 27, 1945, that the incident occurred which took his life but won for him the Medal of Honor. His citation reads, in part: "... as Leader of an assault platoon, serving with Company G 3rd Bn., 27th Marines, 5th Mar. Div., in action against enemy Japanese forces at Iwo Jima.... With the advance of his company toward Hill 362, facing vicious machine gun fire from a forward position guarding the approaches to this key enemy stronghold, Gy. Sgt. Walsh fearlessly charged at the head of his platoon against the Japanese entrenched on the ridge above him, utterly oblivious to the unrelenting fury of hostile automatic weapons and hand grenades employed with fanatic desperation to smash his daring assault. Thrown back by the enemy's savage resistance, he once again led his men in a seemingly impossible attack up the steep rocky slope, boldly defiant of the annihilating streams of bullets which saturated the area, and ... gained the ridge's top only to be subjected to an intense barrage of hand grenades thrown by the remaining Japanese staging a suicidal last stand on the reverse slope. When one of the grenades fell in the midst of his surviving men, huddled together in a small trench, Gy. Sgt. Walsh ... instantly threw himself upon the deadly bomb, absorbing with his own body the full and terrific force of the explosion ... he saved his comrades from injury and possible loss of life and enabled his company to seize and hold this vital enemy position."

WALT, Lewis William. Brigadier General. Director of the Marine Corps Landing Force Development Center, Marine Corps Schools, Quantico, Va.: b. Waubaunsee County, Kans., Feb. 16, 1913. Lewis Walt graduated from high school in Fort Collins, Colo., then entered Colorado State University and was awarded a Bachelor of Science degree in chemistry upon graduation in 1936. He was an enlisted man in the Colorado National Guard from Dec. 1929 to May 1936, and was also a member of the Army ROTC unit at Colorado State University. Upon graduation he was commissioned a second lieutenant in the Army Field Artillery Reserve, but resigned that commission to accept an appointment as a Marine second lieutenant, July 6, 1936. He completed Basic School at Philadelphia, and in Apr. 1937 was assigned to the 6th Mar. Regt. in San Diego, Calif. as a machine gun platoon leader. Embarking for China in Aug. 1937, he took part in the defense of the International Settlement of Shanghai until Feb. 1938, at which time he returned to San Diego. In June 1939, he began his second tour of overseas duty when he was assigned to the MB, Guam, Mariana Is. He was promoted to captain in Dec. 1941. Early in 1942, Walt volunteered to join the 1st Marine Raider Bn., and in Apr. 1942 arrived with the battalion on Samoa. On Aug. 7, 1942, as commander of Co. A, 1st Raider Bn., he landed his company in the assault on Tulagi and Florida islands in the British Solomon Is. He was awarded the Silver Star Medal for conspicuous gallantry during these landings. Following this, he joined the 5th Mar. Regt. on Guadalcanal where he took part in combat first as Regimental Operations

Officer then as CO of the 2nd Bn., 5th Marines. He was promoted to major in Sept. 1942. In Oct. 1942, as Battalion Commander, 2nd Bn., 5th Marines, 1st Mar. Div., he was wounded in action but continued in combat. On Dec. 22, 1942, he was given a spot promotion to lieutenant colonel for distinguished leadership and gallantry in action during the Guadalcanal Campaign. In Dec. 1943, following hospitalization and training in Australia, Lt. Col. Walt led the 2nd Bn., 5th Marines, in the assault on Cape Gloucester and shortly thereafter was assigned as Regimental Executive Officer. In the middle of this campaign he was ordered to take over command of the 3rd Bn., 5th Marines, during its intense battle for Aogiri Ridge. During this action, he earned his first Navy Cross. Departing Cape Gloucester in late Feb. 1944, he was ordered to the Naval Hospital, Oakland, Calif., for treatment of wounds and malaria. In June 1944, he returned to the Pacific area. That Sept., he participated in the landing on Peleliu as Regimental Executive Officer, 5th Marines. On D-Day he was ordered, again, to take over command of the 3rd Bn., 5th Marines, in the midst of the battle for the beachhead. His second Navy Cross was awarded him during this action. In Nov. 1944, Lt. Col. Walt returned to the States, and the following month assumed duty at MCS, Quantico, as Chief of the Officer Candidates' School, Tactics Section. In July 1946, he joined Troop Training Unit, Pacific, MCB, San Diego, as Battalion Landing Team Instructor. During this assignment, he saw duty in Japan in connection with training 8th Army troops. Assigned to Camp Pendleton in Jan. 1947, he served as Assistant Chief of Staff, G-3, 3rd Mar. Brig., and then as G-3, 1st Mar. Div. In Nov. 1947, he assumed duty as Operations and Training

Officer, 1st Prov. Mar. Brig., on Guam, and served as Chief of Staff of that organization from Feb. to Apr. 1949. Returning to MCS, Quantico, in May 1949, he saw duty as a battalion commander with the Special Training Regiment; and in Sept., he entered the Amphibious Warfare School, Senior Course. On completing the course in June 1950, he remained at MCS serving as Chief of Tactics Section, S-3, and finally, Executive Officer, Basic School. He was promoted to colonel in Nov. 1951. After leaving Quantico, he served from Feb. to Nov. 1952 as Assistant Chief of Staff (Military Operations) on the Staff of the Commander, Amphibious Forces, Pacific Fleet. Ordered to Korea in Nov. 1952, he saw combat with the 1st Mar. Div. until Aug. 1953, serving consecutively as CO, 5th Marines; Assistant Chief of Staff, G-3, and Chief of Staff of the division. The Legion of Merit and Bronze Star Medal, both with Combat "V," were awarded him for exceptionally meritorious service during this assignment. Also, the Korean government awarded Col. Walt the Ulchi Medal and the Ulchi Medal with Silver Star for this period of combat. On arrival at MCS, Quantico, in Aug. 1953, Col. Walt saw duty as Director, Advanced Base Problem Section, Marine Corps Educational Center, through May 1954, followed by duty as CO, Officers' Basic School, until Aug. 1956; and Member of the Advanced Research Group, Marine Corps Educational Center, until June 1957. Transferred to Washington, D.C., Col. Walt served briefly as Head, Detail Branch, Personnel Department, HQMC, until Nov. 1957, when he became Assistant Director of Personnel. He served in the latter capacity until Aug. 1959, then entered the National War College, Washington, D.C., completing the course in June 1960. In July 1960, Col.

Walt began a one-year assignment as Marine Corps Representative on the Joint Advance Study Group of the Joint Chiefs of Staff, Department of Defense, Washington, D.C. Upon completing this assignment, he reported for duty at Camp Lejeune as Assistant Division Commander, 2nd Mar. Div., in June 1961, and was promoted to his present rank of brigadier general in July 1961. In Sept. 1962, Gen. Walt returned to MCS, Quantico, to become Director of the Marine Corps Landing Force Development Center.

WATKINS, Lewis George. Staff Sergeant. Medal of Honor: b. Seneca, S.C., June 6, 1925; d. KIA, Korea, Oct. 7, 1952. S. Sgt. Watkins' citation reads, in part: " . . . Although painfully wounded when a well entrenched hostile force at the crest of a hill engaged the platoon with intense small arms and grenade fire, he gallantly continued to lead his men. Obtaining an automatic rifle from one of the wounded men, he assisted in pinning down an enemy machine gun, holding up the assault. When an enemy grenade landed among S. Sgt. Watkins and several other Marines as they were moving forward through a trench on the hill crest, he immediately pushed his companions aside, placed himself in a position to shield them and picked up the deadly missile in an attempt to throw it outside the trench. Mortally wounded when the grenade exploded in his hand, S. Sgt. Watkins, by his great personal valor in the face of almost certain death, saved the lives of several of his comrades. . . ."

WATSON, Wilson D. Private. Medal of Honor: b. Tuscumbia, Ala., Feb. 18, 1921. Pvt. Watson's citation reads, in part: " . . . serving with the 2nd Bn., 9th Marines, 3rd Mar. Div., during action against enemy Japanese forces on Iwo Jima Feb. 26 and 27, 1945. With his squad abruptly halted by intense fire from enemy fortifications in the high rocky ridges and crags commanding the line of advance, Pvt. Watson boldly rushed one pillbox and fired into the embrasure with his weapon, keeping the enemy pinned down singlehandedly until he was in a position to hurl in a grenade, then running to the rear of the emplacement to destroy the retreating Japanese and enabling his platoon to take its objective. Again pinned down at the foot of a small hill, he dauntlessly scaled the jagged incline under fierce mortar and machine gun barrages and with his assistant automatic rifleman charged the crest of the hill, firing from his hip. Fighting furiously against Japanese troops attacking with grenades and knee mortars from the reverse slope, he stood fearlessly erect in his exposed position to cover the hostile entrenchments and held the hill under savage fire for 15 minutes, killing 60 Japanese before his ammunition was exhausted and his platoon was able to join him."

WEEDE, Richard Garfield. Major General. Chief of Staff, U.S. Military Assistance Command, Viet-Nam: b. Sterling, Kan., Sept. 26, 1911. Richard Weede attended Kansas State Teachers College for two years prior to entering the U.S. Naval Academy in 1931. He was commissioned a Marine second lieutenant upon graduation, June 5, 1935. He completed Basic School at the Philadelphia Navy Yard in Sept. 1935, then served with the 1st Bn. at Quantico, Va. In Oct. 1936, he joined the 2nd Mar. Brig. in San Diego, Calif. While there, he was promoted to first lieutenant in July 1938. That Sept. he embarked for Guam where he served almost two years. He returned to Quan-

tico in July 1940 and was subsequently assigned to the 4th and later the 5th Defense Bns. at Parris Is., S.C. He was promoted to captain in Mar. 1941. Upon the outbreak of WWII, Weede was ordered overseas, joining the 2nd Defense Bn. on American Samoa in Jan. 1942. With the exception of a brief period of instruction in the States, he remained in the Pacific area and served with the 2nd Bn. throughout the war. While overseas, he was promoted to major in May 1942, and to lieutenant colonel in May 1943. As CO of the 5-Inch Artillery Group, Lt. Col. Weede moved to Tarawa in Nov. 1943 in conjunction with the initial landing there, and commanded the group through repeated enemy bombing raids. He became battalion commander in May 1944 prior to his return to the States. After completing Field Artillery School at Fort Sill, Okla., he joined the 2nd Mar. Div. on Saipan in Oct. 1944. As CO of the 2nd Bn., 10th Marines, he took part in combat in the landing on and seizure of Iheya Shima and in the final stages of the Okinawa campaign. For meritorious service on Tarawa and Okinawa, he was awarded the Bronze Star Medal with Combat "V." Lt. Col. Weede returned to the States in July 1945, and the following month was assigned to the Bureau of Ordnance, Navy Department. He departed Washington in Aug. 1947 for MCS, Quantico, where he completed the Senior Course in June 1948, then served consecutively as Supervisory Instructor and Assistant Director of the Junior Course. He was promoted to colonel in June 1950. In May 1951, he joined the 1st Mar. Div. in Korea, where he served in combat as CO, 5th Marines. For outstanding service in this capacity during the period Aug. 5 to Nov. 19, he was awarded the Legion of Merit with Combat "V." Subsequently, as Chief of Staff,

1st Mar. Div. (Reinf.), he was awarded his second Legion of Merit for the period Nov. 26, 1951 to Feb. 10, 1952. His participation in liaison and reconnaissance flights from May 1951 to Jan. 1952 also earned him two Air Medals. In Mar. 1952, Col. Weede returned to HQMC, serving there through Aug. 1952 as a Member of the FMF Organizational Structure Board and of the Naval Examining Board. Enrolling at the Army War College, Carlisle Barracks, Pa., he completed the course in June 1953. In July of that year he returned to MCS to serve a year as a member of the Advanced Research Team. Reassigned to HQMC in July 1954, he served as Assistant G-1 and subsequently served on the Marine Corps Table of Organization Board until July 1956. He was then transferred to Camp Pendleton, Calif., where he served as Chief of Staff, 1st Mar. Div. (Reinf.), through May 1958. Following this, he was named CG, Recruit Training Command, MCRD, San Diego, in June 1958, and was promoted to brigadier general in July 1958. Gen. Weede departed San Diego in Nov. 1959, and later that month assumed command of the 1st Mar. Brig. at Kaneohe Bay, Hawaii. He was promoted to his present rank of major general in Aug. 1961. In Feb. 1962, Gen. Weede relinquished command of the 1st Mar. Brig. and assumed his current assignment in Saigon, Viet-Nam, as Chief of Staff of the newly created U.S. Military Assistance Command.

WELLER, Donald McPherrin. Major General. Deputy Commander, Fleet Marine Force, Pacific, Camp H. M. Smith, Oahu, Hawaii: b. Hartford, Conn., May 1, 1908. After graduation from high school in Pittsburgh, Pa. in 1925, Donald Weller studied for a year at Carnegie Tech before entering the U.S. Naval Academy. Upon graduation, June 5, 1930, he was commissioned a Marine second lieutenant. During his first years of service, he completed the Marine Officers' Basic School and the Infantry Basic Course at MCS, Quantico; served aboard the USS *Arkansas* with the 1st Bn., 10th Marines; and was a detachment officer at MB, Norfolk Navy Yard, Portsmouth, Va. On rejoining the 1st Bn., 10th Marines, he was promoted to first lieutenant in Jan. 1935, and later completed the Army Field Artillery School, Fort Sill, Okla. In June 1937, Lt. Weller went aboard the USS *Tuscaloosa* as commander of the Marine Detachment. He was promoted to captain in Aug. 1937. He served on the *Tuscaloosa* until June 1939. The following month, he again joined the 1st Bn., 10th Marines, at Quantico. After serving there as a battery commander until Sept. 1940, he was named Artillery and Naval Gunfire Advisor on the Staff of the CG, 1st Mar. Brig., and participated in extended Caribbean maneuvers from Oct. 1940 to Mar. 1941. He then returned to Quantico, where he continued to specialize in naval gunfire matters as Assistant Operations Officer of the Amphibious Corps, Atlantic Fleet. He was promoted to major in Jan. 1942, and to lieutenant colonel in Aug. 1942. Lt. Col. Weller departed Quantico for San Diego, Calif. in Sept. 1942, and became Assistant Operations Officer of the Amphibious Corps, Pacific Fleet, the following month. In Jan. 1943, he took command of the 2nd Bn., 12th Marines, 3rd Mar. Div., and a month later embarked with that unit for the Pacific area. He led the 2nd (75mm howitzer) Bn. at Bougainville and Guam. For meritorious achievement in these campaigns, he was awarded the Bronze Star Medal with Combat "V" and a Gold Star in lieu of a second. Following the Guam campaign, he was named

Naval Gunfire Officer, FMF, Pacific, in Aug. 1944. For outstanding service in this capacity during the planning and combat stages of the Iwo Jima invasion, he was awarded the Legion of Merit with Combat "V." He returned to the States in June 1945, then served for six months as Chief of the Naval Gunfire Section, Troop Training Unit, Training Command, Amphibious Forces, Pacific Fleet, in San Diego. Following this, Lt. Col. Weller completed the Army-Navy Staff College in Washington, D.C., and the Instructors' Orientation Course, MCS, Quantico. In June 1946, he began a three-year tour of duty as Chief of the Naval Gunfire Section, MCS, Quantico. While there, he was promoted to colonel in Feb. 1948. Upon his detachment from Quantico, Col. Weller entered the Naval War College, Newport, R.I., in Aug. 1949, and completed his studies there in June 1950. During the next two years, he was stationed at HQMC, Washington, D.C., serving as Chief, Strategic Planning Section; Executive Officer, Division of Plans and Policies; and Chief, Policy Analysis Division, respectively. In July 1952, he reported to Camp Lejeune, N.C. There he served as CO, 10th Marine Artillery Regiment and Artillery Officer, 2nd Mar. Div., until June 1953 when he became Chief of Staff of the 2nd Div. A year later, he returned to Quantico where he became Chief of Staff, MCS, in Aug. 1954. He was promoted to his present rank of major general in July 1958. Departing Washington for the Far East in Aug. 1960, he reported on Okinawa that same month as CG, 3rd Mar. Div. (Reinf.), FMF. He served in this capacity until Sept. 1961, when he assumed his present assignment as Deputy Commander, FMF, Pacific.

WEST, Walter Scott. Private. Medal of Honor: b. Bradford, N.H., Mar. 13, 1872; d. Sept. 1943. Walter West enlisted in the Marine Corps at Boston, Mass. on May 11, 1897. His citation reads, in part: "... while serving on board the USS *Marblehead,* for extraordinary bravery and coolness while cutting the cables leading from Cienfuegos, Cuba, May 11, 1898, under a heavy fire of the enemy...." West was discharged from the Corps on Jan. 20, 1899.

WHARTON, Franklin. Lieutenant Colonel. 3rd Commandant of the Marine Corps — Mar. 7, 1804 to Sept. 1, 1818: b. Philadelphia, Pa., July 23, 1767; d. New York, N.Y., Sept. 1, 1818. Franklin Wharton, whose prominent and wealthy family had played an important part in the development of the American Colonies, was commissioned a captain of Marines on Aug. 3, 1798. His first duty station was MB, Philadelphia; however, after several weeks, he was assigned to the frigate *United States,* where he served as officer in charge of the vessel's Marine Detachment until the close of the undeclared sea war with France in 1801. He returned to Philadelphia as CO of Marines there and, on Mar. 6, 1804, he received word of his promotion to the office of Commandant of the Marine Corps. Capt. Wharton's assignment to succeed his close friend, Lt. Col. William Ward Burrows, as CMC in 1804, was a gigantic undertaking for an officer having only five years experience as a member of the Marine Corps. However, what he may have lacked in military experience was offset by his vitality, diplomacy, and complete faith in his officers and men. The Marine Corps at that time was engaged in America's war with the Barbary States. Commandant Wharton retained policies established by his predecessor; he stressed military discipline and neatness; he also prescribed distinctive uniforms for his officers and men. The Marine Corps Band, organized by Commandant Burrows, reached new heights under Col. Wharton. It participated in virtually every important affair of state held in Washington. Within the continental limits of the United States, Marines were needed in Louisiana where a large force of Spanish troops had been massed at its southwestern boundary. Marines of that era were stationed at New Orleans, which had been designated to become the seat of the "monarchy" proposed by Aaron Burr. Volunteer companies, Marines, and other troops patrolled the streets, ready to suppress any attempt at insurrection. Commandant Wharton also ordered a detachment of Marines to Georgia and Florida in 1811 to cooperate with U.S. Army troops in an attempt to subdue an Indian uprising. Under Col. Wharton, Marines participated in many important engagements during the War of 1812. They saw action at Annapolis, Fort McHenry, Portsmouth, Chaney Is., Bladensburg, and New Orleans, and fought under Gen. Henry Dearborn on the northern frontier. At sea, Marines participated in important naval battles, serving aboard the warships and privateers on the Great Lakes, the Atlantic, and the Pacific. They fought under Commodore Oliver Perry on Lake Erie and under Commodore Isaac Chauncey on Lake Ontario. Aboard the frigate *Constitution,* Marines were important factors in that vessel's victorious battles against the *Guerriere, Java, Levant,* and *Cyane.* Those aboard the *Wasp* saw action in the vessel's engagements with the *Frolic, Reindeer,* and *Avon.* Marines serving aboard the frigate *United States* were commended for their efficiency in its fight with the *Macedonian.* Lt. Col. Commandant Wharton died

Sept. 1, 1818 in New York City and was buried in Old Trinity Church Yard in New York.

Wieseman

WIESEMAN, Frederick Leonard. Major General. CG, 2nd Mar. Div., Camp Lejeune, N.C.: b. Milwaukee, Wis., Mar. 16, 1908. Frederick Wieseman graduated from high school at Palmyra, Wis., in 1925. In Aug. of that year, he joined the Marine Corps, serving as an enlisted man until July 1927, when he was appointed to the U.S. Naval Academy. Upon graduation, he was commissioned a Marine second lieutenant on June 4, 1931. After completing Basic School at Philadelphia, Pa., in 1932, he served with the Marine Corps Rifle and Pistol Team at Quantico. Transferred to the MB, Parris Is., S.C. in Sept. 1932, he served there until Mar.

1934. He was a member of the 1932 Parris Is. Marine football team, coached the basketball team there two seasons, and was head coach of the Quantico Marine football teams of 1935 and 1936. He also served at sea with the Marine Detachment aboard the USS *Minneapolis* from Apr. 1934 to June 1935, when he began three months' service again as a member of the Marine Corps Rifle and Pistol Team, Quantico. He later completed a course at the U.S. Naval Gun Factory Optical School, Washington, D.C., and a tour of duty at the MB, Quantico. He again served at sea from Feb. 1937 to June 1939 aboard the USS *Yorktown,* prior to completing the Amphibious Warfare School, Junior Course, Quantico, in May 1940. The following month he began a third assignment with the Marine Corps Rifle and Pistol Team. From Jan. to Sept. 1941, he saw service in Cuba and at Parris Is. with the 1st Mar. Div. His next assignment was with the 7th Marines, 1st Mar. Div., serving at New River (later Camp Lejeune), N.C., until Mar. 1942 when the unit was detached to the 3rd Mar. Brig. for duty at Samoa. With the 7th Marines, he rejoined the 1st Mar. Div. on Guadalcanal in Sept. 1942, and in Jan. 1943 became Liaison Officer for the 1st Mar. Div. at GHQ, Southwest Pacific Area. Transferred to the 1st Marine Amphibious Corps, he earned the Bronze Star Medal as an Assistant Chief of Staff (Supply) in the Solomon Is. area from Aug. to Dec. 1943. For meritorious service as logistical officer on the Staff of the CG of the 3rd Amphibious Corps from Dec. 1943 to Aug. 1944, during which time he participated in combat operations on Guam, he was awarded the Legion of Merit. Following his return to the States, he was ordered in Oct. 1944 to HQMC, Washington, D.C., where he served two years in the Division of Plans and Policies. Assigned to FMF, Pacific, in Dec. 1946, he served consecutively as Executive Officer and CO of the 7th Service Regt.; as CO of the 12th Service Bn.; and as CO of the 3rd Marines at Tsingtao, China. While there he served as Representative of the Commander, Naval Forces, Western Pacific, in successful negotiations with the Chinese Communists for the release of a Marine plane crew shot down and held prisoner in Shantung Province in 1948. In Oct. 1948, he joined Troop Training Unit, Atlantic, and following duty there entered the Armed Forces Staff College, Norfolk, Va., in Feb. 1949. He completed the course that June. At the beginning of the Korean conflict, he was serving as Chief of the Logistics Section, Marine Corps Educational Center, Quantico. He left Quantico in July 1952, and served as Chief of Staff, 3rd Mar. Div., both at Camp Pendleton, Calif., and in Japan before returning to this country in May 1954. The following month, he returned to Quantico for a one-year tour of duty as a member of the Advanced Research Group. Ordered to HQMC in July 1955, he served as Assistant Fiscal Director until May 1956, when he was named Fiscal Director. He was promoted to brigadier general in July 1956. Departing HQMC in Apr. 1959, Gen. Wieseman reported at Kaneohe Bay, Hawaii, the following month as CG, 1st Mar. Brig. While there, he was promoted to major general in Nov. 1959. On his return to Washington, Gen. Wieseman was assigned as Deputy Chief of Staff (Plans), HQMC, in Jan. 1960. In Nov. 1961, he left HQMC to become CG, 2nd Mar. Div. at Camp Lejeune, N.C.

WILLIAMS, Ernest Calvin. Major. Medal of Honor: b. Sidell, Ill., Aug. 2, 1887;

d. July 31, 1921. Maj. Williams' citation reads, in part: "... for extraordinary heroism in the line of his profession in the face of the enemy at San Francisco deMacoris, Dominican Republic, Nov. 29, 1916...." Against enemy forces, Williams and a dozen men rushed the gate of a fortress. Eight of the men were wounded by rifle fire but Williams pressed on with the remaining four and plunged against the door as it was being closed, forcing an entry to the stronghold, killing the guards and taking command of the fort which held a hundred prisoners. Williams was retired from the Corps as a major on Mar. 22, 1921.

WILLIAMS, Hershel Woodrow. Chief Warrant Officer (USMCR). Medal of Honor: b. Fairmont, W.Va., Oct. 2, 1923. Hershel Williams enlisted in the MCR on May 26, 1943. He left the States on board the MS *Weltevreden* on Dec. 3, 1943 for New Caledonia. In Jan. 1944, he joined the 3rd Mar. Div. at Guadalcanal. He was first attached to Co. C, 21st Marines, and then to HQ Co., 1st Bn., 21st Marines. During July and Aug. 1944, he participated in action against the Japanese at Guam, and in Oct. he rejoined Co. C. Now a sergeant, Williams' next campaign was at Iwo Jima where he won the Medal of Honor. Landing on D-Day, Feb. 21, 1945, the sergeant three days later became a distinguished fighting man. Quick to volunteer his services when U.S. tanks were maneuvering vainly to open a lane for the infantry through a network of reinforced concrete pillboxes, buried mines, and black volcanic sands, Williams daringly went forward alone to attempt the reduction of devastating machine gun fire from the unyielding positions. Covered by only four riflemen, he fought desperately for four hours under terrific enemy small arms fire and

repeatedly returned to his own lines to prepare demolition charges and obtain serviced flame throwers, then struggling back, frequently to the rear of hostile emplacements, to wipe out one position after another. One occasion saw him daringly mounted on a pillbox to insert the nozzle of his flame thrower through the air vent, killing the occupants and silencing the gun. On another occasion, he grimly charged enemy riflemen who attempted to stop him with bayonets and destroyed them with a burst of flame from his weapon. He was wounded in action during that campaign on Mar. 6, 1945.

WILSON, Harold Edward. Master Sergeant. Medal of Honor: b. Birmingham, Ala., Dec. 5, 1921. M. Sgt. Wilson's citation reads, in part: "... while serving as platoon sergeant of a rifle platoon attached to Co. G, 3rd Bn., 1st Marines, 1st Mar. Div. (Reinf.), in action against enemy aggressor forces in Korea on the night of Apr. 23-24, 1951. When the company outpost was overrun by the enemy while his platoon, firing from hastily constructed foxholes, was engaged in resisting the brunt of a fierce mortar, machine gun, grenade and small arms attack launched by hostile forces from high ground under cover of darkness, Sgt. Wilson braved intense fire to assist the survivors back into the line and to direct the treatment of casualties. Although twice wounded by gunfire, in the right arm and the left leg, he refused medical aid for himself and continued to move about among his men, shouting words of encouragement. After receiving further wounds in the head and shoulder as the attack increased in intensity, he again insisted upon remaining with his unit. Unable to use either arm to fire, and with mounting casualties among our forces, he resupplied his men with rifles and ammunition taken from the wounded. Personally reporting to his company commander on several occasions, he requested and received additional assistance when the enemy attack became even more fierce and after placing the reinforcements in strategic positions in the line, directed effective fire until blown off his feet by the bursting of a hostile mortar round in his face. Dazed and suffering from concussion, he still refused medical aid and, despite weakness from loss of blood, moved from foxhole to foxhole, directing fire, resupplying ammunition, rendering first aid and encouraging his men. By his heroic actions in the face of almost certain death, when the unit's ability to hold the disadvantageous position was doubtful, he instilled confidence in his troops, inspiring them to rally repeatedly and turn back the furious assaults. At dawn, after the final attack had been repulsed, he personally accounted for each man in his platoon before walking unassisted one-half mile to the aid station where he submitted to treatment. . . ."

WILSON, Louis Hugh, Jr. Colonel. Medal of Honor: b. Brandon, Miss., Feb. 11, 1920. Louis Wilson enlisted in the MCR in May 1941 and was assigned to active duty in June 1941. Subsequently assigned to Officers' Candidate Class at Quantico, Va., he was commissioned a Marine Reserve second lieutenant on Nov. 1, 1941, then joined the Reserve Officers' Class there. The MCB at San Diego, Calif. was his next stop; there he performed the duties of a platoon leader in the 2nd Mar. Div. On Apr. 10, 1942, he accepted a commission in the regular Marine Corps. He was later appointed a first lieutenant on Oct. 1, 1942. Shipping overseas in Feb. 1943, he was assigned as a company officer to N Co., 9th Marines, 3rd Mar. Div. and in Apr. received his captaincy. Guadalcanal and Efate, New Hebrides Is. were his next two stops before landing on Bougainville, British Solomon Is. on Nov. 1, 1943. He became Executive Officer of the company while on Bougainville. Capt. Wilson returned to Guadalcanal as CO, Co. F, 2nd Bn., 9th Marines the following month. He was in the assault on Guam on July 25 and 26, 1944, during which action he earned the Medal of Honor. His citation reads, in part, ". . . as CO of Co. F, 2nd Bn., 9th Marines, 3rd Mar. Div., in action against enemy Japanese forces at Fonte Hill, Guam, Marianas Is. July 25 and 26, 1944. Ordered to take that portion of the hill within his zone of action, Capt. Wilson initiated his attack in mid-afternoon, pushed up the rugged, open terrain against terrific machine gun and rifle fire for 300 yards and successfully captured the objective. Promptly assuming command of other disorganized units and motorized equipment in addition to his own company and one reinforcing platoon, he organized his night defenses in the face of continuous hostile fire and, although wounded three times during this five-hour period, completed his disposition of men and guns before retiring to the company CP for medical attention. Shortly thereafter, when the enemy launched the first of a series of savage counterattacks lasting all night, he voluntarily rejoined his besieged units and repeatedly exposed himself to the merciless hail of shrapnel and bullets, dashing 50 yards into the open on one occasion to rescue a wounded Marine lying helpless beyond the front lines. Fighting fiercely in hand-to-hand encounters, Wilson led his men in a furiously waged battle for approximately 10 hours, tenaciously holding his line and repelling the fanatically renewed counterthrusts until he succeeded in crushing the last efforts of the hardpressed Japanese early in the following morning. Then, organizing a 17-man patrol, he immediately advanced upon a strategic slope essential to the security of his position and, boldly defying intense mortar, machine gun, and rifle fire which struck down 13 of his men, drove relentlessly forward with the remnants of his patrol to seize the vital ground...." After being wounded during the battle, Wilson was evacuated to the U.S. Naval Hospital, San Diego, Calif., remaining there until Oct. 15 when he returned to duty as CO, D Co., MB, Camp Pendleton, Calif. In Dec. he left for Washington, D.C., as Detachment Commander of the MB and Post Security Officer. On Mar. 15, 1945, he was promoted to major. While serving in that capacity, Maj. Wilson was formally presented the Medal of Honor by the President of the United States. In June 1946, he became Dean of the Marine Corps Institute in Washington, D.C., and later became Assistant Director. Pearl Harbor became his next station in Dec., serving there as Aide-de-Camp to Lt. Gen. Thomas E. Watson, CG, FMF, Pacific. Maj. Wilson returned to the States in Jan. 1949, and shortly after assumed duties as Officer-in-Charge, District HQ Recruiting Station, New York, N.Y. After serving in New York until Aug. 1951, he began a three-year tour of duty at the MCS, Quantico, and while there was promoted to lieutenant colonel in Nov. 1951. At Quantico, Lt. Col. Wilson served consecutively as CO of the 1st Training Bn., Basic School, and CO, Camp Barrett, prior to becoming Executive Officer of the Basic School in Feb. 1953. Then he completed the Senior Course at the MCS in Aug. 1954. The following month, after a brief tour

as a Senior School instructor, he departed for Korea and served as Assistant G-3, 1st Mar. Div. Returning to the States with the division he served as G-3 until Aug. 1955, when he was named CO of the 2nd Bn. 5th Marines. In Mar. 1956, he was ordered to HQMC where he served for two years as head of the Operations Unit, G-3 Division. He was again assigned to Quantico in June 1958, and served as CO of the Training and Test Regt., Basic School, until June 1960, then as CO of the Basic School until July 1961. During this last assignment, he was promoted to colonel in July 1960. From Aug. 1961 until June 1962, Col. Wilson completed the course at the National War College, Washington, D.C. In July 1962, he was assigned to HQMC, and is presently serving as Joint Matters Coordinator, Office of the Deputy Chief of Staff (Plans and Programs).

WILSON, Robert Lee. Private First Class. Medal of Honor: b. Centralia, Ill., May 24, 1921; d. KIA, Tinian, Aug. 3, 1944. P.F.C. Wilson's citation reads, in part: "... with the 2nd Bn., 6th Marines, 2nd Mar. Div., during action against enemy Japanese forces on Tinian Island. As one of a group of Marines advancing through heavy underbrush to neutralize isolated points of resistance, P.F.C. Wilson daringly preceded his companions toward a pile of rocks where Japanese troops were supposed to be hiding. Fully aware of the danger involved, he was moving forward while the remainder of the squad armed with automatic rifles closed together in the rear, when an enemy grenade landed in the midst of the group. Quick to act, P.F.C. Wilson cried a warning to the men and unhesitatingly threw himself on the grenade, heroically sacrificing his own life that the others might live and fulfill their mission."

WINANS, Roswell. Brigadier General. Medal of Honor: b. Brookeville, Ind., Dec. 9, 1887. Roswell Winans, whose combat service goes back to the "Banana Wars" in Central America and in France during WWI, earned the nation's highest military decoration for action during an engagement at Guayacanas in the Dominican Republic on July 3, 1916. Serving there as a first sergeant, he was cited for extraordinary heroism in action against a considerable force of rebels on the line of march of his unit. On Oct. 10, 1912, after serving four years in the U.S. Army, he enlisted in the Marine Corps and rose to the rank of first sergeant, seeing duty during the Mexican, Haitian, and Dominican campaigns, before he was commissioned a second lieutenant during WWI. A captain at the end of that war, Winans served prior to WWII at various Marine posts and stations in the States, as well as taking part in the second Nicaraguan Campaign. He was a colonel at the outbreak of WWII, and was promoted to his present rank upon retirement on Aug. 1, 1946.

WINDRICH, William Gordon. Staff Sergeant. Medal of Honor: b. Chicago, Ill., May 14, 1921; d. KIA, Yudam-ni, Korea, Dec. 2, 1950. William Windrich enlisted in the MCR June 6, 1938, and was ordered to active duty in Nov. 1940. During WWII, he spent 20 months overseas in the south Pacific as a machine gunner. Discharged in Nov. 1945, S. Sgt. Windrich reenlisted in the regular Marine Corps the following Feb. In the summer of 1946 he participated in the atomic bomb tests at Bikini Atoll while serving aboard the USS *Mount McKinley*. During the years after WWII he also served as an NCO of the guard in Washington, D.C., at the Naval Gun Factory and at HQMC, and in China. At the outbreak

of fighting in Korea, Windrich was on military police duty at Camp Pendleton, Calif. He went overseas with the 1st Mar. Brig. and was among the first Marines to see action in Korea. His citation reads, in part: " . . . as a platoon sergeant of Co. I, 3rd Bn., 5th Marines, 1st Mar. Div. (Reinf.), in action against enemy aggressor forces in the vicinity of Yudam-ni, Korea, the night of Dec. 1, 1950. Promptly organizing a squad of men when the enemy launched a sudden, vicious counterattack against the forward elements of his company's position, rendering it untenable, S. Sgt. Windrich, armed with a carbine, spearheaded the assault to the top of the knoll immediately confronting the overwhelming force and, under shattering hostile automatic weapons, mortar, and grenade fire, directed effective fire to hold back the attackers and cover the withdrawal of our troops to commanding ground. With seven of his men struck down during the furious action, and he himself wounded in the head by a bursting grenade, he made his way to his company's position and, organizing a small group of volunteers, returned with them to evacuate the wounded and dying from the frozen hillside, staunchly refusing medical attention himself. Immediately redeploying the remainder of his troops, S. Sgt. Windrich placed them on the left flank of the defensive sector before the enemy again attacked in force. Wounded in the leg during the bitter fight that followed, he bravely fought on with his men, shouting words of encouragement and directing their fire until the attack was repelled. Refusing evacuation although unable to stand, he still continued to direct his platoon in setting up defensive positions until, weakened by the bitter cold, excessive loss of blood and severe pain he lapsed into unconsciousness and died...."

WITEK, Frank Peter. Private First Class. Medal of Honor: b. Derby, Conn., Dec. 10, 1921; d. KIA, Finegayan, Guam, Aug. 3, 1944. P.F.C. Witek's citation reads, in part: "... while serving with the 1st Bn., 9th Marines, 3rd Mar. Div., during the Battle of Finegayan at Guam, Marianas, on Aug. 3, 1944, when his rifle platoon was halted by heavy surprise fire from well-camouflaged enemy positions, P.F.C. Witek daringly remained standing to fire a full magazine from his automatic at pointblank range into a depression housing Japanese troops, killing eight of the enemy and enabling the greater part of his platoon to take cover. During his platoon's withdrawal for consolidation of lines, he remained to safeguard a severely wounded comrade, courageously returning the enemy's fire until the arrival of stretcher bearers and then covering the evacuation by sustained fire as he moved backward toward his own lines. With his platoon again pinned down by a hostile machine gun Witek, on his own initiative, moved forward boldly ahead of the reinforcing tanks and infantry, alternately throwing hand grenades and firing as he advanced to within five to ten yards of the enemy position, destroying the hostile machine-gun emplacement and an additional eight Japanese before he himself was struck down by an enemy rifleman...."

Y

YOUNG, Frank Albert. Sergeant Major. Medal of Honor: b. Milwaukee, Wis., June 22, 1876; d. U.S. Naval Hospital, Mare Is., Calif., Apr. 3, 1941. Prior to his enlistment as a private in the Marine Corps on Aug. 25, 1897, Frank Young had served with the U.S. Cavalry from May 25, 1886 to June 6, 1891. During his first enlistment in the Marine Corps, he participated in the Naval Expedition of Subic Bay, Luzon Is., Sept. 23, 1899, and Rumblon Is., Dec. 16, 1899, in the Philippines. Later, in the siege of Peking, China during the Boxer uprising, he served with special distinction, for which he was awarded the Medal of Honor. His first enlistment in the Marine Corps terminated Sept. 7, 1902, with an excellent discharge. From Jan. 10, 1903 to Jan. 12, 1906, he again served with the 12th U.S. Cavalry. On Jan. 15, 1906, he reenlisted in the Marine Corps and served continuously in the Corps until Oct. 31, 1923, retiring with the rank of sergeant major.

YOUNGDALE, Carl Albert. Brigadier General. Assistant to the Deputy Chief of Staff (Plans and Programs) for Joint Matters, HQMC, Washington, D.C.: b. Gowrie, Iowa, June 23, 1912. Carl Youngdale graduated from Harcourt Consolidated High School, Harcourt, Iowa, in 1930. In June 1936, he received his Bachelor of Science degree from Iowa State University, where he was a member of the ROTC unit for four years. He resigned his Army Reserve commission (Field Artillery) to accept appointment as a second lieutenant in the Marine Corps on July 10, 1936. The following Mar., he completed Basic School at the Philadelphia Navy Yard. The same month he was transferred to the Marine

Detachment, Naval Prison, Portsmouth, N.H., where he served as a detachment officer until June 1938. Assigned to the 1st Mar. Brig., FMF, at Quantico, in July 1938, he served first as an infantry platoon leader in D Company, 1st Bn., 5th Marines, and later as an artillery officer in the A Battery, 1st Bn., 10th Marines. He was promoted to first lieutenant in July 1939. Transferred to the USS *Henderson* in July 1940, Youngdale served aboard that ship for two years as CO of the Marine Detachment. He was promoted to captain in Jan. 1942, and to major in Aug. 1942. From Aug. 1942 until Apr. 1943, Maj. Youngdale served as Officer in Charge of the Artillery School and G-3 of the Training Center at Camp Elliott, Calif. After graduating from the Artillery School, Fort Sill, Okla. in July 1943, he was ordered overseas. He joined the 4th Mar. Div. as CO, 4th Bn., 14th Marines. He was promoted to lieutenant colonel in Mar. 1944, shortly after the battle of Roi-Namur, and subsequently took part in the Saipan, Tinian, and Iwo Jima campaigns. He was awarded the Legion of Merit with Combat "V" for exceptionally meritorious service on Saipan and Tinian in landing his battalion under heavy enemy fire and furnishing artillery support for succeeding waves of invasion troops. Later the Silver Star Medal was awarded him for conspicuous gallantry while leading his reconnaissance party ashore on Iwo Jima under intense enemy fire. In May 1945, he was appointed Regimental Executive Officer of the 14th Marines, and remained with the regiment until Nov. 1945 when he returned to the States. In Jan. 1946, Lt. Col. Youngdale became Executive Officer for the Field Artillery School at Quantico, where he served until Sept. 1947, then graduated from the Senior School, MCS, Quantico, in May 1948. From June 1948 until July 1950, he was assigned as Inspector Instructor of the 2nd 105mm Bn., USMCR, Los Angeles, Calif. Ordered overseas in Aug. 1950, he joined the 11th Marines, 1st Mar. Div., serving as Regimental Executive Officer and later Regimental CO during the landings at Inchon, the capture of Seoul, and the Chosin Reservoir phase of the Korean War. He took over the Artillery Regiment at Hagaru-ri just prior to the advance to Hungnam. For outstanding service in Korea from Aug. to Nov. 1950, and from Nov. 1950 to May 1951, he received two Gold Stars in lieu of a second and third Legion of Merit with Combat "V." In June 1951, he began a two-year assignment on the staff of the Commander in Chief, Pacific Fleet. While serving in this post, he was promoted to colonel in Nov. 1951. In July 1953, he was assigned to the Joint Chiefs of Staff, where he served as Marine Corps Liaison Officer for the Secretariat until July 1955. He then entered the National War College, Washington, D.C., graduating in June 1956. Following graduation he was assigned to the United States European Command, Paris, France, as Chief of Operations Branch, J-3 Division. From Aug. 1958 to June 1961, Col. Youngdale was assigned to the 2nd Mar. Div. FMF, Camp Lejeune, serving successively as Division Chief of Staff, CO of the 10th Marines, and Assistant Division Commander. He was designated Assistant Chief of Staff, G-2, HQMC, in June 1961, and was promoted to brigadier general in Aug. 1961. In May 1962, Gen. Youngdale was designated the Assistant Chief of Staff, G-2 and Assistant Chief of Staff, G-3. He served in this capacity until July 1962, when he became Assistant to the Deputy Chief of Staff (Plans and Programs) for Joint Matters, HQMC.

Z

ZEILIN, Jacob. Brigadier General. 7th Commandant of the Marine Corps: b. Philadelphia, Pa., July 16, 1806; d. Washington, D.C., Nov. 18, 1880. Jacob Zeilin was appointed a second lieutenant in the Marine Corps on Oct. 1, 1831. After completing training in Washington, D.C., his first tours of duty were ashore at the MB, Philadelphia, and at Gosport (Portsmouth), Va. He then served aboard the sloop of war *Erie* in Mar. 1832, after which followed a tour of duty at Charlestown (Boston), Mass. In Aug. 1934, he again joined the sloop *Erie* on a long and eventful voyage that lasted for more than three years. He was promoted to first lieutenant Sept. 12, 1836. From Sept. 1837 to Apr. 1841, Zeilin served at Charlestown, Mass. and New York. In Feb. 1842, he returned to sea duty on board the *Columbus*; during the cruise that followed he spent several months on the Brazil station. Upon the conclusion of this tour of sea duty, and after again serving at important Marine Corps stations on the east coast of the States from 1842 to 1845, he was transferred to duty aboard the frigate *Congress*. During the conquest of California (1846-1847), he took part in the capture and occupation of Santa Barbara and San Pedro early in Aug. 1846, and soon afterward assisted in the first capture of Los Angeles. A few days later, with the Marines of the Squadron, he recaptured San Pedro, which had been lost to the insurgent Californians. In Dec. 1846, when Gen. Kearney's army was beleaguered at San Bernardo Ranch, Calif., Zeilin took a prominent part in its relief and rescue. In Jan. 1847, he served as adjutant of Commodore Stockton's mixed column of sailors, Marines, and volunteers who marched from San Diego and defeated the Californians in the battle of San Gabriel and in the affair at La Mesa. On Jan. 28, 1847, he was appointed Military Commandant of San Diego and served in that capacity until the completion of the conquest of California. Zeilin was promoted to the regular rank of captain on Sept. 14, 1847. During the following few months, together with the Marines of the Pacific Squadron, he participated in the capture of important ports in Lower California and the west coast of Mexico, and served as Fleet Marine Officer of the Pacific Squadron. After the close of the war with Mexico, Zeilin proceeded to Norfolk, Va., where he served for a time, then went to New York. He remained in New York until June 1852, when he was selected to accompany Commodore Perry as Fleet Marine Officer in the famous expedition to Japan in which the Marines took a prominent part. Zeilin himself was the second person to set foot on shore at the formal landing of the naval forces at Yokohama on July 14, 1853. He was also one of those later accorded special honor for his part in the expedition that opened the doors of the Mikado's realm to the outside world. Upon his return from Japan, he was again stationed at Norfolk. This duty was followed by command of the MB, Navy Yard, Washington, D.C. After remaining for a time at Washington, he again went to sea, this time aboard the frigate *Wabash* on the European Station. He remained on this assignment until the year 1859. During the early part of the Civil War, he was on garrison duty in command of MB, first at Philadelphia and later at Washington, D.C. In July 1861, he was on detached duty with the Marine battalion at the Battle of Bull Run and was wounded in that action. Five days later he was appointed to the regular rank of major. In 1863, Maj. Zeilin was given command of the battalion of Marines sent to support the naval force whose mission was the capture of Charleston, S.C. But, because of illness, he returned after a few weeks to garrison duty at MB, Portsmouth, N.H. While serving at Portsmouth he was appointed Colonel Commandant of the Marine Corps on June 10, 1864. His faithful and efficient performance of the duties of Commandant of the Corps during the trying period of the last year of the war and those years immediately following it, is evidenced by the fact that he was promoted to the rank of brigadier general on Mar. 2, 1867. Brig. Gen. Jacob Zeilin retired as CMC on Nov. 1, 1876, after having served more than 45 years as a Marine Corps officer.

ZION, William. Private. Medal of Honor: b. Knightston, Ind., Oct. 23, 1878. William Zion's citation reads, in part: "... for distinguished conduct in the presence of the enemy at Peking, China, July 21 to Aug. 17, 1900...." Pvt. Zion was discharged from the Corps on July 29, 1904.

APPENDIX A

COMMANDANTS OF THE U.S. MARINE CORPS

1. SAMUEL NICHOLAS .... 28 Nov 1775 – Aug 1783
2. WILLIAM WARD BURROWS .... 12 Jul 1798 – 6 Mar 1804
3. FRANKLIN WHARTON .... 7 Mar 1804 – 1 Sep 1818
4. ANTHONY GALE .... 3 Mar 1819 – 8 Oct 1820
5. ARCHIBALD HENDERSON .... 17 Oct 1820 – 6 Jan 1859
6. JOHN HARRIS .... 7 Jan 1859 – 2 May 1864
7. JACOB ZEILIN .... 10 Jun 1864 – 31 Oct 1876
8. CHARLES G. McCAWLEY .... 1 Nov 1876 – 29 Jan 1891
9. CHARLES HEYWOOD .... 30 Jun 1891 – 2 Oct 1903
10. GEORGE F. ELLIOTT .... 3 Oct 1903 – 30 Nov 1910
11. WILLIAM P. BIDDLE .... 3 Feb 1911 – 24 Feb 1914
12. GEORGE BARNETT .... 25 Feb 1914 – 30 Jun 1920
13. JOHN A. LEJEUNE .... 1 Jul 1920 – 4 Mar 1929
14. WENDELL C. NEVILLE .... 5 Mar 1929 – 8 Jul 1930
15. BEN H. FULLER .... 9 Jul 1930 – 28 Feb 1934
16. JOHN H. RUSSELL, JR. .... 1 Mar 1934 – 30 Nov 1936
17. THOMAS HOLCOMB .... 1 Dec 1936 – 31 Dec 1943
18. ALEXANDER A. VANDEGRIFT .... 1 Jan 1944 – 31 Dec 1947
19. CLIFTON B. CATES .... 1 Jan 1948 – 31 Dec 1951
20. LEMUEL C. SHEPHERD, JR. .... 1 Jan 1952 – 31 Dec 1955
21. RANDOLPH McCALL PATE .... 1 Jan 1956 – 31 Dec 1959
22. DAVID M. SHOUP .... 1 Jan 1960 –

APPENDIX B

U. S. MARINE CORPS CHRONOLOGY OF COMBAT ACTIONS IN
WORLD WAR II — (*Courtesy Leatherneck Magazine*, Nov 1950)

Pearl Harbor — Midway   7 Dec 1941

1st Def Bn (less Wake Det)
2nd Eng Bn (less Co C)
3rd Def Bn
4th Def Bn
6th Def Bn
Marine Forces, 14th Naval Dist   7 Dec 1941
Marine Aircraft Gp-21, HQ and SMS
Marine Fighter Sq-211 (rear ech)
Marine Scout Bomber Sq-231
Marine Scout Bomber Sq-232
Marine Transp Sq-252

Guam — Bataan — Corregidor   8 Dec 1941 — 6 May 1942

1st Sep Marine Bn   8 Dec 1941 — 1 Jan 1942
4th Marines   8 Dec 1941 — 6 May 1942
Marine Barracks, Guam   8 Dec 1941 — 9 Dec 1941

Wake Island   8-23 Dec 1941

1st Def Bn (Wake Det)
Marine Fighter Sq-211 (Fwd Ech)   8-23 Dec 1941
Marine Scout Bomber Sq-231 (Adv Ech)

Battle of Midway   3-6 Jun 1942

2nd Raider Bn   4-6 Jun 1942
3rd Defense Bn (3-in AAA Gp only)   4 Jun 1942
6th Def Bn   3-6 Jun 1942
Marine Aircraft Gp-22, HQ & SMS   3-6 Jun 1942
Marine Fighter Sq-221   3-6 Jun 1942
Marine Scout Bomber Sq-241   3-6 Jun 1942

Guadalcanal — Tulagi Landings
(including First Savo)   7-9 Aug 1942

1st Amph Tractor Bn
1st Eng Bn (less Co B)
1st Marines   7-9 Aug 1942
1st Marine Div HQ & Sv Bn

1st Marine Div HQ
1st Mil Police Co
1st Med Bn (less Co C)
1st Parachute Bn
1st Pioneer Bn
1st Raider Bn
1st Scout Co (2nd Plat only)
1st Sv Bn (less Co B)
1st Signal Co
1st Spec Weapons Bn
1st Tank Bn (less Co C)
2nd Amph Tractor Bn (Co A only)   7-9 Aug 1942
2nd Eng Bn (Co A only)
2nd Med Bn (Co D only)
2nd Marines
2nd Marine Div Spl & Sv Troops (Det only)
2nd Pioneer Bn (Co A only)
2nd Sv Bn (Co C only)
2nd Special Weapons Bn
2nd Tank Bn (Co C only)
3rd Def Bn
5th Marines
10th Marines (3rd Bn only)
11th Marines (less 1st Bn)

Capture and Defense of Guadalcanal
10 Aug 1942 — 8 Feb 1943

1st Amph Tractor Bn	10 Aug 1942 – 22 Dec 1942
1st Aviation Eng Bn	18 Sep 1942 – 8 Feb 1943
1st Eng Bn (less Co B)	10 Aug 1942 – 22 Dec 1942
1st Eng Bn (Co B)	18 Sep 1942 – 22 Dec 1942
1st Marines	10 Aug 1942 – 22 Dec 1942
1st Marine Div HQ	10 Aug 1942 – 8 Dec 1942
1st Marine Div HQ & Sv Bn	10 Aug 1942 – 22 Dec 1942
1st Med Bn (less Co C)	10 Aug 1942 – 22 Dec 1942
(Co C)	18 Sep 1942 – 22 Dec 1942
1st Military Police Co	10 Aug 1942 – 22 Dec 1942
1st Parachute Bn	10 Aug 1942 – 18 Sep 1942
1st Pioneer Bn	7 Aug 1942 – 9 Aug 1942
1st Raider Bn	10 Aug 1942 – 16 Oct 1942
1st Scout Co	10 Aug 1942 – 22 Dec 1942
1st Sv Bn (less Co B)	10 Aug 1942 – 22 Dec 1942
(Co B)	18 Sep 1942 – 22 Dec 1942
1st Signal Co	10 Aug 1942 – 22 Dec 1942
1st Special Weapons Bn	10 Aug 1942 – 22 Dec 1942

1st Tank Co (less Co C)	10 Aug 1942 – 22 Dec 1942
2nd Amph Tractor Bn	
(1st Plat, Co A)	15 Sep 1942 – 31 Jan 1943
(HQ Plat, Co A)	4 Oct 1942 – 31 Jan 1943
2nd Aviation Eng Bn	30 Jan 1943 – 8 Feb 1943
2nd Eng Bn (Co A only)	10 Aug 1942 – 8 Feb 1943
2nd Marine Div HQ	4 Jan 1943 – 8 Feb 1943
2nd Marines	10 Aug 1942 – 31 Jan 1943
2nd Marine Div Spl & Sv Troops (Det)	10 Aug 1942 – 31 Jan 1943
2nd Med Bn (Co D only)	10 Aug 1942 – 8 Feb 1943
2nd Pioneer Bn (Co A only)	10 Aug 1942 – 8 Feb 1943
2nd Raider Bn	4 Nov 1942 – 17 Dec 1942
2nd Repl Bn	28 Oct 1942 – 11 Nov 1942
2nd Sv Bn (Co C only)	10 Aug 1942 – 8 Feb 1943
2nd Signal Co	12 Dec 1942 – 8 Feb 1943
2nd Special Weapons Bn	10 Aug 1942 – 8 Feb 1943
2nd Tank Bn (Co C only)	10 Aug 1942 – 8 Feb 1943
3rd Barrage Balloon Sq	8 Sep 1942 – 8 Feb 1943
3rd Def Bn	10 Aug 1942 – 8 Feb 1943
4th Repl Bn	12 Nov 1942 —
5th Def Bn (Det only)	8 Sep 1942 – 15 Jan 1943
5th Marines	10 Aug 1942 – 9 Dec 1942
6th Marines	4 Jan 1943 – 8 Feb 1943
7th Marines	18 Sep 1942 – 5 Jan 1943
8th Marines (1st Bn)	4 Nov 1942 – 31 Jan 1943
(2nd & 3rd Bns)	2 Nov 1942 – 8 Feb 1943
9th Def Bn	30 Nov 1942 – 8 Feb 1943
10th Marines (3rd Bn only)	10 Aug 1942 – 8 Feb 1943
(1st Bn only)	4 Nov 1942 – 8 Feb 1943
(2nd Bn only)	4 Jan 1943 – 8 Feb 1943
11th Def Bn	17 Jan 1943 – 8 Feb 1943
11th Marines (less 1st Bn)	10 Aug 1942 – 22 Dec 1942
(1st Bn)	18 Sep 1942 – 22 Dec 1942
14th Def Bn	15 Jan 1943 – 8 Feb 1943
18th Marines (Co's C & F)	4 Jan 1943 – 8 Feb 1943
1st Marine Air Wing, Hedron (Det)	3 Sep 1942 – 8 Feb 1943
2nd Marine Air Wing, Hedron (Fwd Ech)	26 Dec 1942 – 8 Feb 1943
Marine Aircraft Gp-14, HQ & SMS	16 Oct 1942 – 8 Feb 1943
Marine Aircraft Gp-23, HQ & SMS	
(Fwd Ech)	20 Aug 1942 – 4 Nov 1942
(Rear Ech)	29 Aug 1942 – 4 Nov 1942
Marine Aircraft Gp-25, HQ & SMS	
(Det HQ Sq)	3 Sep 1942 – 8 Feb 1943
(Det SMS)	18 Nov 1942 – 8 Feb 1943
Marine Fighter Sq-112	2 Nov 1942 – 8 Feb 1943
Marine Fighter Sq-121 (Flt Ech)	20 Oct 1942 – 28 Jan 1943

Marine Fighter Sq-122 (Flt Ech)	12 Nov 1942 – 8 Feb 1943
Marine Fighter Sq-123 (Flt Ech)	3 Feb 1943 – 8 Feb 1943
Marine Fighter Sq-124 (Flt Ech)	3 Feb 1943 – 8 Feb 1943
Marine Fighter Sq-131	11 Nov 1942 – 8 Feb 1943
Marine Scout Bomber-132	1 Nov 1942 – 19 Jan 1943
Marine Scout Bomber-141 (Flt Ech)	23 Sep 1942 – 17 Jan 1943
Marine Scout Bomber-142 (Flt Ech)	12 Nov 1942 – 8 Feb 1943
Marine Scout Bomber-144 (Flt Ech)	5 Feb 1943 – 8 Feb 1943
Marine Transp Sq-152 (Flt Ech)	21 Oct 1942 – 8 Feb 1943
Marine Photo Sq-154 (Det Flt Ech)	10 Nov 1942 – 8 Feb 1943
Marine Fighter Sq-212 (Flt Ech)	17 Aug 1942 – 21 Nov 1942
Marine Fighter Sq-223 (Flt Ech)	20 Aug 1942 – 16 Oct 1942
Marine Fighter Sq-224	30 Aug 1922 – 2 Nov 1942
Marine Scout Bomber-231 (Flt Ech)	30 Aug 1942 – 14 Nov 1942
Marine Scout Bomber-232	20 Aug 1942 – 2 Nov 1942
Marine Scout Bomber-233 (Flt Ech)	25 Dec 1942 – 5 Feb 1943
(Grd Ech)	18 Jan 1943 – 8 Feb 1943
Marine Scout Bomber Sq-234 (Flt Ech)	28 Jan 1943 – 8 Feb 1943
Marine Fighter Sq-251 (Flt Ech)	19 Aug 1942 – 8 Feb 1943
Marine Fighter Sq-253	3 Sep 1942 – 8 Feb 1943

Makin Island Raid   17-18 Aug 1942

2nd Raider Bn	17-18 Aug 1942

Battle of Eastern Solomons   23-25 Aug 1942

Marine Fighter Sq-223 (Flt Ech)	23-25 Aug 1942
Marine Scout Bomber Sq-232 (Flt Ech)	

Battle of Cape Esperance (Second Savo)   11-12 Oct 1942

Marine Fighter Sq-121 (Flt Ech)	11-12 Oct 1942
Marine Scout Bomber Sq-141 (Flt Ech)	11-12 Oct 1942
Marine Fighter Sq-223	11-12 Oct 1942
Marine Fighter Sq-224 (Flt Ech)	11-12 Oct 1942
Marine Scout Bomber Sq-231	11-12 Oct 1942
Marine Scout Bomber Sq-232	11-12 Oct 1942

New Georgia—Rendova—Vangunu Occupation   20 Jun 1943 — 31 Aug 1943

1st Raider Bn	5 Jul 1943 – 28 Aug 1943
1st Raider Regt (HQ)	5 Jul 1943 – 28 Aug 1943
2nd Sep Wire Plat	1 Jul 1943 – 31 Aug 1943
4th Raider Bn	21 Jun 1943 – 11 Jul 1943

9th Def Bn	30 Jun 1943 – 31 Aug 1943
10th Def Bn (Tank Plat only)	26 Jul 1943 – 13 Oct 1943
11th Def Bn (Btry E)	14 Jul 1943 – 31 Aug 1943
(Tank Plat)	4 Aug 1943 – 31 Aug 1943
(Btry K)	7 Aug 1943 – 31 Aug 1943
Marine Aircraft Gp-25, HQ & SMS	21 Jun 1943 – 31 Aug 1943
Marine Fighter Sq-121	21 Jun 1943 – 22 Jul 1943
Marine Fighter Sq-122	21 Jun 1943 – 24 Jul 1943
Marine Fighter Sq-124	21 Jun 1943 – 31 Aug 1943
Marine Scout Bomber Sq-132	22 Jun 1943 – 1 Aug 1943
Marine Scout Bomber Sq-141	20 Jun 1943 – 31 Aug 1943
Marine Torpedo Bomber Sq-143	20 Jul 1943 – 29 Aug 1943
Marine Scout Bomber Sq-144	21 Jun 1943 – 1 Aug 1943
Marine Transp Sq-152	20 June 1943 – 5 Aug 1943
Marine Transp Sq-153	20 Jun 1943 – 18 Aug 1943
Marine Fighter Sq-214	22 Jul 1943 – 31 Aug 1943
Marine Fighter Sq-215	25 Jul 1943 – 31 Aug 1943
(Det Grd Ech)	21 Aug 1943 – 31 Aug 1943
Marine Fighter Sq-221	27 Jun 1943 – 24 Aug 1943
Marine Scout Bomber Sq-233	13 Aug 1943 – 31 Aug 1943
Marine Scout Bomber Sq-234	4 Aug 1943 – 31 Aug 1943
Marine Transp Sq-253 (Det Flt Ech)	20 Jun 1943 – 31 Aug 1943

Vella—Lavella Occupation   15 Aug 1943 — 16 Oct 1943

1 Marine Amph Corps HQ (Fwd Ech)	25 Sep 1943 – 16 Oct 1943
1 Marine Amph Corps Med Bn (Co A)	7 Oct 1943 – 16 Oct 1943
1st Marine Amph Corps Motor Transp Bn (Co A)	25 Sep 1943 – 16 Oct 1943
(Co B)	7 Oct 1943 – 16 Oct 1943
1 Marine Amph Corps Signal Bn (Det)	25 Sep 1943 – 16 Oct 1943
1st Med Bn (Det Co A)	25 Sep 1943 – 16 Oct 1943
1st Parachute Bn	4 Oct 1943 – 16 Oct 1943
1st Parachute Regt	4 Oct 1943 – 16 Oct 1943
2nd Parachute Bn	1 Sep 1943 – 16 Oct 1943
3rd Special Weapons Bn (2d Plat, Btry A)	25 Sep 1943 – 16 Oct 1943
4th Base Depot (Co's A & B, Br No 3)	25 Sep 1943 – 16 Oct 1943
4th Def Bn	15 Aug 1943 – 16 Oct 1943
Marine Aircraft Gp-25, HQ & SMS	15 Aug 1943 – 16 Oct 1943
Marine Fighter Sq-123	15 Aug 1943 – 18 Sep 1943
Marine Fighter Sq-124	15 Aug 1943 – 6 Sep 1943
Marine Scout Bomber Sq-141	15 Aug 1943 – 3 Sep 1943
Marine Transp Bomber Sq-143	15 Aug 1943 – 29 Aug 1943
Marine Fighter Sq-214	15 Aug 1943 – 2 Sep 1943
Marine Fighter Sq-215 (Flt Ech)	15 Aug 1943 – 6 Sep 1943
Marine Fighter Sq-221	15 Aug 1943 – 24 Aug 1943
Marine Fighter Sq-222 (Flt Ech)	5 Sep 1943 – 15 Oct 1943

Marine Scout Bomber Sq-232	23 Sep 1943 — 16 Oct 1943
Marine Scout Bomber Sq-233	15 Aug 1943 — 21 Sep 1943
Marine Scout Bomber Sq-234	15 Aug 1943 — 7 Sep 1943
Marine Scout Bomber Sq-235 (Flt Ech)	4 Sep 1943 — 16 Oct 1943
Marine Scout Bomber Sq-236	7 Sep 1943 — 16 Oct 1943
Marine Fighter Sq (N)-531 (Adv Ech)	12 Sep 1943 — 16 Oct 1943
(Rear Ech)	10 Oct 1943 — 16 Oct 1943

Eastern New Guinea Operation
(including Finschlafen, Oro Bay, Milne Bay, and Goodenough Is)   22 Sep 1943 — 17 Feb 1944

1st Amphibious Track Bn	15 Oct 1943 — 25 Dec 1943
1st Marines	22 Sep 1943 — 25 Dec 1943
1st Marine Div HQ	20 Oct 1943 — 31 Dec 1943
1st Marine Div HQ & Sv Bn	15 Oct 1943 — 31 Dec 1943
1st Med Bn	15 Oct 1943 — 25 Dec 1943
1st Military Police Co	15 Oct 1943 — 30 Jan 1944
1st Motor Transp Bn	15 Oct 1943 — 25 Dec 1943
1st Sv Bn	15 Oct 1943 — 30 Jan 1944
1st Special Weapons Bn	15 Oct 1943 — 24 Jan 1944
1st Tank Bn	15 Oct 1943 — 25 Dec 1943
5th Marines	8 Oct 1943 — 28 Dec 1943
7th Marines	20 Oct 1943 — 25 Dec 1943
11th Marines	15 Oct 1943 — 25 Dec 1943
17th Marines (less 3rd Bn)	15 Oct 1943 — 25 Dec 1943
(3rd Bn)	1 Nov 1943 — 25 Dec 1943

Woodlark Island, Occupation and
Consolidation of   30 Jun 1943 — 7 Dec 1943

12th Def Bn	30 Jun 1943 — 7 Dec 1943

Cape Gloucester (New Britain)
Operation   26 Dec 1943 — 1 Mar 1944

1st Amph Tractor Bn	26 Dec 1943 — 1 Mar 1944
1st Marines	26 Dec 1943 — 1 Mar 1944
1st Marine Div HQ	1 Jan 1944 — 1 Mar 1944
1st Med Bn (less Rear Ech)	26 Dec 1943 — 1 Mar 1944
1st Marine Div HQ and Sv Bn	1 Jan 1944 — 1 Mar 1944
1st Military Police Co	31 Jan 1944 — 1 Mar 1944
1st Motor Transp Bn	26 Dec 1943 — 31 Jan 1944
1st Sv Bn	31 Jan 1944 — 1 Mar 1944
1st Special Weapons Bn	25 Jan 1944 — 1 Mar 1944
1st Tank Bn (less Co B)	26 Dec 1943 — 1 Mar 1944

5th Marines	29 Dec 1943 — 15 Jan 1944
7th Marines	26 Dec 1943 — 1 Mar 1944
11th Marines	26 Dec 1943 — 1 Mar 1944
12th Def Bn	26 Dec 1943 — 1 Mar 1944
17th Marines	26 Dec 1943 — 1 Mar 1944

Green Islands Landing   15-19 Feb 1944

1st Marines Air Wing, Hedron	15 Feb 1944 — 19 Feb 1944
Marine Torpedo Bomber Sq-143	15 Feb 1944 — 19 Feb 1944
Marine Fighter Sq-212	15 Feb 1944 — 17 Feb 1944
Marine Fighter Sq-216	15 Feb 1944 — 19 Feb 1944
Marine Fighter Sq-217 (Flt Ech)	15 Feb 1944 — 19 Feb 1944
Marine Fighter Sq-218 (Flt Ech)	15 Feb 1944 — 19 Feb 1944
Marine Fighter Sq (N)-531	15 Feb 1944 — 19 Feb 1944
Marine Scout Bomber Sq-233	15 Feb 1944 — 19 Feb 1944
Marine Scout Bomber Sq-244	15 Feb 1944 — 19 Feb 1944

Treasury Island Landing   27 Oct 1943 — 6 Nov 1943

1st Marine Amph Corps Signal Bn (2nd Plat, Co A)	27 Oct 1943 — 6 Nov 1943
1st Marine Air Wing, Hedron	27 Oct 1943 — 6 Nov 1943
Marine Fighter Sq-212	27 Oct 1943 — 6 Nov 1943
Marine Fighter Sq-215 (Flt Ech)	27 Oct 1943 — 6 Nov 1943
Marine Fighter Sq-221	27 Oct 1943 — 6 Nov 1943
Marine Fighter Sq-531 (N)	27 Oct 1943 — 6 Nov 1943

Choiseul Island Diversion   28 Oct 1943 — 4 Nov 1943

1st Marine Amph Corps Exper Rocket Plat (Det)	28 Oct 1943 — 4 Nov 1943
1st Parachute Regt (Det)	28 Oct 1943 — 4 Nov 1943
2nd Parachute Bn	28 Oct 1943 — 4 Nov 1943
Marine Fighter Sq (N)-531	28 Oct 1943 — 4 Nov 1943

Occupation and Defense of Cape Torokina — Bougainville   1 Nov 1943 — 15 Dec 1943

1 Marine Amph Corps HQ (Adv Ech)	1 Dec 1943 — 15 Dec 1943
1 Marine Amph Corps HQ & Sv Bn (1st Ech)	1 Nov 1943 — 15 Dec 1943
1 Marine Amph Corps HQ & Sv Bn	17 Nov 1943 — 15 Dec 1943
1 Marine Amph Corps Exper Rocket Plat	6 Dec 1943 — 15 Dec 1943
1 Marine Amph Corps Motor Transp Bn (Fwd Ech)	26 Nov 1943 — 15 Dec 1943
1 Marine Amph Corps Signal Bn (Fwd Ech)	1 Nov 1943 — 15 Dec 1943
(1st Ech)	11 Nov 1943 — 15 Dec 1943
(2nd Ech)	13 Nov 1943 — 15 Dec 1943

1st Parachute Bn	23 Nov 1943 — 15 Dec 1943
1st Parachute Regt	4 Dec 1943 — 15 Dec 1943
1st War Dog Plat	1 Nov 1943 — 15 Dec 1943
1st 155mm Arty Bn	1 Nov 1943 — 15 Dec 1943
2nd Raider Bn	1 Nov 1943 — 15 Dec 1943
2nd Raider Regt (Prov)	1 Nov 1943 — 15 Dec 1943
2nd 155mm Arty Bn	16 Nov 1943 — 15 Dec 1943
3rd Amph Tractor Bn	1 Nov 1943 — 15 Dec 1943
3rd Def Bn (1st Ech)	1 Nov 1943 — 15 Dec 1943
(2nd Ech)	11 Nov 1943 — 15 Dec 1943
3rd Marines	1 Nov 1943 — 15 Dec 1943
3rd Marine Div HQ	1 Nov 1943 — 15 Dec 1943
3rd Marine Div HQ & Sv Bn (less dets HQ Co)	1 Nov 1943 — 15 Dec 1943
3rd Marine Div Spl & Sv Troops (Det)	1 Nov 1943 — 15 Dec 1943
3rd Med Bn (less Co E & Dets HQ & Sv Co)	1 Nov 1943 — 15 Dec 1943
3rd Motor Transp Bn	1 Nov 1943 — 15 Dec 1943
3rd Parachute Bn	4 Dec 1943 — 15 Dec 1943
3rd Raider Bn	1 Nov 1943 — 15 Dec 1943
3rd Sep Wire Plat (less Dets)	1 Nov 1943 — 15 Dec 1943
3rd Sv Bn	1 Nov 1943 — 15 Dec 1943
3rd Signal Co	1 Nov 1943 — 15 Dec 1943
3rd Special Weapons Bn	17 Nov 1943 — 15 Dec 1943
3rd Tank Bn	1 Nov 1943 — 15 Dec 1943
4th Base Depot (Dets Branch No 3)	1 Nov 1943 — 15 Dec 1943
9th Marines	1 Nov 1943 — 15 Dec 1943
19th Marines	1 Nov 1943 — 15 Dec 1943
21st Marines (less 2nd & 3rd Bn)	6 Nov 1943 — 15 Dec 1943
21st Marines (2nd Bn)	11 Nov 1943 — 15 Dec 1943
(3rd Bn)	17 Nov 1943 — 15 Dec 1943
1st Marine Air Wing, Hedron	1 Nov 1943 — 15 Dec 1943
Marine Torpedo Bomber Sq-143 (Fwd Ech)	1 Nov 1943 — 30 Nov 1943
Marine Scout Bomber Sq-144 (Flt Ech)	1 Nov 1943 — 22 Nov 1943
Marine Transp Sq-153	1 Nov 1943 — 15 Dec 1943
Marine Fighter Sq-215 (Flt Ech)	1 Nov 1943 — 15 Dec 1943
(Grd Ech)	10 Dec 1943 — 15 Dec 1943
Marine Fighter Sq-221	1 Nov 1943 — 19 Nov 1943
Marine Scout Bomber Sq-232	1 Nov 1943 — 15 Dec 1943
Marine Scout Bomber Sq-244 (Flt Ech)	1 Nov 1943 — 29 Nov 1943
Marine Fighter Sq (N)-531	1 Nov 1943 — 15 Dec 1943

Tarawa (Gilbert Islands)
Operation   13 Nov 1943 — 8 Dec 1943

1 Marine Amph Corps Medium Tank Bn (Co C)	20 Nov 1943 — 24 Nov 1943
2nd Airdrome Bn (Ellice Is)	13 Nov 1943 — 8 Dec 1943
2nd Amph Tractor Bn	20 Nov 1943 — 5 Dec 1943

2nd AT Bn	20 Nov 1943 – 30 Nov 1943
2nd Def Bn	24 Nov 1943 – 8 Dec 1943
2nd Eng Bn	20 Nov 1943 – 24 Nov 1943
2nd Marines	20 Nov 1943 – 24 Nov 1943
2nd Marine Div HQ	20 Nov 1943 – 4 Dec 1943
2nd Marine Div Spl & Sv Troops	20 Nov 1943 – 24 Nov 1943
2nd Med Bn	20 Nov 1943 – 24 Nov 1943
2nd Pioneer Bn	20 Nov 1943 – 24 Nov 1943
2nd Sv Bn	20 Nov 1943 – 24 Nov 1943
2nd Special Weapons Bn	20 Nov 1943 – 24 Nov 1943
2nd Tank Bn	20 Nov 1943 – 24 Nov 1943
V Amph Corps HQ	20 Nov 1943 – 25 Nov 1943
V Amph Corps Recon Co	18 Nov 1943 – 3 Dec 1943
5th Def Bn (Funafuti)	13 Nov 1943 – 8 Dec 1943
6th Marines	20 Nov 1943 – 8 Dec 1943
7th Def Bn	20 Nov 1943 – 8 Dec 1943
8th Def Bn	28 Nov 1943 – 8 Dec 1943
8th Marines	20 Nov 1943 – 24 Nov 1943
10th Marines	20 Nov 1943 – 1 Dec 1943
18th Marines	20 Nov 1943 – 24 Nov 1943
25th Repl Draft	13 Nov 1943 – 8 Dec 1943
Marine Scout Bomber Sq-331 (Det Flt Ech)	30 Nov 1943 – 8 Dec 1943
Marine Transp Sq-353 (Det Flt Ech)	26 Nov 1943 – 8 Dec 1943

Occupation of Kwajalein and Majuro Atolls — 29 Jan 1944 — 8 Feb 1944

1st Armored Amph Bn	1 Feb 1944 – 6 Feb 1944
1st Def Bn	1 Feb 1944 – 8 Feb 1944
1st Joint Assault Signal Co	1 Feb 1944 – 8 Feb 1944
1st Prov Rocket Det	1 Feb 1944 – 8 Feb 1944
2nd Sep Pack Howitzer Bn (Fl Res)	1 Feb 1944 – 4 Feb 1944
2nd Sep Tank Co	31 Jan 1944 – 8 Feb 1944
4th Amph Tractor Bn	1 Feb 1944 – 6 Feb 1944
4th Marine Div HQ	1 Feb 1944 – 8 Feb 1944
4th Marine Div HQ & Sv Bn	1 Feb 1944 – 8 Feb 1944
4th Med Bn	1 Feb 1944 – 8 Feb 1944
4th Motor Transp Bn	1 Feb 1944 – 8 Feb 1944
4th Tank Bn	1 Feb 1944 – 8 Feb 1944
4th Sv Bn	1 Feb 1944 – 8 Feb 1944
4th Special Weapons Bn	1 Feb 1944 – 8 Feb 1944
V Amph Corps HQ	1 Feb 1944 – 7 Feb 1944
V Amph Corps HQ & Sv Bn	1 Feb 1944 – 7 Feb 1944
V Amph Corps Recon Co	30 Jan 1944 – 2 Feb 1944
V Amph Corps Signal Bn	1 Feb 1944 – 7 Feb 1944

V Amph Corps Tactical Gp I (Fl Res) (Consisted of 22d Marines, reinf by Army units)	1 Feb 1944 — 4 Feb 1944
10th Amph Tractor Bn	1 Feb 1944 — 8 Feb 1944
11th Amph Tractor Bn (Co A only)	1 Feb 1944 — 8 Feb 1944
14th Marines	1 Feb 1944 — 8 Feb 1944
15th Def Bn	2 Feb 1944 — 8 Feb 1944
20th Marines	1 Feb 1944 — 8 Feb 1944
22nd Marines (Fl Res)	1 Feb 1944 — 4 Feb 1944
23rd Marines	1 Feb 1944 — 8 Feb 1944
24th Marines	1 Feb 1944 — 8 Feb 1944
25th Marines	1 Feb 1944 — 8 Feb 1944
Marine Aircraft Gp-31, HQ & SMS	7 Feb 1944 — 8 Feb 1944
Marine Fighter Sq-111 (Grd Ech)	7 Feb 1944 — 8 Feb 1944
Marine Fighter Sq-113	2 Feb 1944 — 8 Feb 1944
Marine Scout Bomber Sq-231 (Grd Ech)	3 Feb 1944 — 8 Feb 1944
Marine Fighter Sq-311	7 Feb 1944 — 8 Feb 1944
Marine Fighter Sq-422	2 Feb 1944 — 8 Feb 1944

Occupation of Eniwetok Atoll
(Marshalls)   17 Feb 1944 — 2 Mar 1944

1st Def Bn	17 Feb 1944 — 2 Mar 1944
2nd Sep Eng Co.	17 Feb 1944 — 25 Feb 1944
2nd Sep Med Co	17 Feb 1944 — 25 Feb 1944
2nd Sep Pack How Bn (Fl Res)	17 Feb 1944 — 25 Feb 1944
2nd Sep Tank Co	17 Feb 1944 — 2 Mar 1944
2nd Sep Transp Co	17 Feb 1944 — 25 Feb 1944
4th Tank Bn (Co D Scout only)	17 Feb 1944 — 25 Feb 1944
V Amph Corps Recon Co	17 Feb 1944 — 23 Feb 1944
V Amph Corps Tactical Gp I (Fl Res)	17 Feb 1944 — 2 Mar 1944
10th Def Bn	21 Feb 1944 — 2 Mar1944
22ndMarines	17 Feb 1944 — 25 Feb 1944
Marine Aircraft Warning Sq-1	20 Feb 1944 — 2 Mar. 1944
Marine Aircraft Gp-22,HQ & SMS	20 Feb 1944 — 2 Mar 1944
Marine Fighter Sq-113	17 Feb 1944 — 2 Mar 1944
Marine Fighter Sq-422	17 Feb 1944 — 2 Mar 1944

Capture and Occupation of
Saipan   15 Jun 1944 — 10 Aug 1944

1st Amph Truck Co	15 Jun 1944 — 24 Jul 1944
1st Joint Assault Signal Co	15 Jun 1944 — 24 Jul 1944
1st Prov Rocket Det	15 Jun 1944 — 24 Jul 1944
2nd Amph Tractor Bn	15 Jun 1944 — 24 Jul 1944
2nd Armored Amph Bn	15 Jun 1944 — 24 Jul 1944
2nd Eng Bn	12 Jul 1944 — 10 Aug 1944
2nd Joint Assault Signal Co	15 Jun 1944 — 24 Jul 1944

2nd Marines	15 Jun 1944 — 24 Jul 1944
2nd Marine Div HQ	15 Jun 1944 — 24 Jul 1944
2nd Med Bn (HQ Sv & Co's A, B, and C)	15 Jun 1944 — 10 Aug 1944
(Co's D and E)	15 Jun 1944 — 24 Jul 1944
2nd Motor Transp Bn	15 Jun 1944 — 24 Jul 1944
2nd Pioneer Bn	15 Jun 1944 — 24 Jul 1944
2nd Prov Rocket Det	15 Jun 1944 — 24 Jul 1944
2nd Sv Bn	15 Jun 1944 — 24 Jul 1944
2nd Tank Bn	15 Jun 1944 — 24 Jul 1944
2nd 155mm Howitzer Bn	15 Jun 1944 — 16 Jul 1944
III Amph Corps, Air Delivery Sect (Fwd Ech)	26 Jul 1944 — 10 Aug 1944
4th Marine Div HQ	15 Jun 1944 — 24 Jul 1944
4th Marine Div HQ & Sv Bn	15 Jun 1944 — 24 Jul 1944
4th Med Bn	15 Jul 1944 — 24 Jul 1944
4th Motor Transp Bn	15 Jun 1944 — 24 Jul 1944
4th Sv Bn	15 Jun 1944 — 24 Jul 1944
4th Tank Bn	15 Jun 1944 — 24 Jul 1944
4th 105mm Howitzer Bn	15 Jun 1944 — 24 Jul 1944
V Amph Corps Air Delivery Sect	15 Jun 1944 — 24 Jul 1944
V Amph Corps HQ	15 Jun 1944 — 24 Jul 1944
V Amph Corps HQ & Sv Bn	15 Jun 1944 — 24 Jul 1944
V Amph Corps Med Bn	15 Jun 1944 — 24 Jul 1944
V Amph Corps Motor Transp Co	15 Jun 1944 — 24 Jul 1944
V Amph Corps Prov Eng Gp	15 Jun 1944 — 24 Jul 1944
V Amph Corps LVT Gp	15 Jun 1944 — 24 Jul 1944
V Amph Corps Signal Bn	15 Jun 1944 — 24 Jul 1944
V Amph Corps Recon Bn	15 Jun 1944 — 24 Jul 1944
6th Marines	15 Jun 1944 — 26 Jul 1944
7th Field Depot	15 Jun 1944 — 24 Jul 1944
10th Amph Tractor Bn (less Co A)	15 Jun 1944 — 24 Jul 1944
10th Marines	15 Jun 1944 — 24 Jul 1944
11th Amph Tractor Bn (Co C only)	15 Jun 1944 — 24 Jul 1944
14th Marines	15 Jun 1944 — 24 Jul 1944
18th Marines	15 Jun 1944 — 24 Jul 1944
20th Marines	15 Jun 1944 — 24 Jul 1944
23rd Marines	15 Jun 1944 — 24 Jul 1944
24th Marines	15 Jun 1944 — 24 Jul 1944
25th Marines	15 Jun 1944 — 24 Jul 1944
29th Marines	15 Jun 1944 — 24 Jul 1944
Island Command, Tinian (Adv Detail)	15 Jun 1944 — 24 Jul 1944
Marine Observ Sq-2	17 Jun 1944 — 10 Aug 1944
4th Marine Air Wing (Mar Air Def Det Marianas Area)	17 Jun 1944 — 10 Aug 1944
Aircraft Warning Sq-5	15 Jun 1944 — 10 Aug 1944
Marine Transp Sq-252 (Det Flt Ech)	20 Jun 1944 — 10 Aug 1944
Marine Transp Sq-353	3 Aug 1944 — 10 Aug 1944

Marine Fighter Sq (N)-532 (Adv Ech)   6 Jul 1944 — 10 Aug 1944
Marine Transp Sq-952 (Det Flt Ech)   2 Jul 1944 — 5 Jul 1944

Capture and Occupation of Guam   21 Jul 1944 — 15 Aug 1944

1st Armored Amph Bn	21 Jul 1944 — 13 Aug 1944
1st Base HQ Bn	21 Jul 1944 — 15 Aug 1944
1st Exper Rocket Plat	21 Jul 1944 — 15 Aug 1944
1st Military Police Co	27 Jul 1944 — 15 Aug 1944
1st Prov Marine Brig (HQ & Brig Troops) 1st Prov Brig composed of 4th Marines Reinf and 22nd Marines, Reinf	21 Jul 1944 — 15 Aug 1944
1st Prov Repl Co	21 Jul 1944 — 10 Aug 1944
1st Radio Intell Plat	21 Jul 1944 — 15 Aug 1944
1st Sep Eng Bn	21 Jul 1944 — 15 Aug 1944
1st Sep Wire Plat	21 Jul 1944 — 15 Aug 1944
1st War Dog Plat	21 Jul 1944 — 15 Aug 1944
1st 105mm Arty Bn (Howitzer)	21 Jul 1944 — 15 Aug 1944
2nd Ammunition Co	21 Jul 1944 — 15 Aug 1944
2nd Aviation Eng Bn	21 Jul 1944 — 15 Aug 1944
2nd Sep Eng Bn	21 Jul 1944 — 15 Aug 1944
2nd War Dog Plat	21 Jul 1944 — 15 Aug 1944
2nd 155mm Howitzer Bn	21 Jul 1944 — 15 Aug 1944
3rd Amph Tractor Bn	21 Jul 1944 — 15 Aug 1944
3rd Joint Assault Signal Co	21 Jul 1944 — 15 Aug 1944
III Amph Corps Air Delivery Sect (Fwd Ech)	8 Aug 1944 — 15 Aug 1944
III Amph Corps Arty HQ	21 Jul 1944 — 12 Aug 1944
III Amph Corps HQ	21 Jul 1944 — 12 Aug 1944
III Amph Corps HQ & Sv Bn	21 Jul 1944 — 15 Aug 1944
III Amph Corps Med Bn (Rein)	21 Jul 1944 — 15 Aug 1944
III Amph Corps Motor Transp Bn	21 Jul 1944 — 15 Aug 1944
III Amph Corps Signal Bn	21 Jul 1944 — 15 Aug 1944
3rd Marines	21 Jul 1944 — 15 Aug 1944
3rd Marine Div HQ	21 Jul 1944 — 15 Aug 1944
3rd Marine Div HQ & Sv Bn (less Dets) (HQ Bn)	21 Jul 1944 — 15 Aug 1944
3rd Marine Div Spl & Sv Troops (Dets)	21 Jul 1944 — 15 Aug 1944
3rd Med Bn (less Co E and Dets HQ and Sv Co)	21 Jul 1944 — 15 Aug 1944
3rd Motor Transp Bn	21 Jul 1944 — 15 Aug 1944
3rd Sv Bn	21 Jul 1944 — 15 Aug 1944
3rd Tank Bn	21 Jul 1944 — 15 Aug 1944
3rd War Dog Plat	21 Jul 1944 — 15 Aug 1944
4th Ammunition Co	21 Jul 1944 — 15 Aug 1944
4th Amph Tractor Bn	21 Jul 1944 — 15 Aug 1944
4th Marines	21 Jul 1944 — 15 Aug 1944
V Amph Corps HQ	13 Aug 1944 — 15 Aug 1944

V Amph Corps HQ & Sv Bn	21 Jul 1944 — 15 Aug 1944
V Amph Corps Signal Bn	21 Jul 1944 — 15 Aug 1944
5th Field Depot (less rear ech)	21 Jul 1944 — 15 Aug 1944
7th 155mm Arty Bn	21 Jul 1944 — 15 Aug 1944
9th AAA Bn (1st Ech only)	21 Jul 1944 — 15 Aug 1944
9th Def Bn (less dets)	21 Jul 1944 — 15 Aug 1944
9th Marines	21 Jul 1944 — 15 Aug 1944
10th Amph Tractor Bn (Co A only)	21 Jul 1944 — 15 Aug 1944
11th Amph Tractor Bn (Co A only)	21 Jul 1944 — 15 Aug 1944
12th Marines	21 Jul 1944 — 15 Aug 1944
14th Def Bn (less Sea Coast Arty Gp)	21 Jul 1944 — 15 Aug 1944
14th AAA Bn	21 Jul 1944 — 15 Aug 1944
19th Marines	21 Jul 1944 — 15 Aug 1944
21st Marines	21 Jul 1944 — 15 Aug 1944
22nd Marines	21 Jul 1944 — 15 Aug 1944
Island Command, Guam	26 Jul 1944 — 15 Aug 1944
Marine Observ Sq-1 (Grd Ech)	21 Jul 1944 — 15 Aug 1944
(Flt Ech)	30 Jul 1944 — 15 Aug 1944
Aircraft Warning Sq-2	21 Jul 1944 — 15 Aug 1944
4th Marine Aircraft Wing (Mar Air Def Det, Marianas Area)	17 Jun 1944 — 15 Aug 1944
Marine Aircraft Gp-21, HQ & SMS (Fwd Ech)	27 Jul 1944 — 15 Aug 1944
Marine Fighter Sq-217 (Det Grd Ech)	30 Jul 1944 — 15 Aug 1944
(Remainder Sq)	4 Aug 1944 — 15 Aug 1944
Marine Fighter Sq-225	30 Jul 1944 — 15 Aug 1944
Marine Transp Sq-252 (Det Flt Ech)	21 Jul 1944 — 15 Aug 1944
Marine Transp Sq-353	3 Aug 1944 — 10 Aug 1944
Marine Fighter Sq (N)-532 (Adv Ech)	21 Jul 1944 — 10 Aug 1944
(Rear Ech)	21 Jul 1944 — 10 Aug 1944
Marine Fighter Sq (N)-534 (Adv Ech)	29 Jul 1944 — 15 Aug 1944
(Flt Ech)	4 Aug 1944 — 15 Aug 1944

Capture and Occupation of Tinian 24 Jul 1944 — 10 Aug 1944

1st Amph Truck Co	24 Jul 1944 — 10 Aug 1944
1st Joint Assault Signal Co	24 Jul 1944 — 7 Aug 1944
1st Prov Rocket Det	24 Jul 1944 — 7 Aug 1944
2nd Amph Tractor Bn	24 Jul 1944 — 10 Aug 1944
2nd Amph Truck Co	24 Jul 1944 — 7 Aug 1944
2nd Armored Amph Bn	24 Jul 1944 — 10 Aug 1944
2nd Base HQ Bn	2 Aug 1944 — 10 Aug 1944
2nd Joint Assault Signal Co	24 Jul 1944 — 10 Aug 1944
2nd Marines	24 Jul 1944 — 10 Aug 1944
2nd Marine Div HQ	24 Jul 1944 — 10 Aug 1944
2nd Med Bn (Co's D and E)	24 Jul 1944 — 10 Aug 1944

2nd Med Tractor Bn	24 Jul 1944 – 10 Aug 1944
2nd Prov Rocket Det	24 Jul 1944 – 10 Aug 1944
2nd Sv Bn	24 Jul 1944 – 10 Aug 1944
2nd Tank Bn	24 Jul 1944 – 10 Aug 1944
4th Marine Div HQ	24 Jul 1944 – 7 Aug 1944
4th Marine Div HQ & Sv Bn	24 Jul 1944 – 7 Aug 1944
4th Med Bn (Co's D and E)	24 Jul 1944 – 7 Aug 1944
4th Motor Transp Bn	24 Jul 1944 – 7 Aug 1944
4th Sv Bn	24 Jul 1944 – 7 Aug 1944
4th Tank Bn	24 Jul 1944 – 7 Aug 1944
4th 105mm Howitzer Bn	24 Jul 1944 – 7 Aug 1944
5th Amph Tractor Bn	24 Jul 1944 – 10 Aug 1944
V Amph Corps Air Det Sect	24 Jul 1944 – 10 Aug 1944
V Amph Corps Amph Recon Bn	24 Jul 1944 – 10 Aug 1944
V Amph Corps HQ	24 Jul 1944 – 10 Aug 1944
V Amph Corps Med Bn (less Co's B and C, Det HQ & Sv Co)	24 Jul 1944 – 7 Aug 1944
V Amph Corps Motor Transp Bn	24 Jul 1944 – 7 Aug 1944
V Amph Corps Prov Eng Gp	24 Jul 1944 – 7 Aug 1944
V Amph Corps Prov LVT Gp	24 Jul 1944 – 7 Aug 1944
V Amph Corps Signal Bn	24 Jul 1944 – 7 Aug 1944
6th Marines (less 2nd Bn)	26 Jul 1944 – 10 Aug 1944
(2nd Bn)	24 Jul 1944 – 8 Aug 1944
7th Field Depot	24 Jul 1944 – 10 Aug 1944
8th Marines	24 Jul 1944 – 10 Aug 1944
10th Amph Tractor Bn (less Co A)	24 Jul 1944 – 7 Aug 1944
10th Marines (less 2nd Bn)	24 Jul 1944 – 10 Aug 1944
11th Amph Tractor Bn (Co C only)	24 Jul 1944 – 7 Aug 1944
14th Marines	24 Jul 1944 – 7 Aug 1944
17th AAA Bn	2 Aug 1944 – 10 Aug 1944
18th Marines	24 Jul 1944 – 10 Aug 1944
20th Marines	24 Jul 1944 – 10 Aug 1944
23rd Marines	24 Jul 1944 – 10 Aug 1944
24th Marines	24 Jul 1944 – 10 Aug 1944
25th Marines	24 Jul 1944 – 7 Aug 1944
29th Marines	24 Jul 1944 – 10 Aug 1944
Island Command (Adv Detail)	29 Jul 1944 – 10 Aug 1944
Marine Observ Sq-2	24 Jul 1944 – 10 Aug 1944
Marine Observ Sq-4	24 Jul 1944 – 10 Aug 1944
Marine Transp Sq-252 (Det Flt Ech)	24 Jul 1944 – 10 Aug 1944
Marine Transp Sq-353	3 Aug 1944 – 10 Aug 1944

Capture and Occupation of Southern Palau Island   15 Sep 1944 — 14 Oct 1944

1st Amph Tractor Bn	15 Sep 1944 – 14 Oct 1944

1st Eng Bn	15 Sep 1944 — 14 Oct 1944
1st Marines	15 Sep 1944 — 20 Oct 1944
1st Marine Div HQ	15 Sep 1944 — 14 Oct 1944
1st Marine Div HQ & Sv Bn	15 Sep 1944 — 2 Oct 1944
1st Med Bn	15 Sep 1944 — 2 Oct 1944
1st Motor Transp Bn	14 Sep 1944 — 2 Oct 1944
1st Pioneer Bn	15 Sep 1944 — 14 Oct 1944
1st Sv Bn	15 Sep 1944 — 2 Oct 1944
1st Tank Bn	15 Sep 1944 — 14 Oct 1944
2nd Radio Intell Plat	15 Sep 1944 — 14 Oct 1944
III Amph Corps, Air Delivery Sect (Fwd Ech)	15 Sep 1944 — 14 Oct 1944
III Amph Corps HQ	15 Sep 1944 —14 Oct 1944
3rd Armored Amph Bn	15 Sep 1944 — 14 Oct 1944
3rd Base HQ Bn	22 Sep 1944 — 14 Oct 1944
3rd 155mm Art Bn	15 Sep 1944 — 14 Oct 1944
4th Joint Assault Signal Co	15 Sep 1944 — 14 Oct 1944
4th War Dog Plat	15 Sep 1944 — 14 Oct 1944
5th Marines	15 Sep 1944 — 14 Oct 1944
5th Sep Wire Plat	15 Sep 1944 — 14 Oct 1944
5th War Dog Plat	15 Sep 1944 — 14 Oct 1944
6th Amph Tractor Bn	15 Sep 1944 — 14 Oct 1944
6th Sep Wire Plat	15 Sep 1944 — 14 Oct 1944
7th AAA Bn	15 Sep 1944 — 14 Oct 1944
7th Marines	15 Sep 1944 — 14 Oct 1944
8th Amph Tractor Bn	15 Sep 1944 — 14 Oct 1944
8th 155mm Art Bn	15 Sep 1944 — 14 Oct 1944
11th Marines	15 Sep 1944 — 14 Oct 1944
12th AAA Bn	15 Sep 1944 — 14 Oct 1944
16th Field Depot	15 Sep 1944 — 14 Oct 1944
Administrative Command FMF, Pacific	15 Sep 1944 — 10 Oct 1944
Island Command, Peleliu (1st Ech)	15 Sep 1944 — 14 Oct 1944
2nd Marine Aircraft Wing, Hedron	24 Sep 1944 — 14 Oct 1944
3rd Marine Observ Sq (Fwd Ech)	15 Sep 1944 — 14 Oct 1944
Marine Aircraft Gp Sq-11, HQ & SMS (Fwd Ech)	15 Sep 1944 — 14 Oct 1944
(Rear Ech)	25 Sep 1944 — 14 Oct 1944
Marine Fighter Sq-144 (Grd Ech)	1 Sep 1944 — 14 Oct 1944
(Flt Ech)	26 Sep 1944 — 14 Oct 1944
Marine Fighter Sq-121 (Grd Ech)	15 Sep 1944 — 14 Oct 1944
Marine Fighter Sq-122 (Grd Ech)	15 Sep 1944 — 14 Oct 1944
(Flt Ech)	10 Oct 1944 — 14 Oct 1944
Marine Torpedo Bomber Sq-134 (Grd Ech)	20 Sep 1944 — 14 Oct 1944
(Flt Ech)	6 Oct 1944 — 14 Oct 1944
Marine Transp Sq-353	6 Oct 1944 — 14 Oct 1944
Marine Fighter Sq (N)-541 (Grd Ech)	15 Sep 1944 — 14 Oct 1944
(Flt Ech)	24 Sep 1944 — 14 Oct 1944
Marine Transp Sq-952	1 Oct 1944 — 14 Oct 1944

Zamboanga, Mindanao, Southern Philippine Campaign (Army)

Marine Air Wing-1, Hedron	10 Mar 1945 — 4 Jul 1945
Air Warning Sq-3	17 Apr 1945 — 4 Jul 1945
Air Warning Sq-4	10 Mar 1945 — 4 Jul 1945
Marine Aircraft Gp-12, HQ & SMS	10 Mar 1945 — 4 Jul 1945
Marine Aircraft Gp-24, HQ & SMS	17 Apr 1945 — 4 Jul 1945
Marine Aircraft Gp-32, HQ & SMS	10 Mar 1945 — 4 Jul 1945
Marine Fighter Sq-115	10 Mar 1945 — 4 Jul 1945
Marine Scout Bomber Sq-133	17 Apr 1945 — 4 Jul 1945
Marine Scout Bomber Sq-142	11 Mar 1945 — 4 Jul 1945
Marine Fighter Sq-211	10 Mar 1945 — 4 Jul 1945
Marine Fighter Sq-218	10 Mar 1945 — 4 Jul 1945
Marine Scout Bomber Sq-236	17 Mar 1945 — 4 Jul 1945
Marine Scout Bomber Sq-241	17 Apr 1945 — 4 Jul 1945
Marine Scout Bomber Sq-243	17 Mar 1945 — 4 Jul 1945
Marine Scout Bomber Sq-244	17 Apr 1945 — 4 Jul 1945
Marine Fighter Sq-313	10 Mar 1945 — 1 Jun 1945
Marine Scout Bomber Sq-341	17 Mar 1945 — 4 Jul 1945
Marine Bomber Sq-611	17 Mar 1945 — 4 Jul 1945

Cebu, Negros, Samar, Leyte Campaign (Army)

Marine Aircraft Gp-14, HQ & SMS	11 Jan 1945 — 28 May 1945
Marine Fighter Sq-212	19 Jan 1945 — 14 May 1945
Marine Fighter Sq-222	2 Apr 1945 — 14 May 1945
Marine Fighter Sq-223	19 Jan 1945 — 15 May 1945
Marine Fighter Sq-251	2 Apr 1945 — 1 May 1945
Marine Fighter Sq-313	3 Dec 1945 — 15 Mar 1945

Leyte Operation (only)

2nd Joint Assault Signal Co (Air Liaison)	20 Oct 1944 — 29 Nov 1944
3rd Joint Assault Signal Co (Air Liaison)	20 Oct 1944 — 29 Nov 1944
VAC Arty HQ (Air Sect)	20 Oct 1944 — 29 Nov 1944
Det, Air Liaisons Sec VAC	10 Oct 1944 — 29 Nov 1944
5th 155mm How Bn VAC Arty	20 Oct 1944 — 13 Dec 1944
11th 155mm Gun Bn, VAC Arty	20 Oct 1944 — 29 Nov 1944
Marine Aircraft Gp-25, HQ & SMS	30 Oct 1944 — 16 Dec 1944
Marine Fighter Sq-115	3 Dec 1944 — 16 Dec 1944
Marine Fighter Sq-211	5 Dec 1944 — 11 Dec 1944
Marine Fighter Sq-218	5 Dec 1944 — 16 Dec 1944
Marine Fighter Sq (N)-541	3 Dec 1944 — 16 Dec 1944

Dagupan, Luzon Campaign (Army)

Marine Aircraft Gp-24, HQ & SMS	11 Jan 1945 — 8 Apr 1945

Marine Aircraft Gp-32, HQ & SMS	27 Jan 1945 — 22 Feb 1945
Marine Scout Bomber Sq-133	22 Jan 1945 — 9 Apr 1945
Marine Scout Bomber Sq-142	22 Jan 1945 — 23 Mar 1945
Marine Scout Bomber Sq-236	11 Jan 1945 — 23 Mar 1945
Marine Scout Bomber Sq-241	22 Jan 1945 — 14 Apr 1945
Marine Scout Bomber Sq-243	22 Jan 1945 — 25 Mar 1945
Marine Scout Bomber Sq-244	22 Jan 1945 — 16 Apr 1945
Marine Scout Bomber Sq-341	22 Jan 1945 — 24 Mar 1945

Luzon Operation (only)

Marine Aircraft Gp-25, HQ & SMS	17 Dec 1944 — 1 Apr 1945
Marine Fighter Sq-115	17 Dec 1944 — 9 Mar 1945
Marine Fighter Sq-124 (aboard USS *Essex*)	3 Jan 1945 — 22 Jan 1945
Marine Fighter Sq-211	12 Dec 1944 — 9 Mar 1945
Marine Fighter Sq-212	11 Jan 1945 — 18 Jan 1945
Marine Fighter Sq-213 (aboard USS *Essex*)	3 Jan 1945 — 22 Jan 1945
Marine Fighter Sq-218	17 Dec 1944 — 9 Mar 1945
Marine Fighter Sq-222	11 Jan 1945 — 1 Apr 1945
Marine Fighter Sq-223	12 Jan 1945 — 18 Jan 1945
Marine Fighter Sq-251	3 Jan 1945 — 1 Apr 1945
Marine Fighter Sq (N)-541	17 Dec 1944 — 8 Jan 1945

Borneo (Balikpapen) Operation

Marine Corps Aviation Sv Det-1 (Fwd Ech aboard USS *Block Island*)	26 Jan 1945 — 6 Jul 1945
Marine Corps Aviation Sv Det-2 (Fwd Ech aboard USS *Gilbert Islands*)	26 Jun 1945 — 6 Jul 1945
Marine Torpedo Bomber Sq-143	26 Jun 1945 — 6 Jul 1945
Marine Scout Bomber Sq-233	26 Jan 1945 — 6 Jul 1945
Marine Fighter Sq-512 (aboard USS *Gilbert Islands*)	26 Jun 1945 — 6 Jul 1945

Assault and Occupation of Iwo Jima   15 Feb 1945 — 16 Mar 1945

1st Joint Assault Signal Co	19 Feb 1945 — 16 Mar 1945
1st Prov Field Arty Gp (H& Btry)	19 Feb 1945 — 16 Mar 1945
1st Prov Rocket Det	19 Feb 1945 — 16 Mar 1945
1st Radio Intell Plat	19 Feb 1945 — 16 Mar 1945
2nd Armored Amph Bn	19 Feb 1945 — 16 Mar 1945
2nd Bomb Disposal Co	19 Feb 1945 — 16 Mar 1945
2nd Sep Eng Bn	19 Feb 1945 — 16 Mar 1945
2nd Sep Topographic Co	19 Feb 1945 — 16 Mar 1945
2nd 155mm Howitzer Bn	19 Feb 1945 — 16 Mar 1945
3rd Amph Track Bn	19 Feb 1945 — 16 Mar 1945
3rd Eng Bn (less Co C)	19 Feb 1945 — 16 Mar 1945
(Co C, Fl Res)	19 Feb 1945 — 5 Mar 1945

3rd Joint Assault Signal Co (less Det)	18 Feb 1945 – 16 Mar 1945
(Det Fl Res)	19 Feb 1945 – 5 Mar 1945
3rd Marines (Fl Res)	19 Feb 1945 – 5 Mar 1945
3rd Marine Div HQ	19 Feb 1945 – 16 Mar 1945
3rd Marine Div HQ & Sv Bn (less Dets HQ & Co)	19 Feb 1945 – 16 Mar 1945
3rd Marine Div Spl & Sv Troops (Dets)	19 Feb 1945 – 16 Mar 1945
3rd Med Bn (less Co C)	19 Feb 1945 – 16 Mar 1945
(Co C, Fl Res)	19 Feb 1945 – 5 Mar 1945
3rd Motor Transp Bn (less Co C)	19 Feb 1945 – 16 Mar 1945
(Co C, Fl Res)	19 Feb 1945 – 5 Mar 1945
3rd Pioneer Bn (less Co C)	19 Feb 1945 – 16 Mar 1945
(Co C, Fl Res)	19 Feb 1945 – 5 Mar 1945
3rd Prov Rocket Det	19 Feb 1945 – 16 Mar 1945
3rd Military Police Co	19 Feb 1945 – 16 Mar 1945
3rd Sv Bn (less dets)	19 Feb 1945 – 16 Mar 1945
3rd Tank Bn	19 Feb 1945 – 16 Mar 1945
3rd War Dog Plat	19 Feb 1945 – 16 Mar 1945
4th Amph Truck Co	19 Feb 1945 – 16 Mar 1945
4th Eng Bn	19 Feb 1945 – 16 Mar 1945
4th Marine Div HQ	19 Feb 1945 – 16 Mar 1945
4th Marine Div HQ & Sv Bn	19 Feb 1945 – 16 Mar 1945
4th Med Bn	19 Feb 1945 – 16 Mar 1945
4th Motor Transp Bn	19 Feb 1945 – 16 Mar 1945
4th Pioneer Bn	19 Feb 1945 – 16 Mar 1945
4th Sv Bn	19 Feb 1945 – 16 Mar 1945
4th Tank Bn	19 Feb 1945 – 16 Mar 1945
4th 155mm Howitzer Bn	19 Feb 1945 – 16 Mar 1945
5th Amph Tractor Bn	19 Feb 1945 – 16 Mar 1945
5th Amph Truck Co	19 Feb 1945 – 16 Mar 1945
5th Eng Bn	19 Feb 1945 – 16 Mar 1945
5th Joint Assault Signal Co	19 Feb 1945 – 16 Mar 1945
V Amph Corps Air Delivery Sect	19 Feb 1945 – 16 Mar 1945
V Amph Corps Arty HQ	19 Feb 1945 – 16 Mar 1945
V Amph Corps HQ	19 Feb 1945 – 16 Mar 1945
V Amph Corps HQ & Sv Bn	19 Feb 1945 – 16 Mar 1945
V Amph Corps Med Bn	19 Feb 1945 – 16 Mar 1945
V Amph Corps Motor Transp Co	19 Feb 1945 – 16 Mar 1945
V Amph Corps Prov LVT Gp	19 Feb 1945 – 16 Mar 1945
V Amph Corps Signal Bn	19 Feb 1945 – 16 Mar 1945
V Amph Corps Shore Party (Comm Unit)	19 Feb 1945 – 16 Mar 1945
V Amph Corps Evac Hospital No 1	19 Feb 1945 – 16 Mar 1945
5th Div HQ	19 Feb 1945 – 16 Mar 1945
5th Med Bn	19 Feb 1945 – 16 Mar 1945
5th Motor Transp Bn	19 Feb 1945 – 16 Mar 1945
5th Pioneer Bn	19 Feb 1945 – 16 Mar 1945
5th Sv Bn	19 Feb 1945 – 16 Mar 1945

5th Shore Party Regt	19 Feb 1945 — 16 Mar 1945
5th Tank Bn	19 Feb 1945 — 16 Mar 1945
6th War Dog Plat	19 Feb 1945 — 16 Mar 1945
7th War Dog Plat	19 Feb 1945 — 16 Mar 1945
8th Ammunition Co	19 Feb 1945 — 16 Mar 1945
8th Field Depot	19 Feb 1945 — 16 Mar 1945
9th Marines	19 Feb 1945 — 16 Mar 1945
10th Amph Tractor Bn	19 Feb 1945 — 16 Mar 1945
11th Amph Tractor Bn	19 Feb 1945 — 16 Mar 1945
12th Marines	19 Feb 1945 — 16 Mar 1945
13th Marines	19 Feb 1945 — 16 Mar 1945
14th Marines	19 Feb 1945 — 16 Mar 1945
23rd Marines	19 Feb 1945 — 16 Mar 1945
24th Marines	19 Feb 1945 — 16 Mar 1945
24th Repl Draft	19 Feb 1945 — 16 Mar 1945
25th Marines	19 Feb 1945 — 16 Mar 1945
26th Marines	19 Feb 1945 — 16 Mar 1945
27th Marines	19 Feb 1945 — 16 Mar 1945
28th Marines	19 Feb 1945 — 16 Mar 1945
28th Repl Draft (less Dets)	19 Feb 1945 — 16 Mar 1945
(Dets Fl Res)	19 Feb 1945 — 5 Mar 1945
30th Repl Draft	19 Feb 1945 — 16 Mar 1945
31st Repl Draft	19 Feb 1945 — 16 Mar 1945
33rd Depot Co	19 Feb 1945 — 16 Mar 1945
34th Depot Co	19 Feb 1945 — 16 Mar 1945
34th Repl Draft (less Dets)	19 Feb 1945 — 16 Mar 1945
(Det Fl Res)	19 Feb 1945 — 5 Mar 1945
36th Depot Co	19 Feb 1945 — 16 Mar 1945
Amph Recon Bn FMF Pac (Co B only)	19 Feb 1945 — 16 Mar 1945
Landing Force Assault Signal Comm Unit-1	19 Feb 1945 — 16 Mar 1945
Marine Observ Sq-1 (Fwd Ech)	19 Feb 1945 — 8 Mar 1945
Marine Observ Sq-4	19 Feb 1945 — 16 Mar 1945
Marine Observ Sq-5	19 Feb 1945 — 16 Mar 1945
Marine Fighter Sq-112 (Fwd Ech aboard USS *Bennington*)	15 Feb 1945 — 4 Mar 1945
Marine Fighter Sq-123 (Fwd Ech aboard USS *Bennington*)	15 Feb 1945 — 4 Mar 1945
Marine Fighter Sq-124	15 Feb 1945 — 4 Mar 1945
Marine Fighter Sq 213	15 Feb 1945 — 4 Mar 1945
Marine Fighter Sq-216 (Fwd Ech aboard USS *Wasp*)	15 Feb 1945 — 4 Mar 1945
Marine Fighter Sq-217 (Fwd Ech aboard USS *Wasp*)	15 Feb 1945 — 4 Mar 1945
Marine Fighter Sq-221 (Fwd Ech aboard USS *Bunker Hill*)	15 Feb 1945 — 4 Mar 1945
Marine Torpedo Bomber Sq-242 (Fwd Ech)	8 Mar 1945 — 16 Mar 1945

Marine Transp Sq-252	3 Mar 1945 — 9 Mar 1945
Marine Transp Sq-253	3 Mar 1945 — 16 Mar 1945
Marine Transp Sq-353	8 Mar 1945 — 15 Mar 1945
Marine Fighter Sq-451 (Fwd Ech aboard USS *Bunker Hill*)	15 Feb 1945 — 4 Mar 1945
Marine Bombing Sq-612	15 Feb 1945 — 16 Mar 1945
Marine Transp Sq-952	1 Mar 1945 — 16 Mar 1945

Assault and Occupation of Okinawa Gunto
1 Apr 1945 — 30 Jun 1945

1st Amph Tractor Bn	1 Apr 1945 — 30 Jun 1945
1st Amored Amph Bn	1 Apr 1945 — 30 Jun 1945
1st Bomb Disposal Co	1 Apr 1945 — 30 Jun 1945
1st Eng Bn	1 Apr 1945 — 30 Jun 1945
1st Joint Assault Signal Co	1 Apr 1945 — 30 Jun 1945
1st Marines	1 Apr 1945 — 30 Jun 1945
1st Marine Div HQ	1 Apr 1945 — 30 Jun 1945
1st Marine Div HQ & Sv Bn	1 Apr 1945 — 30 Jun 1945
1st Med Bn	1 Apr 1945 — 30 Jun 1945
1st Military Police Bn, FMF	1 Apr 1945 — 30 Jun 1945
1st Motor Transp Bn	1 Apr 1945 — 30 Jun 1945
1st Pioneer Bn	1 Apr 1945 — 30 Jun 1945
1st Prov AAA Gp (HQ)	2 Apr 1945 — 30 Jun 1945
1st Sep Eng Bn	1 Apr 1945 — 30 Jun 1945
1st Sep Topographic Co	1 Apr 1945 — 30 Jun 1945
1st War Dog Plat	1 Apr 1945 — 30 Jun 1945
1st 155mm Arty Bn	1 Apr 1945 — 30 Jun 1945
2nd AAA Bn	3 Apr 1945 — 30 Jun 1945
2nd Amph Tractor Bn (Fl Res)	1 Apr 1945 — 10 Apr 1945
2nd Amph Tractor Bn	1 Jun 1945 — 30 Jun 1945
2nd Amph Truck Co (Fl Res)	1 Apr 1945 — 10 Apr 1945
2nd Eng Bn (Fl Res) (Co C only)	1 Jun 1945 — 30 Jun 1945
2nd Joint Assault Signal Co (Fl Res)	1 Apr 1945 — 10 Apr 1945
2nd Marines	1 Apr 1945 — 10 Apr 1945
2nd Marine Div HQ (Fl Res)	1 Apr 1945 — 10 Apr 1945
(Det only)	1 Jun 1945 — 30 Jun 1945
2nd Med Bn (Fl Res)	1 Apr 1945 — 10 Apr 1945
(Co E only)	1 Jun 1945 — 30 Jun 1945
2nd Motor Transp Bn (Fl Res)	1 Apr 1945 — 10 Apr 1945
(Co B only)	1 Jun 1945 — 30 Jun 1945
2nd Pioneer Bn (Fl Res)	1 Apr 1945 — 10 Apr 1945
(Co A only)	1 Jun 1945 — 30 Jun 1945
2nd Military Police Co (3rd Plat)	1 Jun 1945 — 30 Jun 1945
2nd Prov Field Arty Gp HQ	1 Apr 1945 — 30 Jun 1945
2nd Prov Rocket Det (Fl Res)	1 Apr 1945 — 10 Apr 1945
(3rd Sect only)	1 Jun 1945 — 30 Jun 1945

2nd Sv Co (Fl Res)	1 Apr 1945 — 10 Apr 1945
(2nd Plat, Ord C, & 3rd Plat S&S Co)	1 Jun 1945 — 30 Jun 1945
2nd Tank Bn (Fl Res)	1 Apr 1945 — 10 Apr 1945
(Co A only)	1 Jun 1945 — 30 Jun 1945
2nd War Dog Plat (Fl Res)	1 Apr 1945 — 10 Apr 1945
3rd Ammunition Co	1 Apr 1945 — 30 Jun 1945
3rd Armored Amph Bn	1 Apr 1945 — 30 Jun 1945
III Amph Corps Air Del Sect (Fwd Ech)	11 Apr 1945 — 30 Jun 1945
III Amph Corps Arty HQ	1 Apr 1945 — 30 Jun 1945
III Amph Corps HQ	1 Apr 1945 — 30 Jun 1945
III Amph Corps Med Bn	1 Apr 1945 — 30 Jun 1945
III Amph Corps Signal Bn	1 Apr 1945 — 30 Jun 1945
3rd Sep Laundry Plat	1 Apr 1945 — 30 Jun 1945
3rd Sep Radio Intell Plat	1 Apr 1945 — 30 Jun 1945
3rd 155mm Arty Bn	1 Apr 1945 — 30 Jun 1945
4th Amph Tractor Bn	1 Apr 1945 — 30 Jun 1945
4th Joint Assault Signal Co	1 Apr 1945 — 30 Jun 1945
4th Prov Rocket Det	1 Apr 1945 — 30 Jun 1945
4th Sep Laundry Plat (Fl Res)	1 Apr 1945 — 10 Apr 1945
4th War Dog Plat	1 Apr 1945 — 30 Jun 1945
5th AAA Bn	3 May 1945 — 30 Jun 1945
5th Depot Co	1 Apr 1945 — 30 Jun 1945
5th Marines	1 Apr 1945 — 30 Jun 1945
5th Prov Rocket Det	1 Apr 1945 — 30 Jun 1945
5th Sep Laundry Plat	1 Apr 1945 — 30 Jun 1945
6th Amph Truck Co	1 Apr 1945 — 30 Jun 1945
6th Eng Bn	1 Apr 1945 — 30 Jun 1945
6th Joint Assault Signal Co	1 Apr 1945 — 30 Jun 1945
6th Marines	1 Apr 1945 — 30 Apr 1945
6th Marine Div HQ	1 Apr 1945 — 30 Jun 1945
6th Med Bn	1 Apr 1945 — 30 Jun 1945
6th Motor Transp Bn	1 Apr 1945 — 30 Jun 1945
6th Pioneer Bn	1 Apr 1945 — 30 Jun 1945
6th Sv Bn	1 Apr 1945 — 30 Jun 1945
6th Tank Bn	1 Apr 1945 — 30 Jun 1945
6th 155mm Howitzer Bn	1 Apr 1945 — 30 Jun 1945
7th Marines	1 Apr 1945 — 30 Jun 1945
7th Sep Laundry Plat	1 Apr 1945 — 30 Jun 1945
7th 155mm Arty Bn	1 Apr 1945 — 30 Jun 1945
8th AAA Bn (1st Ech)	17 May 1945 — 30 Jun 1945
(2nd Ech)	3 May 1945 — 30 Jun 1945
(3rd Ech)	3 Jun 1945 — 30 Jun 1945
8th Amph Tractor Bn	1 Apr 1945 — 30 Jun 1945
8th Marines (Fl Res)	1 Apr 1945 — 10 Apr 1945
8th Marines	1 Jun 1945 — 30 Jun 1945
8th 155mm Arty Bn	1 Apr 1945 — 30 Jun 1945

9th Amph Tractor Bn	1 Apr 1945 — 30 Jun 1945
9th 155mm Arty Bn	1 Apr 1945 — 30 Jun 1945
10th Marines (Fl Res)	1 Apr 1945 — 10 Apr 1945
(2nd Bn only)	1 Jun 1945 — 30 Jun 1945
11th Marines	1 Apr 1945 — 30 Jun 1945
11th Motor Transp Bn	1 Apr 1945 — 30 Jun 1945
15th Marines	1 Apr 1945 — 30 Jun 1945
16th AAA Bn (Adv Ech)	4 Apr 1945 — 30 Jun 1945
(2nd Ech)	1 May 1945 — 30 Jun 1945
(3rd Ech)	27 May 1945 — 30 Jun 1945
22nd Marines	1 Apr 1945 — 30 Jun 1945
26th Repl Draft (less Rear Ech)	1 Apr 1945 — 13 May 1945
29th Marines	1 Apr 1945 — 30 Jun 1945
29th Repl Draft	1 Apr 1945 — 30 Jun 1945
32nd Repl Draft	1 Apr 1945 — 30 Jun 1945
33rd Repl Draft	1 Apr 1945 — 17 May 1945
35th Repl Draft (Fl Res)	1 Apr 1945 — 10 Apr 1945
41st Repl Draft (Fl Res)	1 Apr 1945 — 10 Apr 1945
46th Repl Draft	17 May 1945
54th Repl Draft	27 May 1945
55th Repl Draft	10 Jun 1945 — 11 Jun 1945
57th Repl Draft	27 May 1945 — 29 May 1945
62nd Repl Draft	10 Jun 1945 — 11 Jun 1945
63rd Repl Draft	27 May 1945 — 11 Jun 1945
Aircraft Warning Sq-1	18 Apr 1945 — 30 Jun 1945
Landing Force Assault Signal Comm Units 1, 2, and 3	1 Apr 1945 — 30 Jun 1945
MCASD — 1 (Fwd Ech aboard USS *Block Island*)	10 May 1945 — 16 Jun 1945
Marine Air Wing — 2	1 Apr 1945 — 30 Jun 1945
(Rear Ech)	1 May 1945 — 30 Jun 1945
MCASD — 2 (Fwd Ech aboard USS *Gilbert Island*)	21 May 1945 — 16 Jun 1945
Marine Observ Sq-3	1 Apr 1945 — 30 Jun 1945
Aircraft Warning Sq-6	17 Apr 1945 — 30 Jun 1945
Marine Observ Sq-6	1 Apr 1945 — 30 Jun 1945
Aircraft Warning Sq-7	1 Apr 1945 — 30 Jun 1945
Marine Observ Sq-7	6 May 1945 — 30 Jun 1945
Aircraft Warning Sq-8	6 May 1945 — 30 Jun 1945
Marine Aircraft Gp-14, HQ & SMS	29 May 1945 — 30 Jun 1945
Marine Aircraft Gp-22, HQ & SMS (Fwd Ech)	2 May 1945 — 30 Jun 1945
(Rear Ech)	12 May 1945 — 30 Jun 1945
MarineAircraft Gp-31, HQ & SMS	1 Apr 1945 — 30 Jun 1945
Marine Aircraft Gp-33, HQ & SMS	1 Apr 1945 — 30 Jun 1945
Marine Aircraft Gp-43, Hedron	1 Apr 1945 — 30 Jun 1945
Marine Fighter Sq-113, (Grd Ech)	6 May 1945 — 30 Jun 1945
(Flt Ech)	21 May 1945 — 30 Jun 1945
Marine Fighter Sq-131 (Grd Ech)	29 May 1945 — 30 Jun 1945

(Flt Ech)	29 May 1945 – 30 Jun 1945
Marine Transp Sq-143	7 Jun 1945 – 8 Jun 1945
Marine Fighter Sq-212 (Fwd Ech)	29 May 1945 – 30 Jun 1945
(Rear Ech)	7 Jun 1945 – 30 Jun 1945
Marine Fighter Sq-222 (Grd Ech)	29 May 1945 – 30 Jun 1945
(Flt Ech)	10 Jun 1945 – 30 Jun 1945
Marine Fighter Sq-223 (Flt Ech)	11 Jun 1945 – 30 Jun 1945
(Grd Ech)	24 Jun 1945 – 30 Jun 1945
Marine Fighter Sq-224	2 Apr 1945 – 30 Jun 1945
(Rear Ech)	1 May 1945 – 30 Jun 1945
Marine Scout Bomber Sq-223 (Fwd Ech)	1 Apr 1945 – 30 Jun 1945
(Rear Ech)	1 May 1945 – 30 Jun 1945
Marine Scout Bomber Sq-233 (Rear Ech)	
(aboard USS *Block Island*)	1 May 1945 – 30 Jun 1945
Marine Transp Sq-252	18 Apr 1945 – 30 Jun 1945
Marine Transp Sq-253	18 Apr 1945 – 30 Jun 1945
Marine Fighter Sq-311 (Flt Ech)	6 Apr 1945 – 30 Jun 1945
(Rear Ech)	1 May 1945 – 30 Jun 1945
Marine Fighter Sq-312 (Assault Ech)	2 Apr 1945 – 30 Jun 1945
(Flt Ech)	9 Apr 1945 – 30 Jun 1945
Marine Fighter Sq-313	2 Jun 1945 – 30 Jun 1945
Marine Fighter Sq-314 (Grd Ech)	6 May 1945 – 30 Jun 1945
(Flt Ech)	24 May 1945 – 30 Jun 1945
Marine Fighter Sq-322 (Grd Ech)	2 Apr 1945 – 30 Jun 1945
Marine Fighter Sq-322	9 Apr 1945 – 30 Jun 1945
Marine Fighter Sq-323 (Grd Ech)	2 Apr 1945 – 30 Jun 1945
(Flt Ech)	9 Apr 1945 – 30 Jun 1945
Marine Transp Sq-353	19 Apr 1945 – 30 Jun 1945
Marine Photo Sq-354	29 Jun 1945 – 30 Jun 1945
Marine Fighter Sq-422 (Grd Ech)	6 May 1945 – 30 Jun 1945
(Flt Ech)	23 May 1945 – 30 Jun 1945
Marine Fighter Sq-441 (Grd Ech)	2 Apr 1945 – 30 Jun 1945
(Flt Ech)	7 Apr 1945 – 30 Jun 1945
Marine Fighter Sq-511 (aboard USS *Block Island*)	3 May 1945 – 30 Jun 1945
Marine Fighter Sq-512 (aboard	
USS *Gilbert Islands*)	21 May 1945 – 16 Jun 1945
Marine Fighter Sq (N)-533 (Flt Ech)	10 May 1945 – 30 Jun 1945
(Grd Ech)	30 May 1945 – 30 Jun 1945
Marine Fighter Sq (N)-542 (Grd Ech)	1 Apr 1945 – 30 Jun 1945
(Flt Ech)	7 Apr 1945 – 30 Jun 1945
Marine Fighter Sq (N)-543	
(Assault Ech)	1 Apr 1945 – 30 Jun 1945
(Flt Ech)	6 Apr 1945 – 30 Jun 1945
(Rear Ech)	1 May 1945 – 30 Jun 1945
Marine Bomber Sq-611 (Det Flt Ech)	6 Jun 1945 – 10 Jun 1945
Marine Transp Sq-952	22 Apr 1945 – 30 Jun 1945
Marine Transp Sq-953 (Det Flt Ech)	29 May 1945 – 31 May 1945

Occupation of North China

1st Assault Signal Co
1st Marine Ammunition Co
1st Marine Div
1st Military Police Bn, FMF, Pac
1st Recon Co
1st Sep Eng Bn
1st Signal Co
111 Amph Corps
3rd Amph Truck Co
3rd Marine Brig
1st Salvage Plat, 3rd Salvage Repair Co
3rd Sep HQ & Supply Co (Prov)
3rd Sep Laundry Plat
3rd Sep Radio Intell Plat
4th Bakery Plat (Prov)
4th Rocket Det (Prov, FMF, Pac)
4th Salvage Repair Co (Prov)
4th Sep Radio Intell Plat
5th Sep Laundry Plat
6th Amph Truck Co
6th Bakery Plat (Prov)
6th Marine Div
7th Sep Laundry Plat
7th Sv Regt

11th Motor Transp Bn, FMF, Pac
3rd Bn, (Reinf), 12th Marines
12th Marine Ammunition Co
12th Sv Bn
20th Marine Depot Co
37th Marine Depot Co
38th Marine Depot Co
Marine Air Gp-25
Marine Air Gp-32
Marine Fighter Sq-115
Marine Scout Bomber Sq-134
Marine Transp Sq-152
Marine Transp Sq-153
Marine Fighter Sq-211
Marine Fighter Sq-218
Marine Scout Bomber Sq-244
Marine Transp Sq-252
Marine Transp Sq-253
Marine Scout Bomber Sq-343
Marine Transp Sq-352
Marine Bomber Sq-413
Marine Fighter Sq (N)-533
Marine Fighter Sq (N)-541
Marine Bomber Sq-611

Occupation of Japan

2nd Marine Div
2nd Sep Eng Bn
2nd Sep Guard Bn, FMF, Pac
2nd Sep HQ & Sup Co (Prov)
2nd War Dog Plat
3rd Fleet Marine Landing Force (Task Unit 31, 32, composed of Marine Dets of ships of the 3rd Fleet)
3rd Military Police Bn (Prov)
Regimental Combat Team-4
4th Separate Laundry Plat
V Amph Corps
5th Amph Truck Co
5th Assault Signal Co
5th Marine Div
5th Sep Radio Intell Plat
6th Marine Div
6th Marine Ammunition Co
6th Sep Laundry Plat
6th War Dog Plat
8th Marines

8th Marine Ammunition Co
8th Sep Laundry Plat
8th Sv Regt
10th Marines
10th Marine Ammunition Co
12th Motor Transp Bn (Prov)
13th Marines
20th Amph Truck Bn
24th Marine Depot Co
26th Marines
27th Marines
28th Marines
33rd Marine Depot Co
34th Marine Depot Co
36th Marine Depot Co
42nd Marine Depot Co
43rd Marine Depot Co
Prov Marine Air Base Sq, Omura, Japan.
HQ Sq, Marine Operating Gp-1
Marine Observ Sq-2
Landing Force Assault Signal Comm Unit No. 4
Marine Observ Sq-5
Marine Air Warning Sq-9
Marine Air Warning Sq-12
HQ Sq & SMS, Mag-22
HQ Sq & SMS, Mag-31
Marine Fighter Sq-113
Marine Torpedo Bomber Sq-131
Marine Fighter Sq-224
Marine Transp Sq-252
Marine Transp Sq-253
Marine Fighter Sq-311
Marine Fighter Sq-314
Marine Transp Sq-353
Marine Fighter Sq-422
Marine Fighter Sq-441
Marine Fighter Sq (N)-542
Marine Fighter Sq (N)-543
Marine Bomber Sq-612
Marine Transp Sq-952

Presidential Unit Citation

1st Def Bn, Wake Det
1st Def Bn
Marine Fighter Sq-211 of MAW-21
8 – 22 Dec 1941

Marine Aircraft Gp-22
Midway Islands
June 1942

       ◦   ●   ◦

1st Marine Div, Reinf
Guadalcanal
7 Aug — 9 Dec 1942
    (2nd PUC — Assault and seizure of Peleliu and Ngesebus, Palau
    Islands, 15 — 29 Sep 1944)
    (3rd PUC — Okinawa, 1 Apr — 21 Jun 1945

       ◦   ◦   ◦

Marine Fighter Sq-214
Guadalcanal
7 Apr 1943

       ◦   ◦   ◦

2nd Marine Div, Reinf
Tarawa Atoll, Gilbert Islands
20 — 24 Nov 1943

       ◦   ◦   ◦

4th Marine Div, Reinf
Saipan and Tinian
15 Jun — 1 Aug 1944

       ◦   ◦   ◦

3rd Marine Div, Reinf (serving as 3rd Combat Team)
Guam
21 Jul — 10 Aug 1944

       ◦   ◦   ◦

5th Amph Corps Assault Troops, Reinf
Iwo Jima
19 — 28 Feb 1945

       ◦   ◦   ◦

6th Marine Div, Reinf
Okinawa
1 Apr — 21 Jun 1945

       ◦   ◦   ◦

Marine Observ Sq-3
Okinawa
2 Apr — 21 Jun 1945

       ◦   ◦   ◦

2nd Marine Aircraft Wing
Okinawa, Shima and Ryukyus campaign
4 Apr — 14 Jul 1945

Navy Unit Commendation

Amph Recon Bn, FMF, Pac
19 — 26 Nov 1943 — Gilbert Islands

20 Jan — 23 Feb 1944 — Marshall Islands
15 Jun — 4 Aug 1944 — Marianas Islands
26 Mar — 24 Jul 1945 — Ryukyus Islands

❉   ❉   ❉

11th Marine Regt, 1st Marine Div
26 Dec 1943 — 30 Apr 1944 — Cape Gloucester, New Britain

❉   ❉   ❉

1st Prov Marine Brig
21 Jul — 10 Aug 1944 — Guam, Marianas Islands
1st Sep Eng Bn
10 Dec 1942 — 27 Feb 1943 — Guadalcanal
20 Aug 1944 — 24 Mar 1945 — Tinian

❉   ❉   ❉

14 Apr — 2 Sep 1945 — Okinawa

❉   ❉   ❉

9th Marine Def Bn
30 Nov 1942 — 20 May 1943 (date of last enemy aerial attack) Guadalcanal
30 Jun — 7 Nov 1943 (date of last enemy aerial attack) (Tank plats of the
    10th and 11th Def Bns attached during this period) Rendova and
    New Georgia Area
21 Jul — 20 Aug 1944 — Guam

❉   ❉   ❉

6th Def Bn, FMF
Jun 1942 — Midway

❉   ❉   ❉

V Amph Corps, Reinf, Support Troops
19 — 28 Feb 1945 — Iwo Jima

❉   ❉   ❉

3rd Amph Corps Signal Bn
1 Nov 1943 — 21 Jun 1945 — Bougainville, Guam, Palau, Okinawa

❉   ❉   ❉

3rd Bn, 10th Marines, 2nd Marine Div, FMF
7 Jul 1944 — Saipan

❉   ❉   ❉

3rd Marines, 3rd Marine Div
1 Nov — 22 Dec 1943 — Empress Augusta Bay Beachhead, Bougainville,
    British Solomon Islands

❉   ❉   ❉

12th Marines, 3rd Marine Div
1 Nov 1943 — 12 Jan 1944 — Empress Augusta Bay Beachhead,
    Bougainville, British Solomon Islands
21 Jul — 10 Aug 1944 — Guam, Marianas Islands

❉   ❉   ❉

21st Marines, Reinf, serving as 21st Regimental Combat
    Team, 3rd Marine Div
21 July — 10 Aug 1944 — Guam, Marianas Islands

278